Sociology in India

Sociology in India

Intellectual and Institutional Practices

Edited by

MAITRAYEE CHAUDHURI

RAWAT PUBLICATIONS

Jaipur • New Delhi • Bangalore • Guwahati • Kolkata

ISBN 978-81-316-0350-5 (HB)

Reprinted, 2025

Published by
Prem Rawat for **Rawat Publications**
Satyam Apts, Sector 3, Jawahar Nagar, Jaipur 302 004 (India)
Phone: 0141 265 1748 / 7006 Fax: 0141 265 1748
E-mail: info@rawatbooks.com
Website: www.rawatbooks.com

New Delhi Office
4858/24, Ansari Road, Daryaganj, New Delhi 110 002
Phone: 011 2326 3290

Also at *Bangalore, Guwahati* and *Kolkata*

Typeset by Rawat Computers, Jaipur
Printed at Nice Printing Press, New Delhi

For my students

Contents

PART III : Sociology in Professional Institutions: Global Brands and Disciplinary Marginality

PART IV : New Sites and Modes of Doing Sociology

PART V : Tracking Concepts: Of Intellectual Journeys

Acknowledgement

This volume represents writings of predominantly young scholars working in diverse and sometimes challenging and difficult conditions. This volume is a testimony of their efforts to record, reflect and critique the conditions within which they produce and disseminate knowledge.

This book could not have been ever imagined without the diversity and richness of classroom experiences across the country. This deserves special mention and acknowledgement for it draws attention to the symbiotic link between teaching and research – a link that many of the current developments mentioned in the book may sever. This book in many senses therefore rests on the collective experiences of scholars spread across India. The list of people and institutions to whom I am indebted are therefore far too many to mention by name.

However, I would like to specially record my thanks to the Centre for the Study of Social Systems, Jawaharlal Nehru University where I have learnt the practice of sociology and which supported me in my initial effort to organize the workshop in January 2007 that paved the way for bringing out this volume. My special thanks to Professor Avijit Pathak, who was the chairperson then, and without whose persuasion I may not have tried to organize it. I also thank all my teachers and colleagues from the Centre for helping me – first to hold the workshop and then for sustaining their faith in the belief that this academic endeavour will definitely succeed. I thank ICSSR for granting me financial support to hold the workshop. It would have been impossible to invite the scholars from different parts of the country without its assistance. My sincere thanks to the staff of CSSS who helped me hold the workshop and provided assistance to see the book through.

Colleagues outside the Centre had no less a role in sustaining my interest and belief in the project. My sincere thanks to Professor Virginius Xaxa to so readily agree to allow me to reproduce his article. I would like to specially mention Professor Ari Sitas for taking the trouble to actually read through the manuscript and affirm faith in the project. And, my very special thanks to my students Jesna Jayachandran, Suchita Chakraborty, Mahima Verma, Jyoti Sinha, M.N. Sanil and Debabrata Baral, for their help. Needless to say the shortcomings are all mine.

The Contributors

A.K. Nongkynrih is Associate Professor of Sociology in the North-Eastern Hill University, Shillong (Meghalaya). His areas of interest are sociology of rural development, sociology of organizations, and sociology of tribes/indigenous peoples. He is also a facilitator of participatory development and participatory research, and works in close collaboration with local, national and international organizations, such as the International Fund for Agricultural Development, Rome and others.

Amites Mukhopadhyay has been teaching sociology at the University of Kalyani in West Bengal for more than a decade. His areas of interests are: anthropology of development with particular reference to coastal Sundarbans, competing perspectives on development and resource use, ethnographies of state and civil society, and colonial and postcolonial histories in South Asian context. Among his recent works are 'Negotiating Development: Nuclear Episode in the Sundarbans of West Bengal' in *Anthropology Matters* (www.anthropologymatters.com) and *Social Justice in the Sundarbans* as part of a volume on *Enlightenment and Social Justice*, edited by Pradip Bose and Samir Das. He has been a Commonwealth awardee and completed his PhD in anthropology of development from University of London. At present, he is carrying out a collaborative project on experiences of democracy in Indian states with the Department of Political Science, University of Calcutta.

Archana Prasad teaches sociology at the Kamala Nehru College, Delhi University. Her area of interest is gender and labour studies. She is also closely associated with developmental work for women in an NGO for a decade now. Her doctoral work on *Social Audit and Labour Reorganization in a Globalized India* is in the process of publication.

Dalia Chakrabarti has been teaching at the Department of Sociology, Jadavpur University, Kolkata since 2005. She taught earlier at Presidency College, Kolkata for eight years – the college she had topped from in sociology from Calcutta University. She is the author of *Colonial Clerks: A Social History of Deprivation and Domination.* She has also been actively engaged in organizing workshops and seminars apart from being involved in syllabus revision. She has also been the Coordinator of Certificate Course on Applied Sociology under the UGC's Career Oriented Programme.

Kushal Deb teaches at the Department of Humanities and Social Sciences, IIT, Mumbai. He earlier taught at the Department of Sociology, University of Pune. His areas of interest are urban studies, multiculturalism and sociological theory. He has edited two volumes: *Urban Studies in India* and *Mapping Multiculturalism.*

Madhu Sharan has been a sociology student from Delhi University and Jawaharlal Nehru University, New Delhi. She has a rich experience in the pedagogy of sociology, issues of microfinance and empowerment of women, marginality, gender and mental health. She has worked as Project Director of Microfinance in Hand-in-Hand, Tamil Nadu. Since 2007 she has been working as Executive Director in the Banyan Academy of Mental Health (BALM) in Chennai, overseeing research, training and short-term courses on marginality, mental health and gender.

Maitrayee Chaudhuri teaches sociology at the Centre for the Study of Social Systems, School of Social Sciences, Jawaharlal Nehru University, New Delhi. She has written and published widely in the areas of gender, culture, globalization and media. Her works include: *Feminism in India*, *The Women's Movement in India: Reform and Revival* and *The Practice of Sociology*. She has been interested in pedagogy and has also been involved in writing school textbooks in sociology for NCERT.

Manish Thakur is Assistant Professor, Department of Public Policy and Management , Indian Institute of Management, Kolkata. He earlier taught for a decade at Goa University and was Adjunct Faculty at the Indian Institute of Management, Kozhikode between 2004–2006. He has written extensively in the area of rural sociology and has been interested in questions pertaining to the practice of sociology for long. His other area of work is politics-society interface and issues in political culture.

Pushpesh Kumar has been teaching for over a decade in Nanded University, Maharashtra. He has published widely in the area of gender, tribes and kinship. He has also been a regular contributor to the *Sociological Bulletin*, *Economic and Political Weekly* and *Contributions to Indian Sociology*. He was awarded the Professor M.N. Srinivas Award for Young Sociologists in 2005. He was at the Anthropology Department, LSE under British Academy Visiting Fellowship from June to September 2009.

R. Santhosh is currently working as Assistant Director in Centre for Study of Social Exclusion and Inclusive Policy, Mangalore University. He has completed his PhD in sociology from the Institute for Social and Economic Change, Bangalore. His research interests include ethnic mobilization, identity politics, Muslim identity, social exclusion and globalization.

Ramanuj Ganguly is Reader at the Department of Sociology in West Bengal State University, Barasat, Kolkata. Earlier, he was Senior Lecturer in Sociology, Maharani Kasiswari College, and Guest Lecturer, College of Nursing, Asia Heart Foundation, R.N. Tagore Institute of Cardiac Sciences, Kolkata. He is also Associate Managing Editor of *Bharatiya Samajik Chintan*, quarterly journal of Indian Academy of Social Sciences, Allahabad. He has recently published a textbook of sociology in Bengali.

Ravi Kumar teaches at the Department of Sociology, Jamia Millia Islamia, New Delhi. He has written over a dozen articles and papers on education, communalism, and politics. His publications include *The Politics of Imperialism and Counterstrategies*, *The Crisis of Elementary Education in India, Global Neoliberalism and Education and its*

Consequences. He specializes in social movements, identity politics, social theory, and sociology of knowledge.

Rukmini Sen has taught courses in Sociology, Disability and Law, Law and Social Change at the West Bengal National University of Juridical Sciences, Kolkata since 2002. Her doctoral work is on tracing a culture of silence in Bengali women's autobiographies. At present, she is associated with the Centre for Women's Development Studies, New Delhi, working on the interface between gender, violence and legal terrains. She has also published a few articles in reputed journals.

Santosh Kr. Singh has a PhD from the Centre for the Study of Social Systems, Jawaharlal Nehru University, New Delhi. Presently, he is Assistant Professor in the Department of Sociology, Government College for Girls, Chandigarh. He has contributed chapters in a few edited volumes on issues concerning globalization and religious identities in India. He is also a member, scientific board, *International Journal on Humanistic Ideology*, a biannual journal published by the Cluj University Press, Romania, and contributes regularly in popular press on issues of critical social relevance. His areas of interest are sociology of agribusiness, globalization and local identities and religion.

Shaji Varghese is at present with Meta-i Technologies Pvt. Ltd., a Bangalore-based company providing educational testing and assessment services. He did his postgraduation from University of Hyderabad. His major area of interest is sociology of education. He earlier taught at the Department of Sociology at Christ College, Bangalore. He was also the recipient of the International Policy Fellowship of the Open Society Institute, Budapest in 2003, for a research project on Civil Society Organizations in the Primary Education Space in India.

Subrat K. Nanda currently teaches at the Department of RDAP, NEHU, Tura Campus, Tura, Meghalaya. He was earlier Lecturer in Sociology, Department of Extension, NEHU, SASRD, Medziphema, Nagaland from 1988 to1995 and Senior Lecturer in Sociology, Department of Sociology, Pachhunga University College, NEHU, Aizwal. His area of specialization has been ethnic and nationality questions an area in which he has published extensively.

Virginius Xaxa is Professor of Sociology at the Delhi School of Economics, University of Delhi, and was holding the Rajiv Gandhi Chair for Contemporary Studies at North-Eastern Hill University, Shillong. He is the author of *Economic Dualism and Structure of Class: A Study in Plantation and Subsistence Settings in North Bengal*, and co-author of *Tea Plantation Labour in India* and *State, Society and Tribes: Issues in Post-Colonial India.*

V. Sujatha teaches at the Centre for the Study of Social Systems, Jawaharlal Nehru University, New Delhi. She taught at the Department of Sociology, University of Goa prior to joining JNU. She has worked on sociology of medicine with particular reference to indigenous medicine in India and her book, *Health by the People: Sociology of Medical Lore* was published in 2003. She also works on sociology of knowledge.

Vivek Kumar teaches sociology at the Centre for the Study of Social Systems, Jawaharlal Nehru University, New Delhi. He was earlier Lecturer at the Unit for Sociology of Education, Tata Institute of Social Sciences, Mumbai. He has also written extensively apart from being active in the Dalit movement. He has published five books – three in English and two in Hindi. *Dalit Leadership in India*, *India's Roaring Revolution: Dalit Assertion and New Horizons* and *Bahujan Samaj Party and Dalit Assertion in Uttar Pradesh* are his books in English. His books in Hindi are: *Bahujan Samaj Party avm Sanrachnatmak Parivartan* and *Dalit Samaj: Purani Samasyaen, Nai Akanchyen.*

1

Introduction

The central task of this book is to capture illustratively some of the ongoing institutional and intellectual practices in sociological teaching and research. Some of the practices are old, some new. This volume therefore is not about changes alone, nor just about continuities, but the curious manner in which the already extant issues pertaining to sociology in India have acquired new forms and directions. For instance, the concerns which Indian sociologists have so often raised about the uneven quality of teaching and research, about the language of instruction and absence of appropriate textbooks, about the mechanical use of alien concepts and the idea of indigenous categories, remain. But they also acquire new dimensions. For instance, textbooks are now quizzed from new perspectives such as feminist or dalit. These new intellectual insights are closely linked to 'local' social and political movements. The very idea of an Indian society, the primary object of inquiry for mainstream Indian sociology, is thus looked at anew. We shall see later how this practice of methodological nationalism comes under scrutiny from quite another source, namely globalization and the purported withdrawal of the state and the increasingly interconnected nature of contemporary society.

Old debates, rehearsed many times over in Indian sociology about pure versus applied sociology, about linking or delinking with state policies, remain.[1] In older debates the key trepidation appeared to be whether the practice of sociology ought to be autonomous or not of state policies. The debate now gets both compounded and reconfigured with the retreat of the state as the central actor and the entry of a host of new actors with a proliferation of non-state institutions, such as national and international non-governmental organizations (NGOs), corporations and transnational research foundations.[2] In this transformed globalized context, the institutional and intellectual meaning of 'autonomy' and 'relevance' necessarily gets redefined.

What has changed also is the manner in which 'local' issues are impinged upon by global agendas. For example, dalit sociology acquires a global presence, linking up with global discourses on race, discrimination and exclusion. Tribal sociology engages with global debates on indigenous people. The term 'indigenous' has come to occupy wide currency in general in the deliberations of the international agencies such as the ILO and UN bodies, and particularly after the declaration of the year 1993 as the international year of the indigenous people (Xaxa*). Feminist sociology in India, however 'locally' rooted, has to perforce link/delink with global feminisms (Chaudhuri*). Ideas about 'grassroot' and 'community', self-evidently with 'local' roots resonate with global debates on the same (Mukhopadhyay*). Peter Berger has an interesting observation on what he describes as the globalization of the Western intelligentsia, what he calls "not so felicitously, the 'faculty club culture' ... carried by a variety of vehicles: academic networks, foundations, non-governmental organizations (NGOs), some governmental and intergovernmental agencies" (Berger, 2003: 4). There is an elite sector of the emerging global culture he argues, which sometimes merge with the business culture, and sometimes is in tension with it. "It too seeks actively and creates markets throughout the world, but the products it promotes are not those of multinational corporations but the ideas and behaviours invented by Western (mostly American) intellectuals, such as the ideologies of human rights, feminism, environmentalism, and of multiculturalism, as well as the politics and lifestyles that embody these ideologies" (ibid.).

It is not difficult to contest the idea that the ideologies of human rights, feminism, environmentalism, and multiculturalism are 'creations' of American intellectuals. The body of Indian 'nationalist' and ideas from 'outside the nationalist framework', its tensions and conflicts would be helpful in this regard.[3] What one can however readily recognize is that there has been a certain appropriation of both intellectual concepts and institutional functioning by a new 'global' or 'market' or 'corporate' vision that would necessarily have its impact on how the various ideologies mentioned above get reconstructed. That the American vision remains a dominant one within the present form of appropriation, I would think, holds true still at this point in history. I have argued elsewhere and in quite other contexts how studies of American Indians or American Koreans are effortlessly transcribed as Indian or Korean studies per se (Chaudhuri, 1998). I have also argued that feminism in India is either seen as an exotic other or as intrinsically lacking (Chaudhuri, 2004). The significant point here is that often this is done in deference to multicultural sensibilities and 'difference'.

The current context of globalization and India's own story within this, the immediate propelling reason for the volume, has further compounded this matter of 'appropriation' for, far too often, as the volume would seek to show, it appears as a free flow of ideas, a give-and-take of perspectives, rather than hegemony. Perhaps to describe this process as analogous to 'glocal' strategies, increasingly adopted by corporations, may not be entirely inappropriate. For indeed it is a double-edged weapon. In both instances greater visibility and recognition is made possible to 'other cultures' or 'other academics' as the case may be. What I argue is of serious import is the manner in which the content and form of both 'culture' and 'academic discourse' gets reconfigured. Readers may find both parts III and V of this volume instructive in this regard.

It is not my intent to debate the idea or the process of globalization. I simply proceed with the assumption that there are remarkable changes that have been having serious impact on our academia in general, and on the intellectual and institutional practice of sociology in India, in particular. I introduce the concept of globalization with caution for it immediately brings in questions of definitions, political perspectives and contentions. While debates on globalization are not central to this volume, it is only in order that I clarify that the focus of this volume is only on those aspects of globalization which I argue have been transforming higher education in general and liberal arts in particular. It is in this context that I seek to identify below the challenges that globalization throws up for the earlier nationalist framework within which higher education was visualized, and within which much of sociology in India was being practised.

I

The Argument: Challenges to the Nationalist Framework

The central understanding that informs this volume is that the role of higher education in modern societies, often seen as coterminous with nation-states, is of immense significance. And, within higher education, social sciences and liberal arts held a special space. However, at different points in the trajectory of capital, class formations and nations, the place and role of the social sciences tends to get redefined. I would therefore contend strongly that a fruitful way of seeking to understand the changing practices of sociology in India is to locate them in the context of the changing nature of capitalism, nationalism, the state and social movements in India.

An argument that I wish to make and one that the volume generally hopes to communicate, is that the historical context of 21st century globalization marks a shift from a capitalism of an earlier era, which despite its essentially global nature, operated with what one can be termed a nationalist framework. The changing character of corporations has to be understood likewise. The days of largely nation-based capitalism have changed. The capitalist class therefore marks a shift from being a national capitalist class to a transnational one. No better example than the contemporary case of Indian capitalist class can exist.[4]

The nation and the state have been looked at afresh in the current context of globalization. Further, and this is the central argument that the volume seeks to communicate, is that the nationalist framework has been under attack from two apparently opposing fronts, one 'local social movements' and the other 'global capital'. If we start with the 'local' challenge, a dalit view asks where was the dalit in the imagined Hindu order, or in the imagined nationalist framework (Vivek Kumar*). A tribal critique argues that while the principle of 'territoriality' is accepted widely as a basis for claiming identity as a nation, it is curiously denied in the case of tribals (Xaxa*). Likewise, the exclusive nature of the nationalist framework of gender has been a central theme in the feminist critique (Chaudhuri*). On the other hand, the imperatives of global capital also demand major changes in the nationalist framework as almost all the chapters in Part III on Sociology in Professional Institutions and Part IV on New Sites of Knowledge Production, show. This should not suggest however that the local critiques stemming from often radical social movements, women, tribal, caste or class, are in turn unaffected by the transformative potential of global capital. Indeed, often, both are at work redefining the parameters of the nationalist framework. My contention is that in some way the appropriation of academic discourse that I mentioned above could be fruitfully seen in this fashion.

The intellectual interrogations have emerged from local/national and often radical political and social movements but a point that I seek to describe is that in the current context of globalization, they too have been impacted by both global developments and sometimes appropriated by hegemonic corporate voices. For instance, the practice of social compliance audit (SCA) in the corporate sector has far-reaching implications for the labour movement (Prasad*). Radical issues in the present conjecture tend to be domesticated within the parameters of funded research (Ravi Kumar*; Chaudhuri*). The account of how a concept like 'community' alters and gets redefined draws attention to this trend in intellectual practice (Mukhopadhyay*) while the mapping of the idea of 'autonomy' indicates similar changes in institutional practice (Varghese and Santhosh*). Below I seek to develop this broad argument further with a rough attempt of what one means by nationalist vision of the university and a national public sphere.

The University and the National Public Sphere

The relationship between the university and the nation-state, which began in early 19th century Europe, was defined along three different but interconnected axes: (1) the training of students for advanced positions in the state bureaucracy or the civil society (professionals); (2) the production of advanced knowledge through research that would, directly or indirectly, serve the national community; and (3) the development of an ethos of self-cultivation and intellectual identity formation for which the German idealists introduced the term *Bildung* (Bruford, 1975). They held the practice of exclusive training in a specialized discipline, such as law or medicine, in low esteem since it was oriented primarily towards practical goals without raising the intellectual self-consciousness of the student. More recently, and nearer home the report of the Committee to Advise on Renovation and

Rejuvenation of Higher Education (henceforth CARRHE), 2009 has argued against a single discipline university, e.g., the National Law University[5] as being antithetical to the spirit of a university (CARRHE, 2009: 4).

A point of contention that is invariably raised in India today about higher education and globalization is the question of privatization. This somehow suggests that state universities are necessarily national universities. The paradigm of the national university cannot simply be reduced to the state university or the question of funding by agencies of the state. Rather, it is more important to consider the national university in terms of its complete integration into the intellectual life of the nation. Put differently, the national model defines itself vis-à-vis a national public sphere, both in cultural and political terms. The students ought to be perceived as academic citizens whose education is related not only to the needs of the state (administration) but also to the needs of the civil society (Schelling, 1966). Martha Nussbaum's recent proposal to reinvigorate the American undergraduate curriculum clearly invokes the idea of the education of citizens, and although she is quite critical of older definitions of the national community, she reconnects her project to the political nation, that is, however, defined in multicultural terms (Nussbaum, 1997: 90–91). In our own Indian context this implies that it is possible to be critical of the nationalist framework that has been exclusive,[6] yet argue for a democratic and inclusive political nation, a just world order without necessarily dropping the national project entirely.

My key contention is that what is taking place in contemporary India is a reframing of what constitutes the national project. For the moment we go with the idea that the liberal concept of the public sphere is essential for the emergence of the modern national university (Habermas, 1989). The question that looms large in present-day India is what happens when "the public sphere itself has openly transcended national borders and reflects global concerns" (Hohendahl, 2005: 89), or:

> ...Put differently, what happens to the university when it has to define its mission in transnational terms? I argue that this relatively new situation has changed the way the university looks at and assesses its resources as well as its achievements. *It can no longer be satisfied with the task of serving the nation. Instead, it develops a global map*

> *for its mission and negotiates its role within a broader international public sphere.* This transition entails not only new opportunities but also new and different responsibilities that could possibly conflict with the idea of a traditional, national university (ibid.: emphasis mine).

At one level global concerns such as global peace or global ecology are indeed more desirable than narrow national concerns. The crux of the matter however lies in who defines 'global concerns'. I argue that what is presently taking place is an apparently unchallenged ascendancy of the corporate vision in defining both the 'national' and the 'global'. For Brand India is the new 'nationalist and global vision'. It is the dominant public discourse.[7] The national bourgeoisie and the transnational capitalist class cannot possibly pursue the same agenda. My contention is that India is undergoing precisely this conflict and negotiation of very different visions of the nation and what it represents. Not surprisingly, we have had a serious look at our state of higher education. The report of CARRHE was submitted on March 1, 2009. It begins with an idea of the university, not so different from the idea of freedom articulated by Hohendahl in the western context. I quote:

> A university is a place where new ideas germinate, strike roots and grow tall and sturdy. It is a unique space, which covers the entire universe of knowledge. It is a place where creative minds converge, interact with each other and construct visions of new realities. Established notions of truth are challenged in the pursuit of knowledge (CARRHE, 2009: 9).

This invocation of "the university ... as the trustee of the humanist traditions of the world" (ibid.: 10) is accompanied by a somewhat contrary view that "university education is no longer viewed as a good in itself, but also as the stepping-stone into a higher orbit of the job market, where the student expects a concrete monetary return, and consequently in this perception, the university of today is expected to be in tune with the emerging needs of the society" (ibid.: 9–10). For university education is no longer a place only for socially privileged students and therefore the matter of employability and skills becomes even more crucial. I have no quarrel with this affirmation of democratic principles. But I would like to argue that this formulation seems to suggest that the humanist tradition of university education is essentially an elite project. As this volume goes to show some of the most interesting conceptual challenges to mainstream Indian sociology have come from the margins (Part V). An equally important point however is that our penchant to be politically correct ought not to blind us to the fact that the practice of sociology, whether in the centre or on the margins (Part II), is often dismal and banal. Indeed, some may question the very validity of including the ordinary banal everyday teaching of sociology in a volume such as this. I strongly argue that if one were to overlook the mundane, dreary, unimaginative practice of everyday sociology in classrooms spread across the country, he or she would miss the essential point about sociology and its irrelevance. But for the moment to return to the CARRHE report which argues that in order to bring back the humanist project of universities, "universities have to be autonomous spaces" (ibid.). The quote below illustrates how this *autonomy* needs to be defined and operationalized:

> Universities need the *autonomy* to operate in a healthy competitive setting. The leadership of the university must be driven by the objectives of the institution and draw on government only for macro policies. They need to set their own policies and thereby experiment with strategies on university governance. They need to be accountable to the various stakeholders – *the society, government, students, recruiters, alumini etc.* (CARRHE, 2009: 61: emphasis mine).

Significantly, the question of autonomy is privileged, but as argued earlier key concepts get reconfigured. Also discernible is a reframing of what constitutes the nation. As the quote suggests, does naming a set of disparate stakeholders constitute the nation? I would like to argue that this formulation of the university being accountable to the above mentioned stakeholders serves two purposes. On the one hand, it emphasizes accountability and democratic participation. On the other, it erodes the very content of accountability by deflecting the point that these stakeholders are unequally poised and unequally able to influence the content and structure of higher education. Surely, corporate recruiters would be in a better position to call the shots than students.

At this point, one needs to reiterate that corporate heads today are not just feted for their achievements in the corporate sphere in India, but they are also seen as intellectual visionaries who would know what is best for education in the country. The corporate vision has become the legitimate national vision though a certain degree of unease may have started to be felt even within state and corporate structures. C.N. Rao, Scientific Advisor to Prime Minister, once commented that "if you are worried about economic competitiveness and not worried about scientific competitiveness, then I think the future will be bleak" (*The Times of India*, July 23rd 2006). Kiran Karnik, NASSCOM president too, while reiterating that "the future of India is linked to the knowledge industries, and our success in these depends upon how well we nurture and grow our human resources" warned how "it is important not to convert professional education into polytechnic training" (Karnik, 2005: 10).

In this new world of pragmatism, theoretical and ideological debates are seen with some relief as remnants of a well-rid past. Teaching is seen as a tool but not really something that cannot be replaced with other means that could range from virtual teaching to online programmes. The teacher-student relationship is transformed to that of a service provider-customer one (Varghese and Santhosh*). Criticisms about armchair academics and teachers become sharper when the academic disciplines happen to be social sciences or humanities. The need of the hour is therefore to redesign disciplines to be more 'useful'. Critical debates in the public sphere certainly falls outside the ambit of the 'useful'. Contrast this with Humayun Kabir's take in the context of India in the 1950s.

> Higher education – as distinct from professional training – is abstract and often has no direct relation to the practical problems of life. *Its abstractness is however its saving virtue, for it gives to such education a universal aspect* (Kabir, 1956: 186; emphasis mine, cited in Chakrabarti*).

In the new context of 'useful' knowledge, of skill enhancement and market competitiveness sure victims are the four practices that distinguish a liberal arts education, namely, critical thinking, examination of life, encounters with difference, and free exchange of ideas. A liberally educated person should be capable of principled judgement, seeking to understand the origins, context and implications of any area of study, rather than looking exclusively at its application. This volume seeks to collectively argue that the sociological tradition is potentially able to be at the forefront of liberal education.

The issue of applied knowledge vis-a-vis liberal education can however be seen differently from the perspective of the excluded. This is evident from V. Sujatha's chapter in this volume, which refers to the body of critical commentary on the 'uselessness' of traditional, contemplative Brahminical knowledge. This, it was argued, deterred it from aligning knowledge to work and action. Intellectual energy was thereby expended on thoroughly gratuitous tasks such as the defining of rules of touchability, seeability and approachability. Besides they denigrated Pariahs and others who could have contributed to the making of such a need-based knowledge but who were prevented from doing so by a system that allowed them no access to learning. Vivek Kumar also makes a similar argument. I cannot possibly enter the larger though sharply contested debate of the democratizing potential of globalization for the previously excluded sections like the dalits and the tribals, but a mention of this in the context of corporate policies and its implications for the traditionally excluded section, is perhaps warranted (Omvedt, 2005; Hensman, 2004).

Fully conscious of the class/caste/gendered nature of knowledge, I would still argue for a possibility of a critical practice of sociology that necessarily has to negotiate with 'useful' knowledge but not always in an immediate, tangible sense of immediate application. I say 'not always' for no one can deny the imperatives that a people in dire state have, and which Nongkynrih vividly portrays in his paper in this book. As he rightly asks does the sociologist watch people die. This theme of relevance I return a little later when I seek to address some of the other themes that surface through the chapters. As mentioned earlier, many of these like that of relevance cut across the sections into which the book has been divided. I address these themes immediately after the next section that which provides a synoptic account of the book.

II

A Synoptic View of the Book

This book is divided into five broad sections. Needless to say, there are many overlapping themes that run through the book and cannot be contained within any one section. **Section I** *Society and Sociology* seeks to show the many ways that an academic discipline such as sociology is linked to wider societal processes. V. Sujatha*, Dalia Chakrabarti* and A.K. Nongkynrih* address this relationship from very different perspectives. They inadvertently also help to show how regions are different, how public discourses are different, how social dynamics vary and how they all impinge on the practice of sociology – be it syllabus making or social resistance to sociology or a possible relationship between academic sociology and the wider society

Section II *Sociology in the Margins* focuses on the uneven nature of the practice of sociology in India and the great divide between centres and peripheries. At the same time, they note that considerable differences exist within the margins just as they do within the metropolis. Regions have their own specificities and histories, hierarchies and discriminations. And, any description of even the nitty-gritty details of everyday teaching, dictating notes, examining, writing textbooks, building curriculum and negotiating in decision-making bodies involve engaging with a world outside the institution.[8] If chapters by Pushpesh Kumar* and Santosh Singh succeed in bringing alive the mundane and everyday practice of sociology in the regions, they also capture the angst and pathos of our unequal and hierarchical educational system. Subrat Nanda* puts across the story of sociology/social anthropology in North-East India and draws attention to the conceptual hegemony of an idea of Indian society, with which mainstream Indian sociology operates, and which in no small way alienates students from the discipline.

Section III *Sociology in Professional Institutions* seeks to map the actual practice of teaching sociology in professional institutions, namely, Engineering, Law, Management and Nursing. The central point that Manish Thakur*, Ramanuj Ganguly*, Rukmini Sen* and Kushal Deb* makes is that sociology as a discipline is marginal in these institutions while the institutions themselves (unlike the ones depicted in Section II) are often seen and projected as the competitive face of global India. What is also discernible in these accounts is the manner in which a shift has taken place in the institutional visions of an IIM or IIT, once more closely linked to the nationalist vision of the Nehruvian period to one more conducive to a global, transnational one.[9]

Section IV *New Sites and Modes of Doing Sociology* maps new sites and practices of sociology in globalizing India. The new sites include research institutes and non-governmental organizations (NGOs), the corporate sector and autonomous colleges. The new practices refer to the growing body of project-driven research in the research institutions and NGOs (Ravi Kumar*), the new practice of social compliance audit

(SCA) in the corporate sector (Archana Prasad*) the new orientations in teaching sociology in autonomous colleges (Varghese and Santhosh*) and the rise of corporate sociology in place of sociology in even traditional universities (Madhu Sharan*). These chapters foreground the tensions between employability and critical awareness – the twin goals of liberal education.

Section V, *Tracking Concepts* looks at the intellectual and institutional journey of some salient sociological concepts like caste (Vivek Kumar*), tribe (Xaxa*) gender (Chaudhuri*) and community (Mukhopadhyay*). They collectively show how intellectual ideas and sociological concepts are constitutive of larger political processes, whether that of local/national social movements or of globalization and the increasing role of international institutions.

III

Of Relevance and Autonomy, of Skills and Marketability

Each of the chapters in the book has its own distinct tale to narrate. Together, however, they have a broader story to communicate about the changes and continuities in the institutional and intellectual practices in sociology. I find it productive to locate this within the broader framework of change that I outlined earlier, namely, the transformations in the trajectory of capital and a shift from a national capitalist class to a transnational capitalist class with deep implications for the manner that the nation gets restructured and imagined, on the one hand, and the challenges to redefine a hegemonic and exclusivist idea of the nation by political movements of previously marginalized sections, on the other. The central argument has been that in this process, the role of the social sciences gets redefined as do matters of intellectual relevance and institutional autonomy of sociology – our key object of inquiry in this book. I attempt below two things: (i) a very quick and necessarily shorthand account of the major ways that relevance and autonomy have been debated in the practice of sociology in India; and (ii) a sketch of broad trends in the growth of skill-based knowledge and market competitiveness with its often detrimental consequences for critical liberal education. A significant argument that this volume seeks to make is that sociology has a key role within liberal education. For we "maintain that the teaching of sociology is justified insofar as a liberal education is assumed to have a more than etymological connection with intellectual liberation" (Berger, 1966: 198). This understanding of sociology, I contend, is the basic premise upon which this book rests and therefore not surprisingly emerges as a crucial theme in the exposition below.

Matters of Relevance and Autonomy: Shifting Debates

A persistent question in the practice of sociology in India has been the matter of relevance. The meaning of the term 'relevant' has however never been either self-evident or agreed upon. A brief foray into some of the debates within Indian sociology may help us appreciate what 'relevance' can mean in different contexts. "In the late 1960s, the social sciences in India were astir in search of a direction and an identity. Phrases like 'science and swaraj' were in the air" (Saberwal, 1980: 10). Decolonization and nationalization were the tasks at hand. J.P.S. Uberoi elaborates:

> Every swarajist should recognize what are the essential precondition, under this system, for the advancement of universal science in our environment. *Until we can concentrate on decolonization, learn to nationalize our problems and take our poverty seriously, we shall continue to be both colonial and unoriginal* (1968: 123; emphasis mine).

This changed over the next decade as did "the scene in international politics". "Even though the social sciences in India began to be financed relatively well, the Young Turks of yesteryear discovered that greater insulation was not synonymous with better growth; that autonomy – personal and collective – could be stagnative as easily as creative" (Saberwal, 1980: 10).

Reading through the debates of the 1970s, one is struck by the fact that the entire issue of autonomy and freedom of social science research was primarily geared vis-a-vis state funding. Savyasachi Bhattacharya, writing in 1972, thus observes that the problems of autonomy "...would also apply to the situation of the social science consultant vis-à-vis the corporate sector. In fact, such possibilities are likely to be far greater and more pernicious. But *links between social science work and the private sector have not yet been established in a big way*" (1972: 39; emphasis mine).

At the turn of the 21st century, the scene had entirely changed:

> Forced to go where the funding is, the sociologists' research priorities and criteria of relevance are determined by the sponsoring agencies,

> whether government or, *increasingly the big extra – and multinational funding agencies.* Each has its attendant hazards, *but in either case the role of sociology as social engineering is likely to prevail*, for every project – if it is not to be deemed infructuous – is expected to yield a clear set of policy implications and recommendations. Cross-country comparative projects, though often lushly funded tend to be devised without consultation with the Indian partners who are merely expected to execute the Indian 'country study' according to a *predetermined protocol* (Uberoi, 2000: 19; emphasis mine).

In many ways this book seeks to depict institutional and intellectual practices in sociology in India a decade after tangible changes had already started to be felt in the changing criteria of relevance and research priorities in sociology. A predetermined protocol and the conduct of free and autonomous research do not sit easily as evident in many of the chapters in the volume.

Skill-based Knowledge and Market Competitiveness

Globalization has indeed opened up new avenues for employment for sociology graduates as evident from many of the chapters in this volume. That employability is an important issue for students is an unquestionable fact and its 'relevance' in a hugely unequal society, such as ours, cannot be overemphasized. The observation made in the report of CARRHE (2009) is noteworthy in this regard:

> The slow but increasing democratization of higher education in India has meant that the university is no longer the preserve of the children of the elite, or of the educated/professional middle class. As more youngsters from a different segment of society enter the universities, they look at higher education as a means to transcend the class barriers. Consequently, *university education is no longer viewed as a good in itself, but also as the stepping stone into a higher orbit of the job market, where the student expects a concrete monetary return*, and consequently in this perception, the university of today is expected to be in tune with the emerging needs of society (CARRHE, 2009: 9; emphasis mine).

There are clear signs that sociology skills are in growing demand by research institutions or what Ravi Kumar* calls the NKCs and by corporations and NGOs as Madhu Sharan* and Archana Prasad* note. Marginal or otherwise premier law, management and technology institutes too require sociology. Most contributors to this volume have mentioned the recent trend in teaching as well as in research on skill-based education and the pressing need for market competitiveness. This is a concern that any student would have. As Ramanuj Ganguly* observes, a major concern among the nursing students too is their apprehension about the applicability of the knowledge learnt in college in a health sector undergoing rapid technological changes and market guided policy revisions.

Madhu Sharan* argues in the context of Tamil Nadu that two developments seem to be driving this change towards greater marketability of sociology: a pronounced increase in the importance of corporate social responsibility (CSR) and Human Resource Management (HRM) in corporations. There is also a greater awareness of the need to create an appropriate disaster management strategy, especially in the wake of the devastation caused by tsunami in December 2004. An increased demand for individuals to handle CSR and HRM portfolios in these large firms has led to a simultaneous increase in demand for students with backgrounds in Social Sciences. Those recruited are expected to carry out research, understand, relate to and engage the wider community for development programmes for their firms and to secure a good brand image. It has also led to a new branch in Social Sciences called 'Corporate Ethnography' to equip individuals to study, understand and handle issues of HRM and social development in the corporate firms. Several colleges in Chennai offer courses in 'Corporate Sociology' in their undergraduate and postgraduate streams while Madras University has introduced a full-time postgraduate course, also called 'Corporate Sociology'.

Accompanying this growth of market demand is also a concerted effort on the part of both the state and international institutions to recast education. Ravi Kumar* illustrates how the discourse and practice of education is being actively recast by international institutions, such as the World Bank, which see this world as one where "knowledge supplants physical capital as the source of present (and future) wealth" and "the quality of knowledge generated within higher education institutions, and its availability to the wider economy, is becoming increasingly critical to national competitiveness" in the global economy (World Bank: 2000: 9). This is in keeping with the broader argument I make of a shift from a nationalist framework to a global/transnational one.

Before we move on, a quick recap of some aspects of sociology's marketability may be helpful. First, there is clearly a growing demand for sociology, for corporate ethnography, for evaluation research, for social audit to mention the most obvious. And, the demand is global, for instance, the growth of the 'global professional activist' in the context of gender development (Chaudhuri*). Madhu Sharan* refers to the emergence of the corporate ethnographer while a global study notes that:

> It is not surprising to find among the INGOs, for example, professionally trained social scientists among its leadership, and social scientists within the employ of multinational corporations. A company as wealthy as Coca-Cola can boast of having fifty cultural anthropologists, sociologists, behavioural psychologists, and ethnographers on staff working on matters relating to strategic marketing (Hunter and Yates, 2003: 338).

Second, this demand requires certain sociological/anthropological skills, a kind of quick ethnography in some cases, and in many cases, basic survey methods and some quantitative analysis. Third, it leads to very different sets of criteria as the model for evaluating liberal arts and social science programmes as Varghese and G. Santosh* observe. Programmes in IT and management studies become the legitimate model. The new criteria for evaluating the significance of a discipline are externally the employability of students and internally the capacity to generate revenue. As Giroux (2005) points out, globally "...cost efficiency, restructuring and downsizing have become code words to tie education more closely to the ideological and economic imperatives of the labor market. This is evident, for instance, in the current conservative assessment of liberal arts programs as ideologically expendable and economically unfeasible". In the immediate context of the college, Varghese and Santosh* observe that this trend inevitably leads to a stratification of departments, students and disciplinary knowledge. Despite greater employability, sociology cannot compete on par with commerce or economics when the success of an academic programme in the college is assessed on the basis of revenue generation, employability of the students, industry demand, on-campus recruitment etc. These new contexts offer not only new possibilities to the practice of sociology, but also a whole new series of challenges and predicaments.

Fourth, *this leads to* the recasting of the teacher to a 'service provider' and the student to a 'customer'. The overall objective of education is reduced to the production of individuals with skills and attitudes required by the market economy. Increasing marginalization of teachers is amounting to what Naidoo and Jamieson call 'distortion of pedagogic relations' and that is likely to be corrosive of both sides of the relationships (Naidoo and Jamieson, 2005). Fifth, the organizational restructuring based on market competitiveness in autonomous educational institutions create hurdles for socially and economically weaker sections to claim access to these centres of learning. A similar economic logic also leads to disciplinary hierarchies, where disciplines espousing humanistic perspectives such as sociology are subordinated to more instrumental and market-oriented disciplines.

Indian sociology has been aware that this growing 'marketability' is a double-edged weapon. As Yogendra Singh writes, "the globalization and liberalization of the economy also creates new opportunities and demands for certain types of skills and education, which may pull away an increasing number of scholars and students from liberal and humanistic social sciences such as sociology" (1986: 11). He, however, fears that vocationalizing sociology would invariably disturb the core of *sociological training*... which is to "inculcate in them *the ability to critically comprehend the place of these forces in the scheme of social order* from a critical-historical perspective" (ibid.: 13 emphasis mine). Or else we will be swamped by a discourse of sociology/social science, which is only about quantifying, organizing and evaluating techniques. This not only provides the authority by which action is justified but it also supplies an idiom by which "the work" is accomplished on a day-to-day basis whether they are corporations conducting "pre-research", NGOs evaluations, or "women employing statistical analysis to evaluate the effectiveness of USAID" (Hunter and Yates, 2003: 337).

Not surprisingly, Kushal Deb* teaching sociology in a globalized IIT finds it an onerous though stirring task. I draw from his chapter to capture his Rip Van Winkle like experience:

> ...in the midst of an overwhelming technological ambience, my disciplinary and research interests seemed out of place... I accept that those who want to specialize in applied fields, which are directly related to the technological sphere, should be encouraged to do so.

> Networking and getting massive funding for projects remain important because these activities get the discipline visibility and employment for those research students who are without fellowships. But those like me who cannot hold CEP courses, do consultancies or get massive projects also have a place within that framework. We are doing a very crucial job. We are training future technologists to think critically, to be sensitive to the conditions of the poor and oppressed sections of our society and inculcating in them secular and humanitarian values.

What Kushal Deb is arguing for and what the volume is more broadly seeking to do is a plea for the practice of sociology that helps not just critical thinking but endows basic democratic and egalitarian values. This perspective one has contended so far is under attack from a vision exclusively oriented to skill enhancement and market competitiveness. I would however also strongly argue that this tradition of liberal humanist education has long been under attack, even within what I refer to as the nationalist framework. The single most compelling reason for this has been the poor and alienating quality of sociology taught. A very important need exists to shift the discussion of relevance from the realm of marketability to matters of disconnects between the lived society and the taught sociology, between the idiom of sociology and language of society and social thought, and between the richness of sociological classics and the deadening wordiness of notebooks. I argue too that we need to discuss the world of ordinary banal sociology not just because it is widespread in the institutional and intellectual practice of sociology, but also because only by addressing it we can hope to change it.

IV

Banal Sociology and the Question of Relevance

I return here to the context that propelled my earlier venture into *The Practice of Sociology*. I quote:

> The single most important concern that motivated envisaging a project such as this was a feeling that there was something amiss with how and what we teach. ...There was a strong feeling that the students could not make/teachers could not communicate *one*, the connections between the sociology they studied and the society they lived in, and *two*, between theory papers and papers on Indian

society or for that matter between any one paper and another (Chaudhuri, 2003: 1).

Many of the issues that were addressed in the book such as the relevance of sociology, its image and employment opportunities, the skills that the discipline endows us with the relationship between sociology, society and the self, the theoretical and conceptual apparatus that has dominated Indian sociology and its implications for substantive research – reappear here. And, I reiterate again that "any attempt however to address these queries... have to invariably draw their analysis away from the classroom, from the academia to the larger world outside. In this important sense, the kind of sociology visualized here in the pages of this volume challenges the arbitrary divide between the word and the world" (ibid). This volume carries this task forward. I attempt below a schematic account of the many reasons that go into the making of the poor self worth of sociology and its wide reputation as being irrelevant.

For many postgraduates in social sciences and sociology in India, as so many of the authors here bring out poignantly, the degree is only relevant so far as it yields social prestige in communitarian and kinship domains. In many cases it does not even fetch them a job. Yet in the perception of the students, having a degree is certainly better than not having one. As Santosh Singh* observes of a college in Uttarakhand where he taught, that in the last more than two decades, its most productive and tangible impact appears to have been to "make" the daughters of the area more eligible for marriage for its largely migrant male population! Pushpesh Kumar* likewise refers to the prevalent joke that many men and women who pursue postgraduation in sociology and other social sciences do so in order to mention this in their wedding invitation cards! He writes that most of the rural male students opt for sociology as they think that they can easily look after their agricultural operations at home along with their sociology course. The girls who opt for sociology assume it is easier as they already know what is to be known about family, marriage and kinship – standard topics in a sociology course.

Pushpesh Kumar* recalls how disturbing is it to hear that some of the NET and SET qualified students in sociology are doing manual jobs in factories to sustain themselves. There is nothing else that they can do with their sociology degree, if they do not get a teaching job locally. This is not an easy task as recruitments in local colleges are often linked to 'cash transaction'. That sociology graduates are not easily employable has been running theme in any discussion about sociology in India (Unnithan et al., 1967). V. Sujatha* too mentions the "high social value" of the M.A. degree and its latent social function. Sociology seems to perform a crucial social function in the university setting in such situations. It provides a soft option for the first/second generation learners by virtue of being 'general' (less technical) and by virtue of dealing with the familiar thing called society. This degree becomes the social and cultural capital for the marginalized. The story as Subrat Nanda* notes is not very different in the otherwise distinct North-East. Students mostly opt for sociology to get a general academic degree or to get into the single career option of teaching the subject in colleges and universities. Ramanuj Ganguly* likewise comments that sociology is still seen as having little direct relevance to nursing.

Is this story of the everyday ordinariness of doing sociology irrelevant to our debate about the 'weightier' matters of critical sociology? I do not think so. Central to this volume is the belief that sociology and society are interconnected, and that knowledge is socially produced and consumed. Surely, the poor state of research and teaching of sociology in many parts does not fall outside the purview of sociological investigation. Surely too, there is a necessary connect between the wider educational policies and the extant hierarchy of disciplines, between centres of excellence and margins of mediocrity. What relevance can sociology have if it fails to even transmit bare skills and make students employable. The possibility of critical sociology is a remote possibility. Should one conclude hastily that teachers and students in such settings do not "think", do not "reflect" and are inherently "uncritical". The existence of rich local debates, social movements and social thought which so many chapters refer to clearly suggest otherwise. Explanation for the emaciated state of sociology lies therefore in an inability on our part to grasp and communicate the interrogative spirit of the sociological perspective which alone would make it possible for us to engage with and integrate local traditions of social thought and sociological theory.

The state of higher education in India is uneven and unequal. We have pockets of excellence, most often read as centres of technology, management and law – the skills that global capital requires. The 'humanities' or 'arts' streams in schools[10] have always been considered the refuge of those who can do no better, cannot manage science or commerce, and are usually girls. Many 'leading' schools actually no longer offer humanities as an option after the class X. Two dominant ideas circulate in middle-class India, namely, the utter 'uselessness' of subjects such as social studies; and that the only skill required for it is learning by rote and memorizing vast amount of information. The story ends there. Its only redeeming feature is the purported mass of disparate information that it contains. As Madhu Sharan* notes:

> Most still feel that Sociology is a very general subject regarding the 'sociability of people' and since it is so general, there is no need to study it. The comments from a senior faculty member at MOP Vaishnav College teaching Sociology for over 10 years, perhaps sums up the attitude of the society in Tamilnadu towards Sociology, "the status of Sociology in Tamilnadu can only go up if the name of the course is changed from 'Sociology' to 'B.Sc. Social Engineering' as anything to do with 'science' and 'engineering' has a lot of value."

The above comment draws attention to two very significant points: one, the hierarchy of disciplines and the hegemony of technology, and two, the self-evident commonness of sociology. It is no easy task to confront with these two ideologically deep-rooted and potent ideas. Nor can they be challenged with the kind of sociology that Pushpesh Kumar* and Santosh Singh* describe. It needs serious engagement with the discipline, with theoretical and philosophical questions so central to sociology. It also needs exposure to serious sociology texts. And, finally, it needs mastery of the discipline and a willingness to communicate the sociological imagination that can then connect personal problems with public issues.

Dalia Chakrabarti* observes how dictated notes turn the students into copying machines without any power of intervention. If the notes are not updated, then, it is more pernicious. Prepared notes to be dictated by a teacher also destroy his or her ability to argue more effectively. *Notes received either in classroom or in tutorial homes are substandard because these are very often dilutions of serious textbooks, or do not have critical points of departure, or are usually close-ended, and usually inhibit learner's initiative to learn something through his or her own intellectual efforts* (emphasis mine).

Classroom transactions have a very important role in the devalued and battered state that sociology finds itself in so many places. Neither self nor society, nor the relationship between the two, gets discovered. Instead, there is a vague sense of dull, wordy information that has to be memorized and upon which one will be tested. In such a situation, it is the 'wordiness' itself that may provide a sense of worthiness to sociology. V. Sujatha* has already outlined why examinations make more sense in such a context. Santosh Singh* too makes a similar observation: "...patterned answers are easy to evaluate".

The travesty that our "note books" are, have a huge role to play in perpetuating the idea of sociology as a dull, pedantic subject that deals with society. This is very important but unfortunately still only part of the story. There is a conceptual issue here about the idea of Indian society, the central object of inquiry for much of Indian sociology is today under serious questioning for its exclusive and discriminating character. It will be evident from the exposition below that when the 'society and self' in the textbook and the 'society and self' of students do not match, a kindling of the sociological imagination is impossible. Subrat Nanda's chapter* problematizes the very idea of a homogeneous Indian society that can be grasped by the triad of caste, religion and family. He notes that tribal students of the region express discomfort and a sense of disconnect in understanding and assimilating several aspects of *Indian Sociology* or *Society in India* as the contents of this course mostly focus on the mainstream Hindu social institutions, culture, values, religious order, etc., with very little or no reference to the peripheral and minority societies of the North-East. The 'text view' of Indian society is mainly derived from the indological and the scriptural sources, which mainly depict the Hindu social system. Likewise, the 'field view' of Indian society, which is derived from several 'village studies', reflects the mainstream Hindu social institutions and values to a great extent. Many scholars do not accept the expression 'Indian society' or 'Indian social system' and would rather use the expression "forms of social life in India".

This critique is developed more extensively by Vivek Kumar* who argues that while the Hindu social order as taught in the sociology classes is a 'social construct', yet teachers across the country portray it as a given. Further, he contends that the deliberate and forced inclusion of groups within the so-called Hindu social order led to the virtual erasure of their distinct belief system, worldview and life styles.

Accompanying this was also a cognitive blackout of dalit worldview, their icons, movements in the sociology taught at different levels of the educational system. Only the rise of the dalit movement and studies forced Indian sociologists to take note of dalits. As we witness many counter-narratives to the extant dominant one, the possibilities of bridging some disconnects between diverse selves and society may occur. At the same time, it is important to recognize the dangers of narratives which are mirror reflections of the hegemonic one.

Indian sociology is perhaps more self-conscious today than it ever were about how social orders are constructed. We learn from Amites Mukhopadhyay* how discourses of aboriginality and primitivism operating in colonial labour market made possible ethnic stereotyping of labourers and fetishized the correspondence between aboriginality and physical strength as a crucial element in the construction of adivasi personhood. And, from Virginius Xaxa,* the political and intellectual dimensions that mark the complex journey of the concepts of 'adivasi', 'tribes' and 'indigeneity'.

If the very construction of an 'Indian society' fails to connect with students, it is not surprising that the medium of English language through which it is communicated in many parts makes the task even more complex. This issue of the difficulties of teaching/reading sociology in English is encountered in every region of India. That the more privileged section usually is competent in the language further compounds the complex hierarchies at work. This contentious issue has been differently raised by the authors of this volume. Pushpesh Kumar*, in his observation that the local students when taught in English felt "that this is not their sociology – their sociology is that which is taught in mother tongue and 'rooted in their own culture', touches upon the critical link between culture and language, so central to a sociological/anthropological approach". V. Sujatha* describes the process whereby candidates from the *muffasil* entering higher education in social science learn English and also imbibe the disengaged standpoint that the disciplines demand as 'neo-sanskritization' in the university system. In many regions the textbooks are in English. In many they are not. In both cases the quality of textbooks is questionable. As Pushpesh Kumar* writes, the sociology of local text books is coloured by the predominantly upper caste worldview of the authors, and buttressed by the continuing domination of the functionalist paradigm. I think, this combination has had an enormous import on the teaching of sociology. Unfortunately, there are no counter texts[11] referred by teachers and students of sociology to challenge this. Pushpesh Kumar* further observes that this seems ironical in a context where there is a strong dalit movement in the region, a visible and vibrant public culture with five to six local newspapers debating dalit issues. The city has also seen the development of a dalit counter-culture defined in terms of their marriage rituals, worship and festivals. Sociology teachers however have not responded to this development as of any particular interest. I would argue that this is the failure of our system which has been unable to communicate either the passion or the potential of sociology as a discipline. For, the entire discipline, not unlike many other cognate social sciences in India, is simply seen as a sum of sub-standard questions and ready-to-be learned answers. Available guidebooks are the only source of sociology.

Indeed, the disconnect between social thought and sociology is a crucial point that V. Sujatha* makes. Hence, while debate as a mode of public expression called *Patti manram*, between two parties with a judge who declares the winner on the basis of better argument, is quite central to Tamil culture, it leaves the classroom bereft of its influence. She thus feels that because of barriers of linguistic expression, the written annual examination becomes acceptable as it facilitates prior preparation and memorizing the answers, ironically, especially on theory. She further argues that though publication of textbook material in regional languages would have helped

> ...the fact remains that the conceptual concerns of formal sociology such as relation between individual and society, debates about holism and atomism, rationality and sentiment and the like, in themselves did not hold student's interest. Even in substantive courses on religion, caste and social change, *academic writing in the sociological style that speaks about everything from nowhere was difficult for students to inculcate* (Sujatha, emphasis mine).

There are two points being made here. One that abstract debates may not hold interest to students. And, two, that students do not connect to academic writing in the sociological style that speaks about everything from nowhere. I would argue that there is no inherent quality of deterrence that abstractions have. However, the 'sociological style', the language from 'nowhere' does not invite spontaneous response. This is in contrast to the language from somewhere as in the case of the voices of the dalits, the tribals, women, ethnic minorities, backward regions that increasingly challenge the mainstream contours of sociology. Unfortunately, as Sujatha* observes, disciplinary sociology has not been able to establish a symbiotic relationship with the social thought of the regions. This is compounded by the fact that disciplinary sociology itself is often reduced to 'guidebooks' with not even a family resemblance to the discipline.

V

Conclusion: In Defence of Sociology

My effort in this introduction is a somewhat ungainly effort to capture what has been described as the multitude of hierarchies within which sociology is practised in contemporary India (Varghese and Santhosh*). In their words "these diversities of contexts emerge from a number of factors including the diverse geographic locations, medium of instruction, rural/urban disparities, caste/class composition of the students, specific traditions and histories of certain centres of learning...". The task of addressing the institutional and intellectual practices of sociology in India is thus a difficult though necessary task. The task is rendered even more difficult because contemporary India is witness to many diverse developments – both global and local. I have argued that some of the new developments linked to globalization, which privilege skill enhancement and market competitiveness may, even if unwittingly, erode the critical thrust of sociology. I however contend that there have been other serious and persisting reasons that have worn down the strength and vibrancy of the sociological perspective. Salient among them is the state of sociological teaching and research that I have sought to capture above. There is an urgent need to reaffirm the critical possibility of sociology, which the authors of the volume believe in, notwithstanding the banality that may mark the practice of sociology in ours and in many other parts of the world. In Kushal Deb's* words:

> I had instantly taken to Sociology because it seemed to possess a strong subversive potential. Its strength seemed to lie in its ability to unravel the relations of power and domination implicit in everyday life, and in social processes and institutions. The insights one got into

the nuances of human relations, and working of various social/political/economic institutions was for me enlightening and gave me a certain sense of emancipation.

I take this opportunity to return to Peter Berger to reiterate the power of the sociological perspective:

> ...*the teaching of sociology is justified insofar as a liberal education is assumed to have a more than etymological connection with intellectual liberation.* Where this assumption does not exist, where education is understood as purely technical or professional terms, let sociology be eliminated from the curriculum. It will only interfere with the smooth operation of the latter, provided, of course, that sociology has not also been emasculated in accordance with the educational ethos prevailing in such situations. Where, however, the assumption still holds, *sociology is justified by the belief that it is better to be conscious than unconscious and that consciousness is a condition of freedom.* (Berger, 1966: 198; emphasis mine).

I would also like to push the point that the theoretical openness of sociology, seen as a lack especially versus a discipline like economics, is 'useful'. "One of the great advantages of sociology in the context of a democratic conversation is precisely its openness. The self-reflexivity of individuals is also reflected in that of the discipline itself..." (Lauder, et al., 2004: 8).

As I come to the end of this introductory chapter, I hope, the volume will help in some small way to articulate a sociology of sociology that "explores both the micro-politics of everyday life and the macro-politics of institutional silencing and exclusion" inspired by Bourdieu who had sought to direct "the sociological and historical gaze back on the disciplinary habitus itself" with a "lens not only for seeing what is passed over, for bringing "the undiscussed into discussion," but also for understanding the disabling (as opposed to enabling) constraints and soft censorships that social fields place on those who labour within them (Topper, 2005: 157–58).

Notes

* References to authors' writings in this volume have been marked with an asterisk (*)

1. See Mukerji (1952), Unnithan et al. (1967), J.P.S Uberoi (1968), Singh (1973), Saberwal (1979), Dhanagare (1980), Jayaram (1980), Saberwal (1980), Singh, (1986), Oommen and Mukherji, (1988), Thapan (1991), Giri (1992), P. Uberoi (2000), Shah (2000, 2005), Sundar et al. (2000), Beteille (1972, 2003) and Chaudhuri (2003).
2. See TFR 2000; WDR 1998/99.
3. See works by Pandita Ramabai, Bhagat Singh, Periyar, Gandhi, Ambedkar, Nehru to mention but a bare few. Also relevant in this context is a delink between Indian social thought and the institutional practice of sociology, which many of the chapters take up. See in particular V. Sujatha, Pushpesh Kumar and Vivek Kumar.
4. Almost every other day newspapers are flush with stories of Indian business buying off corporations globally, e.g., the case of the Tatas buying off Corus, Lakshmi Mittal, Indian citizen, British resident's deal with the French steel giant Arcelor are just the more popularly known cases.
5. See Rukmini Sen*.
6. The exclusivist understanding of Indian society in sociology has been critiqued in many of the chapters in this volume.
7. I have argued earlier how advertisements since the 1990s have redefined Indian media and thereby public discourse. See Chaudhuri (2000, 2001, 2005). In recent years I see indications that the academia too may play a similar role.
8. See Amites Mukhopadhya's* reference to the need to incorporate "community capacity building" in the curriculum and Nongkynrih's* comment on including SHGs within the curriculum.
9. Manish Kumar's* perceptive analysis of the visions of IIM over the decades provides us a window to observe this shift.
10. See the National Curriculum Framework (NCF) (NCERT) 2005.
11. The NCERT Class XII textbooks in sociology (2009) have attempted a somewhat different rendering of sociology textbooks.

References

Berger, Peter L. 1966. *Invitation to Sociology: A Humanistic Perspective.* Harmondsworth: Penguin.

—. 2003. "Introduction: The Cultural Dynamics of Globalisation" in Peter L. Berger and Samuel P. Huntington (eds.), *Many Globalizations: Cultural Diversity in the Contemporary World.* Oxford: Oxford University Press, pp. 1–16.

Beteille, Andre. 1972. "The Problem" *Seminar* 157 September, pp. 10–14.

—. 2003 "Newness in Sociological Enquiry" in Maitrayee Chaudhuri (ed) *The Practice of Sociology*. New Delhi: Orient Longman, pp. 403–419.

Bhattacharya, Sabyasachi. 1972. "All the ifs" *Seminar* 157 September pp. 37–40.

Bottomore, T.B. 1975. *Sociology as Social Criticism*. London: George Allen & Unwin.

Bruford, Walter H. 1975. *The German Tradition of Self-Cultivation: Bildung from Humboldt to Thomas Mann*. London: Cambridge University Press.

Chatterjee, Partha. 2002. "Institutional Context of Social Science Research in South Asia" *Economic and Political Weekly* August 31, 2002. pp. 3604–3612.

Chaudhuri, Maitrayee. 1998. "Among My Own in Another Culture: Meeting the Asian Indian American" in Meenakshi Thapan (ed.) *Anthropological Journeys: Reflections From the Field*. New Delhi: Orient Longman.

—. 2000. "'Feminism' in Print Media" *Indian Journal of Gender Studies*, 7:2 pp. 263–288

—. 2001. "Gender and Advertisements: The Rhetoric of Globalisation", *Women's Studies International Forum* Vol. 24 No3/4 pp. 373–385.

—. 2003. *The Practice of Sociology*. New Delhi: Orient Longman.

—. 2004. *Feminism in India*. New Delhi: Kali/Women Unlimited.

—. 2005. "A Question of Choice: Advertisements, Media and Democracy" in Bernard Bel et al. (eds) *Media and Mediation Communication Processes* Vol. 1. New Delhi: Sage, pp. 199–226.

Dhanagare, D.N. 1980. "Search for Identity" *Seminar* 254 on 'Studying our Society' pp. 23–26.

—. 1993. *Themes and Perspectives in Indian Sociology*. Jaipur: Rawat.

—. 2003. Social Policy Concerns in Indian Sociology, Presidential Address, XXIX All India Sociological Conference, Indian Sociological Society.

Giri, Ananta. 1992. "Creating a Community of Discourse in Sociology in India." *Economic and Political Weekly* 28 (29–30) pp. 1538–39.

Giroux, Henry A. and Patrick Shannon. 1997. *Education and Cultural Studies: Toward a Performative Practice*. New York: Routledge.

Gouldner, Alvin. 1973. *For Sociology: Renewal and Critique in Sociology Today*. Harmondsworth: Penguin.

Habermas, Jurgen. 1989. *The Structural Transformation of the Public Sphere*. Cambridge, Mass: MIT Press.

Hegde, Sasheej. 1989. "On Sociology in/of India: Towards a Discursive Deviation". *Social Scientist* 175–6. pp. 93–108.

Hunter, James Davison and Joshua Yates. 2003. "In the Vanguard of Globalization: The World of American Globalizers" in Berger and Huntington op. cit., pp. 323–357.

Hensman, Rohini. 2004. "Capitalism Without Borders" *Economic and Political Weekly* March 6, pp. 1030–34.

Hohendahl, Peter Uwe. 2005. "The Transnational University and the Global Public Sphere" in Max Pensky (ed) *Globalising Critical Theory*. Lanham: Rowman and Littlefield Publications, pp. 89–112.

Kothari, Rajni. 1972. "In Search of a Role" *Seminar* 157, September, pp. 17–23.

Jayaram, N. 1998. "The Social Reality" *Seminar* 254 on 'Studying Our Society' pp. 18–22.

Joshi, P.C. 1972. "The Question of Relevance" *Seminar* 157 September pp.24–29.

Karnik, Karan. 2005. *The Hindu*, July 18th.

Krishnaraj, Maithreyi. 2005. "Research in Women Studies: Need for a Critical Appraisal" *Economic and Political Weekly* July 9th Vol. XL No. 28. pp.3008–3017.

Lauder, Hugh, Philip Brown and A. Halsey. 2004. "Sociology and Political Arithmetic: Some Principles of a New Policy Science", *The British Journal of Sociology* Vol. 55, No. 1, March, pp. 3–22.

Lynd, Robert S. 1939. *Knowledge for What?* New Jersey: Princeton University Press.

Mills, C. Wright. 1959. *The Sociological Imagination*. London: OUP.

Mukerji, D.P. 1952. "Sociology in Independent India" *Sociological Bulletin* 1(1)

Nandy, Ashis. 1972. "Conspiracy of Incompetence" *Seminar* 157 September. pp. 30–2.

Naidoo, Rajni and Ian Jamieson 2005 'Empowering Participants or Corroding Learning? Towards a Research Agenda on the Impact on Students Consumerism in Higher Education' *Journal of Education Policy* 20, 3, 276–81.

Naik, J.P. 1972. " Status and Potential" " *Seminar* 157 September, pp. 15–16.

Narlikar, Jayant V. 2005. "Reaching for the Stars" *The Times of India*. July 30th, p. 24.

Nussbaum, Martha C. 1997. *Cultivating Humanity: A Classical Defence of Reform in Liberal Education*. Cambridge, Mass.: Harvard University Press.

Omvedt, Gail, 2005. "Capitalism and Globalisation, Dalits and Adivasis", *Economic and Political Weekly* 40: 47, 19th–25th November, pp. 4881–4884.

Oommen, T.K. 2000. "Professionals Without Professionalism" *Seminar* 495. November 2000. pp. 24–28.

Oommen, T.K. and Partha Mukherji (eds). 1988. *Indian Sociology: Reflections and Introspections.* Bombay: Popular Prakashan.

Saberwal, Satish. 1980. "For Renewal" *Seminar* 254 on 'Studying our Society' pp. 1218.

Schelling, F.W.J. 1966. *On University Studies,* trans. E.S. Morgan, ed. Norbert Guterman. Athens: Ohio University Press.

Shah, A.M. 2000. "Sociology in a Regional Context" *Seminar* 495 November 2000, pp. 45–49.

—. 2005. "Higher Education and Research: Roots of Mediocrity" *Economic and Political Weekly* (XL: 22823) May 28–June 4th. pp. 2234-2242.

Singh, Yogendra. 1986. *Indian Sociology.* New Delhi: Vistaar.

Sundar, Nandini, Satish Deshpande and Patricia Uberoi. 2000. "Indian Anthropology and Sociology: Towards a History". *Economic and Political Weekly* 35(24) 10th June .

Topper, Keith. 2005. *The Disorder of Political Inquiry.* Cambridge: Harvard University Press.

Thapan, Meenakshi. 1991. "Sociology in India: A View from Within" *Economic and Political Weekly* 26(19): 11 May. pp. 1229–34.

Uberoi, J.P.S. 1968. "Science and Swaraj" *Contributions to Indian Sociology* n.s.2: 1968:119–23.

Uberoi, Patricia. 2000. "*Déjà vu*" *Seminar* 495 November, pp. 14–19.

Unnithan, T.K.N., Yogendra Singh, Narendra Singhi and Indra Deva (eds). *Sociology for India.* New Delhi: Prentice-Hall India, 1967.

Documents

Report of the Task Force on Higher Education in Developing Countries (TFR), (Published by the World Bank, Washington, D.C. 2000) This report is also available via the internet, at http:/www.tfhe.net The report is called 'Higher Education and Developing Countries: Peril and Promise.'

'Knowledge for Development' World Bank's World Development Report (WDR 1998/99) (Published for the World Bank by Oxford University Press, 1999).

National Curriculum Framework Review (NCERT, 2005).

Report of "The Committee to Advise on Renovation and Rejuvenation of Higher Education" (CARRHE) 2009.

Part I

Sociology and Society: Different Takes

Links between the historical specificities of a society and the discipline of sociology, whose overt intent is the 'study of society', are manifold, complex and reciprocal. This is the central argument that informs this section though each of the three chapters may appear to deal with very disparate themes, for instance, the relationship between sociology and social thought in Tamil Nadu; academic sociology and developmental needs in Meghalaya; and society in West Bengal and the making of a sociology syllabus. Both the dominant social formations, be it colonialism or the extant class/caste system as well as the counter-hegemonic challenges to it, impinge upon the making and acceptance of an academic discipline such as sociology. Likewise, the existing power structure of society is implicated into the very making of a syllabus, an entity otherwise seen widely as a neutral set of topics whose sole reason to exist appear to be the possible examination questions that it can generate. On the other hand, sociologists have perforce to rework and rethink their relationship to society and the people that they seek to study by exploring possible relationship between academic sociology and the wider society.

2

Disciplinary Trajectories and Social Trends

Sociology and Social Thought in Tamil Nadu

V. SUJATHA

A crisis in social sciences in the past decade has been noted by surveys in India (Chatterjee, 2002). Compared to the situation in 1950–75, the period after 1980 has been one of lull in terms of disciplinary output and theoretical development. Partha Chatterjee (2000) attributes this situation to the fall in state funding for higher education. The effect is manifest in the poor quality and quantity of research work. Thus, there is a temporal factor in the performance of social science from a rather glorious past with the not so glorious present.

Apart from the temporal aspect, Chatterjee (ibid.) also finds a problem with the spatial distribution of performance. It is disconcerting that while there are about 423 social science departments and three dozen research institutes throughout the country, bulk of the research output is concentrated in few institutions in the capital. Chatterjee also mentions that there have always been poor performers right from the beginning, such as the institutions in south India. The survey on the state of social sciences in the south (Pandian, 2002) draws attention to the theoretically sophisticated debates in the South Indian literary circles by non-formal academics. However, apart from pointing out to the "hegemonic presence of English as the language of social science practice in India" (ibid.: 3617), he does not engage with the question at any length.

In spite of a focus on a narrow set of institutional factors, this and similar reports of the state of social sciences in India are guided by a genuine concern for disciplinary growth. With regard to temporal factors, a major concern is about funded projects that undermine critical theoretical engagement. As regards the spatial distribution, the accounts are tacitly informed by a notion of centre and periphery. They explain poor performance in terms of financial resources, institutional lapses and the lack of will for quality research and teaching in the *muffasil*/periphery. While the university system which the disciplines inhabit is certainly affected by factors like resource availability and motivation for research and teaching, these are factors internal to the institution. The institution is located in a larger social milieu from which it draws its candidates and the social composition of the populace has a bearing both on institutional and disciplinary performance. The performance of disciplines, especially those in the social sciences, cannot therefore be attributed only to institutional factors. With the exception of Deshpande (2002; 2008) who draws our attention to larger societal trends and highlights the complex nature of social dynamics in the country, other reports fail to locate the discussion in a larger context.

There are a host of presuppositions that underlie such institutional accounts of disciplinary trajectories. First, the belief that a body of knowledge once created or transplanted in an institution – be it sociology or history – will have to continue stably, irrespective of social transformations. Secondly, reporting the institutional factors alone in a pan-Indian or global review is based on the presumption that disciplines have a uniform character that could be replicated in all similar institutions, irrespective of social context. Thirdly and importantly, when we say that social sciences have not done well in Asia and a host of other countries in the southern part of the globe, we are left only with Europe and America that seem to have done well. If a large section of the world is not doing very well in the discipline, then, do we not interrogate the discipline? Thus, the status reports seem to be status quo reports in which the discipline is taken for granted and there is no scope to examine if non-performance in a discipline is an indicator either of the lack of its social purpose or its rejection by the dominant section of society in the region concerned. Fourthly, observations about the concentration of research output in few premier social science institutions in the country are based on the presupposition that inclination for a subject/discipline ought to be moderately spread throughout a given society. The reasons for imbalance are sought in factors internal to the university system without interrogating the relation between social thought of a region and its social science.

When we examine a larger canvas, say a region or culture, we could ask *how the discipline performs* among people of different social background. The point is that even within the framework of university education, not all disciplines share a similar position in the social consciousness of the people of a region. Different social and historical factors condition the acceptance of certain forms of disciplinary knowledge by certain social groups. We therefore need a more nuanced perspective to examine disciplinary trajectories in relation to cultural perspectives of the dominant sections of society in any particular region.

This paper is an attempt to examine the situation of sociology in Tamil Nadu based on the assumption that social science disciplines are not epistemologically neutral and that performance of disciplines cannot be accounted for only by recounting institutional factors, particularly in social science, which is heavily conditioned by language. This is true of both international and intra-national differences in academic performance.

Accordingly, the paper seeks to examine, from a sociology of knowledge perspective, why social sciences, specifically sociology, occupy an insignificant position in Tamil Nadu. The case of Tamil Nadu is particularly interesting because it is one region in the country where the social sciences, except economics, have not had a good track record from the beginning, in terms of enrolment at M.Phil and PhD level, research output in peer reviewed journals and the number of books/textbooks published through publishing companies of national repute. While the case of West Bengal where the social sciences have done particularly well right from the beginning would be an interesting counterpoint in this regard, by virtue of being an explorative attempt, this study is limited to Tamil Nadu. Some cursory references to the case of Bengal would be resorted to in order to highlight key points.

This paper draws on status reports of the discipline, interviews with professors and students in Tamil Nadu and reflexive engagement with the discipline as a student of sociology from Tamil Nadu and is organized in four sections: one, setting out the position of sociology in Tamil Nadu, second, looking at the function and associated characteristics of the discipline in the region, third, setting out the relation between worldview and sociology, highlighting key themes in the social thought in the Tamil region during the 18th–19th century, and lastly, an attempt to look at the relation between knowledge, structural positions of protagonists and their interests.

I

Sociology in Tamil Nadu

As we know, independent sociology departments in India started in a big way only after the 1950s. In Tamil Nadu, Annamalai University in Chidambaram was the first to launch the undergraduate (henceforth UG) course in sociology in 1954 and the postgraduate (henceforth PG) course in 1957. The PG curriculum laid stress on theory, Indian society, methodology and social statistics. Rural sociology, industrial sociology and labour welfare were some of the areas of interest on which M.A. dissertations were submitted.

The department of social sciences in Madras University was established in 1966, but the independent department of sociology came about only in 1976 after four failed attempts since 1917 (Sundaram, 2007). It was finally possible only in 1975 when the new Vice Chancellor of Madras University, Professor Malcolm Adiseshiah closed down the department of social sciences and created independent departments of economics, political science and sociology (ibid.). Around the same time the Madurai Kamaraj University in Madurai and the Bharathiar University in Coimbatore established their PG departments of sociology in 1976 and 1977 respectively under the semester pattern. Five more universities introduced sociology later. At present, there are about eight universities in Tamil Nadu that offer postgraduation and doctoral research in sociology apart from the MIDS that offers doctoral and postdoctoral research facilities.

The M.A. sociology curriculum, when it was launched in 1976 in Madras University, emphasized the primacy of 'ideas' from classical sociology. The first board of studies meeting of the department, which consisted of members from Delhi, Bombay and Mysore, resolved to adopt 'book-centred critical pedagogy of sociology of ideas' and 'a quest for the social' as opposed to the field view based on anthropological orientation (ibid.). The sociology of ideas model, rather than social anthropology based on fieldwork, was thus the chosen model for curriculum development in M.A. sociology in the other universities in Tamil Nadu as well.

Enrolment and Pedagogy

In Tamil Nadu, ever since its introduction in the university, student enrolment for postgraduate degree in sociology in general has been low, varying between a maximum of fifteen to about two students per year. While the applied and engineering sciences, economics and history have had many seekers in the same universities, sociology has not attracted many students.

Whether enrolments were small or large, the disciplinary content of sociology and its theories did not seem to appeal to the students. As is true of most departments in regional universities, the language of the sociology texts is English and this has been a major barrier to learning. Class presentation as mode of internal assessment would not work here because of barriers of linguistic expression, though debate as a mode of public expression called *Patti manram*[1] has been quite central to Tamil culture. The written annual examination would be acceptable because it facilitates prior preparation and memorizing the answers, especially on theory. Memorizing essays for a discipline like sociology may seem inappropriate to modern sensibilities but it has been an accepted method of learning among Tamil youth[2]. Publication of textbook material in regional languages would have certainly contributed to the appeal of the subject, but academic writing in the sociological style that speaks about everything from nowhere was also difficult for students to inculcate.

This is reflected in the number of registrations for PhD in sociology which has not been very high in most institutions in Tamil Nadu. Even when there were higher M.A. enrolments, it had not translated into greater numbers at the PhD level. For instance, during the twenty-year period from 1979–99, a premier institute in the region, MIDS had a total of 36 students registered for PhD (in social sciences in general, the proportion in sociology is much smaller) out of which 18 had dropped out (Pandian, 2002). At Madras University, during the twenty-year period 1966–85, there were 7 Ph.Ds. in sociology and in 1985 there were 10 people registered for PhD (Sundaram, 1985). The department of sociology at Madurai Kamaraj University has had during the thirty-year period 1976–2006 about 25 PhD students (MKU website).

A common and important reason for poor performance of sociology at higher levels is that the PG degrees in sociology do not fetch jobs. But, the social value of the M.A. degree in social sciences is high in other South Indian states and it is a crucial vehicle of social mobility. In Tamil Nadu, however, unlike other South Indian states, M.A. sociology did not have much social value either. Here, the upwardly mobile sections of society have chosen to empower themselves through salaried jobs in government and private institutions. Science and technology courses for upper echelons of the society and polytechnic and a host of other technical, semi-professional courses like catering, hotel management and travel services for the upcoming sections have been the preferred avenues of employment. The preference for job-oriented education reflects that here educational achievement is expected to culminate in economic achievement in terms of a stable job. M.A. degrees that do not open the door for employment are not valued even as a residual option.

It is important to note that few colleges affiliated to the university offer sociology at the UG level. Tamil Nadu has the highest number of private colleges in the country, but they all in part professional or vocational education, where aspiring Tamil youth from villages and towns would like to go. How do we explain this indifference of Tamil Nadu to disciplinary sociology? A look at the social thought in Tamil Nadu in the last two centuries would give us some clues. But before that we must consider the relation between social thought and sociology itself.

II

Social Thought and Sociology

The use of the concept 'world view of sociology' by Yogendra Singh (2004) is a suitable entry point into the question of the relationship between social thought and sociology. By world view he means the normative and ideological constructions about societal reality prevalent at a particular time period from which sociology draws its categories and domain assumptions. The relation between social thought and sociology lies at the basis of the European self-understanding of emergence of the discipline and is spelt out time and again in accounts of origin of sociology. Thus, Weber highlighted the disenchantment of the world and the process of rationalization as precondition (Bauman, 1978) to the emergence of sociology which is then a more formal, perfected and systematically articulated form of the prevalent world view. The emergence of an economy based on capitalism and the secular state with the individual citizen as its subject is cited as a factor in the historical birth of the self-conscious individual in modern Europe. But, such a self-presentation of European thought that sociology is the product of its modernity is wrought with several difficulties which we will not go into. Suffice to point out whether anybody could talk of one 'world view' of Europe in the first place. What about the blacks, ethnic and racial minorities, immigrants and their world views and social history? What happened to their social knowledge during centuries of slavery which characterized the emergence of European modernity? Did the societal self-awareness not include them as to produce a notable sociological thinker worthy of inclusion in the curriculum? Was it the actual world view of elite intellectuals that was universalized by institutional replication? These questions have been avoided in mainstream theories linking modernity and birth of social science, which have constituted the oppression as an object of enquiry without including the oppressed as subjects/knowers in sociological knowledge.

In any case, sociology derives its strength by being rooted in a world view or what we may call as the (dominant) social thought of the times. In the words of Yogendra Singh, "The historical and pedagogic situation of sociological worldview links sociology deeper with the 'language of sources' which the public articulate, as well as the design and play of the artist, the literati and the philosophers which mirror sociological concern in a generalized, cognitive and evocative form. There is, and there has always existed, as says Bourdieu, a closer relationship of correspondence, both cognitive and appreciative between the 'spontaneous sociology' of the literary forms and the 'scientific sociology' resulting from 'socio-analysis' of reality by sociologists." (2004: 27–28)

The world view of a society in the sense of its concerns in art, literature and philosophy thus bears upon its sociology to a large extent and the relation between the two has been central to both the genres of intellectual activity. Bourdieu and Wacquant (1992) suggested disciplinary reflexivity as a measure to maintain the relation with the 'language of the sources' and guard against reification of sociological categories. In Bourdieu's formulation, however, 'the sources' speak in one 'language'; there is no scope here for many coexisting languages and world views and the relations of power between them.

Yogendra Singh identifies the problem when he says, "for a time the theoretic concerns overwhelmed the sociological practices in teaching and research, and as sociology gained recognition from the public, the ruling elite and the intelligentsia, its orientation became more formal than normative. To some extent, this dilemma is inherent in the very principles and operations which distinguish theory from the worldview of sociology" (2004: 28).

The dilemma, as we can guess, is particularly acute in the regions characterized by heterogeneity in which the relation between social thought and sociology becomes problematic. Consider the situation of Tamil Nadu that has been the site of major social transformation and political activism during the 20th century.[3] An overview of the intellectual orientation in relation to the key players in social arena may strengthen our argument.

Socio-cultural Concerns in 18th Century Madras Presidency

The Tamil region is one of the regions where printing made its debut as early as 1679, initiated by missionary scholars both Jesuit and Lutheran in their missionary zeal for proselytization. By 1712, the number of books published in Tamil was 266, far greater than in other languages in the country – Persian (100) and Bengali (84) (Blackburn, 2003).

What was interesting was apart from the translation of biblical scriptures in Tamil, missionaries also wrote original treatises in Tamil verse setting out their philosophy. Another remarkable development was the collection and publication of folk tales effectively used by the missionary scholars, such as the one that took a dig at the Hindu missionary order[4] (Blackburn, 2003: 63).

At the same time, we have to note the rise of Saiva siddhanta as a counter movement that appropriated the rhetoric and methodological skills of the missionaries to spread its philosophy of Tamil Advaita; its adherents were the *Vellalas*, an agricultural community. Ramalinga (1823–74), a saint, proposed a heretical variety of Saivism that was deeply influenced by Christian notions of peace and charity as well as

Islamic conceptions of piety. In some sense Ramalinga's life represented the creative encounter of Hinduism with the forces of change that beset Tamil region (Geetha and Rajadurai, 1998). The challenge to religious orthodoxy from the heretic and popular traditions combined with the birth of new literary practices in Tamil and the emerging histories of the Tamil language as against Sanskrit during the late 18th century are considered as key landmarks in the emergence of a new Tamil selfhood (ibid.).

In Bengal, on the other hand, more than half of the publications in print were new texts by the westernized elites that debated different aspects of the interface between tradition and modernity (Roy, 1996). The social elites in Bengal had begun to opt for English education and the growth of English literacy was a striking 100 per cent during 1891–1901 (Chatterjee, 1996). There has been parallel growth of 'societies of learning' which published material on natural sciences and the liberal arts. Here, by 1820s, "the new intelligentsia was already engaging with the modern disciplines of knowledge" (ibid.: 12). Such an engagement was facilitated by the intellectual background of the new literati in Bengal, which was grounded in traditional systems of philosophy like *Nyaya and in Tarkasastra.* Translations of scientific and mathematical texts from European languages and debates on social philosophies such as Comte's positivism were not uncommon during this period in Bengal.

Discussing a treatise on a modern science of politics by Anandachandra Mitra (1854–1903), Chatterjee observes, "Echoing the familiar sentiments of the new intelligentsia, he says that as long as the object of education remains only the acquisition of certain money making skills, there is no possibility of serious discussion on the philosophical principles of science" (ibid.: 106). Thus, there seems to have been an emphasis on philosophical debates rather than a concern with the ordinary.

While our aim here is not a comparative analysis of Bengal and Tamil Nadu, it is illustrative to see the differences between the protagonists of change and their social thought. As we proceed we would see how viewpoints on issues such as philosophy versus crafts, knowledge and skill, vary with the social profile of the protagonists in the two regions. Crucial to this discussion is an understanding of occupational mobility and consequent structural changes.

By the turn of the 19th century, when the Bhadraloks of Bengal were engaged in philosophical debates on science and tradition, the Brahmins of Tamil Nadu were already trying their hands in business and industry, apart from holding government posts by virtue of their English education. For instance, the *Kallidaikuruchi* Brahmins started moneylending for trade in agricultural produce. Brahmin youth employed in British engineering and automobile firms acquired technical skills on the job and started their own units. The Hindu newsprint of Kasturi Iyengar (1878), Sundaram Iyengar's TVS group (1908), Seshasayee brothers who started with *muffasil* bus service during World War I and moved to engineering industry, Krishnamachari's TTK group (1928), Anantaramakrishnan's Amalgamations group (1938), and other companies like Enfield and Standard Motors in Madras are some examples of Brahmin entrepreneurship that started with engineering and automobile industry during this period (Damodaran, 2008). This was also the trend with the landed agricultural castes in the Kongu region of the south which by the late 18th century ventured into commercial cotton cultivation and started their own ginning units which later became textile mills that has turned the Coimbatore region into the Manchester of the south. Notwithstanding the notion that the elite Bengalis inclined towards intellectual engagements were indifferent to trade and business, their sustenance in business was constrained by a host of historical factors (ibid.). Even the northern Brahmins and the landed agricultural castes, with few notable exceptions, do not seem to have particularly distinguished themselves in business. Thus, there has been a steady movement toward industry in the Tamil region though business and financial transactions largely proceeded through kin networks in the early phases (ibid.). Certain sections of the depressed castes in the region were also freed from the confines of feudal ties through Protestant missionary education and work in overseas tea plantations.

In the Madras region, by late 19th century, a very different discourse emerged. The entry of various castes into industry had created a demand for educational institutions. With the establishment of Madras University in 1857, the preponderance of Brahmins in higher education that ensured their positions in the administration came to be discussed by various caste associations in the region (Radhakrishnan, 1993). In 1881, government estimates revealed that there was only one member from other Hindu communities to every

125 Brahmins with F.A. and B.A. degrees (ibid.). By then caste associations of various non-Brahmin communities had begun to file independent petitions against Brahmin dominance and the prioritization of the liberal arts and languages over the crafts. Against the background of these structural tensions, one could see the emergence of a non-Brahmin world view.

Social Thought in the Tamil Region in the 19th–20th Century

Notable among those perspectives in late 19th century Madras, was a dalit-subaltern perspective spearheaded by Iyothee Thass (1845–1914) "a Tamil savant, siddha medical practitioner and socio-political activist some fifty years before the mass diksha at Nagpur" (Aloysius, 2004: 17). In his initiative, modern Tamil Buddhism came to be formulated in the Sakya Buddhist Society in 1898 in Madras under the encouragement of Colonel Olcott of the Theosophical Society. In fact, this Tamil Buddhism of early 19th century is said to have culminated in the consistently articulated movement led by Babasaheb Ambedkar in the forties (ibid.). The weekly Tamil magazine *Oru Paisa Tamilan* (One Paisa Tamilian) was started from Madras in 1907 and published a sustained critique of Brahmanic ritualism, myth making and superstitions. The movement had an urban bias and it spread through the deployment of poetic literature in Tamil.

Tamil Buddhism sought to reject both the secular atheism of the European enlightenment and Brahmanical ritualism and sought to maintain a middle path by devaluing ritual without disputing transcendence (Aloysius, 1998: 108). Iyothee Thass rejected Sanskrit language and its philosophies and advanced a strong critique of Brahmanic texts, behaviour and practices. He described all Brahmanical learning as unproductive and passive in that it encouraged laziness (Geetha and Rajadurai, 1998). In his view, such a mode of knowing had several implications. "Firstly, the Brahmins' contemplative knowledge deterred him from aligning that knowledge to work and action. Intellectual energy was thereby expended on thoroughly gratuitous tasks such as the defining of rules of touchability, seeability and approachability. Secondly, through the centuries, the arts of religious enquiry, useless and irrelevant as they were, had been developed in all their subtlety and differences such that there were a plethora of creeds, each advancing its own claims on truth and wisdom. In addition to the creeds of the past, there had come to be new ones, the Brahmo Samaj, being one of them."[5]

According to Iyothee Thass, modern degrees like B.A. and M.A. had only created a vast constituency of disaffected and restless intellectuals, who because of the failure to put their knowledge to practical use for a honest living, were led to agitate, hold meetings and show off their learning. He further argued that the useless knowledge systems of the Brahmins "impractical and internally inconsistent, had lead to a consequent underdevelopment of the practical arts of agronomy, irrigation and transport. Besides the labouring Pariahs and others who could have contributed to the making of such a needs-based knowledge had been prevented from doing so by a system that allowed them no access to learning" (cited in Geetha and Rajadurai, 1998)

Thass criticized swadeshi nationalism on the grounds that it was delinked from labour and had no viable alternatives to alleviate economic misery. He argued that the British government was a neutral arbiter in the caste-ridden Indian society and often helped the British officials track down rebellious Congressmen.

In the realm of language, the debates focused more on the power relation between Sanskrit and Tamil rather than on the relation between Tamil and English. The sense of 'difference' between the Aryan and Dravidian cultures was already disseminated by the Orientalists on the one side and the Protestant missionary scholars on the other, who wrote on the Dravidian kinship and languages. By the early 20th century, the dominant sections of Tamil society abandoned the search for an alternative religious paradigm. Instead they opted for a political offensive against the Brahmin community informed by *pagutharivu* (rationality) and *naathigam* (atheism).

The formation of the Justice Party was to demonstrate the essential difference of the non-Brahmin, who could evolve a culture, with its own values and conventions based on the ancient Dravidian principle of equality. Among the areas of reform taken up by the non-Brahmin movement was education. In their writings during the year 1917 the leaders of the movement criticized the government policy of overemphasis on secondary and higher education in favour of the Brahmins and the neglect of primary education that would benefit the labouring castes. Thus, there was a situation where graduates were manufactured in thousands while primary education was in shambles. Arguing that "a few very highly educated individuals cannot constitute a nation", they pointed out how Madras University encouraged Sanskrit learning against the vernaculars of the masses and how public funds were devoted to the study of a dead language while money cannot be found for primary education which is of utmost importance to the ordinary people. One of the key leaders in the early phases, Theagoraya Chetty, remarked at the pathetic state of technical education in relation to the arts and philosophies which had no practical value. He compared Japan's highly skilled workforce brought about by their superior education system and argued:

> Why is this so? In British India with a population of 255 million, the universities have 36,000 students pursuing a literary course, while only 12,000 study in technical schools, which teach mostly typewriting, book-keeping, short hand, etc., Japan, on the other hand, with a population of 51 million, has only 7,500 students pursuing a literary course in its universities whereas 29,00,000 pupils attend technical schools (Geetha and Rajadurai, 1998: 131).

The non-Brahmin leaders envisaged an educational model which would educate the vast but illiterate people into virtues of citizenship and also teach them a useful trade. In this mission, primary education was seen as an important component though not sufficient. Technical education was important to equip students to earn a living and learn new skills necessary to keep pace with a changing world. New techniques of agriculture and trade were the need of the hour.

The Justicites could not succeed is introducing all the reforms in education but by 1923 secured an enlargement of the Madras University Senate that included a representation of various communities. Talks of reservation of seats in government institutions that began in the late 19th century materialized by 1921, thereby ushering the displacement of Brahmins and other forward communities from public institutions. Geetha and Rajadurai (1998: 135) point out how the educational model put forth by the Justicites was not "merely a means to gain access to the precincts of the government. Rather, it envisaged learning as a continual process integrally linked to work and labour". They cite the testimony presented by the Secretary of the Vishwakarma Mahajana Conference in 1916 which outlined the difficulties of students of industrial and artisanal classes to pursue technical education in the foreign countries even when they had the skills because they lacked formal literacy.

As Geetha and Rajadurai argue, the non-Brahmin castes had become aware of the hiatus between formal literacy, which many of them could not meet and 'a certain kind of experiential and guild' knowledge which they knew they possessed. *Hence, their plea that education and work, labour and knowledge cohere with each other'* (1998: 135, emphasis mine). The leaders of the non-Brahmin movement saw their communities as the producing communities having a material stake in the speedy industrialization of the country. Drawing attention to the growth of Bombay – the premier city of India – Varadarajulu Naidu, a leader of the movement, remarked:

> A barren island becoming the premier city of India! What was the cause of this greatness? It is not Sanskrit literature, it is not the world-admired Sankara's philosophy, it is not [even] the political greatness we are hankering for which made Bombay great. It is enterprise – the enterprise of a small community – the Parsees (cited in Geetha and Rajadurai, 1998: 135).

The non-Brahmin movement spearheaded by the Justice Party did include the Adi Dravidas in order to evolve a singular opposition to Brahmins, but in practice this was not possible because of the thorny relationship of the non-Brahmin landowning castes to the labouring Adi Dravidas. So, a coherent non-Brahmin front conscious of their economic and political interests got consolidated only by early 20th century.

The evolving non-Brahmin sentiment was strengthened by the well formulated discourse of E.V. Ramaswamy Periyar, an erstwhile Congressman inspired by Gandhian ideals of prohibition of liquor, abolition of untouchability and spinning (Geetha and Rajadurai, 1998). His idea of *samadharma* (equality) based on self-respect sought to encompass the marginalized – both women and the depressed classes – and was different from the condescending tone of many a (Brahmin) Gandhian. He strongly advocated communal representation in the electorate and the need for non-Brahmins to occupy strategic positions in the government.

After a stint with some Brahmin scholars at Hyderabad and with mendicants in Kashi, Periyar was unsparing in pointing out the anomalies in Hinduism in particular, and religion, in general. Periyar dealt with great sarcasm and with various events and characters of the Puranas. He argued that "owners of knowledge, unlike owners of wealth were not subject to contingencies arising out of trade, famine, marauding kings and wars and at all times could mediate and construct their authority as supreme" (cited in ibid.: 376).

Periyar advocated the acceptance of a religious world view consistent with the principle of self-respect, such as Buddhism or Islam. He thought that all temples and *mutts* be demolished and turned into schools and factories. While Congressmen were debating the temple entry of the Adi Dravidas, Periyar argued that they demand access to public wells. Based on his conceptualization of the relation between private property, sexuality and caste, he advanced a theory of marriage and family as a contractual arrangement and evolved the institution of self-respect marriages, including remarriage of divorcees and widows. He was an ardent supporter of contraception for woman that gave her the right over herself, of course, apart from education.

Periyar's idea of *samadharma* or equality had a set of economic correlates but was founded to be a principle of social equality based on the self-respect of each individual. Proportional representation in government services, access to public spaces, property, education and employment were stressed and the principles of (Marxian) socialism were incorporated under the banner of *Podhu Udaimai* (common ownership of property). His trip to Russia helped him observe the socialist movement and its strategies. He argued that the worker's question in our country was implicated in the caste system and hence was more complex than the European situation.

Periyar was highly critical of the Gandhian khadi movement and the bid to strengthen the handicrafts which he saw was one way of keeping the artisanal classes in cumbersome, labour-intensive occupations. Besides, it was an inefficient form of production. He underscored the need for improved skills in the use of machines pointing out how technology would offer leisure in the life of the artisans that they could utilize in many ways.

By the 1940s the self-respect movement had crystallized into the Dravidar Kazhagam (DK) whose young followers carried forward a programme for Dravidian nationalism having rejected the Indian independence of 15 August 1947. But its call to the left parties did not meet with positive response from the CPI because it found that the DK was not sufficiently socialist in composition; it was supported by wealthy non-Brahmin merchants and landlords.

III

Sociology and the Politicization of non-Brahmanism

After independence, the polarities that the self-respect movement highlighted acquired a largely political character. DK saw the 'northern Bania-Brahmin complex' as its prime opponent and launched the anti-Hindi agitation. This period was also characterized by violent attacks on the Brahmins by DK activists.

The formation of Tamil Nadu state and the emergence of various factions espousing the Dravidian ideology are other developments. Coterminous with these developments is the erosion of the social content of the movement. Its fight for the abolition of caste and gender inequities gave away to political assertion and parochialism of few non-Brahmin castes to the exclusion of the Adi Dravidas. The widespread prevalence of untouchability[6] and atrocities against dalits by non-Brahmin communities (Viswanathan, 2005) in contemporary Tamil Nadu testifies to the obliteration of the social aspect of the non-Brahmin movement. Even during Periyar's time, the oppressive attitude of non-Brahmins towards the dalits within the DK was a major problem, but was not articulated.

This is also true of the position of women in Tamil society. The Dravidian parties sidelined Periyar's radical ideas about women's freedom and his critique of the Tamil literary corpus for eulogizing chastity as a value only for women (Anandi, 2003). Only those aspects of his thought that facilitated the claim of men of the landed castes to political power were selectively appropriated. By achieving higher proportion of reservation than the rest of the country, the backward classes consolidated their hold on government positions and educational institutions, sustaining the ostracism and ridicule of 'Brahminism' in political rhetoric and public discussion.

But the horizontal unification of the non-Brahmin communities, their disdain for philosophy, their emphasis on the relation between work and knowledge and their demand for technical and skill-based education had come to constitute the world view of Tamil society. In the Tamil Nadu of the seventies and eighties, the aspirations of the socially mobile sections was thus to empower themselves through technical skill and salaried jobs in the private sector. While this would be true of most regions in the country, a well-articulated set of ideas in the public domain and an explicit agenda of education and empowerment unfolded in the social thought of the non-Brahmin movement in Tamil Nadu.

The problem in devising a sociology curriculum that is sensitive to the concerns of the time is evident in the discussion about restructuring the syllabus in the late eighties. The committee appointed by the Tamil Nadu government for restructuring UG and PG courses in universities opined in 1989, that "the grammar of sociology as expounded by founding fathers does not address some of the emergent issues in the west (let alone the orient)".[7] Quoting from Alvin Gouldner, the report says that task of sociologists "is to see themselves as they see other people. It is nothing but heightened self-awareness among sociologists". Accordingly, the report recommends a course on 'Social Analysis' as an intermediary between theory and empiricism. Social analysis should facilitate students to bring in analytical insights into the study of actual social issues and has since been introduced as a compulsory paper in M.A. throughout the state.

Further, the committee mentions that it would be a futile task to engage with the theory of society in itself, yet it would not be possible to tailor sociology to job profiles. Therefore, it recommends that the application aspect of the university courses be improved and courses like rural sociology, urban sociology and urban development, industrial sociology and personnel relations, social planning, social statistics and social demography become compulsory courses in the M.A. The curricular focus is here quite different from that of the metropolitan sociology departments in the capital.

Sundaram's interesting distinction between frontyard and backyard institutions is helpful in understanding the character of sociology in different institutions. The first point of distinction is the domain of operation. Research for publication is a central component of frontyard institutions. They have a strong theoretical component and get their research work published in peer reviewed journals. We can see that frontyard institutions fulfil the manifest academic function, while the backyard institutions are engaged in producing reports for government departments, or other funding agencies and their work has more of a descriptive and evaluative component.

Frontyard and backyard difference may also be observed in the realm of pedagogy: "The teachers who teach the issues of society are the backyard sociologists while the teachers who develop the teaching to go beyond the substantive issues by conceptualizing the theoretical and methodological frameworks are the frontyard sociologists" (email interview in 2007 (b)). Further, backyard sociologists rarely refer to original sources in sociological theory and rely on simpler bazaar notes in teaching. Thirdly, Sundaram highlights the disciplinary concerns when he adds, "Many teachers in sociology simply describe the issue, for example, the incidence and characterization of child labour. While some others after substantiating child labour, can conceptualize how society produces child labour and how production is constructed by the issue of child labour" (ibid.). Sundaram points out that Durkheim thus took up the social issue of suicide, but went beyond description to discover its social causes. Backyard sociology however is not 'backward' sociology as Sundaram hastens to clarify. A frontyard teacher does it, as she/he has the social and cultural capital, and he/she is addressing a different audience.

It is evident that frontyard institutions would have a totally different set of priorities based on the presumed autonomy of sociology from concerns of applicability. They would engage in meta-theoretical questions like tradition and modernity, identity, rationality and the like, and would not consider it 'hard core' sociology to be doing something on social analysis, social problems and social planning. In frontyard sociology, there is a translation of real problems into sociological problems through a theoretical engagement with underlying forms of sociality and this calls for a disengagement with the given. Social sections, which are undergoing transformation and are implicated in the process of mobility, probably adopt different modes of intellectual engagement with the 'social'.

Import of modern technology and market economy and fostering educational institutions that cater to the market, has been the strategy of the dominant classes in the Tamil region.[8] As the university system has been slow to respond, private engineering colleges have mushroomed. Presently, there are 271 self-financing engineering colleges in Tamil Nadu, the highest in the country, producing about 1.1 lakh engineers per year (*The Hindu*, June 2008). In fact, most of the (non-Brahmin) caste associations run their own group of professional colleges where 35 per cent[9] of the seats are filled on payment. As for sociology, it has been accepted only in so far as it could provide a viable career option. Our point is substantiated by the fact that two years ago, the university department in Chennai introduced M.A.

corporate sociology and an autonomous college opened M.A. in medical sociology in collaboration with private hospitals and have been successful in terms of both enrolment and placement. This also explains why industrial sociology and personnel management is an important course in M.A. sociology in most of the South Indian universities whereas sociology of science and technology never made its debut here.

Strengthening the government primary and secondary school education in Tamil medium has brought many more sections of the population into the ambit of school education. For the same reason social science disciplines that require English language skills like philosophy, sociology and political science have not been favoured even as soft options in Tamil Nadu unlike the other South Indian states. Professional courses like engineering and polytechnic that do not necessarily require proficiency in English and are based on technical skill and logical abilities, are in popular demand. Interestingly, the research methodology course in the M.A. sociology programme in Tamil Nadu universities is heavily based on survey/quantitative techniques, unlike in the metropolitan sociology departments where the focus is on methods like narratives and in-depth interview whose application in research is heavily conditioned by writing skills in English.

It is important to note that disciplinary sociology in Tamil Nadu even after the non-Brahmin movement continues to be alienated from the literary and social thought of the region. In the Tamil Nadu of the 1980s, non-academic writers, CPI and non-Brahmin activists in Tamil literary circles were writing in what is called 'small' non-commercial literary magazines (*siru pathirikaigal*). They wrote in Tamil on European schools of analysis like structuralism, Marxism and existentialism; translations and commentaries on these paradigms abound the Tamil literary productions. Later, Sri Lankan and NRI Tamil writers, and professors of Tamil in foreign universities, started actively contributing to the Tamil intellectual magazines whose current circulation and e-presence is turning out to be significant as this sector is moving out of the non-commercial mode. Critical analyses of ethnic and caste conflicts, debates between dalit and backward class literary genres, film criticism, social history of Tamil sub-regions, biographies and life histories and, of course, commentaries on the works of

European/American social and literary theorists get published in the 'small non-popular magazine' sector in Tamil. However, in the past four decades, there has been no link whatsoever between these initiatives and the social science academy at the university in the Tamil region. Banerjee (2008) claims that this is true of Bengal as well, yet in comparison to the Tamil region, some links have been forged in the Malayalam and Bengali institutions. Kerala and Bengal have generated regional sociological journals in English to foster the connection between debates in the regional language and English. Regional variations in the nature of the connection between social thought and sociology thus bring out the nuanced interplay of class, language, political movements and the social organization of the university.

IV

Conclusion: Knowledge and Interest

The foregoing account is intended to show how interests of the dominant social classes condition at a point in time, the proliferation of disciplinary knowledge in a region notwithstanding the general problems that plague universities in the country. It is pertinent to examine differences in disciplinary trajectories even within the university system because they are indicative of macro trends and changes in perspective. We may well go beyond institutional histories that list landmarks and status reports that present statistics of output; it is time we probe into data for insights on disciplines and the social classes they attract.

Interests and inclinations, however, are not fixed for any social group. Intellectual inclinations of any section are not irreversible; social landscapes and thereby interests do change. But, the connection between historical experience, interests and social knowledge, which sociology applies to other bodies of knowledge like medicine, natural sciences and religion, has never seriously been applied to sociology itself, or if it has, has not informed the accounts of disciplinary trajectories based on the centre periphery framework.

As mentioned earlier, the question about the relation between social thought and disciplinary sociology is not specific to India. In fact, in the Indian context, the debates on social inequality emerged sooner in the process of social transformation, have been far more radical and covered a wider social base than the public sphere in Europe, in spite of enormous regional and linguistic diversity. In western nation-states, on the other hand, the relation between sociology and class ideology has been a thorny issue despite the monolingual mode and smallness of socio-cultural variation. It is common knowledge that in the European context, erudition in philosophy and classical languages endowed the passion and ability on elite thinkers to make sociological theories out of issues emerging from the bourgeoisie public sphere. The Marxists intellectuals in Europe have been sensitive to the issue and have critiqued the bourgeois nature of sociology in which theorizing is divorced from the conditions of labour. Nevertheless, the question as to why the proletariat could not achieve class consciousness on their own and why it had to be infused from outside by bourgeoisie intellectuals are vexed questions even within Marxist thought. The link between social theory, academic practices and social thought has received little attention within the academy in the West, which continues to rest on the rationalization thesis oblivious to the lifeworld of ethnic and racial minorities and immigrants. The influence of class perspective on the academic practices in French social science institutions known for excellence has been noted (Bourdieu, 1988). But it is treated as a problem of bias of an otherwise 'epistemologically neutral' discipline and is resolved by the call for reflexivity (Bourdieu, 1992). Reflexivity and more reflexivity has been the most enlightened response of the discipline to this ontological problem.

The call for indigenity in social science will be devoid of any insight if we do not ask certain foundational questions about the discipline that were never addressed seriously by sociology in the West. Examining different kinds of knowledge of social life, the modes of their expression and the ways on which language, identity and social interests are interwoven, would facilitate an internal critique of the discipline. This is eminently possible in several non-European societies where the simple and unitary model of rationalization/modernization would be problematized by the politico-intellectual assertion and disciplinary trajectories in different regions (Mukherji, 2005). This could help in arriving at a more responsible response to the mutual alienation of social thought and sociology than postmodernism.

Notes

1. *Patti manram* is a debate between two parties with a judge who declares the winner on the basis of better argument. Generally, it is on literary issues. Presently, the Tamil cable channels have made good use of this tradition and conduct Patti manrams on popular social issues, for instance, whether the family or the society (read, state) is more favourable to women, whether youth today are spoilt or not, whether women are loyal to parents or in-laws, and the like.
2. Memorizing textual material has always been privileged method of learning in (south) India. During my work with siddha vaidyas I found that the vaidya would commit to memory more than 100 verses from the siddha medical texts and this was an essential part of the training. Apart from the fact that this was warranted because of the oral nature of the traditions and absence of the culture of writing, memorizing was valued as a cognitive tool that improves memory of details and allows the student to get the basic terminologies right at an young age, without much reflection so that they may be understood or pondered upon when the learner has found the use for them (for details, see Sujatha, 2007). Memorizing Tamil verses and reciting them is an accepted part of language classes. In this sense it is understandable that many of the students would memorise sociological texts, especially the classics and key concepts like dialectical materialism.
3. Historically, Tamil Nadu has been home to a number of religious traditions that it is difficult to locate a consistent Hindu orthodoxy – the five epics in classical Tamil literature were all both Buddhist and Jain contributions. The major corpus on secular social ethics, namely Thirukural was authored by Thiruvalluvar, a Jain poet. The seminal treatise on Tamil grammar Tolkapiam was written by Tolkapiar also a Jain. Further, the siddha spiritual tradition one of whose outcome is a medical system by the same name, was a heterodox tradition in that the authors were mendicants from diverse social background and they formulated a systematic conceptualization of the body and soul which was different from conventional ideals of *moksha.* Siddha notion of the body and self has been found to be the basis of the world view of the Tamils in historical accounts (Irshick, 2003).
4. *Paramartha Guruvin Katai* (the story of Guru Simpleton in a Hindu ashram), a bilingual text (Tamil and English) combining Tamil oral tales and European story literature, plus the authors imagination was published in London in 1822.
5. Iyothee Thass as paraphrased by V. Geetha and Rajadurai (1998: 66).
6. The segregation of dalits by providing government housing in colonies away from the main village, two glass system in public tea shops and attacking dalit contesters in panchayat elections, have always been happening during the term of the Dravidian parties. In a row over the wall

erected against dalit settlement in a village in Madurai, the ruling party has remained complacent. See Tamil magazine *Kalachuvadu,* June 2008 issue for details.

7. Report of the sub-committee to the high level committee of Government of Tamil Nadu to restructure the syllabus of the UG and PG courses in Tamil Nadu Universities, 1989, p. 15.
8. Also see Madhu Sharan's chapter in this volume for a contemporary analysis of trends in Tamil Nadu (ch. 14).
9. In fact, the proportion of payment seats in relation to seats allotted on merit in private engineering colleges is matter of huge debate in Tamil Nadu, involving conflict between ruling and coalition parties (*Dinamani*, 7 June 2008). Inevitably, the Chief Minister has to intervene because private colleges engage in hard bargaining and refuse to hand over payment seats for merit allotment. Even at the rate of Rs 32,500 per student fixed by the government, the colleges earned Rs 125 crore per year on payment seats and the fee has doubled since 2008 (*The Hindu*, 7 June 2008).

References

Anandi, S. 2003. "The Women's Question in the Dravidian Movement: c1925–1948", in Anupama Rao (ed.), *Gender and Caste*. New Delhi: Women Unlimited and Kali for Women, pp. 141–163.

Aloysius, G. 1998. *Religion as Emancipatory Identity: A Buddhist Movement among Tamils under Colonialism*. New Delhi: The Christian Institute for the Study of Religion and Society and New Age Publishers.

—. 2004. *Dalit-Subaltern Emergence in Religio-Cultural Subjectivity: Iyothee Thassar and Emancipatory Buddhism*. New Delhi: Critical Quest.

Banerjee, Parthasarathi. 2008. "Interlocutions with Social Studies and Society as the Objects of Inquiry: Language of Traditional Pundits in Nineteenth Century Bengal", in Sabyasachi Bhattacharya (ed.), *Development of Modern Indian Thought and the Social Sciences*. New Delhi: Centre for Studies in Civilization and Oxford University Press.

Bauman, Zygmunt. 1978. *Hermeneutics and Social Science*. London: Hutchinson and Company.

Berger, Peter. 1963. *An Invitation to Sociology: A Humanistic Perspective*. London: Penguin Books Limited.

Blackburn, Stuart. 2003. *Print, Folklore and Nationalism in Colonial South India*. New Delhi: Permanent Black.

Bourdieu, Pierre. 1988. *Homo Academicus*. Cambridge: Polity Press.

—. and L.J.D. Wacquant. 1992. *An Invitation to Reflexive Sociology*. Chicago: Chicago University Press.

Burawoy, Micheal. 2007. "The Future of Sociology", *Sociological Bulletin*, Vol. 56 (3), pp. 339–354.

Chatterjee, Partha. 1996. *Texts of Power: Emerging Disciplines in Colonial Bengal*. Calcutta: Samya Books.

—. 2002. "Institutional Context of Social Science Research in South Asia", *Economic and Political Weekly*, Vol. 37 (35), pp. 3604–3612.

Damodaran, Harish. 2008. *India's New Capitalists: Caste, Business and Industry in a Modern Nation*. New Delhi: Permanent Black in association with New India Foundation, Ranikhet.

Deshpande, Satish. 2002. "Social Science Research Capacity in Asia: Some Questions for Discussion", *Economic and Political Weekly*, Vol. 37 (35), pp. 3628–3630.

—. 2008. "Declining Simplistic Narratives", in Overview of the Recommendations of the VI Review Committee of the ICSSR. *Economic and Political Weekly*, Vol. 43 (5), pp. 25–28.

Geetha, V. and S.V. Rajadurai. 1998. *Towards a Non-Brahmin Millennium: From Iyothee Thass to Periyar*. Calcutta: Samya Books.

Guru, Gopal and V. Geetha. 2000. "New Phase of Dalit-Bahujan Intellectual Activity", *Economic and Political Weekly*, Vol. XXXV (3), pp. 130–134.

Irshick, Eugene. 2003. "Conversations in Tarangambadi: Caring for the Self in Early Eighteenth Century South India", *Comparative Studies of South Asia, Africa and the Middle-East*, Vol. 23 (1 and 2).

Mannheim, Karl. 1982. *Structures of Thinking*. London: Routledge.

Mukherji, Partha N. 2005. "Sociology in South Asia: Indigenisation as Universalizing Social Science", *Sociological Bulletin*, Vol. 54 (3), pp. 311–324.

Pandian, M.S.S. 2002. "Social Sciences in South India: A Survey", *Economic and Political Weekly*, Vol. XXXVII (35), pp. 3613–3627.

Radhakrishnan, P. 1993. "Communal Representation in Tamil Nadu, 1850–1916: The Pre-Non-Brahmin Phase", *Economic and Political Weekly*, Vol. XXVII (31), pp. 1585–1597.

Roy, Tapti. 1996. "Disciplining the Printed Text: Colonial and Nationalist Surveillance of Bengali Literature", in Partha Chatterjee (ed.), *Texts of Power Emerging Disciplines in Colonial Bengal*. Calcutta: Samya Books, pp. 30–62.

Singh, Yogendra. 2004. *Ideology and Theory in Indian Sociology*. Jaipur: Rawat Publications.

Sujatha, V. 2007. "Pluralism in Indian Medicine: Medical Lore as a Genre of Medical Knowledge", *Contributions to Indian Sociology*. Vol. 41, pp. 169–202.

Sundaram, D. 1985. Trends and Gaps in Research in the Department of Sociology of the University of Madras. Report presented at the Annual Meeting of the Social Science Departments of Southern Universities at MIDS, Chennai.

—. 2007(a). Sociology Education in the University of Madras: A Transition from Social Sciences Education Project, Issues and Perspectives. Unpublished paper presented at the Seminar on 'Formation of Sociology in India: Documenting Knowledge, Scholars, Practices and Institutions', held on 3 and 4 February 2007 at University of Pune, Pune.

—. 2007(b). Interview on email.

Viswanathan, S. 2005. *Dalits in Dravidian Land*. Pondicherry: Navayana Publishing.

3

Sociology, Sociologists, *Seng Samla* and *Seng Kynthei* of Meghalaya

A.K. NONGKYNRIH

This paper is an exploratory study of a case that illustrates a possible relationship between academic sociology within a university setting and organizations that are not for profit in the wider society. The case in discussion is drawn from the Khasi-Jaintia hills in Meghalaya where sociology is taught at both undergraduate and postgraduate levels. One such kind of organizations in Meghalaya is known as *Seng* or *Sein*. There are three groups of *Seng* or *Sein*: *Seng Samla* (youth), *Seng Kynthei or Longkmie* (women), and *Seng Rangbah* (men). Such *Seng* are found only in the Khasi-Jaintia hills of the state of Meghalaya. The academic interest on the *Seng* was an outcome of the formal interaction between the department of sociology at the North-Eastern Hill University (NEHU) and such organizations. From the year 1999 to 2006 the department of sociology initiated the Community Development Extension Programme (CDEP). CDEP was included as part of the Department Research Scheme – a project sponsored by the University Grants Commission, New Delhi. Under CDEP there were many programmes and one of these was on the training of organizations working not for profit. It is out of the initiative under the CDEP that this paper evolved. The decision of including the CDEP as part of the department research support (DRS) was a departmental decision. In the second phase of the DRS, CDEP was discontinued because the thrust of the DRS was on conducting research and organizing workshops.

The objective of this paper is to describe the *Seng*, and see whether the *Seng* fits in the definitional framework of grassroots organizations. In India not-for-profit organizations are of two types: one, the traditional such as caste, ethnic, kinship, village associations etc. Such types of organizations are sanctioned by traditional beliefs and practices; and two, the modern such as professional associations, co-operative societies or development-based organizations. The second type of organizations are defined by law and not necessarily by conceptual terminology and definitions. Under the law, not-for-profit organizations are governed by set of rules and regulations, such as, for example, The Societies Registration Act,1860; The Indian Trusts Act, 1882; The Co-operative Societies Act, 1904: The Trade Union Act, 1926; and Section 25 of The Indian Companies Act, 1956 (Nongkynrih, 2006).

In the north-eastern region of India in general and the state of Meghalaya in particular, the entry of modern organizations such as not-for-profit organizations are of more recent times. The colonization of the hills and the changes which it created led the process of formation of not-for-profit organizations in the region. The advent of religion-based organizations in the region, such as the Christian missionaries of varied denominations, paved the path and the beginning of not-for-profit organizations. The Ramakrishna Mission is another organization that has been working in the region. Further, the state also promoted the formation of such organizations under the law of the state for people wanting to access state's developmental resources have to form organizations and be registered under any of the Acts cited above.

Not-for-profit organizations in the state of Meghalaya are of two broad categories: the unregistered organizations, and the registered organizations. By 'unregistered' we mean those organizations which did not register themselves with the Meghalaya Societies Registration Office, and thus do not have any legal identity. Without legal identity such organizations cannot apply for or receive financial support from the government or other national or international agencies. Such organizations however take up charitable or voluntary programmes. Under this category we can classify organizations into various sub-types such as, clan-based organizations, youth organizations, mother's associations, women's associations, youth associations, women's and men's organizations formed by and under various Christian denominations.

The registered organizations are those which have legal identity and have registered themselves under any one of the following Acts:

(i) The Meghalaya Societies Registration Act, 1976
(ii) The Central Cooperative Societies Act, 1904
(iii) The Indian Trusts Act, 1882
(iv) The Trade Union Act, 1926
(v) Section 25 of the Indian Companies Act, 1956

Registration is mandatory if organizations are interested in obtaining financial support from the government and other national or international agencies (PRIA, 2003: 9). The paper focuses on those organizations, which have registered under the Societies Registration Act. Under this category, organizations are varied and we can divide them into sub-types such as the religion-based organizations and the secular-based organizations (Nongkynrih, 2006).

This paper is broadly divided into three parts. Part one raises the question about the role of sociology in society, particularly in the context of this paper which focuses on the type of interaction and communication between the sociologist and the *Seng*. Part two describes the *Seng* and relates it in the context of the definitional framework of grassroots organizations; and finally the conclusion. The paper is based on both primary and secondary data. Primary data was collected during the period of (1999–2006) from the *Seng* and from the villages they are located, and the secondary data in the form of published materials.

I

Sociology and Sociologists

The role of sociology and sociologists in society has been debated in India for long. Debates of whether or not sociologists should play an active role in society have long existed. Such debates assume more significance in the light of the CDEP, which was initiated and implemented by the department of sociology at the NEHU. This paper in part explores whether this type of initiative falls within the role of sociology. It is a norm for sociologists not to get involved with the ideas, opinions and views prevalent in the field. The question that arises is: should sociologists be concerned only with the intellectual matters of the subject and remain indifferent to whatever is happening in society.

Anthony Giddens (1997) opines that sociology is a subject with important practical implications. It can contribute to social criticism and practical social reform in several ways. For instance, sociology offers groups and individuals an increased opportunity to alter the conditions of their own lives. He further argues that no sociologically sophisticated person can be unaware of the inequalities that exist in the world today, the lack of social justice in many social situations and the deprivations suffered by millions of people. It would be strange if sociologists did not take sides on practical issues, and it would be illogical to try to ban them from drawing their expertise in so doing.

Andre Beteille (2002) argues that sociology serves a larger social purpose through neither social engineering nor social activism but by advancing man's critical understanding of his own circumstances. He further adds, that by analysing the forms and functions of social institutions he/she (sociologist) can help people to gain deeper insight into the true nature of the constraints under which they live. Beteille categorically states that the social activist is by his/her own free choice a partisan, and partisanship undermines the very conditions of sociological enquiry and analysis. In his opinion society is a field of contending values and interests, and the sociologist serves his purpose best by not taking sides in the contention. It is fair mindedness, and not partisanship which defines the value of the sociologist.

The reason that I choose to introduce and highlight the issue of whether sociologists should be 'non-partisan' or 'take sides' is not to pursue the debate further but to outline the context in which the paper can be read. This paper has developed out of the interaction with the community in general and the organizations in particular. It is an interaction that involves both 'taking sides' and being 'non-partisanship'.

It would be difficult for the reader to understand the discussion without providing the background that led the idea and initiating the CDEP by the department of sociology at the NEHU. The interaction between the sociologist and not-for-profit organizations in Meghalaya was not part of the formulated research proposal nor an intended initiative. These were the circumstances at that time in the state of Meghalaya that brought the two together. Not-for-profit organizations from rural areas were searching for ways and means to solve problems such as economic backwardness, illiteracy, health, poverty and unemployment. They were looking for agencies or bodies or individuals who could provide and assist them with alternative ideas, knowledge and skills. The reason that made them search for alternative paths was because the government and political parties were not taking interests in solving problems which affect the rural people in particular. From 1952 onwards political parties have been focusing and concentrating their efforts on the issue of tribal identity. The issue of tribal identity subsumes all other issues and assumed as the most significant agenda. In the process the social development of the people in general and rural areas in particular was neglected.

The issue of tribal identity has been such that the state of Meghalaya has witnessed many sporadic protest movements at different intervals. The politics of tribal identity has been so pervasive that issues of social and economic development of the state hardly figure in public discourse. The rural areas and rural poor are not paid due attention. It seems as if rural areas and the rural poor of the state do not exist, and even today many of the rural areas particularly those without proper connectivity continue to be neglected and are in conditions of abject poverty.

Another dimension which deserves to be presented here is the role of media and the academics. In the opinion of Sanat K. Chakravarty, a journalist, metro newspapers concentrated their attention on insurgency and insecurity, and the projection they give to the outside world is that the north-eastern region is a 'disturbed area' (Chakravarty, 1998). Secondly, if one goes through the academic writings one would find that the issue of tribal identity or ethnicity or protest movements is the major focused subject of discussions.[1] The real situation of the people, particularly those living in rural areas, and their plight of economic backwardness received little attention as compared to issues such as tribal identity or movements.

The interaction of the sociologist with not-for-profit organizations started in 1990 in one of the most economically backward areas of Meghalaya. The area is known as *Khatar Shnong* (*Khatar* means twelve and *Shnong* means village). The 40 villages are clustered into twelve units, and each unit is known as *Raid*. The chief of the *Raid* is called

Sordar. Every village of *Khatar Shnong* has a village council and the *Tymmen Shnong* (headman) is the village leader.

Out of the forty villages, the village of Kongthong was selected for the fieldwork. In January 1990, a pilot visit was conducted in the village and two other neighbouring villages. In the latter part of the year the area was severely affected by gastro-enteritis. It started in one village and soon became an epidemic. I was informed by the villagers about the epidemic. They said that the people required medical assistance. They also informed me that majority of the people from villages have fled and were hiding in the jungle and caves because they feared that the epidemic was a strong supernatural phenomenon. I was also informed that when the gastro-enteritis started it infected only one or two families. Such families went and sought help from the local medicine man. Prayers and rituals were performed appeasing the supernatural forces to cure the problem because people thought that supernatural forces were punishing them. But more and more people lost their lives. It took a while before they changed their minds and sought medical help from outside. By this time, the number of deaths in the area had increased and the situation was getting out of control. Most people had fled away from their villages and searching for them was a problem (Nongkynrih, 2002).

To a student of sociology, the way people responded to a sickness like the gastro-enteritis is a sociologically phenomenon to study and understand. In such a situation, what is the role of sociologists – to investigate the beliefs and practices or assist the villagers? My response was to search for support for the infected people and the area. My involvement did not change my training in sociology or affected my research. By the time the fieldwork was conducted I was no longer a stranger to them, though still considered 'an outsider of the village'. The village was glad to have me and to pursue my fieldwork. Two days later after my arrival in the village, village leaders visited the sub-health centre. It was my temporary home because it was hardly used except on rare occasions when medical staffs of the health department of the Meghalaya government visited the village. The interaction started with exchange of pleasantries of where did I come from and which clan did I belong. After a while, after getting to know each other, the village leader asked me, "You trekked on foot for eight hours to reach here, did you not stumble occasionally while trekking on the narrow village-made footpath?" It is a local phrase and means you did not get tired and fed up to come all the way to such a remote village. My reply to them was: even if you stumble and fall occasionally, you trek without looking back. To this reply they laughed and understood why I am there.

I was surprised that residents of the village addressed me as *Babu* (meaning teacher). I came to know that village leaders had informed others that I am a teacher at NEHU. One evening I invited one of the village leaders and requested him to share with me about who coined the word *'Babu'* for me. He narrated that after meeting me they had a meeting and one of the agendas was how to address me. The reason was because "you are 'an outsider of the village' and an 'insider by matrilineal descent'. In our village, residents have their own kinship terminologies, and we could not place you anywhere. We came up with solution of giving you the title 'Babu' which you are and because the word is neutral and respectable. According to our customs, it is impolite to address guests of the village by name".

The incident and the research work in the area led to closer interaction with the local organization known as *Khatar Shnong Socio-Organisation* (KSO). When you live and also belonged to small communities, people get to know much faster about you than you can probably think. Gradually, individuals and leaders of not-for-profit organizations from rural areas began to contact and visit the department of sociology. The interaction started informally for eight years. Formally, the interaction started in 1999 and officially terminated in 2006.[2]

It is important to explain the reasons for my involvement, a sociologist with not-for-profit organizations of the society. It is difficult to detach oneself from the society even though one may be a sociologist. This is particularly more so if by birth you are a member of the society where you live and work. The Khasi society has the practice where individuals are expected to contribute to the welfare and development of the people. The contribution depends on the capacity of individuals. In this case it is expected that the sociologist can contribute by disseminating information, knowledge and skills. In such society any one refusing to assist or disseminate information and knowledge would suffer from a social stigma locally referred to as *Sarong* meaning proud and arrogant. No member of the society would like to be known as a *Sarong* person. Secondly, it is also my academic interest and desire to understand about such organisations at the village level.

II

Communication and Transferring of Knowledge

The formal interaction between not-for-profit organizations and the sociologist was carried out by adopting various processes. Such processes involve techniques of communication in the transferring of sociological knowledge. The transferring of sociological knowledge was a challenge because the audience consists of persons without any background of sociology, and most of them have completed only high school education. Rarely have we had leaders of organizations with graduate degree.

The first of the process of the interaction was deciding about monthly meetings and held on the last Saturdays of the month, and the duration of such meetings was of four hours each. The first meeting was held for identification of issues by participants. The sociologist facilitate the process and out of the total number of issues identified by participants prioritized the issues. The prioritized issues were separated into two groups: those which the sociologist could provide the inputs, and those which needed the support of experts or agencies from outside the discipline. The issues which have been handled by the sociologist were information about government policies and schemes, meaning of social development, self-help groups, empowerment of women, report writing and the method of organizing training or conducting awareness programmes. Monthwise training on each of the issues was organized.

The second group of issues was handled by resource persons from outside, and the issues were micro-credit skills-based training; rural entrepreneurship development, organizational management, leadership skills and procedure of accounting system. Most of the training conducted by outside experts was in the form of classroom lectures and discussions. The interaction between organizations and experts from various government departments, training institutes, banks and other agencies enlarged the scope of training opportunities for organizations. It also led to building of network, and because of this process they received support from government departments and other agencies.

Coming back to the training process adopted by the sociologist, on the issue of information about government schemes, there was no need of training except supplying them with the relevant published materials acquired from the Meghalaya government. In the case of other issues highlighted above except the participatory learning and action, the process followed was classroom lectures and group work. In classroom lectures the concept or term or meaning of the subject matter was explained by outlining the main points and with many examples. This was followed by group work where participants were divided into ten peer groups and each group examined the subject matter. The duration of group work was one hour.

The process of examining the subject matter was done by providing participants with what they should be doing such as identifying what they have understood about the concept or term or meaning; what they have learned and whether or not they can apply in their work; and what difficulties they faced in understanding the subject matter. Each group selected a chairperson whose role was that of guiding the discussion and ensuring that every group member gets an equal opportunity in sharing their views and opinions. The group also selected one member as its presenter. After an hour of meeting each group shared it discussions. The facilitator took over after group presentations and clarified the points raised. The participatory learning and action (PLA) training is a different type of knowledge. The knowledge was disseminated by combining classrooms lectures and group exercises. The duration of the training was four days and a group of 30 participants per batch.

There are two examples which we can share about the transferring and communication of knowledge and skills to participants. First is the application of analytical knowledge and skills in diagnosing problems; and the second is the application of the concept of self-help groups (SHGs) as the model of solving problems related with income generation in particular. It is important to point out that at that time we were the few persons besides the Bosco Reach-Out (a developmental wing of the Salesians of Don Bosco, Guwahati) who adopted the idea and initiated the formation of SHGs in Khasi-Jaintia hills.

Coming back to the discussion on the application of analytical knowledge and skills, sociology was useful in the sense that it assisted the sociologist in training participants who had no background in sociology. The first process was applied by asking them to identify causes of economic backwardness. Causes were listed randomly and followed by compounding of such causes into specific areas such as political, economic, religion, family and kinship, and government departments. For each specific area and causes related with it the participants were divided into groups and an in-depth analysis of such causes was done. It is process which enhanced the analytical knowledge of participants and enabled them to move from the general to the specific. The process was applied with the intention of identifying actual cause(s). Such analytical exercises provide the path and strategy for local interventions. One of the strategies that was adopted and applied for enhancing livelihoods of families in villages was the concept of SHGs.

In sociology we are taught about group and the two types of group are formal and informal. The concept of group is understood by the sociologist. Sociologically, participants could not define group but they understood the term 'group'. In Khasi-Jaintia society the word 'group' in English is equivalent to the local word *Kynhun*. All types of village activities are carried out collectively. The collective is separated into *Kynhun*, and each *Kynhun* has a leader and the team is assigned with specific task. The challenges we confronted were because we had to form SHGs. The training provided the scope for both the sociologist and participants in understanding the concept, and designing the process of promotion of SHGs in rural areas. Initially, the formation of SHGs took time because it was a new concept and gradually people accepted and formed such groups.

III

The *Seng Samla* and *Seng Kynthei* or *Longkmie*

The word *Seng* in Khasi means to establish or to lay foundation, and in this case it would mean an association or organization. According to the beliefs and practices of the Khasi-Jaintia society, the position and role of male and female members of the society are defined by age sets and sex. Age sets is a socially defined category and not counted in the number of years from the date and year of birth. There are five groups of age sets: (i) *Khunlung* meaning infant of both sexes; (ii) *Khynnah* are children of both sexes; (iii) *Samla* are youth, and *Samla Kynthei* are female youth and *Samla Shynrang* are male youth; (iv) *Rangbah* are grown-up men and *Longkmie* are married women; and (v) *Tymmen* are aged persons of both sexes. The society does not give any responsibility to those belonging in groups (i) and (ii) above. They enjoy special care and protection from the elder members of the society. It should be noted here that the word *Kynthei* means female in general and when we use *Longkmie* it means married women.

The members of the society belonging to groups (iii), (iv) and (v) have specific role and responsibilities. To understand the role and responsibilities of these groups, the example from the village (*Shnong*) would be most appropriate. A *Shnong* is comprised of families residing in it and it has a definite boundary. The village council (*Dorbar Shnong*) is the village authority that administers village affairs. The village council is a composition of adult male members or *Rangbah* from every family residing in the village. Every *Rangbah* inducted in the village council is a life member. Every village council elects from amongst the *Rangbah* a *Tymmen Shnong* (headman) as its representative head. He functions on the basis of consensus. Women (*Longkmie*) and youth (*Samla*) of both sexes are passive participants.

The village council is the decision-making body and it organizes the activities of the village collectively. Women and youth do not attend the village council meetings, yet both are active participants in village activities. Over generations it has been the practice of the Khasi-Jaintia society to give women and youth specific responsibilities. Traditionally, it is the village council that organizes and divides their work. To illustrate the point, the following example is self-explanatory: When a member of the village dies, the headman organizes the men, women and youth collectively and each group (*Kynhun*) is entrusted with a specific task. The men would be responsible in the preparation of the coffin and the cremation or burial ground. The women prepare and assist the bereaved family members and their kinsfolk who are from outside the village by preparing food, cleaning the house and taking care of the home of the bereaved. The young people would be divided into two groups: the male youth assist the men and *Longkmie* in making arrangements and are the night vigil party in the bereaved home; while their female counterparts serve food and assist the women. Such division of work is similarly followed in the case of village festivals or marriages, etc.

The idea of separating the groups and organizing them, and giving each group their responsibilities, is an old practice. The shift from the traditional system of group formation into an organization with some of the features from the modern type of organization is a later development. It is difficult to exactly point out when it started but the critical factor causing the change began after the colonization of the hills. On the basis of the interaction we found that there are many *Seng Samla* and *Seng Kynthei* or *Longkmie* throughout the four districts. It is also interesting to note that such organizations are easy to identify from which village they are because the name of the village is added to it. If the village is *Mawphan*, the women's organization would be called *Seng Longkmie Mawphan*, and youth organization would be similarly named as *Seng Samla Mawphan*.

IV

Aspects of Change in the *Seng Longkmie* and *Seng Samla*

The *Seng* of both women and youth today have a written constitution. From amongst the members they elect office bearers like the president, secretary, treasurer etc., and they have the executive committee too. They organize the annual general meetings, maintain the proceedings and accounts books and organize various types of activities for the youth or women and for the general population of the village. For example, *Seng Samla* organizes annual sports meet and cultural programmes like dancing and short play competition, and also takes part in the inter-club football tournaments outside the village. In the case of *Seng Longkmie* much of their work has been associated with the programmes of the social welfare department and social issues like banning of sale of alcohol and drunkenness. For organising such activities funds are generated locally from the contributions of the members, donation from village councils and individual donors from the village. The amount of funds generated is small, and most of the *Seng* survive on the volunteering spirit of its members. Office bearers are neither part-time nor full-time workers, and there is no monetary benefit for the service they rendered. The spirit and values of community service is the factor that keeps them active.

There are two aspects in the modernizing process of the *Seng* (women and youth) which deals with the village council and their role in the village. One, they need the consent and approval of the village council and the headman for such *Seng* are under the authority of the village council. They function as semi-autonomous bodies in the village, and are permitted to apply for outside support such as government departments and other agencies. Two, the incorporation of modern forms of organization in the *Seng* do not affect their traditional roles in the village. They continue to fulfil those roles besides initiating other types of developmental activities.

From the year 1998 onwards there has been a number of changes in the activities of these *Seng,* because of the training organized under the CDEP. *Seng Samla* is more involved in social and developmental programmes. Programmes such as environmental awareness, youth leadership, dissemination of information on government schemes, health education, formation of SHGs, skill-based training and rural entrepreneurship programmes are being organized. We have selected the case of one *Seng Samla* as an example and shown how it has been trying to reduce poverty in its village (see Box 1).

The women's organizations is becoming more active in organizing developmental programmes for the village in general and women in particular. One of the initiatives taken by women's organizations is their fight against the sale and consumption of alcohol in villages. Even village councils give due recognition for the efforts they are making. As an illustration the *Seng Kynthei* from Jaintia hills is presented here (see Box 2).

The transformation of the *Seng* at the village level also catalyzed the transformation at another level. In the early years of the 1990s the village-based *Seng* collectively organized into a network. Such networks of *Seng* are called *Ka Lympung.* Literally it means a ground or *Ka Synjuk* meaning to combine. *Seng Samla* of different villages organized themselves under a network known as *Ka Synjuk Ki Seng Samla Shnong,* and the women organizations of different villages also created an umbrella organization. We have selected *Ka Lympung Ki Seng Kynthei* as an example.

In 1992 a group of women leaders from different villages of Shillong city and from the outskirts of the city met, discussed and decided the formation of a network called *Ka Lympung Ki Seng Kynthei.* The purpose was to bring together like-minded women's organizations on one platform for voicing common issues pertaining to women and children. The network was an umbrella of more than 60 *Seng* of women from the Khasi-Jaintia hills district. Since 1992 the network has been raising public issues concerning women's health, consumer rights, women's rights and the fight against corruption. In collaboration with

Box 1

Seng Samla Diskiangpungsior of West Khasi Hills

Diskiangpungsior village is located in the West Khasi Hills District of the state of Meghalaya. Before the year 1996 majority of the working population were engaged as daily wage labourers with timber contractors. The villages opted for such occupation because it fetches hard cash on a weekly basis. On the 12 December of 1996, the Supreme Court of India passed the Order of banning timber trade in the whole country. The working population and their families of the village were not prepared when the ban was imposed on the district. The whole village was caught unaware and suffered from a loss of weekly income. The people did not know what to do next or how to deal with the situation. There was problem of food security because for many years their agricultural land was left fallow and uncultivated nor did they save enough money from the wages as timber labourers.

Like most of Khasi-Jaintia villages the youth of this village are active in their traditional roles. The ban of timber trade affected them as it affected their families. The village leaders and elders do not know how to respond or act to the impending situation and problem of food insecurity. The youth acted by organising themselves and formed the *Seng Samla Diskiangpungsior.* The youth leaders discussed with village leaders and got the consent and approval. This was followed by registration with the government.

The youth leaders came to know of the CDEP and joined the interaction programme. Series of interactions between the CDEP and the village took place. In such interaction the idea of forming Self-Help Groups (SHGs) was discussed and people were keen to experiment. Youth leaders were trained and they promoted and formed Self-Help Groups (SHGs) in the village. With the formation of SHGs the organisation contacted various government departments and agencies for support. This process led to the gradual change in the life of the people because skill-based training was provided in the area of horticulture, agriculture and vermi-composting. Out of the three skills trained, the most beneficial is vermi composting. The SHGs of the village developed it into a micro-enterprise.

The SHGs under the leadership of the youth organisation are generating income by selling the compost at the rate of Rs 8 per kilogram. Today, the organisation is known for the business in vermi composting. Besides the vermi composting unit, the organisation has introduced large-scale production of turmeric as part of the economic activity and for sustaining the livelihoods of the people. The organisation is also promoting plantation of fruit trees, medicinal plants, patchouli, and vegetables. These activities have contributed towards sustainable generation of income for the poor people.

Box 2

Ka Seng Kynjoh Shaphrang Ki Kynthei Kyndong Tuber

Kyndong Tuber is a village where majority of women are poor and illiterate. They are active and would play their traditional role as a group when needed by the village council. In such activities of the village they would informally discuss about their plight of poverty and that of the village. This went on for two or three years, and in the year 1995 few women of the village and only with two members knowing how to write decided to form the village organisation of the women. The constitution was prepared and approved, and office bearers were elected. The village council was formed and got the consent and approval from it, and the organisation was registered the same year.

After the formation of the organisation, the general body took the resolution to solve the problem of low income generation. Under the banner of the organisation a plot of land was taken on annual lease. The organisation had dialogued and sought the support of the owner who is from the village for token annual rent. The organisation organised the women into groups: those who work on the land and cultivated vegetables; and those who weaved. Out of such activities women are earning extra income by selling their produce in the market.

the village-based women's *Seng* it has also been organizing awareness programmes on mother and child's health, women's participation in decision-making bodies, and formation of SHGs and self-employment.

There are many more such networks across the Khasi-Jaintia hills. The network affiliation is voluntary and the village-based *Seng* maintains its own autonomy. The affiliation is temporary and an affiliated *Seng* can withdraw from the network any time.

V

Are *Seng Samla* or *Seng Longkmie* Grassroots Organizations?

In the preceding discussions we have sought to explain the nature of the *Seng Samla* and *Seng Kynthei.* Do these *Seng* fit in the definitional framework of grassroots organizations?

Grassroots organizations are informal or formal groups that are created within a particular community to specifically meet the needs of people of the community. They can be viewed as non-governmental organizations, although they do not tend to have a high degree of formality and connectedness to other organizations. They are locally based and generally work without any control of state or political parties, being most responsible and accountable to the group itself. They organize around any issue, such as cultural or environmental, although most are formed by disadvantaged group for economic and survival purposes (Zeller and Vyortinkin, 2004: 440). Berry (2006:6) argues that grassroots organizations are formed from within a community to address the locally perceived needs of that community. They address those needs indigenously defined by the community in sustainable, locally relevant and participatory ways.

According to Smith (1997), grassroots associations are those locally based and basically autonomous, volunteer-run, non-profit groups that have an official membership of volunteers. These have several common characteristics as: recruitment of members or people is based on common interest and background, thus membership in homogenous; members interact face-to-face which strengthen solidarity among them; the level of mobilization and participation of members is high, thus contributing to volunteering; create high internal cohesion and solidarity among members, thus providing mutual support and care; develops an effective ideology explaining the situation of the members and what the association will do to improve this situation, thus providing purposive incentives to members; and they persist overtime so that their goals can be achieved at least gradually in effecting change in their members and non-members.

On the basis of the definitions cited above, we can summarize that grassroots organizations are created within a particular community and/or territory; membership is local, and members come from common background or with common problem; are autonomous and locally based; formal structure exists and interaction among members is more informal than formal; volunteering is the key factor that sustains it; and no specific issues affecting the community and the members are taken up. The term 'autonomous' has specific meaning for grassroots organizations. It means grassroots organisations possess a large degree of self-governance and can determine their own decisions and actions.

If we examine the *Seng Samla* and *Seng Longkmie*, we find that they largely fit in the definition. Both types of *Seng* are formed at the village level, and members are hailed from the village. They have formal structure of an organization and their style of functioning is more informal than formal. They do not depend solely on the written rules and regulations. From amongst the members they elect their office bearers, who share the responsibilities of the organization and function on voluntary basis without spending all their time in the affairs of the organization. Funds are raised locally from the village and they do not necessarily depend only on membership contribution. The Seng organizes programmes or takes up activities concerning the needs and requirements of the village, and also assists the village council and the people when called upon. Thus, the *Seng Samla* or *Seng Longkmie* can be considered as grassroots organizations.

VI

Conclusion

This paper perhaps foregrounds the fact that the context not only defines the action of social actors of society, but also significantly influences the sociologist and the direction of sociological research. The context in this case is the Khasi-Jaintia society of Meghalaya, and there are three aspects that define it: one, issues such as tribal identity and protest movements dominate the public domain, as a result of which issues affecting the livelihoods of rural areas are neglected; two, rural-based not-for-profit organizations responds to this neglect by looking for alternative solutions; and three, the tensions that has to be negotiated by a sociologist who has been taught to be guided by the 'scientific tenets' of the discipline, but who is also a member of the society bound by its own customary beliefs and practices. Such is the nature of the context that the person would not be in a position to be one without also being the other.

The context also produces sociological knowledge, and such knowledge has been useful in understanding the impact of modernization in Khasi-Jaintia society. The formation of modern not-for-profit organizations in society, and the emergence and transformation of the *Seng* in particular from these processes can only be understood in this context. The transformation is an interesting development where the traditional group (*Kynhun*) gets converted into a *Seng* (not-for-profit organization). The transformation did not affect its traditional role because *Seng* continues to retain it as a part of the collective. The *Seng* as of today is a bridge between the old and the new.

Another aspect of the process of transformation of *Seng* is the formation of networks, which started in the early part of the 1990s. The formation of many networks across Khasi-Jaintia hills has expanded its territorial limits. The context of common problems or issues was the factor that brought them together and further helped them demand from the state government and other political bodies for solutions. This process itself led to the emergence of a pan-*Seng* identity in the state of Meghalaya – a new development.

The *Seng* of a village or of a network extending beyond the village plays different types of roles and initiates different types of social and developmental programmes in rural areas as we observed in the case of Meghalaya. Besides the aspects discussed above, the paper brings into focus the village because that is where the *Seng* is located. One of the observations is that most of village studies conducted in (India) have looked at the economy, religion, polity, family and kinship, caste, stratification, etc. Such village studies have contributed much to the sociological understanding of Indian society and towards the growth of sociology of India. However, such village studies have also left some sociological issues unattended, for example, informal and formal groups, not-for-profit organizations and other such formations. Based on the paper we found that groups (formal or informal) and not-for-profit organizations are part of village life. The inclusion of such groups or organizations in village studies would not only contribute towards richer sociological knowledge but would also enhance sociological understanding of Indian society.

Acknowledgement

I am grateful to the Prof Maitrayee Chaudhuri, Centre for the Study of Social Systems, School of Social Sciences, Jawaharlal Nehru University, New Delhi, for the comments and suggestions, and to Prof L.S. Gassah, Department of Political Science, North-Eastern Hill University, Shillong, for going through the paper and editing it. The interpretation is mine and for any error only I am responsible.

Notes

1. See Nikhlesh Kumar (1999), David R. Syiemlieh (2000), L.S. Gassah (1999); J.P. Singh et al. (1998), Niklesh Kumar (2006), NEIHA (1993 and 1997), Sheila Bora and S.D. Goswami (2007) and J.D. Bimal (2006).

2. In 1999, the University Grants Commission (UGC), New Delhi, the department of sociology under the Department Research Support (DRS) got the Special Assistance Programme (SAP). Under the DRS, it was accepted by the department that besides research, the informal interactions with organizations was formally accepted and function under the name of Community Development Extension Programme (CDEP).
3. I am grateful to Prof A.C. Sinha, Professor of Sociology (Retd.) from NEHU, and Dr I. Lanu Aier, Department of Sociology, NEHU for the valuable information on the introduction of the discipline of sociology at the undergraduate level.

References

Baruah, A.K. (ed.) 1993. Proceedings of the North East India Political Science Association. Shillong: North East India Political Science Association.

Baviskar, B.S. 2001. "NGOs and Civil Society in India", *Sociological Bulletin*, 50 (1): 3–15.

Berry, Jo de. 2006. "Exploring the Concept of Community: Implications for NGOs Management", in CVO International Working Paper 8, Centre for Civil Society, London School of Economics.

Beteille, Andre. 2002. *Sociology: Essays and Approach and Method.* New Delhi: Oxford University Press.

Bora, Sheila and S.D. Goswami (eds.). 2007. *Youth at the Crossroads: A Study of North East India.* Guwahati: DVS Publishers.

Chakravarty, Sanat K. 1998. "The Trend in Journalism in India's Northeast", in J.P. Singh et al. (eds.), *Trends in Social Sciences and Humanities in North East India (1947–97).* New Delhi: Regency Publications.

Dhanagare, D.N. 1993. *Themes and Perspectives in Indian Sociology.* Jaipur: Rawat Publications.

Deb, Bimal J. (ed.), 2006. *Ethnic Issues, Secularism and Conflict Resolution in North East India.* New Delhi: Concept Publishing Company.

—. 1997. Proceedings of the North East India Political Science Association. Shillong: North East India Political Science Association.

Department of Sociology. Profile of the Department. Shillong: North Eastern Hill University.

Gassah, L.S. 1999. *Survey of Research in Political Science on North East India.* New Delhi: Regency Publications.

Giddens, Anthony. 1997. *Sociology.* United Kingdom: Polity Press.

Kumar, Nikhlesh. 1999. *Survey of Research in Sociology and Social Anthropology on North East India.* New Delhi: Regency Publications.

—. 2005. "Identity Politics in the Hill Tribal Communities in the North Eastern Region", *Sociological Bulletin*, 54 (2): 195–217.

Nongkynrih, A.K. 2006. "Understanding Volunteering: The Case of Khasi-Jaintia Society in Meghalaya", *Sociological Bulletin*, 55 (1): 91–107.

—. 2002. *Human Development in Khatar Shnong.* Shillong: F. Nongkynrih.

North Eastern Hill University. 2003–2004. Thirtieth Annual Report. Shillong: North Eastern Hill University.

Participatory Research in Asia. 2003. *Exploring the Non-Profit Sector in India: Some Glimpses from Meghalaya.* New Delhi: Participatory Research in Asia.

Smith, David Horton. 1997. "Grassroots Associations are Important: Some Theory and Review of the Impact of Literature", *Non-profit and Voluntary Sector Quarterly*, 26: 269–306.

Slattery, Martin. 2003. *Key Ideas in Sociology.* United Kingdom: Nelson Thornes Ltd.

Singh, J.P. et al. (eds.), 1998. *Trends in Social Sciences and Humanities in North East India (1947–97).* New Delhi: Regency Publications.

Society for Participatory Research. 2003. *Exploring the Non-Profit Sector in India: Some Glimpses from Meghalaya.* New Delhi: The Johns Hopkins University.

Syiemlieh, David R. 2000. *Survey of Research in History on North East India.* New Delhi: Regency Publications.

Voluntary Action Network India. 1995. *Non-Governmental Organisations: Guidelines for Good Policy and Practice.* London: The Commonwealth Foundation.

Zellerer, Evelyn and Dmitry Vyortkin. 2004. "Women's Grassroots Struggles for Empowerment in the Republic of Kazakhstan", *Social Politics*, 11 (3): 439–464.

4

The Making of a Syllabus

An Issue beyond Academics

DALIA CHAKRABARTI

The making and revising of a syllabus is often thought of as a process, involved only with the content of an intellectual discipline, little to do with the wider dynamics of society. In this paper I seek to show the inextricable links between society and the making of syllabi. My case in point is the undergraduate Sociology (Honours) syllabus of Calcutta University. This paper intends to discuss the imperatives of syllabus formulation and revisions, the persistence and change of its content, the various obstacles to change, and the overall consequences, both intended and unintended, of such revisions.

Syllabus is not merely a set of topics to be taught in a particular course. It is a communication tool to convey the general purpose of the course and the manner in which it will be carried out (Smith and Razzouk, 1993: 215). Such knowledge is structured keeping in mind levels of school and college education. It is organized in terms of papers, each paper having units, and each unit having a set of topics. I argue that these set the parameters of imparting and receiving knowledge. Each syllabus is thus a kind of cognitive map. Reflective teachers seek to show how the papers, their units and the topics represent different but related aspects of the discipline, itself in a process of continuous growth. But, for the most part a syllabus is regarded as merely a bunch of topics whose sole reason to exist is that eventually a set of questions will be set on them.

My acquaintance with this syllabus dates back to my days at Presidency College (affiliated to University of Calcutta), initially as a student of sociology undergraduate class (1989–1992) and later as a teacher of the same department for eight long years (1997–2005). Apart from my own experience as a student and then as a teacher I have relied heavily on the experiences of some retired teachers, familiar both with the making and transmitting of the syllabi. I personally have been drawn towards this 'problem' because a wide and publicly expressed feeling exists in Kolkata that Calcutta University lags behind because it does not regularly introduce new courses or revision in its syllabi. Interestingly, even before 1947 there were complaints of deteriorating standards of Calcutta University (Kabir, 1956: 110). The 'decline legend' exerts considerable pressure on syllabus revision. The National Assessment and Accreditation Council (NAAC) of the University Grants Commission (UGC), in its grading system for universities, allots 15 marks out of a total score of 100 for the curriculum. This indicates the significance accorded to syllabus making and its revision as a pedagogical tool. But, unfortunately, the prevailing reward structure in the discipline is very heavily biased against teaching (Deshpande, 1994: 575). There is therefore a relative lack of serious deliberation on the methods and aids of teaching. Furthermore, India's policy of quantitative expansion of college education since independence has often been unaccompanied by measures to assure quality. The problem is more acute in case of 'soft' disciplines such as sociology (Beteille, 1996; Pathak, 2003)

In my attempt to explain a particular course design I have taken into account the larger forces at work in society – the global, the national and the sub-national levels. Global intellectual power has mainly been exercised by British sociological scholarship in the colonial period and American sociology, particularly after the pre-eminent influence of Talcott Parsons. For a ready example, the book by MacIver and Page was the single most important text for undergraduate as well as postgraduate courses for long in Calcutta University. Review of syllabus itself is often spurred on by new theoretical insights and a new crop of research in the western academia reflected of what has been described as 'a captive mind' (Alatas, 1972: 11–12). The obvious consequence of western domination is a confrontation between sociology as a secular understanding of a modern (European-North American) social order and a largely traditional social order resting on theologically sanctioned ascriptive inequality. This has provoked a debate over the wisdom of using western categories for understanding Indian society. For example, Pathak (2004: 35) calls for an alternative perspective on modernity – a soft or humble modernity – questioning the 'cognitive certainty' inherent in Eurocentric notion of the same. Wallerstein asserts: "If social science is to make any progress in the twenty-first century, it must overcome the Eurocentric heritage which has distorted its analyses and its capacity to deal with the problems of the contemporary world" (1997: 22). But, the impact of the West, in a sense, is inevitable. By the very logic of globalization, today's social sciences are bound to tie up the local and the national with the global (Mukherji, 2005: 158). Unfortunately, this relation is not a case of reciprocal mutuality. Coming to the national and the sub-national level, apart from the traditional Brahmanical hegemonic influence, which has been contested widely by dalit scholarship,[1] there has not been very serious complaints about interference, political or otherwise, in teaching or research in Indian universities. "This is largely because of the many layers of institutions of self-regulation that have been established in the Indian academic world" (Chatterjee, 2002: 94). But, occasionally, like in some phases of left rule in some states of the Indian Union, or during the NDA rule at the national level, there was political bickering over autonomy of the education system.[2] Before we proceed to map the revision of the syllabus, it is in order to briefly allude to the institutional history of the discipline in Calcutta University as well as the broader context of the state policies within which the discipline is practised.

I

Institutional Histories, Policies and Practices

The history of sociology, as a discipline, in India can be traced to the introduction of the subject at a postgraduate level in 1917, and at an undergraduate level after independence in the University of Bombay. The honours course in sociology was introduced in Calcutta University as late as the early 1980s. By that time the national-level debate over feasibility of sociology undergraduate course was almost over.[3] The delayed introduction is surprising in view of the fact that as early as in 1851, when, at the instance of Mouat, the Bethune Society was founded in Calcutta for the consideration and discussion of questions connected with literature and science, it reared up a sociological section (Ray and Gupta, 1957: 125). The introduction of new disciplines usually depends on the role of some key individuals which in the case of sociology did not quite happen. According to the Calcutta University statute, undergraduate colleges affiliated to it cannot offer courses unless the university itself has such a teaching department. In 1957, the university appointed Shyama Prasad Mukherjee as Professor of Sociology in order to expedite the opening up of a full-fledged department. In 1964–65, the university invited an American Professor Noel P. Gist with the same intention. However, the department came into being only in 1978, much later than Kalyani University in West Bengal. The government, which funds education, is usually reluctant to introduce new disciplines because of recurring expenses involved.

The teaching of sociology has a long history in this university, introduced as a course in the economics department in 1917 (DuttaGupta, 1969: 102). Sir B.N. Seal used to deliver occasional lectures on 'Comparative Sociology' at the department of philosophy. Benoy Kumar Sarkar and Radhakamal Mukherjee taught sociology at this institution. A hundred marks paper on sociology in 800 marks Political Science (Honours) course, introduced in 1960, gave students a larger exposure to the subject. However, it was only in the 1980s that it was introduced at the undergraduate level as an honours course. As mentioned earlier, individuals do play a key role in pushing through new courses. But, at the same time, their role is constrained by the larger framework of state policies and often local/regional power play.

Education in India had been a provincial subject since 1921 under the direct control of an elected minister responsible to the state legislature. Education in independent India is, however, a state subject and therefore no uniform policy in the teaching of sociology could emerge. This was considered problematic in the initial years of post-independent era. Humayun Kabir once commented that "the absence of a common system of national education has been one of the main reasons why so many Indians exhibit even today a regional, linguistic or communal outlook" (1956: 110). But, this perception had changed over time. In the late 1970s, the regional workshops organized by UGC categorically stated the undesirability of a completely standardized uniform structure of syllabi for all regions of the country, although a basic minimum was felt essential (Singh, 1977). The UGC Curriculum Development Committee in Sociology (2000–01) critically reviewed the structure, orientation and contents of the existing curricula. The problems identified were: (i) lack of adequate correspondence between the changing social reality and the content and orientation of existing courses in sociology; (ii) lack of thematic continuity, and analytical progression in the curriculum from one level to the next; and (iii) problematic classroom-centred pedagogic practice – a combination of monologic lectures and dictation of notes.

In case of the syllabus under consideration I found that in recent years it has been updated at reasonable intervals. But since the syllabi is almost entirely drawn upon western liberal sociology and relies on sociology textbooks written by western authors primarily for their students, a lack of correspondence exists between the changing Indian social reality and the content and orientation of extent courses in sociology. Even the book by T.B. Bottomore titled *Sociology: A Guide to the Literature*, commissioned by the UNESCO for use by the Indian students, has reference to the Indian social institutions and processes as an appendage to the bulk of the discussion on western sociological categories and theories. The situation has been changing since 1980s. So far as the second issue identified by the UGC is concerned, it is not entirely true that in sociology teaching at school, college and university levels, there is no thematic continuity and analytical progression. The third problem is very much present in West Bengal, completely undermining the possibility of developing creativity and a critical perspective among students. I believe that the problems identified by the UGC are in no way peculiar to sociology. These are true about the other social sciences like Political Science. The malaise of classroom-centred pedagogic practice of monologic lectures and dictation of notes affects teaching even of the natural sciences. But, there are significant exceptions in terms of both institutions and individual teachers. A continuous reference to lived experience brings the discipline alive. Dictated notes turn the students into copying machines without any power of intervention. Notes received either in classroom or tutorial homes are sub-standard because these are very often dilutions of serious textbooks, or do not have critical points of departure, or are usually are close-ended, and inhibit learner's initiative to learn something through his/her own intellectual efforts.

The influence of non-academic considerations in administering education is another serious problem. Some of the members of the syllabus-framing agent, i.e., the Board of Studies of Sociology, attached to the Undergraduate Council of Calcutta University, admit that the members of the syllabus-making committees have often been chosen with a quiet attention to his or her political position and not because a certain kind of syllabus (contentwise) is wanted. Thus, the Board of Studies becomes a space for politics, either in the normal sense of the term or personal politics of the 'gate-keepers'. A Board of Studies is always a power centre dispensing privileges, like setting questions or examining answer scripts, or even opening up of avenues for publishing guide books. These very often strengthen aspirations for mobility among the teachers. Not only does Board politics centre on who gets on to these committees, at another level it also functions to exclude candidates who might be considered undesirable. It is always helpful for a convener or a chairman of a Board if he or she is assured of ready agreement. 'Like-minded' may mean that all the Board members are rather orthodox in their choice of papers to be studied, or apprehensive about making bold changes in a syllabus. Formation of such an in-group can be based on personal bonds, or a certain ideological similarity, real or feigned, or partisanship, or a combination of all these. In the last two or three decades there has been an effort to ensure representation of teachers from various types of colleges like elite college, city-based college, rural or semi-rural college in order to democratize the structure of a Board. This is also a political decision. While framing the syllabus, apart from the cognitive content of it, the Board has to keep in mind a number of other issues like the paucity of teaching and reading materials, their poor standards, the lack of a strong tutorial system in teaching methods, student's over-reliance on sub-standard notes, lack of standard materials of teaching in Bengali, poorly equipped libraries, crowded classrooms, the paucity of staff, and consequently, the heavy load of teaching hours for teachers.

It is customary here that after every reframing of syllabus a workshop must be organized. The purpose is to inform the college teachers about the logic behind the change, and to provide them with a guideline regarding the method of teaching as well as the texts and references required to teach the courses. Interaction in such workshops often leads to constructive changes. For example, some participants of the same workshop urged the Board to increase the marks allotted for fieldwork, which was subsequently conceded. The University of Calcutta, as a pro-student move, published model questions booklet for three-year B.A. (Honours) course under the new syllabus, introduced from the academic session 2003–04. Many of us doubted the efficacy of the flat essay-type questions, to generate the necessary interest and passion in students.

II

Contents and Contexts

In this section I attempt to indicate the manner in which both institutional and intellectual contexts impinge on the making of a syllabus. Despite several revisions in the undergraduate syllabus of sociology being taught at Calcutta University (four revisions since the 1980s) some core courses/papers persist, e.g., Introductory Sociology and Basic Concepts, Western Classical Thought, Indian Sociological Thinkers, Indian Society and Social Issues, and Research Methodology. Papers on Introductory Sociology and Basic Concepts provide a strong foundation. The course on 'Western Classical Thought', is organized and taught in a way that creates a mindset among the students that all aspects of non-western society can be entirely understood by blind-folded application of western categories and theoretical insights. Similarly, the course on 'Indian Sociological Thinkers' reflects a Brahmanical preoccupation with tradition. Incidentally, the same are the core courses for undergraduate programme in sociology specified in UGC Model Curriculum (2001: 5). Changes are basically of two types: (i) inclusion or rejection of a course; and (ii) reorganization of a course. Assuming that the sequential arrangement of papers in the syllabus is suggestive of the significance of a course, we trace the changes in the placement of the course on 'History of Sociological Thought' (100 marks) in different syllabi. It was the very first paper in undergraduate Sociology (Honours) course in the 1981 syllabus. In two subsequent revisions (one in 1990 and the other in 1995) it was relegated to the position of third paper. In 2002 revision it became the second paper. The primacy of this paper indicates how far teaching in social sciences is shaped by modernization ideals emanating from encounters with the western traditions. Coming to the topics of this paper I find that the precursors of sociology have over time become less important. Comte, Spencer, Marx, Durkheim, Weber and Pareto are the common thinkers in successive syllabi. Since 1990 onwards, precise specification of sub-themes had become a standard practice. In 1990 Simmel and Formal Sociology and Elitist Tradition in Sociology, i.e.,

Mosca, Pareto, Michels and Mills were included under Western Academic Tradition, i.e., the first half (50 marks) of paper on 'History of Sociological Thought'. Though the former was retained in subsequent revision, elitist tradition was dropped in 1995. A very radical, or perhaps populist, attempt to shed the load of the syllabus had been made in 2002. The items so far taught in a single 100 marks paper (containing two halves/groups) had been distributed in three groups (each 50 marks) of two 100 marks papers.

The change in the emphasis given to Marx in different syllabi is a pointer to the ideological orientation of the key individuals in the syllabus-revision committee. Political philosophies of communism and socialism were at the centre of intellectual reflections in Bengal from an early date. It is reported that students of M.A. history in Calcutta University were asked to discuss the goals of communism as early as in 1870 (Chakrabarti, unpublished section of doctoral thesis). But engagement with serious Marxism in the sense of teaching critical debates within Marxist is largely absent going by both the content of undergraduate and postgraduate syllabi. Marxism is taught but generally from a pro-Marxist standpoint. It is difficult to establish whether this is due to any apprehension about a political backlash. In 1981 syllabus Marx was not only one among many classical thinkers in the first half of paper I (History of Sociological Thought), there was also an entire 100 marks paper (paper V) on 'Sociology of Marx'. In 1990 revision it was reduced to only second half (50 marks) of 'History of Sociological Thought' paper. Another significant development was, unlike the previous syllabus, that it ended with a critical note on Marxian thought. This was retained in the 1995 revision. In 2002, interestingly, there was a single topic on Marx in the syllabus (though containing many sub-themes) and the debate between the Marxist and the non-Marxist sociology was conspicuous by its absence. It shows a remarkable change in the attitude towards Marx on the part of Bengali intellectuals. First, there was uncritical devotion, then a critical appraisal and of late a dispassionate remembrance. The devotion reflects the orthodox Marxist orientation of the Bengali intellectual elites of the early 1980s. That was a time when the leftist government came to the power in the state after a prolonged and hard political struggle with the rightist Congress party. In this struggle they followed the Marxist ideology as well as Marxist political tactics. Eventually, the fall of socialist countries in Russia and East Europe in late 1980s, adoption of the principle of market economy by communist China, and the beginning of the era of liberalization of Indian economy under the pressure of World Bank in the form of Structural Adjustment Programme (SAP) gave rise to an ambivalence in the attitude to Marx in a state ruled by the Marxist elites. It is however difficult to argue with conviction that an altered position on Marxist orthodoxy at the political level in the state led to a reduction in the study space allotted to Marxist sociology.

Since 1990 onwards, sociological theory constituted an important segment of undergraduate Sociology (Honours) syllabus of Calcutta University. In the syllabus of 1990 we find a long list of theories like functional theory, conflict theory, exchange theory, symbolic interactionism, role theory, phenomenology and ethnomethodology – all in a single half (50 marks) of paper I. In 1995 the burden had been substantially reduced by dropping role theory altogether and scaling down the depth of phenomenology and ethnomethodology by only a brief introduction to these theories. But, in 2002, a full 100 marks paper on 'Sociological Theory' was framed. Along with the conventional theories, critical sociology, feminist sociology and postmodern sociology were included whereas role theory, phenomenology and ethnomethodology were dropped. The course on 'Sociological Theory' needs to be contextualized historically and focused more in terms of certain common and significant issues and themes to enable students to draw meaningful linkages and apply them in a similar context of transition in India today. This task has been primarily left to the capability of the course teacher. The new additions reveal a re-orientation of the experts. And, this is certainly in tune with the changing world-view of the ruling elite of West Bengal. These new theories emerged in the West by the late 70s and 80s. But, from an orthodox Marxist standpoint, all these formulations were then perceived as 'bourgeois' developments. The same attitude was there towards the discipline itself, explaining its late arrival and a very slow growth in the state until recently.

'An Introduction to Sociology', as a discipline, was included in paper II (Principles of Sociology) in 1981 syllabus. The main purpose of this paper was to create a feel of the discipline by projecting it as a way of thinking as well as an attitude of mind. It contained items like nature of sociology, concepts, processes, models of society in sociological analysis, social institutions and social change. The first half of paper I 'Issues' in 1990 syllabus dealt with the substantive as well as cognitive interests of sociology, its scientific frame, various levels, its intellectual presuppositions, and academic and practical significance. Basic social structures and processes were allotted to paper II. In the next 1995 revision, two 100 marks papers (I and II) were allotted for 'General Sociology'. Some new social developments and trends, such as social interaction and everyday life, ethnicity and race, media and communication, globalizing of social life, were included. Different aspects of globalization were brought into focus. The trend continued. In 2002, for the first time, we see a separate conceptual item on gender and sexuality. Awareness about gender issues was also evident from themes like gender and stratification, women and work, political participation of women, gender and the educational system, women's movements etc., found in different papers of the same syllabus. Though in all previous syllabi concepts like culture, society and individual and the debate on social control vs. individual freedom were found, it was only in revision of 2002 'personal life' was included along with family and marriage. The Board of Studies of Sociology appears to be flexible and open but still a lot was there to incorporate, for example, the social institution of entertainment, so vital to contemporary consumerism.

All four syllabi contain sections on Indian society. Yogendra Singh (1977), the convener of the subject panel of UGC in the 1970s, reported that in all four regional workshops there was a national consensus that the cognitive contents of the courses must primarily be grounded into the Indian concrete reality and its history. The same was recommended by Ginsberg at the UNESCO Round Table on sociology teaching. He said that the courses should be introduced dealing with the structure of the country in which the course is incorporated. The framers of Calcutta University syllabus too believed that it was from the cultural specificity of India that sociology must draw its strength. In all four revisions the starting point was a common theme – unity and diversity in Indian society. Until about the 1970s, India's diversity was taken to be a symptom of its weakness. Nationalist Indians always tried to emphasize the unity of India, ignoring her diversity. M.N. Srinivas (1992: 4–5) describes how in the 1940s elites used to react to even inquiries about the existence of diversity in Indian society. However, since the beginning of the mid-1980s, "we have ...

moved into a situation when people want to record the diversities" (Jha, 2005: 402).

Lists of topics reveal how India has been perceived in terms of the continuity and change of its structures and processes over time. We may identify a shift from the intellectual orientation of 1940s, i.e., a "humanistic scholarly approach, which emphasized (i) the textual view of India in a timeless perspective of its tradition; (ii) an administrator's perspective, looking at Indian reality through censuses, settlement reports and surveys, treating it as a system of discrete entities that could be 'scientifically' classified for analysis and control; (iii) a tradition of village economic studies with focus upon rural social structure; and (iv) an anthropological approach studying institutions in India from a comparative holistic point of view" (Singh, 1988: 41). Obviously, the underlying purpose of such colonial ethnocentric orientation was to civilize India following the progressive model of West. But, the context has been changed radically in the closing years of 20th century in post-independent India. The 1980s, when the first undergraduate sociology syllabus of Calcutta University was framed, marked the beginning of a new era. Since then, India, as a nation, started facing a 'critical mass of acute problems', which were typically social in nature. Secessionist movements based on ethnic or religious identity, intrusion of caste questions into a supposedly caste-neutral urban middle class milieu and elevation of the communal problem to the centre of national politics created an awareness in and outside of the intellectual circle about the indispensability of sociology to understand and negotiate all these challenges (Deshpande, 1994: 576). It not only improved the prestige and position of the discipline, but also had a definite impact on the content of the sociology syllabus. Themes, recurrently found in all revisions, are village, caste, class, tribe, family and kinship, scheduled caste and tribe and backward classes, secularism and communalism, problems of national integration, population problem, industrialization and urbanization and its consequences etc. A significant inclusion was panchayat system in India and West Bengal. The obvious purpose was to make the curriculum rooted in the social history of the region. The 2002 syllabus elaborated it further by incorporating municipality, local bodies and social change, and the relation between civil society and the state. The 1990 syllabus contained a full 100 marks paper on 'Social Movements in India'. Besides problematizing the concept of social movement, it dealt with the concrete cases of new social movements.

Few social problems were included in the 1995 syllabus such as child abuse, youth problems and environment issues. In 2002 violence against women, old age problems, poverty, illiteracy, globalization and ecological crisis in India were introduced. The content of this paper reveals a typical left radicalism as it presents Indian society in terms of inequality, exploitation and hegemonic relation. The specificity of Bengali leftists becomes apparent in their inclination towards institutional set-up of parliamentary democracy as indicated in themes like panchayat, relation between state and civil society etc. It also indicates the growing maturity of Indian sociologists, who have successfully moved beyond earlier definition of sociology as a branch of knowledge that merely studies India in terms of the caste system, or the village structure or through the prism of India's majority religion – Hinduism (Patel, 2007: 3). The Brahmanic preoccupation of sociologists in the formative period of Indian sociology, which privileged the study of traditional Indian society and its institutions in the language of persistence and continuity, eventually gives way to an urge to go beyond the tradition-modernity binary and understand the diverse structures and processes, their relations, strains in relations and changes in contemporary India. The probable reasons why there has not been a serious challenge to hegemonic Brahmanical preoccupations in this syllabus are the still marginal presence of dalit students. Further possibly, even students who flaunt their progressive predisposition quietly accept this preoccupation with tradition. Some teachers however self-consciously reflect on this focus on tradition. Syllabuswise, studies on dalit movement are part of the course. Also, considerations on the indological approach give at least an indirect opportunity to comment on the primacy attributed to tradition.

The rise of subaltern studies in Bengal is a significant intellectual development, which also motivates some teachers to take a critical stand. Among the contemporary sociologists, Pathak (1998) strongly recommends a study of Indian modernity – its evolution, contradictions, ambiguities and possibilities. Social history writings by Partha Chatterjee, Ashis Nandy, Sumit Sarkar and Bhikhu Parekh should be taken as texts. Even themes like alternative modernity and development, alternative use of science and technology, alternative ways of distributing our resources (Shiva, 1988; Guha 1994) have been proposed by today's sociologists for incorporation in the syllabus. Unfortunately, the syllabi under consideration have not yet been able to fulfil all these requirements. Beteille's critique of the study of Indian society in general holds true for Calcutta University undergraduate syllabus too. He accepts that the study of Indian society has advanced a great deal in the last 40–50 years, but it has advanced more as a branch of Indian studies than as a branch of sociology. For sociology, by its very nature is a comparative science (Beteille, 2006: 209).

Indian sociological thought is another constant and one of the unique features of the sociology undergraduate syllabi framed by the University of Calcutta. In the syllabus of 1981 it was the second half of the very first paper. It covered a wider range of topics. The concept of society in India (ancient, medieval and modern), modern Indian thinkers, modern social institutions, and pioneers of Indian sociology like Dhurjati Prasad Mukerji, Radhakamal Mukerjee, G.S. Ghurye and Benoy Kumar Sarkar, were included. In the next revision in 1990 there was a significant relocation of its position, i.e., first half of sixth paper. To some extent the same thinkers were retained though in a more organized way. Since 1995 onwards a tendency to trim down the syllabus can be identified in this paper too. It just focused on the four Indian sociologists mentioned above, replacing the narrative on institutional development of sociology in India. A reorganization was done in 2002. Radhakamal Mukerjee, known for his philosophical and metaphysical positions, was dropped, while the other three sociologists were retained. Among the new items included were thinkers like Bhupendra Nath Dutt, and Ambedkar (dropped shortly citing the issue of non-availability of material on them) and approaches to the study of Indian society. The course on Indian thinkers is important because the founding fathers of Indian sociology offered a critique to the western orientalist paradigms of study of Indian society, suitable for serving the missionary and administrative interests of the colonial rulers. They initiated the trend of interpreting Indian reality with indigenous concepts, the so-called ethnosociology (Jayaram, 1998: 238). It was their frame of analysis of Indian society, which was largely adopted in the syllabi under focus. But there is a major difference too that needs to be taken note of.

The secular orientation of the intellectuals of Bengal gets reflected in their making of sociology syllabus. This marks a point of divergence from the religious orientation of the founders of Indian sociology. G.S. Ghurye, D.P. Mukerji and B.K. Sarkar, with varying emphasis, did focus on tradition and project Hinduism as a unifying force. On the whole, the paper on 'Indian Sociologists' proves (a) an attempt by Bengali intellectuals to develop a truly national system of education combining the heritage of Indian with the western system of knowledge; (b) an acceptance of the grand narrative of progress inherent in the writings of founders of Indian sociology; and (c) an inclination towards abstract theorization of broader realities like civilization, nation/society etc. However, adequate attention was not paid to their distinctiveness vis-à-vis western sociology for this was not formally an integral part of the syllabus. I would argue therefore that the real purpose of their inclusion has not been served. Emphasis should be given on what the present generation of students can derive from their works. For instance, Ghurye worked on costume, on sex habits of middle class, and all the thinkers extensively used and analysed Indian art and literature. But unfortunately these works were not considered, despite the fact that sociology of art and literature, of dress and fashion are very much in things today. Not surprisingly, today's generation of students fail to relate to these thinkers.

'Research Methods' (50 marks) and 'Social Statistics' (50 marks) always constituted the fourth paper. Nature, typology and steps of sociological research, need for statistics in sociological research, diagrammatic presentation of statistical data, and sampling are the common themes in this paper. In the 1990 revision some relevant concepts like hypothesis, causality, validity and reliability, and some relevant issues like objectivity, relation between research and theory, issue of social policy, and ethics were added to the 'methodology' section. In the 1995 revision a topic on 'humanist method' and on the 'significance of life documents' was incorporated. But, the syllabus is still deficient in creating adequate awareness about the worth of qualitative research, in which memories, folk tales, local histories, visuals as well as literary creations can be taken as important sociological data. This explains the near-total absence of the use of qualitative method by the undergraduate honours students in their own field works. The prestige of positivistic science in Bengali intellectual circle is so entrenched that even in the mouthpiece journals of leftist political parties we regularly come across statistical data based serious write-ups. Among the social sciences, only in sociology course at both the undergraduate and postgraduate levels there are papers on research methodology inclusive of statistics. Ethnography does not figure in the syllabus at the undergraduate level, though as mentioned above, the humanist method is one topic, which allows development of a critique on the positivist method and methodology. Qualitative approach is now being taught at the postgraduate level. At the level of researches in social science institutions in Calcutta, some scholars do indeed use ethnography and other qualitative methods. But there is a perceptible dislike of postmodernism among older sociologists committed to a Marxist mode of production analysis.

Looking back into the history of this course, it is found that before independence sociology was taught in the broader framework of social philosophy and social thought. The impact of French and British positivistic tradition was not that powerful then. A full course in research methodology or in the philosophy of social sciences was not taught either in Bombay or Lucknow University. But, after independence in the 1950s, during the time of rapid expansion of sociology teaching and increasing popularity of the subject, American influence on Indian sociology brought in new awareness about tools and methods for the empirical analysis of social institutions. Two factors contributed to the development and victory of the positivistic instrumental ethos of sociology in India. First, the strategic social science studies conducted during the Second World War using American innovations in methodologies, and second, the projection of sociology as a policy science in India (the contribution of Douglas Ensminger, Director of Ford Foundation in India from 1951 to 1970 was immense in this regard) (Singh, 1988: 45). Today, when a range of software packages meant for social research is readily available, there is not enough justification for an elaborate course on statistics. It was only in 2002, fieldwork and dissertation of 20 (later 30) marks was included reducing little bit the portion of statistics. The major impetus behind it was to rectify a perennial problem, i.e., teaching methods without any practical exercises.

Initially, many special sociology courses were offered. But, the current members of the Board are inclined to do away with it in favour of greater exposure to basic theory and thought. The UGC model suggests the same, i.e., a general orientation of the discipline for the undergraduate students and further specialization for postgraduate students. The presence of allied fields in sociology curriculum had a historical background. It was only since 1930s that sociology as a full-fledged discipline emerged in India. Earlier, sociology was always combined either with economics (Bombay University and Lucknow University at M.A. level), or philosophy (Mysore University at B.A. level as an elective subject) or political science. In the Calcutta University syllabus of 1981 we find 'Social Psychology' (50 marks) paper, which was dropped in subsequent revision. 'Social Planning with an Emphasis on India's Five-Year Planning' was another 50 marks paper in the same syllabus. That was a time when coming to power in 1977 the CPM-dominated left-coalition moved away from a policy of fomenting class struggle to reformism for the sake of a stable governance. With the waning of the significance of public sector and state planning, experts felt no need for the continuation of the paper on planning in the nineties. Similarly, in the syllabus of 1990 there was a 50 marks paper on 'Social Demography', and in 1995 there was one on 'Political Sociology' – both subsequently, dropped. But, unlike these, a 50 marks paper on 'Social Anthropology' persisted for quite a long time. It was introduced in the very first syllabus in 1981 and discontinued only in 2002. The explanation probably lies in the typical social composition of Indian society. In this paper, apart from a general introduction to the anthropological concepts and themes, there were sections on Indian tribes. Political triumph of the mainstream, subsuming different identities and local uniqueness within its fold, has become the characteristic feature of today's globalized world.

Hence, even in Third World countries like India, the difference between sociology and social anthropology increasingly gets blurred. Actually, Indian sociology and anthropology emerged from a colonial construction, which privileged the pre-modern over the modern. Hence, Beteille points out a persistent confusion in separating the fields of sociology and anthropology in India. Probing into the institutional background I have traced another reason behind the persistence of social anthropology. In 1921, a department of anthropology was established at Calcutta University, where lecturership in ethnography was created. In this department eminent sociologists and social anthropologists D.N. Majumdar and N.K. Bose had their early initiation in anthropology. The same was true at the all-India level. Ghurye was trained as social anthropologist and was appointed to the chair in sociology. Hence, experts with anthropology background or having ethnographic research experience always recommended an anthropology course for students of sociology in India. Sociology in West

Bengal has always been associated with social anthropology. For a large number of years social anthropology was taught as a part of the undergraduate honours course and the postgraduate course. Later, in order to create more space for sociology proper, the course has been redesigned to retain social anthropological perspective as one way of understanding sociological issues. Typically, this complementary nature finds expression in pre-modern/postmodern differentiation at the levels of social process and social structure. The fact that studies by M.N. Srinivas, Andre Beteille and Nirmal Kumar Bose are taught at both the levels, is proof enough that there is no hiatus between the two disciplines. T.B. Bottomore's pointer that we need to know and apply both the disciplines in order to understand India has been well taken by sociologists and sociology teachers in West Bengal.

Another special paper in 1981 syllabus was 'Sociology of Organization and Labour', which was discontinued in the next revision only. In this paper there was a substantial section on India in general and West Bengal in particular. Topics listed include labour legislations and their implementation in India, trade union organizations, their role in welfare of workers, history of the trade union movement in West Bengal, impact of grant of trade union rights to government employees, modern organizations in villages, like banks or rural credit societies, impact of panchayat in the life of villagers, and relation of these bodies with state bureaucracies. All these were the focused themes of the ruling left regime in West Bengal. In the electoral success of the left coalition the unionized workers and the government employees played very critical role. Operation *Barga*, establishment of three-tier panchayat system, and bringing teachers in government-aided schools under the direct government employment were the prime factors strengthening their political position and popularity. Since 1990s onwards, a well-penetrated left government started shifting its priorities of development – a focus on village, land reform and panchayat has been replaced by that on industry and, for that matter, foreign direct investment. It explains, to an extent, the reorganization of course structure under the influence of contemporary dominant ideology.

On the whole, significant changes noticed in the successive syllabi are: (i) emphasis on abstract theories has been supplemented by preoccupation with frontier issues; (ii) a shift from special sociology, e.g., a full 100 marks paper on 'Marx' or a course on 'Social Anthropology', to a more general course in sociology; and (iii) a focus on independent research projects to be carried out by each student. Critics point out that the loss of specialized focus snaps the wider linkages between sociology and other social sciences. Sociology, after all, is the study of relations. Creating an abstracted domain of sociology may not do full justice to the discipline itself. Among the framers of syllabus, in course of my interview with a few, I find a concern about the need to stay tuned to contemporary changes in western sociology. In case of specifying the texts and references in the syllabus, apart from the standard of the book, its availability in the market often becomes a deciding factor. For example, in the 2002 syllabus, the first and the fourth editions of Giddens' *Sociology* were cited as texts just because of its availability. However, there has been no formal provision for reading the classics. This is left to individual teacher's capability and the intellectual receptivity and curiosity of students. Another tendency is a deliberate attempt to cut down the size of the syllabus. The Board had the opinion that in their attempt to modernize the courses they should not make it unnecessarily heavy. But, the question is whether this is a populist measure to endorse mediocrity at the cost of the rigour of knowledge. The content of syllabi also reflects a paradigm shift at the epistemological level, which has definite linkage with the political orientation of the ruling left parties of West Bengal. Marxist framework of emancipatory rationality holds the key to the ability on the part of the intellectuals with predominantly leftist orientation to perceive Indian society in terms of conflicts and tensions. That explains the inclusion of various social movements, revolutionary struggles and social problems in the syllabi. This critical and reflexive discourse of society provides the students with the ability to connect their sociological knowledge with the everyday world they inhabit. Left Front's recent inclination towards market-responsive 'bourgeois' development, leaving behind the orthodox Marxist line of socialist development too, has its impact on the current syllabus. In 1980s we find a heavy emphasis on Marxist sociology. The teaching of A.R. Desai's works has a similar explanation. But eventually, despite the evident attempts by the so-called progressive scholars to counter-balance liberal or, what was pejoratively called 'bourgeois' sociology, the predominant place has now been that of a liberal sociology as evident by the range of classical sociologists in sociology courses, in the courses on sociological theory and on methodology, and by the choice of textbooks and references.

III

Change and Resistance

Changes are not always easy to introduce. Only the 'elemental fear of the new', borrowing D.P. Mukerji words, may account for the stiff resistance towards almost every attempt to bring about changes, e.g., (i) introducing new texts like those by Giddens, Berger or Ritzer etc., replacing MacIver and Page or Davis; and (ii) exposing students to contemporary themes like globalization, new theoretical developments like feminist theory or postmodernism or thinkers like Ambedkar. Even in the workshop organized after the reframing in 2002, the issue of Giddens as a text was raised. One made a caustic comment that "radicalism of Bengali culture is evident from its literature, film, drama, even painting, but sociology in Bengal is absolutely devoid of it. The only sign of radicalism in sociology is the inclusion of Marx in the syllabus". The most frequently cited excuse to resist incorporation of new and complex themes was that the students would find it difficult to understand. Easy syllabus and lenient evaluation make sociology a 'soft' discipline. Often resistance comes on the ground that there is not enough time to cover the given syllabus. In the workshop organized in 2004 jointly by Presidency College and Under Graduate Council of Sociology in order to sensitize undergraduate teachers about the new syllabus of 2002, a sizeable number of college teachers express their reservation against the inclusion of thinkers like Bhupendranath Datta and Ambedkar in the paper on 'Sociological Thought' on the ground of time factor and non-availability of adequate reading material. There was even an informal decision not to teach them in the class and not to set questions on them for the time being. These thinkers were subsequently dropped from the syllabus. This apart, personal rivalry among the members and political puritanism in their world view, are the possible reasons why the curriculum fails to fully satisfy the promise of this living subject.

One way of understanding a syllabus is to analyse its content and its change by contextualizing it in the changing social milieu. Another related way is to directly ask the framers about their intentions and motivations and also their current perceptions about it. Majority of the members of the Board, interviewed, stated that while structuring the syllabus, they gave prime importance to the understanding of the discipline. Intellectual capability of the target students came next to it. All of them agreed that the issue of availability of textbooks and reference books was vital, but a somehow manageable problem. Most of them could recall several instances of difference of opinion in the Board, for example, on the issue of globalization, on Indian thinkers, or regarding inclusion of contemporary books. One categorically mentioned that differences were usually resolved simply by not accepting any proposal for change. Another lamented the fact that there was always either defeat or compromised victory. But, there was an altogether different version coming from a very senior member. He could not recall any strong difference of opinion. He said that the possibility was ruled out by careful composition of the Board. Only 'like-minded' individuals – friends and colleagues – who were also democratic in spirit, were included. The relatively junior teachers, he found, normally endorsed suggestions coming from the seniors. The initiative for syllabus updating, following a majority opinion, usually came from the postgraduate department. One veteran member of the Board identified UGC model curriculum as an important guiding principle today. Though the undergraduate teachers (three from government and non-government colleges each) always outnumbered the postgraduate teachers (the chairperson, and three members) in the syllabus revision committee, the latter's opinion carried greater weight. All the college teachers, whom I have interviewed, felt that the committee should formally meet the undergraduate teachers to explain them the changes. Though customary, many a times, it did not happen. Majority of the current and the retired members of the Board felt that a policy change with regard to what was to be taught was the prime justification for the revision of syllabus. Only a few believed that a change in the composition of the committee was the main reason. While reflecting on the successive syllabi, one teacher questioned the logic behind the organization of the courses. As an illustration, the current placement of theory paper was cited. In the 2002 revision, paper on 'Sociological Theory' was pushed back from second paper to sixth paper (part I to part III). Thus, the thought-theory composite, useful and necessary for the students to grasp the connection, was broken. But, another member justified it on the ground that only the intellectually mature students in the third year could understand the abstract theories. Some young members of the Board blamed the seniors' tendency to include their areas of academic interest in the curriculum. It emerged from the interviews that lack of knowledge about emergent concerns of sociology made an average teacher lukewarm to the idea of syllabus change. There was fear too that they would have to study afresh. Teachers could not agree on the factor(s) subverting a forward-looking syllabus. Some held the practice of dictation of notes in lieu of teaching in the class responsible. Others blamed the practice of handing over photocopies, or continuing teaching on the basis of study material for the discarded syllabus. On the whole, a lack of initiative, on the part of teachers, was identified by the teachers as the worst problem. There were notes of appreciation too. I quote one such response: "The successive syllabi have been of high order as indicated by the rate of success of our students in the two universities in Delhi, TISS, Pune University, and from the informal feedbacks from teachers of these institutions, as well as by some of our students doing excellent research in SOAS, Cambridge, and major American universities like Harvard, Illinois etc."

IV

Conclusion

In West Bengal the dominant Marxist discourse of freedom and equality, to a certain extent, holds the twin hegemonic ideology – the traditional Brahmanical (based on caste exclusion) and the modern colonial (based on market exclusion) in control. But, since 1990s, as India has entered into the spell of liberalization, the market becomes a factor to reckon with in every sphere of life, including academics. The primacy of market is unambiguously stated in the World Bank's recommendation of structural reform of the Indian economy. It categorically asks to make "the education system as a whole more responsive to market needs", as well as to ensure "expanding access to education that fosters critical thinking and learning skills for all, not just the elites" (Dahlman and Utz, 2005: 10). This is in complete contradiction with the position of Humayun Kabir in the context of India in 1950s. He wrote: "Higher education – as distinct from professional training – is abstract and often has no direct relation to the practical problems of life. Its abstractness is however its saving virtue, for it gives to such education a universal aspect" (Kabir, 1956: 186).

Even a more or less politically secure leftist regime in West Bengal bows under it. The threat perception is explicit when Yogendra Singh writes: "the globalization and liberalization of the economy also creates new opportunities and demands for certain types of skills and education, which may pull away an increasing number of scholars and students from liberal and humanistic social sciences such as sociology" (Singh, 1996:11). He doubts the possibility of vocationalizing sociology without disturbing its core. He argues that "sociological training... should not only enable its students to cope up with the market forces but inculcate in them the ability to critically comprehend the place of these forces in the scheme of social order from a critical-historical perspective" (ibid.: 13).

The undergraduate sociology syllabus of Calcutta University appears to be partially responsive to the changed world situation, though without any pragmatic commitment to instrumental capitalistic ethos. The increase in the range and depth of papér on theory can be noted as evidence. It retains with rigour the analytical reflexivity and criticality, typical of a social science discipline by exposing students to diversities and contradictions like (i) classical theories (e.g., functionalism) as well as contemporary formulations (e.g., postmodern theories); (ii) conventional status-quoist positions (e.g., Davis and Moore on social stratification) as well as radical stances (e.g., Marx's theory of class); western hegemonic positions (e.g., Parsons' grand narrative), western counter-hegemonic reactions (e.g., Wallerstein's theory) as well as critical perspectives emanating from the Indian or the Third World situation (like the subaltern perspective); abstract conceptualization of social structures and processes as well as an emphasis on empirical investigation of particular and local concrete realities (e.g., a 30 marks field investigation and dissertation in B.A. Honours) course. One serious lacuna in the current syllabus is the near-total absence of a regional orientation. Jha (2005: 402) maintains that a regional sociology can equip sociologists with the knowledge of peoples and cultures that could be useful to the expanding market and media. All the previous syllabi contained a few items specific to West Bengal, but the 2002 revision focuses mostly on pan-Indian situation even where acknowledging diversities in of Indian societal realities. The ultimate purpose of any stream of knowledge is to develop creative faculties of the students and to widen the horizon of experience. The real test of undergraduate sociology syllabus is not merely to act as a feeder for M.A. sociology course, but to train the students to be able to understand the society or relation they live in and remake it, if needed. I believe, the syllabi, under investigation, has not yet been able to fulfil this promise.

Notes

1. See Vivek Kumar's chapter in this volume. Also see Rodrigues (2003).
2. In the last three decades there has been a strong perception in West Bengal, not only on the part of opposition politicians but also on the part of the civil society, that recruitment to positions of higher academic administration like Vice-Chancellors has been guided by partisan choice, that education cell within the ruling party acts as the gate-keeper, and that social science teaching is somewhat ideologized. On the other hand, the left public intellectuals have accused BJP's saffronization of education.
3. For some scholars, the imprecise boundary of sociology, its loose terminology, its ill-defined methods, hazy and multiple nature of sociological theory made the teaching of sociology difficult at the undergraduate level of studies (Beteille, 1973). For others, 'the under-graduate students do show considerable enthusiasm and excitement in seeing villages, slums and tribes. They are full of questions, and it is only appropriate that their curiosity is given the right direction by proper courses and teaching'. (Rao, 1978)

References

Alatas, Syed Hussein. 1972. "The Captive Mind in Development Studies", *International Social Science Journal*, 24 (1): 9–25.

Beteille, Andre. 2006. "Sociology and Current Affairs", *Sociological Bulletin*, 55 (2): 201–14.

Chakrabarti, D. Clerks: An Exploration in the Social Behaviour of an Occupational Group. Unpublished part of doctoral thesis.

Chatterjee, Partha. 2002. *Social Science Research Capacity in South Asia: A Report.* Vol. 6, New York: Social Science Research Council.

Dahlman, Carl and Anuja Utz. 2005. *India and the Knowledge Economy: Leveraging Strengths and Opportunities: An Overview.* Finance and Private Sector Development Unit of the World Bank's South Asia Region and The World Bank Institute, The World Bank, Washington DC.

Deshpande, S. 1994. "Crisis in Sociology: A Tired Discipline?" *Economic and Political Weekly*, March 5: 575–576.

DuttaGupta, B. 1969. "Teaching of Sociology", in *Modernization of University Teaching: Teaching of Natural and Social Sciences in India*, edited by A.B. Shah, Bombay: Nachiketa Publications, pp. 102–115.

Giddens, A. 1996. "In Defence of Sociology", in *Defence of Sociology: Essays, Interpretations and Rejoinders,* edited by Anthony Giddens, Cambridge: Polity Press, pp. 1–7.

Guha, R. (ed.) 1994. *Social Ecology*. New Delhi: Oxford University Press.

Jayaram, N. 1998. "Challenges to Indian Sociology", *Sociological Bulletin*, 47 (2): 237–241.

Jha, Hetukar. 2005. "Indian Sociology in Crisis: The Need for Regional Orientation", *Sociological Bulletin*, Special Issue on South Asia, Vol. 54, No. 3, September–December, 396–411.

Kabir, H. 1956. *Education in New India.* London: George Allen and Unwin Ltd.

Mukherjee, Ramkrishna. 1979. *Sociology of Indian Sociology*. Bombay: Allied.

Mukherji, Partha Nath. 2005. "For a National Social Science Policy", *Sociological Bulletin*, Vol. 54, No. 2, May–Aug, 155–170

Patel, S. 2007. 'Foreword', in "From Knowledge Production to Knowledge Transmission: Exploring the Learning Context of Sociology at the Undergraduate Level", by Edward Rodrigues, *Occasional Paper Series*, Department of Sociology, University of Pune.

Pathak, A. 1998. *Indian Modernity: Contradictions, Paradoxes and Possibilities.* New Delhi: Gyan.

—. 2004. "Teaching/Learning Sociology: A Critical Engagement with Modernity", *Sociological Bulletin*, Vol. 53, No. 1, Jan–April, 31–48.

Ray, N.R. and P.C. Gupta. 1957. *Hundred Years of the University of Calcutta: 1857–1956.* Calcutta: University of Calcutta Press.

Rodrigues, Edward. 2007. "From Knowledge Production to Knowledge Transmission: Exploring the Learning Context of Sociology at the Undergraduate Level", *Occasional Paper Series*, Department of Sociology, University of Pune.

Shiva, V. 1988. *Staying Alive: Women, Ecology and Survival in India.* New Delhi: Kali for Women.

Singh, Y. 1977. Modernisation of Syllabi in Sociology and Social Anthropology. Report based on Four Regional Workshops organized by the UGC, New Delhi.

—. 1988. "Quest for Relevance: Teaching and Research in Sociology", *The Indian Journal of Social Science*, Vol. 1, No. 1, 41–55.

—. 1996. "Sociology and the Emerging Challenges of Change", *Sociological Bulletin*, 45 (1): 1–14.

Smith, M.F. and N.Y. Razzouk. 1993. "Improving Classroom Communication: The Case of the Course Syllabus", *Journal of Education for Business*, 68 (4): 215–221.

Srinivas, M.N. 1992. 'Foreword', in *People of India: An Introduction* by K.S. Singh (National Series Vol.1), Kolkata: Anthropological Survey of India, pp. 1–12.

University Grants Commission. 2001. Model Curriculum: Sociology.

Wallerstein, Immanuel. 1997. "Euro-centrism and its Avatars: The Dilemmas of Social Science", *Sociological Bulletin*, 46 (1): 21–39.

Part II

Sociology in the Margins: The Local and the Banal

The essays in the section bring into focus sharply the ordinary everyday practice of sociology in the regions, while at the same time pointing out that considerable differences exist within the regions themselves. Indeed, the practice of sociology in the North-East India draws attention to the dangers of methodological nationalism and the urgent need to question it. Further, what may appear to be the margins for a metropolitan university may actually be a centre for some. All the three essays share a sense of wariness with the commonplace and facile practice of sociology in their areas. The image of sociology as easy, obvious and ordinary can be understood partially in light of its traditional poor purchase in the job market. However, this has also a great deal to do with the manner that sociology too readily tends to be reduced to the sociologist's 'natural' common sense. This is a fundamental challenge as well as an area of abiding interest for sociology.

5

Practising Sociology on the Outside Edge

SANTOSH KR. SINGH

This is a reflective account of my own experience of teaching sociology in what I refer to as the 'outside edge', the 'periphery' or the non-metropolitan world, not that they form a homogeneous entity.[1] The idea here is basically to communicate what everyday teaching of sociology means here for the teacher, for the student, and for the wider community. And, the sense of a 'lack' that pervades the practice of sociology in the *muffasil*. The sources of this sense of inadequacy are many and diverse. Some of these draw from the larger story of sociology, others to the larger story of India's higher education, particularly vis-a-vis humanities and some to the unequal content and spread of education across regions, across cities and towns, metros and villages. From the larger story of sociology one can sense the 'lack' as stemming from sociology's quest since Auguste Comte to be a science and never quite being so. From the larger story of higher education in humanities is the complete sense of irrelevance that it can generate. And from the purported hierarchy of academics between the centre and the periphery arise undemocratic practices that go against the very spirit of liberal education. Many of the themes that I touch upon have a long history but some have not only got compounded but have also acquired new shapes in the contemporary context of globalization – be it the fetish for 'applied knowledge' or the buzz about 'infrastructure' as the sure route to improvement in education or the new phenomena of 'placement *melas*' in undergraduate colleges or the new scopes for teachers to be engaged in what some describe as the mushrooming of a 'project-driven culture'.

I

The Two Worlds of Sociology and the Many Hierarchies

The Metropolitan versus the 'Muffasil'

If we look at the development of sociology in India, we can safely argue that there exists two kinds of sociology: one which has prospered in the proximity of a research-friendly environment and in the company of top-ranking academia in metropolitan centres like Delhi, Mumbai etc., while the second survived, sustained and mushroomed at places such as Government Degree College, Syalde, Almora in Uttaranchal where I had the privilege of teaching sociology, which was considered 'easy', 'passable', 'soft' and 'feminine'.[2] I had just left the 'utopia' called JNU (Jawaharlal Nehru University) and lured by the magical charm of the word 'Almora' ended up in a place which was clearly untouched by notions of metropolitan civilization except that the only local *kirana* (grocery) shop there had abundant supply of Pepsi. As I later realized Syalde was a small cluster of villages in one of the remotest part of district Almora where the most posh locality *pakka* residence cost one a princely rent of Rs 400 a month and a bucket of drinking water either cost a monthly 100 rupees to a poor local or arduous daily visit to a distant natural source of water in one of the gorges of the hills. The college was established some two decades back at the initiative of a local politician and continues to operate from a five-room building on a hillock. As always Sociology was among the first few subjects along with History, Political Science and Hindi, which were introduced in the college. The college stands there as the most striking testimony to the absurdities that arise in the name of higher education in India. In the last more than two decades, its most productive and tangible impact has perhaps been to 'make' the daughters of the place more eligible for marriage for its largely migrant male population!

Sociology, I would argue, has been very handy in perpetuating such so called centres of higher learning and in the bargain it has earned the dubious honour of being a 'popular' subject. Sociology is concerned as self-reliant and largely experiential. It does not need a library; caters to the poor and the impoverished multitude of graduate wannabes at a minimum cost. During the final examinations, various *gutkas*, *kunjis* or *guides* in all sizes, shapes and colours flood the local *kirana* shops promising 100 per cent success. The teacher becomes redundant, for chances are that those students who did not follow the patterned answers of these guides would end up with 'poor' marks. After all, paper 'evaluation' is also a business. Patterned answers are easy to evaluate; given that most of the time it is a 'family affair' of the enterprising sociology practitioners.

The most telling experience is of one senior lecturer of one of the colleges who did 'brisk businesses' during paper evaluation time, courtesy his networking with the university examination and evaluation branch. The whole family used to be involved in some way or the other in this exercise. His undergraduate students would correct the papers. Many times postgraduate students joined in to please the 'guru' while his wife and children generously kept the flow of tea and lunch going. His wife, innocent of the 'niceties' involved in examinations, once shared with my wife that for the last so many years he has been giving all the 'exam money' he earns from his hard work to her only and she in turn would invest this earning in making gold ornaments for their growing daughters as part of their dowry. I was mute witness to all this as he happened to be both my landlord and the head of the department! Once seeing the heap of answer sheets lying unattended at his doorstep I volunteered to help but he politely refused. He was a nice person and a master of the mundane. Sociology becomes inconsequential in such cases. Perhaps the most worrisome of such practices is that they are considered the 'normal' in society. This is it. This is not seen as an anomaly.

The vicious cycle thus continues. This is an easy arrangement. Everybody is pleased with it. The student becomes a graduate, the teacher earns more money, college management does not have to bother about library and other infrastructure and the politicians are happy they could add to their manifesto one more achievement without much financial fuss.

The situation is different but not so much in terms of quality in the colleges of Chandigarh where I was to join later. Colleges do have great infrastructural base and other academic facilities but as far as the state of sociology as a discipline is concerned, it remains plagued with the same set of malaise that existed in the colleges of Uttaranchal. If one just looks at the format of the B.A. (Pass) sociology question paper for the annual examinations conducted by the Panjab University, one finds the emphasis is on 'passing' the candidates as out of 100 marks questions worth 40 marks are of objective types and short notes. This, to my mind, encourages those students who join college with no serious purpose to opt for the subject and in turn leads to reconfirming its bad branding. A vast majority of the students here also depend upon the guides and the wide assortment of what are clearly sub-standard textbooks. Similarly, for instance, the syllabus designed by the university for the final year (sociology) pass course mentions the phenomenon of suicide as an example of 'personal disorganization' which is such a serious lapse given that one of the founders of the discipline Emile Durkheim and his magnum opus 'le suicide' so fervently argues it to be a 'social fact'. This is interesting because on the one hand as I have argued at the very start sociology has been keen to be defined as a science yet it has been unable to transmit to the students even the very basic of Durkheim's idea of sociology as a distinct and scientific discipline.

This shows lack of commitment to the discipline on the part of those engaged in designing of the syllabi. But, this is understandable given that the Board of Studies, more often than not, is a product of petty political manoeuvring and bizarre and inconsequential cravings for some name and fame at local level. If the divide between the metropolis and the *muffasil* world of sociology is one divide, there are other hierarchies at work too, for instance, that between universities versus colleges, applied (useful) versus theoretical (useless) knowledge, infrastructure versus critical thinking, generalist versus specialist, science versus humanities.

University for Research, Colleges for Teaching

The relationship between the colleges and the university departments is another sad feature contributing to the marginality of the discipline. Despite being located in close proximity, there is not much communication between the university departments and the colleges except on a few occasions when the colleges organize talks or extension lectures and invite the faculty members from the university, that also annually, when some sort of exchange of ideas take place. For all practical purposes otherwise the two remain insulated from each other. University faculty basks in its taken for granted identity as place of profound research and act superior and distant. To my mind perpetuation of this myth where college is associated primarily with 'teaching' and university departments with 'research' has done serious damage to the academic environment. It has spawned a kind of academic apartheid where college lecturers, many times with a better academic credentials, are treated unfairly. This urge for exclusiveness as displayed by university departments only shows their insecurity and lack of self-belief. The Academic Staff College of Jawaharlal Nehru University in Delhi, for instance, in its orientation and refresher courses, regularly invite college lecturers from various disciplines as resource persons to deliver lectures and the Delhi University has some prominent academicians in its colleges and the university takes pride in it by inviting them for lectures in various departments. Sadly, such instances are rare or simply unthinkable elsewhere. This culture of 'strait jacketedness' and preponderance of hierarchical organizational structures and mindsets have sapped the very essence and the spirit of the discipline. As Game and Metcalfe rightly observed, "Sociology appears to be *contained* in its journals, monographs, lectures, textbooks and university departments, university libraries and academics are treated as repositories of knowledge, and students attend not to produce knowledge but to drink from its cup" (1996: 9). Healthy correspondence in an amicable, non-hierarchized ambience between various academic landscapes will surely benefit the discipline.

Universities are also fast becoming a place of 'networking' for higher mobility and personal aggrandizement by the entrepreneurial academics. Even in universities known for their progressive and enlightened atmosphere for the faculty as well as students, one gets to hear that the thrust is more on 'projecteering' and the classroom teaching is being undermined by some of the faculty members. It is sad that an academician's credentials depend primarily on how many overseas assignments and international projects he or she is handling or involved in. Not that these assignments are not to be engaged in but again the primacy of the teacher-taught interface has to be respected and a balance has to be maintained. Nothing captures the current mood and the changing ethos of sociology more sharply than the increasing trend of 'visiting cards' exchanges among its practitioners, overshadowing the ongoing debate in various seminars and conferences. This is perhaps but just one of the manifestations of change in higher educational practices. The other two that I would like to briefly mention are the buzzwords about applied knowledge and infrastructures being the panacea for better higher education.

'Applied Knowledge' as Useful versus 'Theoretical Knowledge' as Useless

India in these early years of the 21st century is flush with the successes of liberalization, of being branded globally as an economic power. The new context puts heavy premium on pursuits, which would lead to material rewards in terms of jobs, remuneration, desirable lifestyles, etc. In other words, the thrust is on human beings primarily as consumers. Actually, sociology does have a growing significance as a subject with the requisite know-with-all for applied knowledge that can be used by the corporate sector, which needs more finetuned information on the Indian market and desires of what is vouched by most global corporate analysts as the one of the largest nations of consumers. The question that is central for this volume hence is, what role does critical or reflexive sociology have in this context?

These are not abstract questions but real dilemmas which confront a sociology undergraduate student today who finds oneself overawed by the respectability and desirability of other fellow friends who are pursing pure science or commerce or economics. The conspicuous exhibition of this trend in pompous annual 'placement melas' organized and sponsored by corporate houses in colleges where even the brightest students of sociology or history are treated as untouchables, is a grim reminder of a world which is increasingly getting compartmentalized and where newer forms of hierarchies are being manufactured. Heavy rush for courses such as BCA, for instance, in the colleges of Chandigarh in recent years, has left the practitioners of social sciences feeling terribly 'unwanted'.

Some of the most sought after and the prestigious colleges of Chandigarh, where earlier all the seats in all the courses used to be filled in the first few days only, are finding it hard to accept the fact that the seats are lying vacant in conventional undergraduate courses, especially in humanities and arts segment, even weeks after the commencement of admission process. As a result, they have been forced to lower its cut off percentage causing bruised collective ego of the institution. Local media highlighting the demands for more seats in BCA and extension of infrastructure in colleges reflect the mood of the changing times.

Just imagine the enormity of challenge in teaching Karl Marx, for instance, and his thoughts to a group of young, impressionable and restless minds who are constantly fed on the futility of their choice of subjects. As a teacher, one realizes how didactic and sermonizing one sounds, lecturing a group of young but completely demotivated students, at least one-third of them, sitting and staring at you blankly as they have been forced by the compulsion of compulsory 75 per cent attendance.

To understand the mindset of an average student, let us ponder over the following informal conversation which occurred in a classroom comprising final year students of B.A. (Pass) course:

> *Student:* Sir how much salary do you get and since when are you teaching?
>
> *Teacher:* Rs 20,000 per month and I have been teaching for the last eight years.
>
> *Student:* And, how much does the Principal get as she is about to retire?
>
> *Teacher:* Rs 45,000 per month.
>
> *Student:* It is too less. Nowadays in call centre you can earn this much salary even after your graduation. I know a cousin of mine whose starting salary is Rs 50,000 per month.
>
> *Student:* Sir why did you join this job. You speak good English. You could have tried somewhere else. Why teaching?

The conversation reflects the current mood of the society in general and students or the youth in particular. There is a frightening trend of money being considered the only and the most important parameter of judging the worth of any person or a thing. Also, English speaking is considered the defining characteristic of brighter people. Not to be missed here is the surprise and bafflement of the student at the teacher's career choice! It is not to imply that this value orientation glorifying materialism is a new development. What is however new is the unprecedented level of legitimacy and moral sanction that it has acquired. This perhaps explains why India's most prominent icons today are more likely to be from corporate world. The word 'business' no more belongs to the realm of profanity; rather, it is the most sacred profession of new India. There is nothing wrong with this change except that it seems to be contemptuously indifferent to other possibilities of success and other possibilities of meaningful life.

It is in this backdrop that we need to locate the problems involved in teaching a subject like sociology in non-metro or regional locations. It is also equally important here to mention that the words 'metropolitan' and 'centre' which have been used in this paper in contrast with 'periphery', 'non-metro' and 'regional' are merely symbolic and metaphorical and have no territoriality attached to them. That is, if Delhi and Mumbai are centres and metropolitan spaces, say for Chandigarh and Haldwani in Uttarakhand, then Chandigarh in a different context works as 'centre' for a local college in say Moga in Panjab. So, basically, it is about the idea, rather than actual geographical spaces.

Infrastructure versus Critical Thinking

Lately, there has been an exaggerated emphasis on infrastructure development while talking about institution building. The pertinent question here is whether an institution is all about swanky buildings and architectural marvels? An institution is also about its academic culture: its dedicated and enlightened faculty members, its belief in the idea of education and teaching as an emancipatory project. Sadly, the whole thrust in various plan documents on higher education has been on quantitative expansion. The Eleventh Plan and its budgetary allocations reflect the skewed preference for vocational and technical education with the manifest objective of generating 'employability'. Since the report of Dr Radha Krishnan headed University Education Commission (1948–49) to the Kothari Commission (1964–65) to the recent National Knowledge Commission (2006), there have been serious concerns raised about the crisis of quality in higher education, yet in practice and implementation the spirit could never grow beyond letters.

Two issues thus call for attention in this background: one is concerning the state of our existing universities and colleges which have been glories of our past and secondly, the rationale behind the idea of opening new universities in the name of expansion, while many of the existing ones have been left to degenerate. Nowhere is this phenomenon more pronounced and glaring than in Bihar, for example. There is a talk of an ambitious project of opening a university of international standing at Nalanda in Bihar. However, a visit to the once prestigious Patna University and its dilapidated buildings thirsty for even a coating of whitewash since decades delegitimizes the ambition of Nalanda. Similar is the case of Bhagalpur University, where remnants of once famous Vikramshila are witness of how shabbily we have treated our traditional seats of learning.

In a workshop titled 'The Future of the Past: A Century of Higher Education in India' organized by the Academic Staff College of JNU in November 2006, while addressing the gathering of the Principals of some of the eminent colleges from across the country, one of the former vice chancellors of the Rajasthan University recounted the hoary time that he experienced while in office. Rajasthan University, which once upon a time acted as a feeder to the institutions such as JNU when the latter was being founded as many of the stalwarts moved to Delhi, is now in a sink of chaos, mismanagement and academic mediocrity characterized by dominance of money, political mafia and muscle power. Another invitee in that workshop J.M. Lyngdoh, former Chief Election Commissioner of India and who later headed a commission to study the phenomenon of student politics in various universities of India on the recommendation of the Supreme Court, in his address further corroborated to the process of degeneration and rot that had set in these places of higher learning, courtesy political interference in the functioning of the universities. Most of these universities are in deep financial crunch as the major chunk of the UGC budget is consumed by the central universities and the Delhi colleges. Nearly 65 per cent of the UGC budget is utilized for meeting the operating expenses of central universities and the Delhi colleges. The remaining 35 per cent is spent on the 116 eligible state universities and around 5,000 affiliated colleges. Thus, the funding pattern is skewed in favour of a handful of central universities. The bulk of the system (85 per cent), accounted by mainly state university affiliated undergraduate colleges, get very little assistance from the UGC.

There is no problem in the idea of expansion as long as it starts from consolidating and reinforcing the existing institutions and infrastructure and not by sidelining them. Also, the thrust on courses with employability does not necessarily mean complete blackout of the role of social sciences and humanities in the construction and well-being of societies and communities. Further, the agenda of skill imparting education for jobs should not gloss over the fact that the subjects such as history, political science and sociology are very important as they provide the much needed investment in social capital.

Generalist versus Specialist

Since I joined Chandigarh, I have been writing off and on for *The Tribune*, an English newspaper of repute, on various themes confronting society. That so far all my articles have been carried on 'op-ed' page, which is considered prestigious in the journalistic circle. It does give me a sense of accomplishment for being able to create a space for myself as a sociology practitioner beyond my classroom. The reactions of my colleagues at both the colleges and the university ranged from a plain indifference to a rather strange advice of "do not waste your time by writing in the newspapers". One senior colleague actually sounded rather concerned and handed me a piece of advice saying, "do write on dalits or minorities and other such subjects, only then you will be able to make any headway in your career".

It surprised me no end since I never started writing with any such motive. I was merely being responsible and trying to engage in a public debate through these short-takes with my modest background in sociology. I see no necessary dichotomy between public and academic sociology. As Peter L. Berger writes:

> The sociologist moves in the common world of men, close to what most of them would call real. The categories he employs in his analyses are only refinements of the categories by which other men live-power, class, status, race, ethnicity. As a result, there is a deceptive simplicity and obviousness about some sociological investigations. One reads them, nods at the familiar scene, remarks that one has heard all this before and do not people have better things to do than to waste their time on truisms-until one is suddenly brought up against an insight that radically question everything one had previously assumed about the familiar scene. This is the point at which one begins to sense the excitement of sociology (1963: 33).

Sociologists, hence, cannot simply delink from its subjects, no matter how mundane and familiar they may appear. Nor does it serve any purpose if their analyses become the preserves only of some professional journals. The practitioners of sociology will have to therefore enter the debate at all levels, especially when society is faced with some crisis, whether it is in times of caste conflict as it happened recently on the issue of giving reservation benefits to the creamy layer or in times of communal frenzy in Gujarat. What is important is the 'occasion' and not the 'stage'. The reason why in a nursery school located in the campus of the Panjab University where I had taken my son for admission, a senior teacher who was interviewing me looked nonplussed when told that I was a sociology lecturer in one of the government colleges. As she later explained she thought sociology was a subject which was taught only by women.

When Prof M.N. Srinivas died, I was in Uttaranchal. I asked the B.A. (Final) year students about him. It did not surprise me that none had heard of him at all. I was happy to introduce this great sociologist to that group of young students. Some years later I repeated the same question to a group of final year students in Chandigarh and this time it shocked me that the response was similar. Why is the 'periphery' so ignorant of the glories of the 'centre'? Why has there been so little meaningful and concerted effort on the part of the metropolitan academia to rescue sociology from the miasma of mediocrity that envelopes it in majority of the regional centres? One can understand the limitations of those in 'lab-bound' pure sciences and their isolated world with minimum interaction with the common man. But, what stops sociology and its practitioners to mingle and intervene at least in times of crisis faced by the society at large remains a mystery.

Is there a fear of being branded a 'generalist'? Is this distancing a conscious attempt on the part of the mainline sociologists to exhibit their power of knowledge? Or, is it that we are still under the influence of Comtean anxiety and suffer from some kind of inferiority complex vis-à-vis pure sciences and want to imitate their cocooned professional life? That any introductory book on sociology for the undergraduates does have to necessarily, almost ritually, even today have to debate 'why sociology is a science' tells you that the ground beneath our feet is still shaky. The manner in which a young practitioner's attempt at writing in regional newspapers or in vernacular press on issues concerning the community is rubbished as 'non-academic' and an exercise in futility by the so-called professionals underline the same abhorrent propensity to segregate. This to my mind has been one of the major failures of sociology, that is, its delinking from the concerns and crisis of the society.

This is not to say that we do not need to follow professional ethics in our academic practices. But this professionalism has to be sensitive to the anxieties and aspirations of the periphery. It is only then that sociology as a subject will gain legitimacy as a sincere discipline. We need to be proud of our academicians, journals and publications of international repute and standing but in a global world we cannot afford to underestimate the local and regional contexts. Academic landscapes, such as universities and colleges, metropolitan and regional centres, central and peripheral institutions, have to cease to exist as isolated and insulated islands and instead work in tandem and forge an alliance for a more meaningful academic world. For this the non-metropolitan centres at regional locale will have to get in to the 'de-sanskritization' mode and stop perpetuating the 'priesthood' from the centre. The sight of a hapless looking organizer, a senior professor, at a regional centre at the last minute news of non-arrival of a retired professor from JNU who was to deliver the inaugural key note address in one of the annual seminars reflect the unfortunate equation of asymmetry and power play between the metropolitan and regional centres. That more often than not these 'big guns' are arranged by these organizers after months of persuasion to exhibit their clout back home, to score over their opponents in the department shows how deeply embedded is the rot to what some sociologist refer to as 'captive colonial mindset'. No wonder success of a seminar at a regional college or university is primarily measured not by the quality of its debate and proceedings but by the number of these 'biggies' from the 'centre' having 'graced the occasion'.

Science and its Hierarchies

Sociology emerged under the shadow of the great discoveries of natural science. The hegemony of a natural science model on its theory, method and most fundamentally on its aspirations, was enormous. In fact, the French philosopher August Comte who is considered the founder of the discipline first named it 'social physics'. The challenge facing a new discipline for the study of society in the illustrious presence of many other contending disciplinary claimants was not easy. The anxiety to garner legitimacy is apparent in the perpetual obsession for acquiring the status of 'science' for the discipline. This is, however, understandable given the preponderance of science and its mind boggling impact in an age which was studded with path-breaking discoveries and inventions unheard in human history. Sociology slowly but steadily progressed from a marginal to a mainliner discipline. Various theoretical perspectives emerged especially in the process of its engagement with the process of modernization. As the pathologies and contradictions of modernity became sharper in the 20th century sociology, with its critical sensitivity to those at the receiving end of the grand design of human emancipation propagated by the modernization project, emerged as a major stream of knowledge. Phenomenological and ethnomethodological schools provided the much needed balance by countering its earlier preoccupation with and quest for detached and disembodied understanding of social reality. Books, such as *Passionate Sociology*, for instance, by Ann Game and Andrew Metcalfe (1996), not just beautifully argue for a reorientation in the way traditionally sociology have masterfully refused to place itself within the social life it studies but also points towards growing confidence of its practitioners in their calling.

II

The Possibilities

The new global context has indeed posed challenges but it has also offered opportunities for the discipline like sociology. Societies across the world today are witnessing a crisis, which is propelled not so much by the economics but by considerations underlined by ethnic, religious and cultural identity formations. Clearly, the task and responsibility of sociology in this background cannot be overestimated. Indeed, there is pressure on various social science disciplines to make it more 'pragmatic' and 'applied'. But here too we need not shy away from this situation. We can think of new branches and areas of sociology such as 'sociology of advertisement' or 'sociology of call centres'. But this 'newness' should not be merely for the sake of it or at the cost of discipline's past repertoire of knowledge base. As Andre Beteille cautioned, "the problem with us is not that the small amount of good work done by preceding generations is unjustly criticized by succeeding ones, but that it is ignored and then quickly forgotten. In India each generation of sociologists seem eager to start its work on a clean slate with little or no work done before. This amnesia about the work of their predecessor is no less distinctive of Indian sociologists than their failure to innovate" (Beteille, 1997). Yet we need to promote research in areas which are new in its origin, such as mapping the changes in family and household relationships as a result of mobile phones. Not that we are not making an effort. But mere throwing in of terms such as 'globalization' and 'gender' in the syllabus will not do. The myth about sociology as a subject necessarily dealing and documenting exotic details about marriage and caste must be debunked. Both India and the world have changed in many ways and so should sociology. More interdisciplinary and cross-border collaborative spaces and themes for future research should be encouraged without paying more heed than it deserves to the question of individuality of the discipline raised by the purists concerned more about the sanctity of its territory than its survival and growth. If we can bring about this balance of say on the one hand positively responding to the pragmatic pulls and on the other hand, retaining our core commitment to the critical epistemological engagement with the social reality around, we would certainly play an important role in society.

Notes

1. This is a point readers would notice repeatedly appears through the volume.
2. Prior to joining the colleges in Chandigarh the author taught for a couple of years in some of the remotest areas of Uttaranchal, then part of Uttar Pradesh.

References

Berger, Peter L. 1963. *Invitation to Sociology: A Humanistic Perspective.* New York: Penguin Books.

Beteille, Andre. 1997. "Newness in Sociological Enquiry", *Sociological Bulletin,* 46 (1): 97–110.

Game, Ann and Andrew Metcalfe. 1996. *Passionate Sociology.* London: Sage Publications.

6

Sociology in the 'Regional' Backwoods

A Fictional Rendering

PUSHPESH KUMAR

This is a fictional account about the practice of sociology in a regional university. It is therefore in order that I insert the disclaimer that any resemblance to real events or persons is entirely accidental. Practice here connotes the teaching of sociology as well as the perception of the practitioners – the teachers and students about their own discipline. The perceptions are deciphered through anecdotes and interviews. The anecdotes have been gathered over several years by our prime narrator, Raman (pseudonym), who is a teacher of sociology in the region. Raman has his masters and doctoral degrees from a university in a metropolitan centre and hence he is 'destined' to compare practices of sociology in metropolitan and non-metropolitan universities due to his double positioning.[1] The practice of sociology in this context also includes the local production of textbooks in the local language for the consumption of teachers and students. Lastly, in a very limited way, it takes into account the doctoral research through a cursory look at some of the doctoral theses submitted to this university. In both cases actual references will not be given. The first section of the paper attempts to reflect upon the practices through anecdotes and through the narratives collected by interviewing the practitioners. The second section is a critical gazing of the texts written by local sociology teachers and the third section constitutes a very brief comment on the quality of doctoral dissertations submitted to the university.

Before I detail these aspects, it is in order to introduce the reader to a fictionalized socio-cultural landscape. University 'A' is located in a city in western India, a part of which was under the erstwhile princely state of Nizam of Hyderabad and is regarded as one the 'backward' regions. It is largely agrarian with comparatively few migrants from even other parts of the region, leave alone from outside the state. Being a regional university, the large majority of teachers and students belong to the same district and the language of interaction, by and large, is the regional language. The students too are not even from other parts of the state except in the engineering and medical colleges and to some extent in the Business Management Department of the university. The university encourages local students to join different courses. Only 2 per cent seats are reserved for the students from outside the state. Besides this, it has not earned a name within the state itself. Hence, the students from other parts of the state do not usually consider enrolling here an attractive possibility despite the fact that 30 per cent seats are reserved for them. Though the university is a decade old, the colleges within its jurisdiction, which offer graduate and postgraduate courses in sociology, have been there for a long time. These colleges were earlier affiliated to a different university within the same region.

The undergraduate students in the faculty of arts take sociology as one of the three subjects and they enrol themselves in various degree colleges affiliated to the university. The postgraduate students of sociology prefer joining the colleges rather than the university because in the university department, the medium of instruction is English unlike in the colleges where teaching is done in the regional language. While the university department gets only 4–5 students in sociology, the enrolment for postgraduate in sociology course in the colleges runs into hundreds. Even in the university department where the medium of instruction is English, the students prefer to write in their mother tongue and many students express their unease at teaching in English language. This widely held sentiment against English is deployed by the local (college) teachers to campaign against the university department as an *alien* entity. This *does* work because the sociology teachers in the university belong to other states. Apart from Raman who studied in Delhi, there is Prof Doon (pseudonym), who hails from eastern India and heads the department. Dr Chand (pseudonym) also belongs to eastern India and occupies a senior faculty position. Both of them have studied in other regional universities. The fourth person is Dr Kamlesh (pseudonym) who has a postgraduate degree in rural development and a doctoral degree in sociology from outside the region. He has experiences in working with reputed research institutes and voluntary sectors. Almost every other college teacher who teaches undergraduate and postgraduate courses have been trained 'locally'.[2]

Sociology in this university, like many places in India, is perceived as a very 'light' and a 'casual' discipline. It is the last choice for the students. Mohan Rao Jadav is one among the few students who have understood that sociology is a difficult and serious discipline. Mohan Rao has tried to study sociological literature in English, and, at the pursuance of Raman he has read articles from different social science and sociological journals available in the university library. This is the reason for his changed perception about sociology. Before this, he had only read textbooks written and published locally. Now, he brands the local textbooks as 'functionalists'. But, Mohan Rao does not constitute the norm, he is an exception. He recently 'rescued' himself from a local college where he got a faculty position and preferred to work temporarily on a research project in the university department. After getting exposed to better books and literature, he says, he does not enjoy teaching in local colleges where 'new' and critical ideas are discouraged. He thinks that his 'different' sociology will desert him soon if he continues teaching in the local colleges. Now, he cherishes a dream to pursue a career in research as he has turned his back to teaching in local colleges. Unlike Mohan Rao Jadav, most of the students do not want to voluntarily go through the difficulty of reading 'difficult' books and prefer local texts to pass the examinations and get a degree. The only career option available to these students is preparation for NET and SET[3] and try to get a teaching position in some local colleges. They cannot move out for jobs to the places where sociology is taught in English or some other language. Some of them make inroads into B.Ed and M.Ed courses after their postgraduate in sociology as they have more job security in this field than by simply remaining as a sociology postgraduate. It is disturbing to hear that some of the NET and SET qualified students in sociology are doing manual jobs in factories to sustain themselves. As Mohan Rao says, they cannot do anything else with their sociology degree if they do not get a teaching job locally. The recruitments in local colleges are mainly possible if the persons aspiring for lecturership are ready to pay heavy sum to the management (of the college).

Most of the students in sociology here come from rural background. Mohan Rao says that most of the rural male students opting for sociology think that they can easily look after their agricultural operations at home along with their sociology course. Many of such students keep visiting their villages during agricultural season to assist their families and to supervise the agricultural operations in their fields. The girls who opt for sociology think that it is easier to pass examinations as they already know what is family, marriage and kinship – the topics of sociology in popular perception, says Mohan Rao. In the university, one can always hear the joke that many boys and girls who pursue postgraduate in sociology and other social sciences do so in order to mention this in their wedding invitation cards! This satire, however, tells only one side of the story. For many students in social sciences and sociology, having a postgraduate degree yields social prestige in communitarian and kinship domains, even if it does not fetch them a job. In the perception of this group of students, having a degree is certainly better than not having one. Unlike the hard and pure sciences, getting a postgraduate degree in sociology is easier.

To Mohan Rao, doing sociology in English medium is an alien experience. A commerce teacher from the local college was astonished at the very idea of sociology in English medium. He could only imagine sociology in the regional language. It is important to realize that often the medium of instruction used is the basis of placing a discipline in the existing hierarchy of subjects. Mohan Rao comments that the idea of sociology in English medium gave a blow to the superior ego of the commerce teacher! One of the senior college faculty members of sociology attributes the fact that there are very few students in the sociology course in the university department to the teaching of sociology in English medium. The local students consider the very idea of sociology as being taught in English as strange and alien. He points out that the local students feel that this is not their sociology – their sociology is that which is taught in mother tongue and is “rooted in their own culture”. By ‘local culture’ he meant that the person teaching sociology should know the local language and the local norms. Without this, the sociology teacher cannot relate to the local students. In this context, teaching in English becomes a disqualification in the perception of the local students and college teachers. This popular viewpoint empowers the local college teachers to discourage the students to enrol in the university department. One of them advised the faculty members from outside to get "involved in things which are local" in order to attract more students.

The question arises here whether the faculty members in the university, who have migrated from outside and teaching in English medium, are any better than the local people teaching in vernacular? This will be unravelled through anecdotes. The local vs outsider and the English vs. vernacular is only one facet. The deeper journey into the interiors of the practices in both the university department and colleges would reveal that even the people teaching in English have been undermining the discipline because of the lack of professional commitment. By and large, the sociological practitioners remain "submerged into the commonsense of their own environment" (Beteille, 2002).

Besides this, the sociological discourse as revealed from the reading of local textbooks, is coloured by the caste status of the authors, particularly the upper castes. Further, they rarely move out of the functionalist paradigm as rightly pointed out by Mohan Rao Jadav. Unfortunately, there are no counter texts referred by teachers and students of sociology to challenge the upper caste perspectives. This seems ironical as there is a strong dalit activism in this region! The city where the university is located has more than one lakh dalits. Among different dalit castes, the dalits who call themselves as Buddhists, are politically very active and organized. The Buddhists dalits are divided into several factions and political groups. On vital issues such as the reservation for jobs and seats in educational institutes and the desecration of Ambedkar's statue etc., all the different factions come together. There are some 5–6 local newspapers of these different political factions of dalits who substantially focus on their issues. The city dalits have their own counter culture in terms of their marriage rituals, worship, festivals etc. and the city has experienced vehement dalit protests recently. Despite the absence of substantive equality with the upper and middle castes, the urban dalits have been actively participating in the procedural democracy here. Both the local and non-local sociology teachers have not found this phenomenon interesting or exciting![4]

I

Anecdotal Illuminations

The anecdotes shared by Raman helps us understand better what is meant by the 'casualization' of the discipline by the practitioners. Some of them are mentioned here:

Andre Beteille is from here !

Professor Doon, who heads the university department of sociology, once, picked up a conversation with his colleagues over a cup of tea. In order to project his special position in the national sociological fraternity, he began to count his proximity to various icons of Indian sociology. In this swaggering acclaim he made a mention of Andre Beteille referred A.B. as being from the region. His colleagues, who had vaguely heard about Beteille and had never read him, were passive listeners at such moment. Interestingly, Professor Doon is the author of a couple of books and has edited several volumes!

Political economy is subaltern studies!

In the year 2001, the syllabi of PG courses were being revised in the university. In sociology, a new course called 'Political Economy of Development' was being introduced. Professor Doon was with his colleague. While paying tribute to his own scholarship, he thumped the table and leaned forward and said – 'I am the only person who is competent to teach this course'. One of his colleagues intervened and asked, 'please enlighten us what political economy is?' Professor Doon answered in Hindi – '*wahi* subaltern studies'. Prof Doon thus rendered Fredric Engels a contemporary of Ranajit Guha. He also got an opportunity to teach this course! He never misses the yearly conference of Indian Sociological Society!

Paper setting!

In 2002, the teachers from the local colleges were invited in the university to set question papers for the postgraduate courses. They all had come with the 'keys' and 'guides' available in the market to help themselves in this exercise. They were puzzled to see that many thinkers like Foucault, Bourdieu and Habermas, who were included in the syllabus, did not figure in these keys and guides and they found it too difficult to set the question papers. The syllabus was new, and had been taken from the University Grant Commission's (UGC) Curriculum Development Guidelines. The problem of these paper setters was resolved by a suggestion from Professor Doon. The thinkers and concepts were prefixed with 'explain', 'elucidate', 'describe' and 'discuss' and by suffixing with 'illustrate with suitable examples'. There is no surprise when everything goes on smoothly because the examiners are recruited from the same group of paper setters.

Drop the subaltern approach as there are no books!

In 2004, the members of syllabus committee sat in a college to amend the syllabus for graduate students. The UGC Curriculum Development Report mentioned several perspectives on caste, including the subaltern approach. Subaltern approach was new to all. Majority of the members decided that the subaltern approach should be dropped as it would be difficult for them to find books and literatures on this topic. Ironically, the person who took a lead in this 'venture' is a senior faculty member of sociology in a local college belonging to what is euphemistically referred to as 'depressed classes' in India. Somewhat similar experiences have been shared by Jose (2003) about the process of syllabus making by the 'general body' of degree college teachers in Mumbai University where the 'non-availability of teaching material' becomes the basis of 'acceptance' and 'rejection' of certain (innovative) contents in the syllabus.

Jose also mentions that the teachers who suggest that 'syllabi' be made more rigorous are reminded by the Board members that the syllabi restructuring will affect not only the departments in 'elite' South Mumbai colleges but also in the adjoining districts of Thane and Raigadh. The question here arises–'do we necessarily need to keep away the innovative contents of the syllabus from the 'non-elite' learners by considering their socio-cultural background?' With some reservations, it appears that this relentless 'pragmatism' in the context of non-metropolitan centres and 'non-elite' background have gone into creating the 'haves' and 'have-nots' among sociology students and teachers, and has encouraged mediocrity and populism.

The interrelationship!

A question which is asked in final examinations of first semester M.A. students of sociology in the paper 'Perspectives on Indian Society' reads–'elucidate the interrelationship between social institutions like family and kinship in Indian society'.

Structuralism Hegemony and Foucault!

Dr Chand, who works as Reader in Sociology and hails from eastern India, while teaching structuralism of Levi Strauss explained–'structuralism would mean how different structures are linked to each other'. He drew an analogy of the affiliation of the engineering college to the university, in explaining the linkage between two different *structures*! To Dr Chand, different institutions and structures are linked to each other in similar fashion as the college and university in his analogy. While teaching Gramsci's hegemony, he gave the illustration–'you see, when I go to the xerox shop for some work, the shop owner gets up from his chair while offering a seat to me. This is how hegemony can be understood. It appears that the discussion in the class usually follows from what comes to his mind at that moment or sometimes what meaning the reader derives through reading about a thinker.

A young teacher, who is teaching M.A. sociology in a local college, understands Foucault thus (in Hindi) *Foucault gyan, shakti aur vimarsh ki baat karata hai. sochane ki jo dharana hai usko gyan aur shakti ke mdhyam se purane gyan kis tarah se simit hain uska adhayyan karana chahiye.* Translated it means–'Foucault talks about knowledge, power and discourse. He shows how the thinking can be changed with the help of knowledge and power. With the help of new knowledge, one can understand the limitations of the old knowledge'. This young faculty feels that sociological knowledge teaches you how to lead a smooth life, '*sulabhpurvak jine ka marg*'. It enables you to understand the reasons of social problem and with the help of this knowledge, the problems can be solved. In his viewpoint, the social problems arise because people fail to perform their roles in accordance with their status. In his perception, every individual should be responsible and should properly perform his/her role. Though a dalit scholar, teaching in the college, feels strongly against caste and race, he shares the similar views about the social problem – the disharmony between status and roles. This is one fact which all the teachers agree upon.

Foucault and Bourdieu are not Sociologists!

Mohan Rao Jadav took up teaching for few months in a local college. He mentions that in connection with the UGC NACC[5] members' visit, different departments in the college were involved in presenting their respective departments in 'innovative' ways. Sociology department did not lag behind. The sociology teachers decided that the portraits of sociological thinkers should be hung on the wall. Mohan Rao Jadav collected the xerox of different sociological thinkers – the classical and the contemporary. The senior faculty members intervened and removed thinkers like Bourdieu, Habermas, Althusser and Gramsci by saying that these are not sociologists. They only agreed to put up Comte, Durkheim, Weber, Mead and, of course, Marx.

Sociology of Delhi is different!

Raman is always advised to adapt and even come down to the 'level' of the students. Apprehensions are expressed – 'if he teaches in the way what he was taught at his the university in Delhi, no student will follow that'. More than the students, this view is shared by the faculty colleagues. Reading sociological journals and keeping track with the publications is not perceived essential even by those who have a 'different' exposure. For some of the local teachers, the books by Sage, Oxford and Routledge are considered as 'high-fi' and the authors of these books belong to a different class of intellectuals whose works are not meant for local academic consumption. These intellectuals are the elevated 'other', but at the same time they are trivialized as they make no sense to the local requirements. In the words of a senior university faculty who claims to know the dynamics of the local culture well, by virtue of belonging to the same region and linguistic group – *hamara utna standard nahin hai; hame baccho ke hishab se hi literature select kadna padta hai* (our standard is not that high; we have to select literature as per the level of our students). Majority of the faculty members simply close their eyes to the authors and their work who are adored as 'the other' but at once dismissed as 'high-fi'. Some of the local teachers are of the view that such authors write only for students of Delhi, Pune, Mumbai and Hyderabad.

Personal collection, not a felt need!

Teachers do not believe in personal collection of books and articles and hardly spend any money on buying books and journals. Very recently, the vice chancellor of the university made a visit to the sociology department. He asked the faculty members about their requirements for *almirahs* and bookshelves. One of the faculty members remarked – 'no, we do not require any bookshelf etc., we have cupboards in which we have enough space to keep books and other literature'. The fact is that many faculty members do not have personal collections and their cupboards are filled with the dissertations of M.A. students. It is reminiscent of Oommen's (1983: 124) characterization of college teachers as 'instrumental sociologists' who look upon themselves merely as communicators of available knowledge to the students and not as the producers of knowledge.

The above accounts are by no means exhaustive. But, they do give us a glimpse of the world of sociological practices in the university located in a non-metropolitan space. What seems completely missing here is what Beteille (2000) proposes as 'the business of sociology' ... 'teaching as a serious and unremitting effort to open the mind to new facts and new arrangements, and the unsuspected connection among them'.

II

The Local Textbooks: Production and Consumption

In this section I take a look at the texts written in the regional language. I however do not refer to them by name though I do quote extensively from them. These texts are used by teachers for classroom teaching and the students for passing the examinations as well as developing some sense of what sociology is? Here, I primarily focus upon what has been written about family, religion and caste. The articulations in these books are not only commonsensical but highly gendered and dangerously moralist. Most of these books are written by the local sociologists who belong to the upper castes. The dalit sociologists are either indifferent or busy with routine work and have not found time to dismantle these formulations. Though one of them told me that the glorification of *varna* system is wrong, he does not have time to develop a text countering those arguments. He spends more time on evaluation of answers sheets of graduate and postgraduate students.

The 'deliberations' about family, religion, caste and certain other social problems in these textbooks reveal that these sociologists have never been engaged in what Deshpande (2003) describes as squinting. He argues that in any sociological exercise one cannot avoid commonsense but needs to go beyond it, as commonsense constitute unexamined and unconscious beliefs and opinions. He writes, "if commonsense is an abbreviation for the transparent pane of unexamined prejudices, through which we normally view the world, sociology is an abbreviation for abnormal gaze that tries to focus on this pane as well as the world beyond it. Figuratively speaking, therefore, sociologists need to cultivate a sort of double vision or squint" (Deshpande, 2003: 8).

A squinting of these textbooks would suggest that they have the potential to re-strengthen the stereotypes and cultural prejudices of the readers. The dalit students are also reading and reproducing from the same book in expectation of good marks! One of them narrated that if they begin to criticize *varna* and caste and begin to quote Babasaheb Ambedkar, their identity will be easily revealed to the examiner, which may affect his marks. Mohan Rao Jadav says that the dalit teachers are not in majority and most of the college managements are controlled by the upper castes. The move of a dalit teacher to radically criticize caste and *varna* will be interpreted by the management as spreading politics instead of teaching. This makes them to abstain from such an exercise. A student who has memorized lines mugged up from these texts and reproduced the same contents in examination obtained 78 per cent marks. He felt rewarded. Being from upper caste family, nothing in the book disturbed him. Even the dalit students who are little disturbed about caste, found that the 'deliberations' about marriage, family and social problems are fine in these textbooks.[6]

From the Local Textbooks

This section draws from some central themes that these books write about. As illustrative evidence I draw from their observations on religion, nation/nationalism, caste and morality, family and women's freedom.

Religion

A textbook on religion authored by a local female sociologist begins with Hindu religious saying – '*hindu hi sankalpana mulat jatiwachak nasun rashtrawachak aahe*' (p. 37). Translated it would mean–'the concept Hindu has nothing to do with caste; the concept Hindu fundamentally connotes nation'. The author in this book quotes sages and *rishis* and she finds their opinion sociologically authentic! She not only firmly believes in their words but keeps prescribing to the readers a moral standard. She quotes Maharshi Vyas – '*lokyatrarthmewech dharmasya niyamah krita*'. Translating this in Marathi she writes – '*ya jagat lokabhichar nit chalawe manunaach dharma che niyam kele aahe* (translated in English it reads–'dharma has offered some rules so that the everyday affairs of life should run properly'. She opines – '*Maharshi Vyasanche he vichar samajshastriya dristya mahatwapurna wat tat*'. Translated it means – 'This statement of Maharshi Vyas is relevant from sociological point of view'. She writes further – 'religion shows the way how every individual should play 'his' role effectively. In this effective role-playing people come together in a social interaction and, through this interaction, social relation gets formed. It is by this process that society itself is created'.

On the next page she talks about one of the significant functions of Hindu religion as *jiwandhyeyache nishchitikaran* (the fixation of main objectives of life). Hindu religion, in her opinion, is a lot more about Purushartha (masculine conducts). Very central to *purushartha* are – *artha* (economics) and *kama* (sex). This appears to be her own statement as she has not cited anyone. Another function of religion she herself prescribes – '*sadkarma che prerna wa atmaniyantrana*' (religion motivates one to do good *karma* and teaches self-control). Then she goes on to quote Romila Thapar and Deshpande: On the basis of these historians' account she proclaims–'those who inhabited the geographical area called *Saptasindhu* including *adivasi* (tribes) and *ardhaadivasi*[7] are Hindus'. Following this, she quotes Savarkar. In her words – '*swatantryavirya sawarkarani Hindu hi sangyan asach sarwasamaweshak arthane waparli aahe*'. Translated it means – 'the great hero and freedom fighter, Savarkar has also used the nomenclature Hindu in this all inclusive sense'.

In the beginning of the text she talks about Vedas. She writes that in Hindu religion, Vedas assume supreme significance following which she opines – '*veda hi saswat, anadi asun swambhu aahet*'. Translated it means – 'Vedas being perennial and timeless, they are *swambhu* (have born on their own)'.

This description is again followed by the description of *varna* system. In her description, *varna* system appears very 'normal' and 'natural'. And, she does not feel the need for any probing and investigation. She writes about the mythological origin of different *varnas*. She tells in highly sanskritic Marathi – *brahmarupi Viratputrayachya vividh awyawatun char hi verna chi utpatti jhali*' (ibid.). Translated it means – 'from different organs of cosmic body of *Viratputra* originated the four different *varnas*. She seems to be justifying different *varnas* by saying that division of labour is needed for the smooth running of the train of society and stratification is the integral part of any society'. In her words – '*samajacha gada surlit chalnyasathi karyache yatha-yougya wivajan awasyak aste. Astarikaran he kontyahi samajache awibhajya ang tharte*' (ibid.). She goes on to tell the readers the purpose behind *varna* system. She writes –'*vividh gatatil sambandh salokha rahawe wa samajat isthirta wa sangtan rahawe hetch hetu verna vyawastha marg hota*'. Translated it means – 'The motto of *varna* system was to maintain a harmonious relations among different four groups. Following this, she talks about samskar and writes about the purpose of samskar (initiation ceremony) in Hinduism. She writes – '*siddhikarana barobarach vyaktigunanche wardhan karne, tyas unnatimay banawne ya marg abhipret hote*'. Translated it means – 'purification apart, *samskar* enhanced the quality of individual and paved the way for the progress of individuals'.

In the same book, she talks about other religions like Islam and Buddhism as equally functional and accommodative, but she does not find any problem with religion as a social institution. In her interview, she told me that she likes Marx and his concept of historical materialism! In the preface of her book, she writes that no institution can match religion in relieving tensions both at individual and social levels and motivates people to move along socially sanctioned (normative) path. It gives peace and consolation to individuals. She mentions that USA stands as a leading nation in the field of science and technology. Despite this, it is second among the most religious nations in the globe. Here again, no reference is cited.

Nationalism

Many textbooks written by local sociologists emphasize on national integration or they rather assign sociology the task of national integration. In a textbook written by Manoharraoji Bale (pseudonym), referred to both by teachers and students, published in 2005 by a local press, the author deliberates upon social problems. The most prominent social problem for him is linguistic conflict, which is caused by the linguistic diversity of India. Though, he argues that all Indian languages should be preserved, he expresses the need for the acceptance of a common Indian language, in the absence of which the process of national integration will slow down and will be an impossibility. Bale writes – '*amchya desh antargat pratek rajyacha sima prashana kewal bhasha vividhtamule nirman jhali aahe*'. Translated it means – 'in our country, the boundaries between different states are due to linguistic diversity. These linguistic boundaries appear to be a serious problem in his perception. And, he prescribes – '*aaj tar kharya arthane rashtriya ekatmatesathi bhashaekatmatechi atyant aawsyakata aahe*' (today, linguistic unification is a pre-requisite for national integration in true sense of the term). He writes, '*sarwat jyast bhashechya udgam Sanskrit bhashach aahe* (Sanskrit is the source of most of the Indian languages). Bale then talks about *Bhartiye sanskriti* (Indian culture). He poses a question – 'why India was known as Aryavart' And, he attempts to answer – 'because, the Aryans were the first one to arrive in India'. To him, Aryan culture exerted tremendous influence on Indian society and this was the reason that India was known as Aryavart. Without any citation, he claims that ancient sages like Agastya and Parasuram were the courageous and bold men who brought the unification of South and North India. While bestowing masculine virility to the sages Agastya and Parashurama, he writes – '*Agastya aani parashuram ya shahasi purushani dakshin wa uttar yanche sandhijod keli*'.

Bale mentions that India is the land of different castes, tribes and linguistic communities. Despite this diversity, Mother India has bestowed equal love, maternal love, kindness, affection to all. The words he uses in Marathi for maternal love and affection are *prem, watslaya, maya, mamta*, which he attributes to the motherland. This fact, he says, is mentioned in Athrva Veda. He claims that even though Boddh and Jain religions gave impetus to other religions and languages, it is the Sanskrit, the Vedic language, which is very fundamental to the unity of Indian nation. In his words – '*Vedic bhasha hi bharatiya sanskriti chye ekatmateche mul bijach aahe*' (Sanskrit – the Vedic language is the main seed of unification of Indian culture and civilization).

About Indian culture Bale writes that since earlier times several invaders came to India. They include Greek, Hun, Shak, Kushan, Musalman and British. Many of them, in greater or lesser degree, established their political control over India. This did not shake the firm Indian culture however. The great *Bharatiye samskruti* (Indian culture!) rather enfolded within itself all the other cultures and moved ahead without looking back. He analogizes Indian culture with milk and says – 'however much water you mix with the milk, the fundamental form of milk does not change for it absorbs the water within itself.

Bale goes on to state that 'India has sheltered everyone including the theist and the atheist and he also mentions *lafangas*'. *Lafangas* is a colloquial word for loafing people and here he probably uses it for the Muslim invaders.

Caste Morality, Family and Women's Freedom

About caste stratification, Manoharraoji Bale writes – 'every caste nurtures pride about its identity and, therefore, both lower and higher castes live with mutual respect!' Apart from legitimizing caste through his 'invented' theory of 'mutual respect', he appears to be an staunch moralist who is heaping scorn on, what he perceives as the degenerative aspect of urbanization. He perceives that the urban space has ensured male-female equality. In his words, men and women have come close to each other as they work together and they are behaving without any inhibitions. Due to this, love marriages are more prevalent than conventional arranged marriages. But these love marriages are not based on what he calls *vichar vinimay* (exchange of ideas! Poor translation!) but *sharirik garje* (physical needs). This ultimately results in clash between spouses leading to growing rate of divorces. Divorce, according to him, is a burning problem in cities. Divorce leads to disintegration of family, which would ultimately destroy the moral fabric of society. Bale writes – '*stree swatantrayamule stree hi adhik swakchandi wa vyavhichari banat aahe. Ya vyabhicharane guptarog, bhrinhatya*, AIDS, *atmahatyache praman wadhu lagle aahe*'. Translated it means – 'as a result of (women's) freedom, women have become more freedom loving and immoral. Because of their immorality, there has begun a growing incidence of sexual disease, foeticide, AIDS and suicide'.

About marriage, Bale writes – '*samajat dharmik bhawanepeksha langiksukhachi bhawna barich prabhawi jhali aahe*' (in society, the carnal desires have taken over the religious desires). Therefore, marriage is no more treated as a sacred institution; the idea of sexual pleasure dominates today's world. In many texts, including that of Bale's, there are sweeping generalizations about the changing nature of caste and family. One of the local sociologists, Kahalekar (pseudonym), opines in his text on social institutions – 'earlier people had ascribed *varna* status. They were either Brahmin or Kshatriya or Vaishya or Sudra. Now, this ascribed status has given way to achieved status. There seems to be an implicit lamentation about what he perceives as the loss of *varna* system'.

The sociological discourse, inherent in the local texts, reveals that these upper caste sociologists are the prisoners of the social environment in which they are born and in which they grow. The absolute lack of professionalism is reflected in their writings. They seem to be miles away from the works of 'mainstream' sociology.[8] They appear to be assigning themselves the task of moral policing, 'national integration' and sermonising! Most of their findings on the issues like 'disintegration of family' and 'rising divorce rate' reflect their own mental constructs. To them, any social institution in their traditional form is unproblematic; change and transformations are full of implicit and explicit lamentations. They rather unconsciously participate in an orientalist romance about the 'glorious past' of Indian civilization. It is pertinent to quote C. Wright Mills here: "the sociologists who distract attention from power are actually distracting attention from social structure itself" (1959: 81). Mills further writes: "by justifying the arrangement of power and the ascendancy of powerful, images and ideas transform power into authority" (ibid.: 123). Most of the articulations in these texts belong to what Mills calls "the everyday empiricism of commonsense filled with assumptions and stereotypes…" (ibid.). The most tragic part of the story is that the students read and reproduce from these texts. One of them told me, 'I obtained 78 per cent marks in my graduation by reading and mugging up from these texts'.

V

Doctoral Dissertations

Most of the doctoral dissertations submitted to the university can be described in terms of what C. Wright Mills had meant by 'abstracted empiricism'. Mills writes: "as a style of social science, abstracted empiricism is not characterised by any substantive proposition and theories…abstracted empiricisms are systematically ahistorical and non-comparative. Neither in defining their problems, nor in explaining their microscopic findings do they make any use of the basic idea of historical social structure" (ibid.: 58–68). Added to this is the lack of professionalism. In a thesis entitled "Women's Empowerment through Self-Help Group", the scholar quotes the opinions of the UN General Secretary and then Prime Minister Atal Bihari Vajpayee. Both of them have supported to the micro-credit project and the scholar in his thesis appears to be fully agreeing with their opinions. There is no attempt to look at any critical literature on micro-credit though they exist in plenty. About his method of data collection he writes "Primary data is collected by using structured interview schedules consisting of 65 questions by using *participant observations*!". He also mentions that he took 15 blocks for the collection of empirical information!

In the above thesis, one can see separate tables on each aspect, viz. age, education, marital status, caste, and religion of the respondents. The table on family only mentions two types of family – joint and nuclear. A table on p. 130 in the thesis can be reproduced here to demonstrate the kind of abstracted empiricism used by the scholar:

Table 6.1

Participation in Decision-making

Participation	*Frequency*	*Percentage*
Yes	192	64
No	108	36
Total	300	100

This table reflects that only opinions are collected and tabulated. The descriptions are devoid of any deep observation of the processes involved in women's participation in Self-Help Group. In another doctoral dissertation entitled "A Sociological Study of Inter-caste Marriage in N District", the author talks of the functions of marriage. He writes that marriage is significant from the viewpoint of minimizing sexual conflict and immorality. He uses a word in Marathi called *langic astharya* whose literal translation is 'sexual stability'. Further he mentions that marriage has given sexual stability in society and that after marriage the responsibility of the wife falls on the shoulder of a man. This doctoral researcher again has missed the whole anthropological literature and its changing contours on the subject of marriage.[9] A thesis on caste written by a dalit student begins by contesting the Vedic myth on the origins (of caste). But, the scholar subsequently mentions Ghurye more than Ambedkar and there is no attempt to incorporate debates and viewpoints from a rich sociological literature on caste.

In this scenario, continuous and major efforts by powers that be and by practising sociologists have to be made to redeem the state of affairs. My attempt in this chapter is a small effort to capture the world of one kind of sociological practice.

Notes

1. The discussion which followed in the seminar after the presentation of this paper was that the metropolitan centres of learning are not homogeneous in terms of the teaching and research. I am aware of this heterogeneity while making the above formulation. The distinction between metropolitan and non-metropolitan is definitely a broader generalization here, and, completely based on Raman's experiences. It, therefore, eludes any strong claim about this distinction (between metropolitan and non-metropolitan centres). Jose's (2003) paper about the practice of sociology in Mumbai University also reflects in some ways that metropolitan university may not be a homogeneous complex.
2. It means that these teachers have not gone out of even outside the district for their higher studies.
3. NET (National Eligibility Test for Lecturership) and SET (State Eligibility Test for Lecturership) are being organized every year by the University Grants Commission, New Delhi and State Governments respectively.
4. An interesting comparison can be made between this disconnect with the argument that V. Sujatha makes in this volume about the disconnection between a rich history of social thought and theory within the discipline.
5. The University Grants Commission, New Delhi has certain institutional mechanisms to evaluate and grade the universities and colleges in India. NACC (National Assessment and Accreditation Council) is the acronym to designate this mechanism.
6. Moreover, dalits are not a homogenous category in the region even in cultural sense. While the Buddhist dalits are anti-Brahmanical, the Mang caste dalits are culturally more close to Hinduism than to Buddhism. They do not consider Ambedkar as their hero. See Das (1989), O' Hanlon (1988) and Spivak (1985) who caution against a unified subaltern category and point to the fact that there might remain certain continuities between hegemonic discourse and subaltern culture.
7. What she means by *ardhaadivasi* is not clear. According to some Marathi readers it might mean 'primitive tribes' here.

8. By mainstream here I mean, the serious academic works of the sociologists. I do not mean 'mainstream' location.
9. See Comaroff (1980), Leach (1961) and Needham (1971, 1975) for the 'rethinking mood' in anthropology with regard to marriage and kinship. To these anthropologists marriage cannot be always defined in terms of 'manifest conjugal forms', to use Comaroff's (ibid.) phrase. The cross-cultural data do not always suggest this (see Comaroff, 1980). Dube (1997: 109) also writes: "In Thailand and Philippines there does not seem to be such a preoccupation with marriage. Both Buddhism and Christianity allow for theoretical possibility of people remaining single". Cross-cultural comparisons is completely missing in the doctoral works which is due to the limitations of postgraduate teaching where teachers do not bother to look into classical and contemporary 'mainstream' work on any subject. The text books and key in vernacular are coloured with local idioms and phrases and remain considerably commonsensical. All these get carried into the doctoral works of the teachers and students alike.

References

Beteille, Andre. 2002. *Sociology: Essays on Approach and Method.* New Delhi: Oxford University Press.

Comaroff, J.L. (ed.), 1980. *The Meaning of Marriage Payment.* London: Academic Press.

Das, Veena. 1989. "Subaltern as Perspective", in Ranajit Guha (ed.), *Subaltern Studies VI: Writings on South Asian History and Society.* Delhi: Oxford University Press, pp. 310–24.

Deshpande, Satish. 2003. *Contemporary India: A Sociological View.* New Delhi: Penguin.

Dube, Leela. 1997. *Women and Kinship: Comparative Perspective on Gender in South Asia and South East Asia.* New Delhi: Vistaar Publications.

Jose, George. 2003. "Make it Soft and Easy: The Undergraduate Syllabi in Sociology", in Maitrayee Chaudhuri (ed.), *The Practice of Sociology.* New Delhi: Orient Longmans, pp. 97–128.

Kumar, Vivek. 2005. "Situating Dalits in Indian Sociology", *Sociological Bulletin*, Vol. 54, No. 3, pp. 514–32.

Leach, Edmund R. 1961. *Rethinking Anthropology.* London: Athlone Press.

Mills, C. Wright. 1959. *The Sociological Imagination.* New York: Oxford University Press.

Needham, Rodney (ed.) 1971. *Rethinking Kinship and Marriage.* London: Tavistock Publications.

Needham, Rodney. 1975. "Polythetic Classifications: Convergence and Consequences", *Man* (n.s.) 10: 349–69.

Oommen, T.K. 1983. "Sociology in India: Plea for Contextualisation", *Sociological Bulletin*, Vol. 32, No. 2, pp. 111–36.

7

Sociology in Northeast India

A Synoptic View

SUBRAT K. NANDA

This paper, like the other chapters that constitute this section on sociology at the margins, is about one such 'periphery', namely, the northeast. Unlike other peripheries that the section dwells upon, the northeast has its own distinctive history and present. This is not to suggest that issues present in other regions do not prevail here. Or that the history of colonial India and its study of Indian society have not left its imprint on the practice of sociology/social anthropology in contemporary northeast. Indeed, the very fact that anthropology has a much longer institutional history in the northeast with its largely tribal population reveals a colonial legacy. This is a legacy that unfortunately persisted even after India attained independence. That nation-building has been no easy task here, that notions of nationalism have faced serious challenges here, have only compounded this matter. Unfortunately, even when sociology entered institutionally in the universities, the syllabus as this chapter indicates often revealed an unproblematic idea of Indian society, closer to what is considered as the 'book view' of Indian society. It is this context which makes the story of sociology in the northeast of particular significance for it brings home the close connection between institutional and intellectual histories, between sociology and what has been described as methodological nationalism, or the tendency to use the nation and society as coterminous units. The effort in this chapter is limited to bring to notice the specificity of the northeast and the growth of sociology here.

Northeast India, as a geo-political region, comprises the group of eight states of Arunachal Pradesh, Assam, Manipur, Meghalaya, Mizoram, Nagaland, Tripura and Sikkim. Except Sikkim, the rest of the states in the region are geographically contiguous and are commonly referred to as the 'seven sister states'. The region covers an area of about 2.62 lakh sq km, which is 7.9 per cent of India's total geographical area. The population of the region stands at 39,035,582 as per the 2001 census, which is 3.8 per cent of the total population of India. The region shows an average population density of 149 persons per sq km, which is much lower than the all-India average of 313 persons per sq km (GoM, 2004).

Northeast India is distinct in several respects. It is unique in terms of its strategic location and geographical features. It is bounded by Bhutan, Nepal and China in the north, Myanmar (Burma) in the east and the south and Bangladesh in the west and the south. It is connected to the mainland of India through a small corridor of land, popularly called the "chicken's neck". The region has 98 per cent international boundaries on three sides and a small 2 per cent state boundary on the western side bordering the state of West Bengal. The region contains striking socio-cultural and ethnic diversities. The linguistic and the religious composition of the region is extremely plural and complex. The people of the region speak numerous languages, follow diverse cultural patterns and profess several religions and faiths. The people and the cultures of the region in fact combine the trait of both 'Indic' and 'Asiatic' Asia. The region is inhabited by both tribal and non-tribal people. The non-tribal people preponderate in the plains areas, whereas the tribal people dominate the hill areas of the region. Wide-range developmental disparities and socio-economic inequalities exist among both the non-tribal and tribal people of the region. This apart, the region is constantly marked by insurgency, ethnic clashes, political turmoil and turbulence, which is reflective of complex historical and contemporary socio-economic dynamics. Further, various forms of social movements, ranging from socio-religious movements, secessionist and autonomist nationalist movements to human rights and ecological/environmental movements, are seen in the region. These specificities of northeast India need to be stated at the outset for too often, not just in lay discourse but also within sociology there is a tendency to refer to the northeast as a blanket term that too often reveals abysmal ignorance of the region. Much of this paper therefore is a factual account of the sociological specificities of the northeast and the emergence and spread of institutional sociology as a discipline in the area. Important in this account is the very idea of an Indian society and Indian sociology that has often informed the book view of sociology in India.

I

A Sociological Synopsis of the Northeast

Since northeast India represents a unique conglomeration of several non-tribal and tribal societies, the practice of sociology, in whatever way or by whichever institution, has great relevance for the region.[1] Each society in the region has its own distinct value systems, marriage and kinship rules, inheritance rules, customary laws and social practices, gender roles and power structures. Indeed, the forms of social stratification and gender inequality are different among caste-Hindus, plains and hills tribes of the region. Further, the existence of matrilineal system among the Khasi, Garo and Jaintia tribes makes the region to give rise to its own set of issues.[2]

The tribal and non-tribal people of the region speak nearly 200 languages and dialects. The principal non-tribal languages of the region are Assamese, Bengali, Manipuri and Nepali. The major tribal languages spoken in the region are Bodo, Khasi, Garo, Jaintia, Mizo, Karbi, Kuki-Chin, Rabha, Koch, Adi, Apatani, Ao, Angami, Lotha, Sema, Kok-Borok, etc. The existence of numerous languages makes North-East India an interesting linguistic area (Miri, 1982). It is well known that language not only serves as an important means of communication but it also acts as a strong factor in identity formation, maintenance of ethnic boundary, and expression of nationalist sentiments for self-determination.

Most of the languages in the North-East are associated with a specific ancestral/traditional or adopted homeland. The states of Assam, Tripura and Manipur are associated with the languages of Assamese, Bengali and Manipuri (Meitei), respectively. The Mizo language is exclusively identified with the state of Mizoram; but in Nagaland numerous Naga tribal languages such as Ao, Angami, Sema, etc., are spoken in their respective areas, although the spoken language 'Nagamese' serves as the lingua-franca among them. Similarly, in Arunachal Pradesh, several tribal languages such as Adi, Apatani, Monpa, etc., exist side by side. In Meghalaya, the Garo language is spoken in Garo hills and the Khasi and Jaintia languages are spoken in Khasi hills and Jaintia hills, respectively. In Assam, Bengali predominates in the southern part, the Bodo language prevails in the Bodo area and the Karbi language is spoken in the Karbi-Anglong district. In Manipur, the Manipuri (Meitei) language predominates in the Imphal valley, but in the hill areas of the state several Naga and Kuki tribal languages are spoken. Given this association between language and territory, the demands for provincial statehood on the basis of linguistic nationalism or ethno-linguistic identity persist in the region. Further, only five languages from the region, namely, Assamese, Bengali, Bodo, Manipuri (Meitei) and Nepali, are listed in the Eighth Schedule to the Constitution of India. But, despite being used as medium of instruction and studied as a subject in colleges and universities, languages like Khasi, Garo and Mizo are not included in the Eighth Schedule and hence movements for inclusion of such languages in the Eighth Schedule persist in the region.

The tribal issue of the region is complex and different from mainland India. As many as 200 tribes and sub-tribes are found in the region, out of which 120 tribes belong to the scheduled category. Tribal societies here range from the primitive and shifting cultivation type to settled agriculturalist and modern-industrial-urban type. Further, some tribes of the region enjoy the benefits of local self-governance under the Sixth Schedule and some tribes are covered under the provisions of the Fifth Schedule of the Constitution of India. Several tribes of the region like the Tai-Ahom, Chutiya, Moran, Koch Rajbongsi and the plantation tribals have been demanding to be included within the Sixth Schedule and be accorded the status of Scheduled Tribe (ST).

Historically, a turning point in social transformation in the North East is the conversion to Christianity and the spread of English education. The role of Christianity in the region has been decisive in shaping the contemporary northeast. Political transformation in the region occurred due to different political arrangements and territorial reorganizations in the colonial and postcolonial periods and the introduction of the democratic electoral process and local self-governance since independence. The rise of tribal nationalisms played a crucial role in the territorial reorganization of the region in the postcolonial period. Economic transformation in the region began with the introduction of British capital and after independence a host of steps took place that accelerated the links of the region within the national economy.

The region has a literacy rate of 68.5 per cent, which is higher than the all-India average of 64.8 per cent as per the 2001 census of India. Yet, the incidence of poverty and unemployment in the region is especially high in the rural areas. Significantly, most of the people in the region are located in the rural area, only 15.45 per cent live in urban areas (Census of India, 2001). The scale and nature of the issues that demand sociological investigation cannot be overstated.

II

Institutional Spread of Sociology in the Northeast Region

In northeast India the teaching of sociology began in the late 1960s and in the recent one and a half decade it has spread to nearly all parts of the region. As the paper goes on to comment that anthropology preceded sociology in the northeast by decades. Sociology is taught at both the undergraduate and postgraduate levels in some universities and colleges in the region.

In 1948, the first university in northeast India came up in Guwahati city in Assam (AIU 1997). Prior to this, all the undergraduate educational institutions of the region were affiliated to Calcutta University. Subsequently, Guwahati University started academic teaching and research programme in anthropology. The reasons for opening an anthropology department at Guwahati University may be partly attributed to the inheritance of colonial legacy and partly to the massive influence of Calcutta University on the region in colonial days. For politico-administrative interests the colonial administration encouraged ethnographic and ethnological studies of the numerous peoples, races and tribes living in northeast India. It may be recalled that northeast India in colonial period, which was then known as Assam, formed a part of Bengal Presidency till 1874 after its occupation by the British in 1826. Thereafter, the region remained closely linked with Bengal Presidency for all practical purposes. Obviously, Calcutta University, being the premier centre of education in colonial days, enjoyed an eminent position in carrying out ethnographic and anthropological studies of the people living in and around Bengal Presidency. In post-independence times, the department of anthropology at Guwahati University continued on similar lines and carried out anthropological studies of the northeastern societies and communities.

Full-fledged teaching of sociology in the region began with the establishment of sociology department in 1967 at Dibrugarh University in upper Assam. The jurisdiction of Dibrugarh University covers the districts of upper Assam. Apart from imparting postgraduate teaching, the sociology department at Dibrugarh University has also been engaged in research activities on the societies in upper Assam and the adjoining areas of Arunachal Pradesh and Nagaland.

A turning point in university education in Northeast India came when North-Eastern Hill University (NEHU), the first central university in the region, was established in 1973, following the formation of Meghalaya state in accordance with the North-Eastern (Reorganization) Act of 1971. Originally, the jurisdiction of NEHU covered the states of Meghalaya, Nagaland and the union territory of Mizoram (later the state of Mizoram). Its headquarters is located in Meghalaya's capital city of Shillong. In addition to the main campus in Shillong, NEHU initially had campuses located in Medziphema and Kohima in Nagaland and at Aizwal in Mizoram. But, after the formation of Nagaland University in 1994 and Mizoram University in 2001, the jurisdiction of NEHU was confined to Meghalaya and at present only two campuses – Shillong and Tura – exist under NEHU.

Sociology began to be taught at NEHU in 1976 with the opening of the composite department of anthropology and sociology at its Shillong campus. But later an independent department of sociology was established at the Shillong campus of NEHU. The sociology department of NEHU made pioneering efforts to spread undergraduate sociology teaching in the areas under the jurisdiction of NEHU. As a result of these efforts, undergraduate sociology courses at both pass and honours levels were introduced in a few colleges in Shillong city, at Fazal Ali College in Mokokchung in Nagaland and at Pachhunga University College (PUC) in Aizwal, Mizoram. Undergraduate courses in rural sociology were also included in the syllabus of the B.Sc. agriculture students at the School of Agricultural Sciences and Rural Development (SASRD) located in erstwhile Medziphema campus of NEHU. From September 1994 SASRD and Fazal Ali

College came under the jurisdiction of Nagaland University and in June 2001 PUC was placed under Mizoram University. In 1996 a regional campus of NEHU was opened at Tura town in Garo hills areas of Meghalaya. The department of rural development and agricultural production was established at the NEHU Tura campus in July 2002. At this department a few sociological aspects of rural development are taught to the M.Sc. students.

As a premier central university, NEHU was established to pay special attention to the improvement of the social and economic conditions of the people of the hill areas of northeast region. The sociology department of NEHU with its thrust on social change contributed to this goal to some extent by providing sociological manpower necessary for interpreting the social and economic conditions of these people. To facilitate desirable sociological research activities among the students, the sociology department of NEHU has been declared as a department for research support (DRS) under the special assistance programme (SAP) of the University Grants Commission (UGC). The northeast region is a folklorists' paradise. The Centre for Cultural and Creative Studies and the department of sociology at NEHU provide necessary training for the study of folklore and carry out useful research on the indigenous knowledge and oral tradition of the region. It is important to note that from December 2005 NEHU has been declared by UGC as university with potential for excellence (UPE).

In the 1980s three new state universities were set up in the northeast. Manipur University came up in 1980, followed by Arunachal University in 1985 and Tripura University in 1987. But, unfortunately, none of these universities introduced postgraduate sociology teaching in their respective areas. Nevertheless, undergraduate sociology teaching at pass and honours levels exist in a couple of colleges in Imphal in Manipur and at MBB College in Agartala, Tripura. But, despite the existence of several tribal societies in the state of Arunachal Pradesh, no department of sociology has so far started at the Arunachal University. The recently opened department of tribal studies at this university deals with the sociological aspects relating to the tribal people. In Sikkim too, as in the case of Arunachal Pradesh, the teaching of sociology at any level has not started so far. Manipal University (a private university) in Sikkim only focuses on technical and professional courses and not on pure social science subjects. In Assam University the department of sociology was created in 1996 and in Nagaland University in 1997. In Tezpur University, however, the department of sociology started only recently in 2004. In Mizoram, although sociology teaching at undergraduate level continues in some colleges, no department of sociology has yet been started at Mizoram University. Thus, by now, five out of ten universities in the region impart sociology education at both postgraduate and undergraduate levels.

Apart from these universities and colleges, sociological research and training are being pursued at a few social science institutes in the region such as North-Eastern Regional Council of Indian Council of Social Science Research (ICSSR), Shillong; Institute of Peace and Conflict Studies, Guwahati; Tribal Research Institute, Guwahati; Tribal Research Institute, Itanagar; Omeo Kumar Das Institute of Social Change and Development (OKDISCD), Guwahati; and the Indian Institute of Technology (IIT), Guwahati. At IIT, Guwahati sociological courses are taught to the B.Tech students. Sociological courses are also taught to the students of Assam Agricultural University in Jorahat and Central Agricultural University in Imphal. Nursing colleges in different parts of the region also teach a few sociological courses to their students.[3] Quite evidently, there has been institutional spread but as this paper goes on to argue that sociology is not perceived as of any special import either as a career option or as a fruitful research endeavour.

III

Syllabi and Textbooks: Analysing the Intellectual Trends

The above account clearly marks out the distinctive nature of the region. But, looking at the sociology syllabi of some of the universities and colleges of the region, one finds that for the most part, the sociological courses taught elsewhere in India are taught here too. But, like elsewhere in the country, in this region too, sociology of the common person, minorities and the marginalized sections does not find space. For example, NEHU, the oldest central university in the region, follows a sociology syllabus for the postgraduate level, which includes conventional academic courses like Sociological Theories, Methodology of Social Research, Sociology of Family and Kinship, Indian Society, Economy and Society and, Polity and Society, Social Change, Sociology of Religion, Urban Sociology, Theories of Social

Anthropology. Some new courses like Sociology of Development, Sociology of Environment, Sociology of Entrepreneurship Management, and Tribal Movements in India are also included in this syllabus. Similarly, the syllabus followed for undergraduate level includes courses such as Basic Sociological Concepts, Social Change, Society in India, Social Stratification, Social Movements and Social Conflicts, Sociological Thinkers, Rural and Urban Sociology, and Social Inquiry and Social Survey.

It may be noted that some of these traditional and new courses have included a few topics reflecting the specificity of northeast India. For example, the course on family and kinship focuses on matrilineal kinship and family pattern, which is specific to the Khasi, Garo and Jaintia tribes of the region. Similarly, courses on religion, economy and society, polity and society, urban sociology emphasize some of the specificities of the region such as practices of indigenous and modern religions, the diverse land tenure systems, shifting cultivation and tribal economy, community ownership, inheritance of property, traditional power systems, tribal political economy, political leadership and political conflicts and trends in hill urbanization, ethnicity and urbanization, respectively. Further, courses on sociology of development and environment include some of the specific aspects of the region. But major gaps are still found between the specificity of the region and the sociology syllabus or the undergraduate and postgraduate levels. For example, the northeast region is inhabited by both indigenous and migrant peoples, but a specific course on ethnicity and ethnic relations is not found in the NEHU sociology syllabus. Similarly, specific issues of the region like tribe-forest relationship, indigenous medicine and healing practices, faith healing, traditional occupation and livelihood, biodiversity and cultural diversity, empowerment and exclusion have not been properly reflected in the syllabus.

The sociology department at Dibrugarh University also follows a traditional sociology syllabus, although in recent times it has introduced a special paper on Sociology of Northeast India. But, the recently established central universities, viz., Assam University, Nagaland University and Tezpur University, have introduced several new courses in their sociology syllabus in addition to the traditional core courses. For example, the department of sociology at Assam University, for its M.A. sociology programme, offers core courses like Sociological Concepts, Sociological Thinkers, Social Stratification, Social Change, Indian Society, Urban Sociology, Methodology of

Social Research and several optional courses like Sociology of Development, Sociology of Environment, Sociology of Movements, Sociology of Tribal Life, Sociology of Gender, Sociology of Communication, Developmental Problems in Northeast India, Sociology of Minorities and Ethnic Groups, Medical Sociology, and Sociology of Language, Art and Culture. The department mainly undertakes research programme in the areas of ethnicity and multiculturalism, entrepreneurship, gender studies, tribal studies, sociology of northeast India, social and economic life of tea garden workers, communication and mass media, voluntary participation in rural development and health and health behaviour, etc.

At Nagaland University the syllabus for M.A. sociology includes some non-conventional elective/optional courses, apart from traditional core courses. These elective/optional courses are: Sociology of Popular Culture and Mass Communication, Social Marketing, Sociology of Marginalized Communities, Science, Technology and Society, Sociology of Information Society, Study of Indian Diaspora, Sociology of Northeast India, Ethnicity, Pluralism and Nation, Sociology of Health, Sociology of Criminology, Globalization and Society, Comparative Sociology, Sociology of Southeast Asia, Sociology of Ageing, Environment and Society, and Project Planning, Programme Evaluation and Implementation. The sociology department of Tezpur University also offers many non-conventional courses in its syllabus for M.A. sociology. For example, the students have to choose any four from amongst the elective courses, such as Sociology of Medicine, Sociology of Culture and Mass Media, Criminology, Environmental Sociology, Gender and Society and Sociology of Development. Interestingly, the course on Sociology of Northeast India is offered as a core course at this university.

Courses on Sociology of Northeast India and Tribal Studies have been designed not only to study the specificities of the region. The interface between cultural diversity and bio-diversity, prevalence of different indigenous medicine and healing practices and the proximity of some northeast Indian people with the people, culture and society of Southeast Asia have also led to the design of courses like Environmental Sociology, Sociology of Medicine, Comparative Sociology and Sociology of Southeast Asia, respectively. Further, in some core courses, namely, Perspectives on Indian society and Sociology of India, some topics like Sixth Schedule, Panchayati Raj and local self-governance and empowerment of tribal people through autonomous district council and local autonomy have been included to reflect some of the specific aspects of sociology teaching in the northeast region.

But, the students taking sociology at the undergraduate or postgraduate level in the region opt for the subject not because of its growing popularity at the domestic or international level or its high market utility or professional value, but because of the choice students make for its general academic value like any other social science/liberal arts discipline. In other words, for job prospects in terms of the present market requirements, sociology is one of the least offered subjects in the northeast region.

What one would like to emphasize is that tribal students of the region, especially the Christian tribal students, mostly express discomfort and inconvenience in understanding and assimilating several aspects of Indian sociology or society in India as the contents of such course mostly focus on the mainstream Hindu social institutions, culture, values, religious order, etc., with very little or no reference to the peripheral and minority societies of the northeast. Many aspects of mainstream Indian society like caste stratification, 'jajmani 'system', marriage, family and kinship, status of women and gender inequality in Hindu social system and the Hindu religious values like 'dharma', 'karma', 'purusarthas', 'moksha', 'ashramas', etc., appear alien to these students. The difficulty of the tribal students of the region in comprehending these aspects of Indian sociology can be easily noticed while taking classes or evaluating answer scripts on this course. One reason for this difficulty may be attributed to the cultural gaps between the mainstream Hindu society and the tribal societies of the northeast. The Hindu social order reflecting mainly the 'Brahmanical' order or the 'great tradition' is based on a written tradition expressed in pure and 'elaborative sanskritic code', whereas the social order of the northeastern tribes is mainly based on oral or 'little tradition' expressed in 'restrictive folk code'.

It may further be noted that both the 'text view' and the 'field view' of Indian society mostly centre on the mainstream social institutions, value system and cultural practices. The 'text view' of Indian society is mainly derived from the indological and the scriptural sources which mainly depict the Hindu social system. Likewise, the 'field view' of Indian society, which is derived from several village studies, reflects the mainstream Hindu social institutions and values to a great extent. Hence, teaching Indian sociology to the tribal students of northeast India has several limitations and implications. It may be mentioned here that some scholars do not accept the expression 'Indian society' or 'Indian social system'. They prefer to use the expression 'forms of social life in India'. The latter description about Indian sociology seems more apt in the northeastern context.[4]

Another major difficulty in teaching sociology in the northeast region, basically at the undergraduate level, is the lack of proper textbooks on several sociological courses. In the absence of proper sociology textbooks, the students in the region mainly require either full-fledged notes or teaching material in the classroom or depend upon cheap and misleading key books from the market. There is an urgent need to rework the sociological courses with materials far more sympathetic to the intellectual histories, social conditions and cultural traditions of the local societies and communities.

IV

Sociological Research

As far as sociological research is concerned, the specificities of the northeast region is better reflected. Sociology researchers at NEHU, i.e., M.Phil and PhD students and individual faculty members, have mainly focused on the vast canvas of social change taking place in the region They are also engaged in a variety of studies relating to tribal ethnography, tribal religion and culture, changing tribal family structure, status of tribal women amidst change and continuity and tribal development. Issues of ethnicity and identity and conflict patterns reform movements, protest movements and student unrest have been also focused by these sociology researchers.[5]

The sociological research carried out in the region mostly falls into three categories: (a) self-proposed research by students for academic research degrees such as M.Phil and PhD and for postgraduate dissertation; (b) self-proposed research by few individual teachers at universities and colleges and by faculty members at social science institutes; and (c) sponsored research, i.e., research works or research projects sponsored by various funding agencies such as ICSSR, New Delhi, NERC-ICSSR, Shillong, UGC, Anthropological Survey of India (ASI), etc.(Kumar, 1998: 92–98) Most of these sociological research either focuses on the whole region or a particular state or a part of a state of the region. Generally, different aspects of Assamese society, the largest linguistic community in the region, and the social and cultural issues of numerous tribal communities living in different parts of the region are covered by most of these research works (Kumar, 1988: 94).

Ethnographic studies on tribal villages mainly emphasize the structural and cultural characteristics of individual tribes found in the hill areas of the region. Studies covering tribal social, religious, economic, occupational and political institutions, tribal customary laws, traditional belief systems and tribal religions have also been conducted by some researchers. Another notable area of social research in the region has been the impact of Christianity and Christian missionaries on the tribal life of the region. The proliferation of Christianity is one of the distinctive features of the northeast region. In India, besides the south and the east, the northeast represents a major regional concentration of Christianity. Over 50 per cent of the tribal people in the region are Christians (Government of Meghalaya, 2003). Next to family and kinship, the church plays a pivotal role in the social organization of these Christian tribal people. Christianity has not only brought great social and cultural changes among these tribes but also promoted literacy/education and health care among them, developed their language, script and literature, protected their language and culture and spread identity consciousness and political awareness among them.

Research on the status of women has looked at the traditional status of tribal women, the impact of changes and the effects of Christianity on them. It may be noted that the status of women in tribes like Khasi, Garo, Jaintia, Naga, Mizo Kuki, etc., has been changed due to the effects of Christianity, education, nuclear family, modern means of communication and above all, employment in non-agricultural occupations. In the area of socio-political movements researches have mainly focused on tribal separatist nationalism, ethno-nationalism, sub-nationalism or cultural nationalism. Research on the impact of government sponsored development programmes has been also conducted. Some studies are also available on the agricultural practices and land tenure systems, especially in the tribal societies of the region.

It may, however, be noted that significant gaps still exist in the sociological research practice in the northeast region. Geographically, northeast India includes both hills and plains. The hill areas cover 70 per cent of the total area. The plains consist of the Brahmaputra river valley and the Barak river valley located in Assam and the small Imphal valley situated in Manipur. While the non-tribal people are predominantly found in the plains areas, the tribal people are in majority in the hills. Some tribes are also found in the plains areas of the region. On a closer look, however, one finds that much attention has been paid to the study of the tribal communities of the hill areas and very few studies have been conducted on the plains tribes such as the Bodos, Rabhas, Koches, etc., as well as on the Assamese, Bengalis, Nepalis, Manipuris, Marwaris and the Hindi-speaking living in different parts of the region.

Besides, the states of Assam and Arunachal Pradesh contain sizeable migrant tribal people, such as the Santhalis, Mundas and Oraons, who are not included in the ST category in their respective states. But, no substantial sociological works on these migrant tribal communities have been done so far. Similarly, very little attention has been paid to the study of the Scheduled Caste (SC) people, who constitute 6.85 per cent of the total population of the region and are mainly distributed in the plains areas of Assam, Tripura and Manipur (Census of India, 1991).

Further, the impact of Christianity and Christian tribes in the region has been studied to a great extent, but not much attention has been paid to the study of the other religious groups of the region such as the Hindus, the Muslims, the Buddhist and the minority religious groups such as the Jains and the Bahai's people. In Assam, the Hindus constitute 67.13 per cent and the Muslims account for 28.43 per cent of the population. In Tripura, the Hindus account for 86.51 per cent, the Muslims form 7.11 per cent and the Buddhist constitute 4.54 per cent of the population. In Manipur, the Hindus constitute 57.65 per cent and the Muslims form a sizeable minority with 7.29 per cent of the population. In Arunachal Pradesh, the Hindus form 36.99 per cent and the Buddhist constitute 12.83 per cent of the population. Here, most of the tribal groups follow their traditional tribal religion or Tibetan/Myanmar form of Buddhism. In Sikkim, the Hindus constitute 68.47 per cent and the Buddhist form 7.09 per cent of the population, (Government of Meghalaya, 2004). But, unfortunately, not much research works are available on religious groups like Assamese Muslims, Bengali Muslims, Muslim Meiteis, Muslim Khasis, Buddhist or Hindu tribal communities. Further, most of the research done on the northeast region has not followed the comparative perspective in their analysis (Kumar, 19: 46).

As mentioned earlier, some social science research institutes in the region have also been engaged in sociological research, for example, the newly established Omeo Kumar Das Institute of Social Change and Development (OKDISCD) at Guwahati. Its basic objective is to provide academic and professional guidance to agencies, institutions and scholars engaged in social change and development. It has identified several thrust areas of research in view of the historical, cultural, social, economic, political and geographical importance of the region. For example, ethnicity and politics has been identified due to the fact that ever since India's independence the northeast region has been experiencing a large number of movements based on ethnic identities, such as language, religion, tribe, culture and region.

Conclusion

The chapter began with the claim that notwithstanding the specificity of the northeastern context, a great deal is common with what is happening elsewhere. Significantly, the growing presence of non-governmental organizations (NGOs), as both agencies of development and as what has been termed as the New Centres of Knowledge Production (NCKP)[6], can be seen here too. There has also been a proliferation of non-governmental organisation (NGO), community-based organization (CBO) and civil society organization activities in northeast India in past few years. These voluntary organizations, particularly the NGOs, in the region are active in both urban and rural areas and they take up wide range issues, such as human rights protection, environment protection, sustainable development, wildlife protection, preservation of biosphere and biodiversity, people's empowerment and capacity building, people's participation in community and rural development, prevention of child labour and delinquency, helping the destitute and street children, rehabilitation of the drug addicts, running old age homes, implementation of anti-poverty programmes, rural marketing, rural technology, micro-financing and self-income generating schemes, self-help groups and cooperative enterprise, entrepreneurship promotion, training the physically disabled, disaster management, relief management, protection of tribal identity, preservation of cultural heritage, etc. Needles to say, most of these issues are in some ways the basic fodder for sociological enquiry. Unfortunately, no course on the role of NGOs in socio-economic, political and cultural development of the people has been designed by any of the northeast Indian universities. The possibility of accepting the paradigm of both development and evaluation provided by the funding bodies and NGOs by sociological research is more likely than not.

Notes

1. It will be instructive here to refer to Dalia Chakrabarti's chapter in the volume regarding issue of how sociology itself and state policies negotiated with the challenge of 'unity and diversity'.
2. See Tiplut Nongbri (2003).
3. See Ramanuj Ganguly's chapter on teaching sociology in nursing colleges.
4. Comparison with the dalit critique of the Hindu social order will be useful here. See Vivek Kumar's chapter in this volume.
5. A.K. Nongkynrih's chapter in the volume suggests that the over emphasis on issues of ethnicity has led to a neglect on fundamental questions of poverty, development and inequality. See his chapter in this volume.
6. See Ravi Kumar's paper in this volume.

References

Association of Indian Universities. 1997. Universities Handbook, 27th Edition. New Delhi.

Baral, K.C. 2006. "Globalisation and the Tribes of Northeast India", *Indian Folklore*, Serial, No. 22, July.

Census of India. 2001.

Government of Meghalaya (GoM). 2004. Where Do We Stand in Northeast India in 2003. Shillong: Directorate of Economics and Statistics.

Kumar, Nikhlesh. 1997. "Trends in Sociological Research in Northeast India (1947–1997)", in J.P. Singh, R. Gopalakrishanan, L.S. Gassah, D.R. Syiemlieh and C.J. Thomas (eds.), *Trends in Social Sciences and Humanities in Northeast India: 1947–1997*. New Delhi: Regency Publications, pp. 92–98.

Miri, Mrinal (ed.), 1982. *Linguistic Situation in Northeast India*. Shillong: North-Eastern Council for Social Science Research.

Part III

Sociology in Professional Institutions: Global Brands and Disciplinary Marginality

Sociology in professional institutions is located not at the edges but in the very centres. But they lack the disciplinary centrality that is accorded to the main thrust areas of the institutions, be it science and technology in the IITs, management in the IIMs or law in the Law Schools. The story of sociology in Nursing is different and with a much longer history but it still remains marginal for what is essentially a professional degree. Developments in the global market and India's own involvement in the process impacts professional institutions more immediately and directly. The demands for marketable skills dominate policy making here, making issues of relevance, autonomy and market skills intensely contestable. More visible here too are the tensions of the broader shift in educational vision from a nationalist to a transnational framework.

8

Of Mainstream and Margins

Sociology in Indian Institutes of Management (IIMs)

MANISH THAKUR

Since the 1990s, Indian Institutes of Management (IIMs) have been at the very centre of the academic firmament in India, and are reckoned to be the elite business schools having global recognition. At a time when the new generation of professionals is no longer trained in liberal arts colleges and conventional universities, the prestige of IIMs is on the rise. In a way, they appear to have occupied the central place in professional higher education as with every passing year the number of engineering graduates coming to IIMs is on the rise. Even those trained at IITs feel compelled to supplement their professional training with management degrees to enter the high-end corporate job market.[1] While the visibility of IIMs in the 'public' imagination cannot be overstated, the invisibility of sociology in IIMs cannot be more understated. The story of sociology within the IIMs has a long history and exploring the past and present of the practice of sociology within management schools may offer a fresh take into the intellectual and institutional legacies of the discipline.

In this paper, I focus on the place of sociology in IIMs. I begin in a sense from the beginning. Section I draws attention to the fact that IIMs in India were modelled on the lines of American management schools and thereby reflected a similar story so far as the location of sociology within it is concerned. In Section II, I dwell on the peculiar Indian twist to the American model in the early years after independence where the Indian state vision of development, modernization and even democracy seemed core goals of the IIMs. Finally, in Section III, I try to evaluate the practices of the discipline in its varied manifestations – teaching, research, training and consultancy – on the basis of professional experiences of fellow sociologists, irrespective of their location in a separate centre for sociology or in any other interdisciplinary group.

This paper draws both from existing documents of IIMs as well upon interviews apart from my own 'participant observations' as a faculty member. The documents are mainly published institutional data such as annual reports, convocation addresses, directors' speeches at the convocations, booklets, brochures of various types, and other sundry material that IIMs have produced over the years as part of their routine administrative demands and professional packaging terms. I have also interviewed some of the academics in the field of management who have spent considerable time in IIMs, and are familiar with their structure and functioning. Tangentially, I also dwell on as to how the practices of sociology in IIMs relate to those in the universities and other research centres. And, finally, I explore as to how our peers, mainly from the universities, relate to us as sociologists. Evidently, any such exercise cannot claim any hard data for its observations, which are likely to be selective and subjective. At the same time, I assert that what follows is not merely impressionistic but is the outcome of careful scrutiny of different sources of information whatever the form. Moreover, the organization of the material and the derived observations are particularly framed by my current location in an IIM after having taught in a university for a decade. In that sense, I do not claim an insider's authenticity as much as I discount outsider's biases. In order to contextualize the present paper, it is important to bear in mind that my exposure to IIMs is just four years old.

I

Management Schools and the Place of Sociology: The American Model

Sociology, as such, has not been a stranger to the curriculum of the American schools of business and management – a state of affairs, which reflects the high standing of sociology in that country and the strategic importance of Elton Mayo's appointment at the Harvard Business School.[2] Way back in 1960, J.H. Smith could claim that "indeed, the position of sociology in business and management education in the US now seems to be such that it has passed beyond the point at which separate reference needs to be made to it in the curriculum" (Smith, 1960: 103) True, even in the School of Industrial Management at MIT, sociology was present more by way of immersing its separate identity in the interdisciplinary themes. Be that as it may, available evidence suggests that relevance of sociology to the management process has been taken for granted at least in the US, and also to some extent in the UK.

In fact, very often, the case for inclusion of sociology in management curriculum has largely been made on the basis of its achievement in the US where the contributions of Elton Mayo loom large. On the flip side, it has also meant equating industrial sociology with Hawthorne experiments. As a consequence, sociology is looked at as a palliative for industrial conflict and a source of 'social skills' – it has been seen as contributing to solving human (read labour) problems in the industrial societies. In this fashion, sociology justified its limited uses in business schools and/or in management teaching. In the UK, sociology has been projected as being essentially a study of institutions, including a description of representative industrial institutions – the enterprise, the trade union, and the labour market. Besides, it included in its provenance the concept of formal and informal behaviour at workplace and focused on the interaction of industrial with other institutions of society – those of class, politics and education. In a manner of speaking, by providing illustrative material on industrial situations, the industrial problems and their social implications, sociology has managed to sneak in through the backdoor of business schools.

On another plane, sociology has also resorted to the general and oft-repeated justification of its being a liberalizing influence on aspiring managers and contributing to the understanding of the world in which the manager lives and works. The overall claim runs like this: sociology can teach managers something about the social structure of industrial institutions, the social values which sustain them, and the social context in which they function; and that the teaching of this kind is both a liberal element in that it broadens the perspective of the student, and at the same time, a useful one, in that it gives him knowledge which may be relevant to practical decisions (ibid.: 108).

II

The American Model and the Indian Twist

It needs to be stressed that IIMs have been modelled after American business schools. George W. Robbins, the then Associate Dean of the School of Business Administration, University of California, Los Angeles, was the consultant hired by the Planning Commission, who put forward the blueprint for an All-India Institute of Management (Planning Commission 1957, Robbins 1959). In IIMs, people keep referring to the active institutional collaboration between Alfred P. Sloan School of Management, MIT, and the first IIM that was established in Calcutta in 1961. Likewise, the IIM, Ahmedabad was established in 1962 with the active institutional support of the Harvard Business School. Given the overall national drive towards industrialization, IIMs were created with the apparent objectives of (a) meeting the needs of industry, commerce and government for managerial manpower, (b) assisting in the solution of management problems, and (c) developing an indigenous literature on management through an effective programme of teaching, research, consultation and publications.

Many thought management education to be a creative endeavour in the sense of being an essential element in the process of modernization and in the building of a new social and economic order. Given the spirit of the time, the enthronement of professional manager as the chief director of economic activity in the country was seen as a much-awaited progressive development. Some of them were ecstatic in viewing managers as great change agents capable of overcoming our backwardness, and "to change our traditional, underdeveloped society into a modern industrialized one" (IIMC, 1987: 34). For example, Bhaskar Mitter, the first corporate head, and the then chairman of Andrew Yule & Co., to have delivered the 6th convocation address at IIM, Calcutta (on 12 April 1971) appears to be at his rhetorical best in the following excerpts:

> The manager in India has to look upon his work as an intellectual challenge. It is fortunate that many of the best brains in the country today are choosing management as a career, just as at one time the intellectual elite of the country tended to converge towards the ICS. But having come into this profession many of them feel frustrated

> because the routine and drudgery of their work seems far remote from their colleges and institutes. They are inclined to think that their talents are wasted in trying to do humdrum jobs like selling soap or maintaining worn out machines or getting workers to come on time. But it needs to be realized that in a country like ours it is not pure research that plays the most important role in bringing about transformation. *The battle for development has to be fought and won on the shop-floors and in the fields, at the desks, drawing boards and in the market place.* The manager who can organise the campaigns for these battles and win them successfully is making more useful contribution towards the transformation of his country than the abstract theorist (emphasis mine, IIMC, 1987: 40).

The policy makers could not see any conflict of interests between the establishment of IIMs, and the pursuit of socialistic pattern of society as a consensual national goal.[3] Rather, IIMs were expected to professionally contribute to the grand ideal of building a socialistic society where public sectors would occupy the commanding heights.[4] Management training was seen as crucial for the efficient and profitable management of public sector enterprises so that persons from administrative services were gradually replaced by the newly trained managers to cut down delays in decisions and thereby enhance profits and productivity, and contribute to the socialist pattern of society.[5] Indeed, D.R. Gadgil, the then Deputy Chairman of the Planning Commission, remarked that the cadre of business executives and managers to be built with the help of IIMs would help make the much-needed transition from "enterprises managed largely on the model of the administrative department to enterprises managed essentially as autonomous business units" (IIMC, 1987: 17).

There was another implicit ideal animating the enterprise of setting up IIMs – that of facilitating and reinforcing the processes of nascent industrial democratization in the country. Delivering the first convocation address (on 16 May 1966), Sachin Chaudhury, the then Finance Minister of India, lauded the attempt to bring in industrial management on the basis of professional competence for its potential to offset the strong allegiance to family and caste characterising business communities in India. According to him, professional management will limit concentration of control over many firms in a few hands with undesirable social consequences. I need to quote him at length to drive home the elements of the vision that was supposed to impart IIMs its public mandate: "As future industrial managers in a democratic society in the second half of the 20th century, your responsibilities will be much wider than towards shareholders alone, or merely to show a good rate of return on capital invested or to expand the firms concerned. You will have responsibility towards labour, towards others who work with you, and more important of all towards society."[5]

Additionally, the newly minted managers were expected to ensure that the development of the private sector was in keeping with the interest of the community at large: "it is of the utmost importance that the management of private industry and business should also be entrusted increasingly to professional managers rather than to persons whose right to management is based on ownership of personal wealth or the accident of birth" (IIMC, 1987: 4). In essence, the higher ideal of an industrial democracy appears to have animated the vision in the sense of growing separation of purely managerial functions from ownership of capital or wealth. More importantly, the private sector was expected to add to the processes of industrial democratization by entrusting management increasingly to professional people.

Ironically, there was a time when there was palpable academic hesitation about the fitness of management as a taught programme or a distinctive university discipline. Management was considered to be some sort of academic potpourri drawing parasitically on established social sciences and other academic disciplines.[6] By contrast, now, the onus is on sociologists to demonstrate that sociology is a key subject in management. With varying success, sociologists have been offering well-intentioned but suspect mixture of labour problems, trade unions, industrial sociology, and entrepreneurship as their areas of disciplinary expertise and somehow have been managing their presence in IIMs. In fact, one of the sociologists – N.R. Sheth by virtue of his pioneering work in the field of industrial sociology – reached the top when he became the director of IIM, Ahmedabad. And, with that the glory of sociology in IIMs reached its zenith. In retrospect, that does not seem to have either enhanced the value of sociological research in IIMs or the professional profile of sociologists. Even now, any discussion of sociology in IIMs begins and ends with Sheth. One may pose an interesting question: Why Sheth could not manage to accomplish for sociology in the context of management education in India something Mayo did so marvellously in the US. But, that would be not only an unfair comparison but also reduce the complexity concerning the production of the knowledge of the social to the role of a few great sociologists.[7]

III

The Marginality of Sociology

A sense of self-perceived marginalization is all pervasive among a small number of sociologists who teach and research at the IIMs. Their marginal location and the attendant marginalization of the discipline they professionally belong to – sociology in the present context – are inextricably linked. The practitioners of the discipline know only too well that their colleagues offering courses, namely, Production and Inventory Control, Sales and Distribution Management, Strategic Planning and HRM, Optimization Models for Industry, Options, Futures and Derivatives, and even Selected Aspect of Macroeconomics, carry more weight and glamour within the institution as well as outside. The latter rightfully deliberate on the futuristic vision of the institution, its mission and mandate, and we ungrudgingly yield to their right to do so. After all, they are the mainstream. They navigate the flagship programmes of the institution, do consultancy, organize management development (training) programmes (MDPs), and, through their expertise and niche in the academic market place and the corporate sector, bring in money to the institution. To put it bluntly, social sciences in general occupy a marginal location within these institutions of management.

It would be unfair to confine this narrative of marginalization to the design and philosophy of IIMs alone. Interestingly, the mainstream of the discipline (if there is one) bypasses these institutions as potential sites of academic research collaboration. Let's ask ourselves: Does joining an IIM have the same meaning for a sociologist as it has for a management guru? For the latter, coming to these institutions means as if they had arrived in their professions? The same can hardly be said about a sociologist.

There is another angle to this. A sociologist in an IIM cannot bask in the institutional glory in the same way as his/her counterpart, say, in Jawaharlal Nehru University or Delhi School of Economics can and indeed does. In the latter case, the accumulated prestige and the acquired glamour of the institution rub on in the individual professional trajectory of the sociologist. For the one in an IIM, he/she has to acquire that professional prestige by his/her own unaided efforts. In my reading, despite the downgrading of social sciences and liberal disciplines in general in the context of withdrawal of the state, and the increasing competition from the emerging market-friendly disciplines such as management, commerce, software technology etc., sociological research and teaching seem to be firmly anchored in the universities and social science research institutions than in IIMs.

After all, universities nourish and sustain disciplinary traditions through their teaching programmes and research degrees. A university, despite all its limitations, creates future torch bearers of the disciplinary culture by virtue of its focus on postgraduate teaching and subsequent research thus imparting continuity to the traditions of disciplinary learning. An IIM is not meant for offering a postgraduate degree in sociology. Naturally, it does not have in-house prospective researchers who can be trained for PhD research. For its PhD programme (called Fellow Programme in Management or FP in IIM parlance), it has to draw on the same universities which it hardly has any linkages worth its name. No wonder, IIMs fail to attract PhD fellows in sociology despite its brand name and a host of fellowship incentives faring much better than many universities. For example, I was shocked to learn that so far only two doctorates have been awarded under the auspices of the Sociology Group at IIM, Calcutta in its history spanning more than three decades – the first in 1986 and thereafter in 2006!

It is no secret that in an IIM, sociology is seen more as an add-on than some sort of value addition. For a management student, sociology courses are unnecessary deviations from their primary tasks of self-fashioning as future managers. Somehow PhD research, and expectedly faculty research, in IIMs are caught in the quagmire of relevance. Their existential dilemmas emanating from their locations in institutions of management propel sociologists to go for relevant research. Relevance comes to acquire a distinctive applied orientation, and sociology faculty seems to naturally gravitate towards those issues/themes that have relevance in management-related fields. I am not saying that research on these issues is not important, but one fails to understand why someone who is in IIM alone should conduct study in the area of sociology of consumption, or entrepreneurship, or management of rural social change, or general issues related to business, society and management? And, why someone who is placed in an IIM should not research on religion or kinship? After all, Rowena Robinson continues to work in the area of sociology of religion despite having been located in IIT, Bombay and E. Haribabu has continued his research interest in the interface of science, technology and society in a mainstream central university.[8]

In the Company of 'Superiors'

The most fundamental point relates to the inferiority complex being suffered by most sociologists in IIMs who are anyway few and far between. They have to carry the extra burden of proving all the time to themselves and their peers from other disciplines about the scientificity of sociology. They travel the extra mile to convince themselves as well as those around them that sociology is an empirical and scientific discipline, just few rungs below the natural sciences.

Something is inferior to something else in relation to a particular quality provided that quality is highly valued and whose absence is seriously missed regardless of other qualities present. Moving further, one can think of different possibilities: (a) inferiority might make things desirable (e.g., sandpaper because of its inferior smoothness, anthropology because of its ability to meaningful insights in a micro-setting); (b) inferiority may be a simply a matter of indifference; and (c) inferiority may be simply regrettable, nonetheless wanted (e.g., psychiatry is required without its ability to effect quick cures, biology is essential without the lack of internal consistency in its theoretical systems).

Wherever something is inferior-superior with respect to the same attribute, there is a choice to be made between alternatives. That would mean in the context of natural and social sciences (a) banishment, (b) no allocation of resources, (c) discouraging the gifted from social sciences and pushing them for 'superior' pursuits, and (d) withholding respect from social scientists. However, these possibilities are out of question as natural sciences and social sciences cannot be, by any means, regarded as alternatives. Both are needed and neither can be dispensed with. Indisputably, all differences need not lead to hierarchy and inferiority is context bound. Very often, we fail to appreciate this plain proposition that because of these properties, research and analyses in social sciences, hold greater complexity and difficulties, and possibly greater challenge (ibid.: 5–19). They should not be seen as deterrent. Problems presented by the social world are certainly not unimportant, and if they are also difficult to tackle, they ought to attract ample resources and the best minds. Unfortunately, neither is forthcoming.

Many issues bearing on the place of sociology in IIMs go well beyond the internal politics of the institution and are conditioned by extraneous factors outlined in the introduction. Is not it revealing that the Indian government does not mind investing crores of rupees in nano-technology but would act niggardly if asked to commit few lakhs to a research project on the ethnography of state practices? Our honourable members of parliament clap in euphoric celebration when a finance minister announces one time grant of Rs 100 crores for the Indian Institute of Science (IIS), Bangalore. But then, the Ministry of Human Resources of the same government has failed to breathe in new life in social science research institutions working under the auspices of Indian Council of Social Science Research (ICSSR).

So much so that a workshop organized at the IIT, Bombay in November 2006 witnessed a concerted effort to set up a separate organization of the sociologists in technology and management institutions where the lead was taken by the sociologists in the IITs. Many felt that the ISS has been dominated by university/college teachers and researchers and is not the suitable platform for sociologists in management and technology institutions. There is a perception that sociologists in IIMs (and IITs) are not given due professional recognition by their peers in the universities and by those who matter in the discipline.[9]

This perception is borne out by the general perception of the Sociology Group of the IIM, Calcutta. I have been told by many well-wishers that what there is in IIM is not sociology but some unrecognisable hybrid entity.[10] Others have cautioned me against staying too long in IIM lest I get ill-equipped to do any kind of meaningful sociological research. All are well-meaning people – mostly from the discipline – and all of them agree on the fact that IIM is not the right place for a young and promising sociologist. 'Try JNU' or 'D'School', or 'if you want to stay in Kolkata only, at least get into Partha Chatterjee's Centre (Centre for the Study of Social Sciences)' – these are the oft-repeated fragments of conversation I have had ever since I announced my decision to shift to IIM, Calcutta from Goa University.

Sociology in Management Curriculum

For the IIMs, the two-year residential Post-Graduate Programme in Management (PGP) is the flagship programme. Over the years, IIMs have been forced to launch various other tailor-made management programmes to cater to different types of constituencies, such as young executives, army personnel, and senior executives with considerable length of work experience. Also, in some IIMs, there is an amalgamation of core management programme and areas like information technology, public systems management, agri-business etc. Yet, the PGP continues to be the most prestigious brand for the IIMs. A careful scrutiny of the IIM brochures reveals so. For example, the website of the IIM, Bangalore proclaims: "The PGP is designed to enable students to acquire the skills and capabilities that will enable them to reach responsible global positions in management". Likewise, IIM, Lucknow states: "the curriculum is designed to impart knowledge and skills considered essential for managers to operate successfully in the increasingly dynamic and complex environment..."[11]

Even otherwise, within the IIMs, participation in the PGP is taken to be the ultimate source of legitimacy and relevance for the faculty members as well as for the groups/areas they come from. Generally, during the two years of the PGP, two sets of courses are offered: the compulsory package and the elective package. The stated aim of the compulsory courses is to provide the students with the fundamental knowledge, skills and the techniques, contextual understanding, and overall perspective necessary for general management. On the other hand, elective courses have the ostensible purpose of helping students develop an in-depth understanding of areas of their interest. Some typical electives courses in IIMs are generally around the areas of marketing, finance, strategy and international business, operations management, human resources management and information technology.

All the IIMs roughly follow the same format for their PGP programmes even when wordings may vary. For example, the IIM, Indore (a new generation IIM along with IIM, Kozhikode and the youngest in the IIM family) highlights its compulsory package of 22 foundation (core) courses "designed to provide basic knowledge of concepts, tools and techniques in various functional areas and relevant disciplines". It is to be noted that there is strong competition among

IIMs themselves and each IIM tries to outshine the other by packaging its programmes in more market-friendly manner.

Ever since the popular media started ranking business schools in India, including the IIMs, the latter have been under tremendous pressure to maintain their cutting-edge positions. The following excerpts from the IIM, Bangalore website display the deeply ingrained sense of competition to maintain and enhance its reputation:

> The programme [PGP] revolves around the principle that world-class business leaders are not mass-produced; they are nurtured and developed with personalised care and attention, in small work groups and teams, and in a practical, application-oriented user-friendly environment. The programme lays the foundation for conceptual and analytical reasoning, and gives the students an insight into the dynamics of the business environment. *It prepares students to manage and lead in global business scenario which is getting increasingly complex and dynamic.* The programme design is inspired by management practice rather than ivory tower academics (italics mine).

Indeed, the mission statement of IIM, Bangalore gestures towards certain perspective building courses. However, at the level of practice, most of the IIMs fall short of realizing the full potential of their own ideals. For example, IIM, Bangalore rests content by stating that students are encouraged to take up dissertation work and to do a project on contemporary concerns under the guidance of the faculty. In IIM, Ahmedabad, the most prestigious among the IIMs, I came across a course entitled 'Indian Social and Political Environment' as a compulsory course offered during Term 3 (the first year). Another course, 'Understanding Contemporary India' is offered as optional during Term 6. Moreover, IIM, Ahmedabad offers one-year PGP in Public Management and Policy (PGP-PMP). As part of this programme, I could find few interesting course titles under the Core Public Management and Policy Module: Democracy and Development, Societal Change and Development; Governance and Policy Formulation and Implementation; Public Policy Formulation and Implementation; and International Economic Relations. Similarly, Rural Development, Agricultural Development and Rural Environment are some of the course titles being offered as part of the PGP in Agribusiness Management. All these courses can easily lend themselves to sociological perspectives and approaches. At the least, the titles suggest so. But despite repeated requests I have not been provided with course outlines.

Apart from IIM, Ahmedabad, IIM, Calcutta and IIM, Kozhikode are the only two IIMs where sociology courses are offered as part of compulsory package. IIM, Calcutta has a compulsory course for the PGP: Indian Social Structure (Basic Sociological Concepts). Besides, the Sociology Group of the IIM, Calcutta offers a set of elective courses for the PGP. Likewise, IIM, Kozhikode has a compulsory course called 'Social Transformation in India' which is offered in the very first academic term of the PGP itself even when IIM, Kozhikode has no trained sociologist among its faculty members.

In IIM, Indore, there is an interesting course by the name 'Society, Business and Management' started in the year 2000. I have failed to get the detailed course outline but what I learn is that it is being taught by a faculty member trained in law and is oriented towards communicating the new framework for corporate social responsibility. As per the website, this course seeks to develop socially sensitive and technically competent business managers, who can contribute not only to corporate excellence but also cater to the needs of the crucial social sector in India. It also helps to develop the social perspective and social ethics in the minds of the future captains of industry. The website adds:

> The private sector, being the dominant engine of growth, needs to deliver 'economic development and social opportunity' to ensure social justice and equality to achieve the long lasting dream of social harmony and stability. In harnessing the synergy of a new partnership amongst the government, private sector and civil society, and making it a self-enhancing initiative for each one of them, the SBM course of IIM, Indore has a key role to play.

Of all the IIMs, IIM, Lucknow appears to have been least receptive to the practices of sociology in terms of modes of teaching research, including both the intellectual orientations of research and teaching as well as the institutions within which they are done. I cannot do better than to quote the personal communication from a faculty member of IIM, Lucknow: "As far as I know there are no courses being taught which have sociological components, and in the ongoing research I know of, I do not think much of sociological components are there" (14 July 2007). Potentially though, IIM, Lucknow has a stated focus on agribusiness, which lends itself to the tools and the accumulated academic legacy of the discipline. But then, the area is monopolized by economists alone.

Interestingly, the mission statement of the PGP of most IIMs stresses values and social concerns – the typical justifications for sociology courses in the management curriculum. Sample the following from the IIM, Kozhikode:

> Successful management and leadership also involve a potent combination of strategy and values, with the latter weighing in with equal importance according to the Institute's management philosophy. *It is expected and awaited that the alumni of the Institute will be harmonious individuals, socially responsible citizens of tomorrow, in addition to taking up the reins of business and industry.* The stricture on upholding values is, in fact, brought home to the students' right at the beginning of the programme, when they take a unique, compulsory course on "social transformation in India". Some of the other regular courses also have this emphasis in-built in their structures. Thus, the course in Social and Rural Marketing includes visits to rural areas in the state to provide the students with "live" experiences essential for understanding the issues involved (all italics mine).

I fail to understand as to why social sensitivity (and its English language equivalents) is such a key term finding a place in the mission and vision statements of almost all the IIMs. For example, IIM, Ahmedabad describes itself as a "a globally respected institute that shapes management practices in India and abroad by creating new frontiers of knowledge and developing ethical, dependable, entrepreneurial, and socially sensitive leader managers committed to excellence".

Sociological Research at IIMs

IIMs are generally not organized in terms of distinctive disciplinary identities. Except for IIM, Calcutta, no other IIMs have a separate sociology group. IIM, Bangalore comes closer to Calcutta where there is a combined area called 'Economics and Social Sciences' covering mainly the domains of economics, political economy and society, and business law. In IIM, Lucknow, the area called 'Business Environment' has no sociological component, which is equally absent from the area of 'Decision Sciences'. In other IIMs, trained sociologists are generally scattered over areas, such as strategic management, organizational development, entrepreneurship studies, business environment, and marketing with a definite slant towards rural marketing. Agribusiness and public policy groups are theoretically possible institutional homes for sociologists. But, then, the total number of trained sociologists in all the IIMs would hardly touch the double digit. Clearly, there is a problem of scale given the abysmally low strength.

Moreover, sociologists in IIMs are constrained by the lack of a healthy and robust tradition of sociological investigation in the industrial and corporate sectors notwithstanding the sub-discipline of industrial sociology. Surprisingly, even today, there is no accessible text or research literature on the increasingly influential Indian managerial class. One notices similar dearth of literature on the theme of sociology of consumption in India. One needs to sociologically probe as to why the tradition of economic sociology has had such a weak foundation in our country.

Another factor that has a great bearing on the professional profile of sociologists in IIMs is the existing (and dominant) understanding of the scope and purpose of management education. Some of the practitioners of management science themselves have started realizing the need for some sort of traditional liberal education. They have started expressing a sense of unease with the tendency on the part of IIMs to become polytechnic training centres with excessive zeal towards vocational and technical instruction aiming mainly at imparting of techniques and skills on a comparatively narrow front. The disproportionate focus on 'competency-building courses' rather than 'perspective-building' ones expectedly keep sociology on the margins of the curricula at IIMs (personal interview with A. Sreekumar, 28 March 2007).

Administrators deciding resource allocations in a multidisciplinary setting often look at the discipline's real and potential contribution to resource generation. Given the corpus of accumulated knowledge, sociology can hardly assert its suitability for MDPs. Its failure on this count – the failure to organize training programmes and to offer enough consultancy to the corporate sector – further pushes it down in the institutional hierarchy. Most of the IIMs are prone to a sort of turf war where faculty and disciplines work to demonstrate their capabilities of relevance in terms of such institutional criteria as MDPs and consultancy. They are more likely to laugh off a sociologist's venture in the field of MDPs as they are not too sure if such MDPs would attract adequate number of participants to make them profitable to the institute. Even when sociologists are increasingly getting involved in NGOs, consultancies, corporate research and new assignments like social auditing, the public image of sociology as an esoteric discipline dealing with worn out themes like caste and village continues among powers-to-be in IIMs. A colleague of mine (who wants IIM, Calcutta to drop its compulsory course in sociology) is not convinced at all as to how sociology would help someone who is going to be an investment banker or consultant to a multinational financial firm.

More importantly, sociologists in IIMs are ill-disposed (to some extent ill-equipped) to perform tasks expected of them. Most of us come from the universities and the bigger biases of professional socialization generate a 'trained incapacity' to practise sociology in settings like IIMs. We have been brought up on a heavy dose of Nisbet's sociology as an art form (1976) and Bottomore's sociology as social criticism (1974). We have learnt to be apologetic about our meagre accomplishments in terms of offering feasible solutions to real-life problems. We have been taught the subtle intricacies of conceptual distinctions between a social problem and a sociological problem – the latter being our provenance. Our campus culture has communicated to us (of course in not so direct ways) that more removed your ideas and theories are from the real world, the more greater a sociologist you are. Who does not recall the evocative distinction between theoretical Brahmins and empirical Shudras in relation to internal division of labour within Indian sociology?[12] In IIMs, where many may not know what sociology is, and where fellow sociologists are few and far between, such a professional socialization does not encourage productive adaptation and fruitful collaboration.

The roots of this socialization go much deeper and are predicated upon the ingrained asymmetrical reward and prestige systems accruing to theoretical and applied research in the university setting. To some extent, it is related to the very nature of university as an institution. Citing Clark Kerr, Lipset observes that even as academics persistently support local and national social change efforts, they take an opposite stance when the academy itself is the focus of concern. "Few institutions are so conservative as universities about their own affairs. While their members are so liberal about the affairs of others, the more elite the professor, the more liberal he or she is on social issues; but the opposite holds on matters that affect the academy" (1982: 156). Even otherwise, "the bottom line, to use business school language, is that life at the border of sociology and management is not for everyone. It is a comfortable location only if you are willing to move beyond the boundaries of sociology, and at the same time, are inclined to bring sociological ideas into management" (Meyer, 1999: 509–10).

Very often, the pursuit of sponsored or state-promoted research has been seen as a threat to the status of established centres and the integrity of the discipline. There have been fears that too much of encouragement of applied research might slow down the cumulative development of sociological theory and further constrict the already narrowing social and political outlook. Conventional sociologists ensconced in prestigious (and not so prestigious) university departments may find it difficult to move out of the comfort levels that the habitual world of repetitive courses and disciplined classrooms, familiar bodies of literature, research methods and work settings have created for them. To go for a change in institutional sense is unattractive as well as fraught with risk.

In IIMs, sociologists are by force engaged in self-conscious marketing of their discipline and profession as they confront their academic colleagues, administrators, professional competitors from other disciplines, students, the general public, and potential and actual clients. One needs to stress that engagement in applied research (with all its limitations) does not mean that any compromise with the discipline's self-reflexivity.

In a pragmatic sense, extending the scope of the discipline through applied research may be a better professional strategy than rueing the decline in state support for social sciences, or the general decline in the prestige of liberal education, or the public image of sociology. The fear of getting bogged down by applied interests led the professional leaders of the yore to claim a space for knowledge producing activity of the academic kind (see Thakur, 2006).

It is not that applied sociology means less rigorous engagement with the discipline. Heuristically speaking, as DeMartini (1979: 333) argues, there are two types of applied sociology. One tradition of work emphasizes the utilization of the basic empirical methods of the discipline in collecting and gathering information needed to make informed decision or opinion on matters of practical concern. Evaluation research, programme evaluation, cost-benefit analysis and social impact assessment, public opinion polling, market analysis, and community ethnography belong to this genre of work which finds its organizational expressions in entities such as ORG-MARG, A.C. Nielson, Microsoft, and numerous research and advocacy NGOs. The other kind of work utilizes the discipline's concepts in interpreting relevant data, and hopefully in providing a more accurate understanding of social determinants and the possible outcome of proposed social action. Analysis of social problems, policy research and analysis would fit in this variety of applied research.

It is possible to maintain a judicious balance between expectations of IIMs in terms of applied research and training and the conceptual and theoretical rigour of sociology. While continuing to be a perspective-building critical discipline oriented towards understanding of social processes and phenomena shaping the context we live in, sociology can also lend itself to theory-driven, case-based and managerially relevant research. As Petrus and Adamek (1988) suggest, sociologists in IIMs can fruitfully employ their relatively easy, if not unfettered, access to business and their databases, for a wide range of research pertaining to issues such as sociological study of language and culture of business. Likewise, sociologists in IIMs can draw on new economic sociology integrating management research with the core concerns of society and apply some of these ideas from economic sociology to concrete business settings. One fails to understand why such endeavour should be confined to IIMs alone or be the sole preserve of sociologists there. Why should not it be a worthwhile academic endeavour if one extends Appadurai's illustrious work on consumption as a category, or one attempts the study of Indian business environment from a sociological perspective? Yet, as Marshall W. Meyer from the well-known Wharton School, University of Pennsylvania, notes, "the sociological perspective which emphasizes the role of values, institutions and social structures in human behaviour is not fully appreciated and may never be" (1999: 508).

IV

Concluding Remarks

I find no better way than to conclude these tentative reflections on the location of sociological practices in IIMs by presenting a somewhat lengthy quote from Meyer who captures the predicament and the dilemmas sociologists face in institutions like IIMs. Evidently, the status anxiety of sociologists in IIMs emanate from two sources: their perceived role and legitimacy within the institution, and outside, that is, in relation to the professional mainstream in the country. They, in turn, are intimately intertwined with the conceptualizations of the disciplinary practices as an established body of knowledge and as a profession. One starts understanding one's professional alienation within an IIM as one reads Meyer:

> At the core of sociology are an assumption and a suspicion. The assumption is that values, institutions and social structures are central to human behaviour – in other words, that it departs substantially from rational choice or simple utility maximisation. The suspicion is that things are not quite what they seem or as simple as they seem to be – this is what Berger and Luckman called the debunking motif of sociology. Our inclination to question rationality and to look for the unexpected leads us to believe that causation is complex, and, often, contingent, and that good empirical work, whether quantitative or qualitative, is preferable to modelling exercises relying on highly stylised assumptions about human behaviour. Management schools and management curricula are dominated by economics. There is a preference for models over hypothesis testing, with the corollary belief that models derived rigorously from the premise of utility maximisation describe how people ought to behave, even if they do not always behave that way. The preference for models is especially strong among MBA students, who seek answers rather than questions and want to learn about opportunities rather than constraints (1999: 509).

On a different plane, sociologists in IIMs find the absence of the simple realization on the part of fellow (mainstream) sociologists that practices of the discipline differ in varied institutional settings. Rather than making invidious comparisons between types of sociology done in the university (say JNU) and the IIMs (say Calcutta), we need to create spaces for empathetic and thoughtful dialogue among practitioners of the discipline irrespective of the sites of their practices, something this volume has attempted to accomplish. This should augur well for the discipline as it brings under self-reflexive gaze both our strengths and weaknesses, our accomplishments and inadequacies, professional solidity and internal fault lines, and finally, instances of theoretical rigour and imitative empiricism.

Acknowledgements

I would like to thank Professor Maitrayee Chaudhuri for having invited me to contribute this chapter to the volume. In writing this paper I have drawn on the encouragement and generosity of a number of colleagues and friends who shared with me their experiences of teaching and researching at IIMs. In particular, grateful acknowledgements are due to Professors Kalyan Sankar Mandal and Madhu S. Mishra (IIM, Calcutta), Ramnath Narayanswamy (IIM, Bangalore), Rajesh Aithal (IIM, Lucknow), Revathi Srinivasan (IIM, Ahmedabad), Justin Paul (IIM, Indore), A.R. Vasavi (NIAS, Bangalore) and A. Sreekumar (Goa University). Alito, Koshy and Venu – my former colleagues at Goa University – have been a source of many ideas and insights used in this paper. However, the usual disclaimer applies.

Notes

1. For instance, during 1991–93, the percentage of engineering graduates joining the IIM, Calcutta's Postgraduate Programme in Management (PGP) was 73.23 (of which 37.01 per cent were from the IITs). The percentage of the engineering graduates rose to 83.02 during 2003–2005 (of which 27.98 per cent were from the IITs).

   As regards, the placement of IIM graduates in the highest possible salary bracket is concerned, it has become almost customary for all the newspapers (mostly business ones) to report it annually (for instance, see *The Economic Times*, 6 March 2007; *The Financial Express*, 6 February 2007). Even TV news channels like NDTV, STAR, CNN-IBN report it every year during the time campus placement offers are made in the IIMs. Till recently, all IIMs used to flaunt the pay packets of their graduates on their websites to demonstrate their relative prestige and rank. However, owing to the perceived threats to the security of the family members of the graduates placed in high-income brackets, IIM, Bangalore and IIM, Lucknow have decided to discontinue the practice of making salary offers public.
2. Elton Mayo (1880–1949) was one of the key figures involved in Hawthorne Studies and his work laid the foundation for the many later management and organisational thinking. He worked in areas of motivation and commitment, and worker-management relations and came to occupy a legendary status as a pioneer of applied social science, especially in the workplace (see Smith, 1998: 221–49).

3. It is interesting to note that some of the early professors of IIMs (primarily IIM, Calcutta but, to some extent, also IIM, Ahmedabad) were well-known Marxist academics and intellectuals. For an absorbing anecdotal account of IIMs in its early phase see Mitra (2005). This Bengali publication was first serialized in the literary periodical *Desh.* Ashok Mitra was a professor of economics at IIM, Calcutta who served in important positions in the Central Government, and was Finance Minister of West Bengal as well as a member of the Rajya Sabha. The English language readers may refer to Mitra (2007).
4. The hope that a larger number of graduating students from the IIMs would take up jobs in the public sector appeared to be a recurring theme in the convocation addresses of the early phase.
5. Reminding the graduating students of the heavy public investment in their education and exhorting them to contribute to the society at large, Professor S. Nurul Hasan, then Minister of Education, remarked at the seventh convocation (on 15 April 1972):

   > It is, therefore, not enough for the managers of tomorrow, to have the necessary knowledge, expertise, and skills in managerial operations. These they must have to the highest possible extent, but they will need something plus; namely, a wider vision, a sense of social awareness, and social responsibility, an identification with the masses of the people, a deep sympathy for their travails and sufferings, and a passionate commitment to improving their condition in the shortest possible time. They must also learn to subordinate corporate profits, or personal gains, to the development of the economy as a whole, to the promotion of self-reliance in the country, and to the welfare of the suffering millions. I would also request you to dedicate yourself to *the cause of achievement of socialism in our country*, and to utilize all your knowledge, expertise and skills, for building up a better world for the common man of India (emphasis mine IIMC, 1987: 46–47).

6. At the fifth convocation (on 16 May 1970), Dr V.K.R.V. Rao, the then Union Minister of Education, appeared to be giving assurance of professional legitimacy to the passing management graduates of IIM, Calcutta by asserting that "there can be no doubt that management is a profession and like all professions involves both academic and practical training" (IIMC, 1987: 27).
7. Professor Sheth was the director of IIM, Ahmedabad for almost seven years, from 13 July 1984 to 3 May 1991 to be more precise. I thank Shri N.V. Pillai (of IIM, Ahmedabad) for this information.
8. See Haribabu, 2000, 2004; Mallick et al., 2005; Robinson, 1998; Robinson and Clarke, 2007.

9. For example, a colleague of mine at IIM, Calcutta felt that sociologists have largely disowned their brethren from the IIMs, including Professor N.R. Sheth. He recalls how at the XXIX All India Sociological Conference, Maharana Pratap University of Agriculture and Technology, Udaipur, (21–23 December 2003) Professor Sheth, who delivered the M.N. Srinivas Memorial Lecture, was introduced as an outsider to the general sociological.
10. I, for one, would like to believe that this hybridity is primarily substantive. The general context of a management institute calls for a distinctive orientation towards sociological issues/themes that would appeal to the constituency at hand. It is to be noted that there is open bidding for elective courses at IIMs. Hence, a conventional elective course on sociology of family, kinship and marriage may not attract any students.
11. All citations in this section have been taken from the respective websites of the IIMs. These websites are: www.iimahd.ernet.in (for IIM, Ahmedabad; established in 1962); www.iimcal.ac.in (for IIM, Calcutta; established in 1961); www.iiml.ac.in (for IIM, Lucknow; established in 1984), www.iimb.ernet.in (for IIM, Bangalore; established in 1972); www.iimk.ac.in (for IIM, Kozhikode; established in 1987); and www.iimidr.ac.in (for IIM Indore; established in 1987). The announcement for the seventh IIM of the country at Shillong has already been made. It is going to be made functional in the year 2008 (*Business Standard,* 2007).
12. Of course, these observations are based on my personal experiences as a student of M.A. in Sociology at JNU during 1993–95. Yet, we can extend them to the larger world of Indian sociology. At annual gatherings of Indian Sociological Society, we come across practitioners of sociology displaying marked respect to those whom they consider to be theoretically engaged.

References

Bottomore, T.B. 1974. *Sociology as Social Criticism.* New York: Pantheon Books.

Business Standard. 2007. "IIM Shillong to Begin Operations Next Year", 25 July.

DeMartini, Joseph R. 1983. "Sociologists Working in Applied Settings", *Sociological Perspectives,* 26 (3): 341–51.

Deshpande, Satish. 2001. "Disciplinary Predicaments: Sociology and Anthropology in Postcolonial India", *Inter-Asia Cultural Studies,* 2 (2): 1–14.

Freeman, Howard E. and Peter H. Rossi. 1984. "Furthering the Applied Side of Sociology", *American Sociological Review,* 49 (4): 571–80.

Gupta, Dipankar. 1995. "Practising Sociology", *Seminar*, December, pp. 43–47.

Haribabu, E. 2000. "Cognitive Empathy in Inter-disciplinary Research: The Contrasting Attitudes of Plant Breeders and Molecular Biologists towards Rice", *Journal of Biosciences*, 25 (4): 323–30.

—. 2004. "Interests and Meanings: The Socio-technical Process of Application of Biotechnology to Crop Improvement in India", *International Journal of Biotechnology*, 6 (1).

Indian Institute of Management, Calcutta. 1987. 'Management Education and India: Collection of Convocation Addresses 1966–1987' (A Silver Jubilee Publication). Kolkata: IIMC.

—. 2004. 'IIMC: Some Concerns about its Future' (a position paper prepared by Faculty Council, mimeographed). Kolkata: IIMC.

Lipset, Seymour M. 1982. "The Academic Mind at the Top: The Political Behaviour and the Values of Faculty Elite", *Public Opinion Quarterly*, 46: 143–68.

Machlup, Fritz. 1994. "Are the Social Sciences Really Inferior?" in Martin Michael and Lee C. McIntyre (eds.), *Readings in the Philosophy of Social Science*. Massachusetts: The MIT Press, pp. 5–19.

Mallick, Sambit, E. Haribabu and S.G. Kulkarni. 2005. "Debates on Science and Technology in India", *Social Scientist*, 33 (11–12): 49–75.

Meyer, Marshall W. 1999. "Notes from a Border Discipline: Has the Border Become the Center", *Current Sociology*, 28 (5): 507–10.

Mitra, Ashok. 2005. *Apila Chapila* (in Bengali). Kolkata: Ananda Publishers.

—. 2007. *A Prattle's Tale: Bengal, Marxism, Governance.* Kolkata: Samya.

Nisbet, Robert S. 1976. *Sociology as an Art Form.* London: Heinemann.

Petrus, Gene and Raymond J. Adamek. 1988. "Taking the Role of the Other: An Aid to Marketing Applied Sociology", *Teaching Sociology*, 16 (1): 25–33.

Planning Commission. 1957. Second Five Year Plan: Education and Social Services. Delhi: Planning Commission, Government of India.

Robbins, George W. 1959. Recommendations for an All-Indian Institute of Management. New Delhi: The Ford Foundation, mimeographed.

Robinson, Rowena and Sathianathan Clarke (eds.), 2007. *Religious Conversion in India: Modes, Motivations, and Meanings.* New Delhi: Oxford.

Robinson, Rowena. 1998: *Conversion, Continuity and Change: Lived Christianity in Southern Goa.* New Delhi: Sage.

Smith, J.H. 1960. "Sociology and Management Studies", *British Journal of Sociology*, 11 (2): 103–11.

—. 1998. "The Enduring Legacy of Elton Mayo", *Human Relations*, 51: 221–249.

Thakur, Manish. 2006. "Social Scientists or Development Professionals? Research-Policy Interface in a Rural Development Institute", *Review of Development and Change*, 11 (2): 179–200.

The Economic Times. 2007. "IIM-C Students Break Salary Barrier", 6 March.

The Financial Express. 2007. "Best Lateral Placements at IIM-C Likely", 6 February.

9

Nurturing Sociology among Nurses

The Case of West Bengal

RAMANUJ GANGULY

Nursing is one of those professions, which in some sense has the longest unbroken history, evolving from informal charitable work to a formal occupation in a formal organizational or institutional set-up. Nurses are also one of the single largest groups of health professionals in India. In 2004, there were 8,65,135 nurses in India, in comparison to 6,45,825 physicians and 5,92,577 pharmacists.[1] This paper is primarily based on my personal experience of teaching the undergraduate nursing students in a nursing college (located within a major private hospital) in Kolkata since August 2005.

For many teaching sociology in mainstream institutions, it may come as a surprise to learn that sociology has been for long an integral part of sociology in undergraduate nursing courses. For about thirty years in India sociology has got integrated in undergraduate nursing courses, at different levels. It is taught compulsorily along with psychology as part of behavioural sciences. There are two types of courses at undergraduate level in the institute/college where I teach as a guest faculty:

1. Four-Year B.Sc. Nursing Course (Generic) (Entry Level: Higher Secondary: *sociology is taught in the second year, one full paper of 100 marks).*

2. Two-Year Post-Basic B.Sc. Nursing Course (Condensed) (Entry Level: After General Nursing Midwifery Two-Year Course, mostly are in full-time job: *sociology is taught in the second year, one full paper of 100 marks*).

In this paper, which is divided into four parts, I would discuss the case of undergraduate nursing students, mentioned above, who study sociology as part of their curriculum. The first part deals with teaching sociology to students of nursing course at the undergraduate (UG) level. It introduces the context within which nursing courses are located, and also the expectations that the broader society has of it. The second part deals with the reasons that students come to these courses. The third part delves into the experience of curriculum transaction in sociology in nursing courses, that is, the perception and the attitude that the students have about sociology. The last part deals with the limitations and shortcomings that the sociology curriculum has within the nursing course and seeks to chalk out a roadmap for the future by exploring the probable avenues to overcome the limitations, and reformulate strategies.

I

Teaching Sociology to Students of Nursing Course at the Undergraduate Level

The West Bengal University of Health Sciences, Kolkata administers the nursing courses in West Bengal. At undergraduate (UG) level there are two courses offered:

- Post-Basic B.Sc. Nursing Course (condensed two-year course, for students who have already completed three-year General Nursing Midwifery Course, and are mostly working).
- B.Sc. Nursing Course (generic four-year course, for students who have qualified at Higher Secondary level and have also qualified in a State Level Joint Entrance Test).

In both the courses, a paper in sociology is offered with full 100 marks in the second year, with sixty hours of teaching, written examination at the end of the year of 75 marks that include both essay-type and objective-type questions, and 25 marks for internal evaluation through class tests and assessment reports of the students.

Around 70 per cent students in the Post-Basic B.Sc. Nursing Course (henceforth condensed course) belong to the age group 30–40 years, and age of 24 per cent students is more than that. More than 60 per cent of them have average monthly family income of Rs 20,000 and/or more. While 61 per cent of them come from nuclear family with an average family size of 3.73 members, the rest are hailed from Indian joint family with an average family size of 6.84 members. It was found that the students in condensed course mostly (96%) work in government-run hospitals/health centres, thus professionally 59.3 per cent of them are located in metropolitan areas, and 30.6 per cent in small towns or district towns. Professional location of these students was found to be more urban-centred in comparison to their place of origin, because only 39 per cent students come from urban areas, 43 per cent students from sub-urban/semi-urban areas, and the rest 18 per cent from semi-rural/rural areas. Surprisingly, it was found that the significant numbers of students (34.7%) are unmarried. Both students and faculty members in the institute are of the view that the profession of nursing had been in the past a great deterrent for marriage because of the work schedule (rotational duty shift), and the nature of job. Even today, in some communities, it continues to remain stigmatized and poorly evaluated in comparison to other professions for women in case of their marriage.

Entry in B.Sc. Nursing Generic Courses (henceforth, generic course) is through a joint entrance test to be held after completion of Class XII (Higher Secondary). Therefore, the average age of the students ranges between 18 and 22 years, with a one or two exceptions. About 68 per cent of the students were found to be from lower-middle class to middle class background with maximum average monthly family income not exceeding Rs 15,000. All the students are unmarried, and more than 86 per cent of them come from nuclear family with four family members on an average. It was found that the students of generic course are dispersed in terms of their place of residence, with 42 per cent coming from urban areas, 31 per cent from sub-urban areas, and 27 per cent from semi-rural or rural areas. The difference found in the socio-economic background of the generic students from the condensed students is because of the differential entry point/level and procedure in either course. The students of condensed course are mostly permanently placed occupationally, having already completed the General Nursing Midwifery Course, and undertake voluntarily to join the present course for career advancement taking academic leave from their job.

Many issues cropped up in the process of interacting and communicating with the (undergraduate) students. The students were found to be sure about their employability due to severe supply-demand mismatch, but ambivalent about their future role and position in society. The causes responsible for their uncertainty becomes clear as we look deeper into the nature of their concerns.

First, the wide-ranging growth and change taking place in India is acknowledged by the curriculum of nursing. An overt process of commercialization of the health sector is taking place. Medical services, unlike in past, is perceived to be a product to be received in lieu of a fee/charge. Further, with greater possibility of global mobility, a large number of nurses are getting placements in different countries in the Middle East, Europe and North America. Today, the nursing profession is no longer assessed in terms of its specialized task, but is considered as part of a broad spectrum of social relationships, with all the stakeholders – doctors and physicians, hospital managers, pharmaceutical MNCs, patient-consumers and their family members.

Sociology, as a discipline, may be still perceived by many to be of no direct relevance to nursing. Within the nursing sector, however, it is admitted that in contemporary society nursing profession has to use and benefit from a range of cognate disciplines. This will allow nursing profession to adapt to the changing circumstances of the society where the traditional unquestioning deference towards health care professionals is increasingly getting challenged.

Second, for students who are older, especially those pursing the Post-Basic B.Sc. Nursing Course, whose age are usually between 30–40 years, it is not easy to develop a 'sociological imagination'. Their set forms of thinking and professional experience lead to statements such as the following:

> "...how do you expect us to consider the sensitivities and particularities of the patients when we have to cater to 300 per cent more patients than the optimum capacity".

> "...if we are not rough and tough with the patients it is not possible to administer any treatment or care, as the patients come from very poor economic background with hardly any literacy/education. They therefore do not realize either the significance or the necessity of the treatment and care, and we have to make them realize. We see the role of the nurse in this situation is that of a trainer and facilitator rather than primarily a service provider".

> "...you do not know how rigid these rural people are in their conviction, therefore, you are suggesting such measures that are good to hear theoretically, but impossible to implement".

Third, a major apprehension that the nursing students have is regarding the field applicability of the knowledge imparted in their college. They fear the challenges of obsolescence and change taking place in health sector due to technological changes (especially in field of diagnostics and surgery) and market guided policy revisions (like marketing of preventive medical care policies, introduction of measures to reduce time for recuperation, rehabilitation and administration). They doubt the relevance of studying sociology and prefer to opt for advanced courses within the discipline of nursing.

While interacting with students of nursing, it was realized that all their concerns stem from a perceived agony about the viability and/or sustainability of their specialized skills and competences in the market. Further, they felt that the present structure and system does not allow for any upgradation of skills. In this context, when we see the course format, content, organization, and course delivery of sociology in UG courses, we find that they prepare the nursing students about the web of social relationship that exists in the field of health care, but is unable to tackle these practical problems.

The experience of teaching sociology to would-be-nurses and UG students in mainstream education studying sociology as an honours subject is completely different. For the former, sociology is an ancillary subject (as part of behavioural sciences, not integrated as a subject in its own right), thus not part of their main focus or priority, and they yet have to get through it for their nursing degree. The experience of a sociology teacher is starkly different as in a nursing college his/her role is subsidiary, hierarchically placed lower than other faculty members, whereas in a mainstream undergraduate college he/she is perceived as an equal/colleague. In the following section, we would examine further the stated purpose of studying sociology in the curriculum of nursing.

II

Purpose of Studying Sociology in Nursing Courses at the Undergraduate Level

Teaching sociology in the curriculum of nursing is focused more on social issues and problems than on theoretical issues. The course content and organization aims to prepare the nurses to the changing demands made on them by the society. Sociology is not delivered as a subject in its own right. Rather, it is integrated in terms of its functional utility. The stated course description given in the syllabus formulated by the West Bengal University of Health Sciences is that it "is designed to reorient students to sociology related to community and social institutions in India and its relationship with health, illness and nursing".

It is expected that a full paper on sociology would facilitate a broad-based sensitization and training of the nurses, orienting them to the development, functioning and changes in the society, as well in inculcating a human outlook towards the social world around them. The study materials of Behavioural Sciences (for Nursing Course) of School of Health Sciences of Indira Gandhi Open University (BNS-105, 2004: 3–10) give us a perspective about the accepted goal of teaching sociology to the nurses. I draw heavily from the same below:

> In health related professions, the large-scale involvement of the behavioural sciences has been relatively recent, but the trend has been particularly strong. That health has important social, cultural and psychological aspects, as well as physical ones, is no longer seriously debated... If man has to live happily and in peace or at all has to survive, we need to study and integrate all human sciences including behavioural sciences.
>
> ...sociology as applied to medicine owes its origin to the study of relationships between health phenomena and social factors in medical context. A sociological approach to the study of history of medicine gives a better understanding of the past in order to gain insight into the current trends and developments in the sphere of medical science and thus develops an integrated knowledge to relate the life processes to the existing social phenomena and health in a meaningful manner.
>
> ...Manifestation of health problems is the result of much more than the simple cause-effect relationship between organism and host, i.e. human body. Hence, health and diseases cannot be seen in isolation...
>
> ...knowledge of socio-economic complexities and socio-behavioural aspects of people's lives have significant contribution to make for the welfare and well being of people. Thus, it is important for the health professionals to understand the factors that contribute to health and disease, have understanding of socio-economic factors that

> contribute to accessibility of services. It is essential that the health practitioners including nurses have insights into these aspects of patient's lives... (BNS-105, 2004: 3–10)

The training of the students of nursing to engage with the social context is expected to equip them to perform better in their profession. Sociology can help them reflect upon their personal values, making them more tolerant and less judgemental in their action.

A senior nurse and faculty member of the institute provided a different take, as she tried to explain how sociology can help the nursing students:

> ...as migration is a common phenomenon among the nurses, they are expected to come to terms with multiple cultural settings at a very short period. Ethno-centric leanings of the patients in such new settings, as well as their own cultural background often clash and impede the process of adjustment. It is expected that sociology will prepare them to perform in multicultural settings.

We should do well to remember that in 1977, the member states of the World Health Organization (WHO) unanimously adopted the Global Strategy for Health for All (HFA) by the Year 2000 (Resolution WHA 30.43). Health care services were expected to reach the masses at their place of work as well as hearth by the year 2000. Promotion of health and hygiene, prevention of diseases, rehabilitation of people in general, and the underprivileged and marginalized in particular were targeted.

> The eight essential elements and the five principles of primary health care call for preparation of nurses to assume responsibility specially for the provision of first level care in community and thus act as a change agent in bringing about a good quality of life to the people at large. This calls for not only a reorientation of the training programmes but also requires a different approach to view their traditional roles in the context of primary health care by understanding the structural realities in our contemporary Indian society (BNS-105, 2004: 10).

Before proceeding to the next section to discuss the content of the sociology syllabus in nursing courses, it will be useful to step back and look into the opportunities available for the students to take up nursing courses at all-India level as well as in West Bengal:

Table 9.1
Details of Opportunities for Students of Nursing in India (as on 30 September 2006)

Type of Courses	*Total Number of Seats*	*Total Number of Institutes*
General Nursing Midwifery Course	56057	1446
B.Sc. Nursing Course	28119	719
Post-Basic B.Sc. Nursing Course	1703	71
M.Sc. Nursing Course	1282	87
Total	87161	2323

Source: Indian Nursing Council, New Delhi, www.indiannursingcouncil.co.in

Table 9.2
Details of Opportunities for Students of Nursing in West Bengal (as on 30 September 2006)

Type of Courses	*Total Number of Seats*	*Total Number of Institutes*
General Nursing Midwifery Course	1211	37
B.Sc. Nursing Course	220	6
Post-Basic B.Sc. Nursing Course	115	4
M.Sc. Nursing Course	40	2
Total	1586	49

Source: Indian Nursing Council, New Delhi, www.indiannursingcouncil.co.in

The above tables are self-explanatory in terms of types of courses available, quantum of students and number of institutes/colleges offering nursing courses. What is significant is the huge number of students entering each year at different entry level of nursing courses. About 11 per cent undergraduate students of nursing out of total 335 students in West Bengal study in the college where I teach based on whom this paper is drawn.

III

Curriculum Transaction in Sociology in Nursing Courses at the Undergraduate Level

Earlier, in this paper, we had stated that at the UG level there are two courses offered: Post-Basic B.Sc. Nursing Course (condensed two-year course) and B.Sc. Nursing Course (generic four-year course). The West

Bengal University of Health Sciences administers the nursing courses in the state. In the second year, in both the courses, a paper in sociology is offered with full marks of 100. This entails sixty hours of teaching, with written examination of 80 marks at the end of the year that includes essay-type and objective-type questions, and 20 marks for internal evaluation through class tests and assessment reports by students.

There are eight units in Post-Basic B.Sc. Nursing Course, which include: (a) Introduction to Sociology, (b) Individual, Community Socialization, (c) Culture, (d) Social Organization, Groups, Institutions, Rural-Urban Community, Ecology, (e) Social Processes, (f) Social Change: Nature, Factors and Theories, (g) Social Control, and (h) Various Social Problems. What is remarkable is that none of the units has been designed to address the concepts from the angle/orientation of health care. Only four units, namely, Introduction, Culture, Social Change, and Social Problems, included at the very end the phrase "role of the nurse".

Similarly, there are thirteen units in B.Sc. Nursing Course (Generic), which include: (a) Introduction to Sociology, (b) Individual and Society, (c) Culture, (d) Social Groups and Processes, (e) Population, (f) Family and Marriage, (g) Social Stratification, (h) Types of Communities in India, (i) Social Change, (j) Social Organization and Social System, (k) Social Control, and (l) Social Problems. Here also, we see the same practice of making an one line connection between sociology and nursing in eight units, namely, Introduction, Culture, Family and Marriage, Social Stratification, Types of Communities in India, Social Change, Social Control, and Social Problems.

It is clear from the above account that the concepts, conceptual formulations and theories taught within sociology are not integrated with the practices of nursing. Whatever little has been tried is not only grossly insufficient, but also reflects how little thought and application has gone into the preparation of the syllabus. The evaluation procedure also does not leave much scope for the students to explore the possibilities that studying sociology can offer. Not surprisingly, the students find it much easier to learn by rote from tailor-made sub-standard books than to involve themselves with the subject.

The interplay between the diseases (pathogenic agents), people (host who are infected) and health care services requires certain conditions, which can be termed as the physical and social environment.

The above phenomenon can be explained in terms of the following model that we can term as a 'health triad':

Figure 9.1

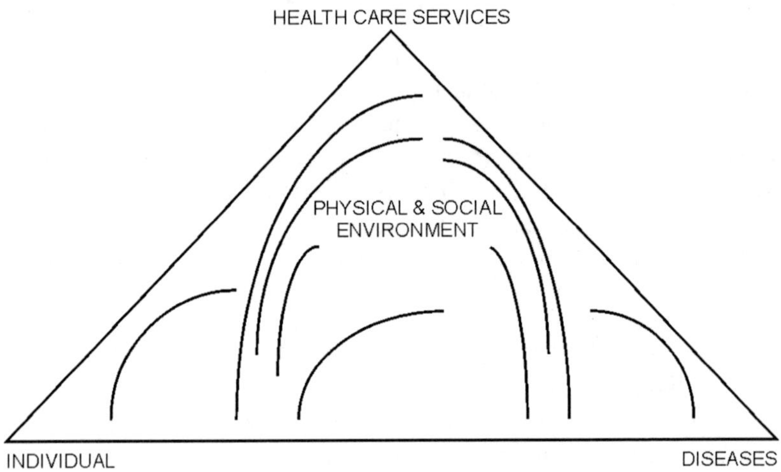

The cultural traits, socio-economic conditions, authority structure, education system and type of residence generally constitute the operational social condition that determines the physical and social environment of a society. Individual, diseases and health care services operate within a particular environment that increases or decreases the probability of and susceptibility to illness in a society. Cockerham (2003: 97–99), while explaining health behaviour and lifestyles, points out that Weber's concepts of "lifestyle, life conduct and life chances", as elaborated in the classic *Economy and Society,* are useful in understanding the intervening socio-economic conditions and positions of the individuals that determine their health lifestyles. Similarly, Pierre Bourdieu's (1984) work points out socio-economic, demographic, socio-psychological and structural variables that work as modifying factors as far as health behaviour and lifestyles are concerned. Bourdieu in his analysis of eating habits and sports preferences describes how a *habitus,* or class-based set of durable dispositions to act in particular ways, shaped particular facets of health lifestyles...The habitus operated to align individual aspirations and expectations with the objective probabilities for actually realizing them typical of people in the same social class. The above theoretical positions can be well explained in terms of the experience in India regarding tackling the disease of tuberculosis (TB).

TB is one of the biggest 'resident' diseases of India; yet solution to tackle it is yet to come despite concerted efforts from the state. The major factors are all located in the mediating sphere of physical and social environment. The relationship between the two was explained by the students of nursing in condensed course, as many have work experience, especially in rural areas:

- low awareness about the symptoms of the disease, mostly caused due to illiteracy and poverty;
- they wait till their conditions to deteriorate;
- explore the possibility of getting cured by local quacks, faith-healers etc.;
- proper diagnosis by a physician takes place very late;
- initial improvement due to medicine is taken to be cure, therefore often discontinuation or irregular administration takes place which aggravates the disease among the people;
- due to misconception about the infectiousness of the disease, social support to the individual dwindle, and often the patients are made to stay in places which are particularly unsuitable for them;
- economically poor background often does not allow patients to rest, the employer-landlord does not allow frequent visits to health centre;
- due to failure in policy and implementation of the government, health centres do not have adequate number of physicians, and adequate quantity of medicines and injection;
- the health service delivery in these places is almost impossible to provide properly because the health centres are very overcrowded, thus neither is it possible for the physicians to diagnose the patients, nor for patients to overcome their inhibitions and talk about their illness; and
- the private health sector is either absent from the scene or charge fees so high that most people are unable to take advantage of the facilities.

Attitude-aspiration-ability (A^3) dystrophy of people in India results in most of the failures in the health care sector. In the above context, we can very well say much that can and should have been included in the syllabus of sociology. For example, the following areas are of cardinal importance that can be looked into:

- Link between social status and health status
- Link between gender differences and physical and mental health
- Link between ethnicity and health
- Link between environment and health
- Link between social context and experience of illness
- Link between globalization and change in health care

We see below how the physical and social environment in which they operate, and lack of proper training in sociology, can adversely affect the nurses in their perception and job performance.

Limitations and Shortcomings

Nurses normally have very little knowledge of the socio-cultural and economic background of most of their future patients. This implies that the nurses who are expected to extensively communicate with the patients have limited or no background knowledge to work well. While studying about any disease/ailment, its symptoms, and cause-effect remedy, a student of nursing remains unaware of the influence of social factors and unhealthy lifestyle of the people that to a great extent is a determinant factor of that disease/ailment. Taking a common example, tuberculosis or gastroenteritis considered endemic in Indian society is treated clinically with chemicals symptomatically, not taking into account the

- living differentials of the communities,
- nature of poverty/deprivation endured,
- income distribution within the household that has gendered inequality, and
- evaluation of a persons quality of life in terms of consumed goods available in market.

Such a fatally flawed approach has allowed the disease to acquire a challenge of huge magnitude in our country. Similarly, we must take into account the fact that rapid urbanization and growth in tertiary/service sector in the last two decades in India have produced social, environmental and dietary changes among the people resulting in increase in cases of hypertension, heart ailments, respiratory problems, obesity and diabetes.

Often it is not realized that even health policy decisions have social implications that affect the nature of competence and sensitivity of health care professionals like the nurses. For example, most of the public and private hospitals are located in urban areas disproportionately catering to the needs of urban rich and middle class, therefore, the exposure of nurses to the rural population is limited and often prejudiced. The following table explicates this:

Table 9.3

Indian Health Sector Indicators

Indicators	*Value/Year*
Physicians (number)	6,45,825 (2004)
Physicians (density per 1,000 population)	0.60 (2004)
Nurses (number)	8,65,135 (2004)
Nurses (density per 1,000 population)	0.80 (2004)
Nurses (number in West Bengal)	23,702 (1999)
Midwives (number)	5,06,924 (2004)
Midwives (density per 1,000 population)	0.47 (2004)
Pharmacists (number)	5,92,577 (2003)
Pharmacists (density per 1,000 population)	0.56 (2003)
Community health workers (number)	50,393 (2004)
Community health workers (density per 1,000 population)	0.05 (2004)
Other health workers (number)	1,101,485 (2003)
Other health workers (density per 1,000 population)	1.03 (2003)
Number of beds in state-run hospitals	3,98,284 (1999)
Number of beds in other hospitals	2,83,359 (1999)

On the other side of the spectrum is the ever-increasing trend of using medical diagnosis to treat lifestyle diseases or of phenomenon that occur physiologically. We can take the example of children from urban households who often complain of lack of attention, that is frequently considered to be psychiatric disorder treated with pharmaceutical drugs. Similarly, a natural phenomenon like menopause catches the imagination of the urban society. Self-medication and word-of-mouth medical prescription is another tendency that is catching up in urban India, not to mention the sprawling field of traditional medicine like *Ayurveda*, *Unani* etc.

Nursing profession, under the circumstances, is not easy. A socially responsible nurse is supposed to have an abiding concern for the health of the patients they take care of, and the health of the community in which they live. Normally, it is seen that as an escape, the nurses adopt a ritualistic mode as a nursing-caring-strategy, which is largely discriminatory, intolerant and non-ethical. One of the students in condensed course stated:

> ...we know it is not possible to attend and provide care to all the patients, as their number is almost always double than the limit and number of staffs always less than allotted. In this scenario if we do not turn indifferent, and sometimes callous, we will simply not survive. Our behaviour can be termed sometimes as haughty and cold because in providing care and administering medicine we are forced to discriminate against common people to accommodate VIP referrals. Principled behaviour and ethics is perceived to be non-cooperation, or mischief, or foolishness...

The downside of the above is that while designing the sociology course it is not realized that the nurses have to be made aware and sensitive of "what it costs to the people needing health care and for what outcome". Sociology as practised among the students of nursing suggest that they continue to remain ignorant about the link between their specialized training and the society they serve as passive workers in the field of health care. Continued absence of awareness of how the practice of health care is cross-cut by the social milieu is making the pursuit of health unsustainable.

IV

A Roadmap for the Future

We now come to the concluding section, where instead of developing a new syllabus, I will try to offer a few broad suggestions to achieve the purpose of empowering the nurses through teaching sociology, which can be further broadened to include all the dimensions of teaching-learning and evaluation.

We can conclude with the following proposals that may help build a front line nursing cadre:

- Instead of a lecture-tutorial set-up, 'problem-based learning' can strengthen sociological imagination among the nursing students, as they will learn to explore and relate issues of real life to sociological concepts and theories. Under the guidance of a 'facilitator', and not a teacher/lecturer, the nursing students as self-directed groups can learn to visualize issues and problems they might encounter by combining individual insights with active and systematic group analysis. This will counter the label of sociology as 'non-mainstream' within the nursing curriculum and thereby initiate a student-centric, activity-based learning of sociology, which may not fare well in subject-knowledge tests but will enhance the social skills of the nurses in health care management.
- Instead of a core disciplinary knowledge, sociology within nursing curriculum should aim for a holistic approach, with engaged pedagogy enhancing critical capacities of the students, providing them with competencies to overcome their social positioning.
- A synergistic combination of didactic learning experiences and faculty supervision will make the practice of sociology within nursing curriculum purposive, activity oriented, and socially constructed, facilitating the integrity and functioning of the health care establishments and organizations. Focusing on value, merit and quality, the practice of sociology has to promote interactive self-learning so that they become confident, flexibly skilled and self-empowered.
- A simple suggestion would be to gather relevant inputs from the current nursing students and qualified nurses through participative process (interactive seminars, brainstorming sessions and workshops) prior to formulating the course, so as to include the concerns of economy, ecology and equity in health care management.
- It will be useful to go beyond the age-old mandated approach to teaching and introduce learning skills that are combined by creative projects, group collaborative activities and problem-solving exercises, extempore oral planning, on-spot decision taking etc.

While formulating the sociology course, we have be sensitive to the needs of the profession and the specific ways that sociological knowledge can be incorporated. Otherwise, sociology within the nursing curriculum will continue to maintain its 'non-mainstream' status. Apart from this we must also recognize the way our taken-for-granted reality impige upon everyday life. This will not happen for the students of nursing until the course design of sociology engages with their concerns and issues.

Note

1. The data is of World Health Organization (WHO) available on WHO Statistical Information System (WHOSIS), http://www.who.int/whosis/database/core/core_select_process.cfm?countries=all&indicators=healthpersonnel visited on 25 June 2007.

References

Behavioural Sciences, BNS-105, 2004. School of Health Sciences, New Delhi: Indira Gandhi Open University.

Bird, Chloe E. et al., 2000. *Handbook of Medical Sociology*, (5th ed.). New Jersey: Prentice Hall.

Cockerham, William C., 2003. *Medical Sociology*, (9th ed.). New Jersey: Pearson.

10

Integrating Sociology in a Law School Curriculum

Discontent, Dilemma, Direction

RUKMINI SEN

There is a strict division that is often made in the Indian academia between social sciences and law. This makes the task of justifying the relevance of sociology an onerous one in law schools. Based on my experience as a sociology teacher within a law school,[1] this paper seeks to provide some understanding of the cultural and academic life of a law school. The special focus is on the obstacles that a sociology teacher faces in a law school and the efforts made to overcome them by creating a 'niche' for the discipline within the legal discourse. As a participant observer, the task here has been to understand how law schools are a product of the global times, as well as examine the different economic and political institutions responsible for the changes in the legal academia. The paper is divided into three sections. In the first section, there is a discussion of the context within which law schools emerged in India, the vision statements of Kolkata law schools over the years, and the theoretical necessity of placing law in a larger social context. The second section discusses lifestyle and student aspiration in Kolkata law schools and its implications for the teaching of a discipline like sociology. The third section emphasizes the importance of law firms and the importance of sociology as an encyclopaedic discipline and its relevance in the legal curriculum. One draws upon the objectives and content of the courses taught in Kolkata law schools.

I

Need for Law Schools and the Vision of Interdisciplinarity

Law schools today are different from law faculty or law colleges that were in existence in India prior to Professor N.R. Madhava Menon's first attempts to establish a law school in Bangalore, which started in 1986. Menon was convinced that the manner in which public interest movements could be sustained in India was through the establishment of independent law schools. The effort to reform legal education in India however was a project that was evident in the Law Commissions' reports or even in the University Education Commission since independence. The 1956 Law Commission Report proposed a structural change in legal education. The Commission argued that students should be subjected to rigorous scientific, theoretical and doctrinal training in law. Criticism was directed towards the faculty as many law departments were being filled by practising lawyers. A change in pedagogy was also suggested along the lines of American law schools using lectures, case law and the Socratic method (Jayanth, 2005: 12).

Interestingly, the Ford Foundation had taken keen interest in Indian legal education since independence and considered India to be a potential ground for furthering higher efficient legal system. An American Professor von Mehren on comparative and international law, in his 1963 report on the state of India's legal institutions, had suggested that a rationale, legal system based on equality and individual liberty governed by fair rules and procedures could not survive in a resource-poor, caste-conscious society (ibid.: 150). Menon, acting as the pioneer of this changing legal academic dynamics, envisioned that faculty members in a law school need to give importance to the case method, implement a problem-based approach to the students, lay emphasis on clinical legal education, and make connections with larger issues concerning legal theory, public policy and social justice. He completed his proposal for revamping Indian legal education in 1982 suggesting a five-year law programme as rigorous as any engineering or medical school curriculum, both of which had a reputation in India for being highly demanding. The project was therefore to restore the lost academic rigour of law and also to make law lucrative for students to take as a career. The first two years in these five years had to be law subjects in combination with social science and humanities subjects. The third and the fourth years would be primarily law subjects and the final year a choice of elective subjects and also a strong clinical component. Thus, the importance of integrating social science subjects with the law subjects was a part of the vision of the law schools. This is what got reflected subsequently in the NUJS brochure (*NUJS Bulletin,* 2000: 2).

The NUJS brochure has consistently written a few words on how the university perceives the role of its students as legal practitioners in the larger society. This vision is based on an understanding of the requirement for the academic interface of law and society in the integrated five-year law curriculum.

Among the objects of the university as stipulated under The West Bengal National University of Juridical Sciences Act, 1999 (Act IX of 1999), the following are important:

- Advancement and dissemination of learning and the knowledge of law and legal processes.
- Studying the role of law and legal processes in national development.
- Developing a sense of responsibility in the student to serve society.
- Promoting interdisciplinary study of law in relation to management, technology and international co-operation.
- Endeavouring to make law and legal processes efficient instruments of social development.

Further, the 2000–01 *NUJS Bulletin* envisioned that:

> Legal education has to be re-christened as 'justice education' if it were to reflect its true mission in society. As medical education is intended to promote 'health' rather than merely to treat diseases, legal education should aim at promoting 'justice' rather than just resolving disputes and ordering relationships. Study of law at NUJS has been based on the assumption that all knowledge leads to the improvement of the quality of the lives of people in general and the underprivileged sections of the society in particular. To be able to analyse and interpret the law critically and to develop abilities to use law as an instrument for making social and economic policies, a law

> student has to cultivate multidisciplinary skills....The curriculum and teaching methods are geared to providing opportunities for learning law-in-society or law-in-development (*NUJS Bulletin*, 2000: 2).

The 2003–04 *NUJS Bulletin* continued with the same vision statement and at the same point of time added new dimensions to the perspective of legal education:

> Globalization and Legal Studies: Indian lawyers with competitive merit would be in great demand by the business community within the country and outside. Lawyering outside courts and litigation, would assume a lot of importance and lawyers would participate more significantly in socio-economic development under a liberal economic regime...NUJS is involved in producing the lawyers and judges of the future who are comfortable to work in a Knowledge Society in which 'law' is expected to assume the role of a mediator in socio-economic transformation, informed by the values of the Indian Constitution; and lawyers will act as social engineers beyond the role of just an agent in a dispute resolution and conflict avoidance would assume centre stage in the new dispensation (Menon, 2003).

Till 2003 it was Professor Madhava Menon who was the Vice-Chancellor of the University and the vision statement of the university definitely reflected the vision of the person who initiated this process of change in the legal academia. Between 2004 and 2007, the section 'From the Desk of the Vice-Chancellor' was written by Professor B.S. Chimni, a Professor of International Law at Jawaharlal Nehru University (JNU) prior to joining NUJS as the Vice-Chancellor.

> NUJS is committed to building a unique environment in which to learn about law and the relationship between law and society...We are encouraging critical thinking and knowledge so that the NUJS students go beyond learning the law by rote to develop a deeper understanding of the place and function of law in society...We seek to sensitize our students to issues of social justice, in particular to the concerns of the marginal and oppressed sections of our society (NUJS Admission Brochure, 2005).

In the report of the Vice Chancellor in 'The First Annual Convocation', 2005 Professor B.S. Chimni emphasized on creating

> [a] law school with a difference. We [in NUJS] do so while being firmly committed to the same objectives of the University. Its distinct

identity is being inter alia created through establishing a university culture that takes pride in promoting democratic practices, through specializing in certain areas of law, and by laying great emphasis on the values of truth and social justice (Chimni, 2005: 8).

Professor M.P. Singh became the Vice-Chancellor in NUJS in February 2007 and he addressed the new 2007 batch of students in their orientation:

> Law is progressively becoming an all-pervasive instrument of social organization and control... law is not a goal in itself but a means to achieve certain goals...If there can be other means, as good as law or better than law for achieving the goals which the law seeks to achieve, we do not fall back on the law all the time for achieving them. We should make as much use of those means as we make the law[2] (Singh, 2007).

The rise of law, sociology and technology would coincide on a similar time frame, which is linked to the rise of the bourgeoisie in western societies. The relation of Enlightenment to the development of sociology involved both a philosophical emphasis on reason, freedom and individualism and the secular concepts of society and social development as objective, collective forces (Swingewood, 1984: 10). Habermas traced the historical trajectory of the juridification process from the claims of individual rights against the sovereign, the democratization of the political order and the guarantee of freedoms and rights against the economic system. This process of juridification actually leads to a change from absolutist bourgeois state to a constitutional bourgeois state to a democratic constitutional state and finally a social welfare state (Deflem, 1996: 7). This perspective to understand the law-society interface provides a large and possibly a critical vision that a simple imperative of practical requirements of institutionally supporting public interest litigation would.

II

Lifestyle Aspirations of Law School Students: Implications for Teaching Sociology

Law schools in India are a product of global industrialization. With the popularity of transnational economic and political structures, the availability of jobs in multinational or national law and corporate firms has become a reality for law students passing out of law schools. It is a choice that students of law schools have to make between lucrative salaries in corporate firms or struggling for years in legal practice in the courts. For many, there is really no choice in the face of peer pressure. Getting a job at a prestigious law firm like Amarchand Mangaldas seems to be the driving force. In the midst of this pre-determined goal, the law schools aim at integrating social science and a critical subject like sociology in the legal curriculum. But this pre-determined goal of recruitment into a law or a corporate firm is a systematic process that is handled by the Campus Recruitment Committee, which has the following processes:

- Contacting firms and inviting them to participate in the recruitment process.
- Compiling a list of firms which have expressed interest in a campus recruitment.
- Vetting of CVs of the students.
- Creating a database of the preference list of the students.
- Organizing pre-placement talks with the firms.
- Dispatch of CVs to the firms a few days before the campus recruitment.
- Two days of campus recruitment.
- Firms are divided in slots so as to prevent job loss.
- Firms conduct interviews and declare the results at the end of their slot.[3]

In spite of getting the job at the most desired law firm, students quit these jobs within two years. Since turnovers are never a problem with the law firms, the quitting of jobs every year never poses a risk to the law firms about services. From the students' perspective the process of 'disillusionment' starts early. Many start leaving law firms after a year or a couple of years and return to higher studies or to litigation. Often exhausted and worn out by the tremendous work pressure they realize that money cannot give them the same prestige that a struggling independent lawyer could acquire after a few years in litigation, or a research scholar could attain through an academic institution. They, however, do not want to acknowledge that there is a process of alienation also. This is mainly because the pay package is such that it camouflages the alienation and the kind of 'exploitation' that these law firms impose on their expert employees. The workload is enormous.

Staying late in office becomes a routine and there are actual instances of encouragement of personal relations to be formed within the office. Not only are the employees expected to stay most of their waking hours of nearly all days of the week in the office, the corporate environments also encourage staying back in the office for the night to meet deadlines.

In this milieu, it was not always easy to explain the relevance of sociology. I attempt below to record the usual set of queries that aries and my responses.

Why should we study sociology in a law school?

In the first semester the course tries to analyse the social context of the law, thus debunking the insulated and neutral 'black letter' construction of law. In this course in sociology the intrinsic interrelatedness of law and society is highlighted. One of the major functions of law is maintenance of social order. Law is also perceived as an instrument of social engineering. This dual role of law in maintaining order and initiating change or responding to changes in society is analysed in this course. Simultaneously, the critical perspective in understanding the role of law in society is also addressed in different modules. Focusing primarily on the questions of order and change, consensus and conflict in different social institutions and processes, law is used as an example to show the connections between social and legal development.

As laid down in the objectives of the study material given to students, the major purposes of studying sociology in the first year of a law school curriculum are:

- To comprehend that law is a part of society and all aspects of society are in continuous engagement with the law.
- To understand the essential sociological concepts and their connection with law.
- To grasp the preliminary sociological theoretical positions and also study how classical sociologists had made this interface between society and law.

This course, besides giving an introduction to the discipline of sociology, was meant to be a basis for the development of preliminary sociological insights into future courses on 'Family Law' and 'Criminal Law' and some optional courses like 'Health Law' and 'Media Law'. The second semester course on 'Inequality, Law and Social Movements' includes Indian social stratification, movements or collective mobilization of different stratified groups to pressurize the state to make new laws or change existing laws, all with the aim of establishing equality and empowering the discriminated sections of the Indian society. It has to be admitted at the outset that this course has identified only four categories of the marginalized – class, women, caste and tribes. The objectives of this course as laid down in its study material are:

- To discuss the history of inequality, provide a brief overview of the changing trajectory of the movements of the different marginalized groups, and to outline how the state has responded in terms of laws.
- To discuss the different constitutional provisions, separate legislations, and international human rights documents targeting these marginalized groups and ensuring rights to each of these categories.
- To facilitate the students to make connections between what they study in this module and what they will later study in Constitutional Law I, Labour Law, Gender and Law or International Human Rights Law.
- To discuss what syllabus should be framed that would attract law students.

Sociology is easy to study, because it is like commonsense

A general statement made by many in a law school is that sociology has been critiqued to be a 'trespasser' and most of the disciplines feel threatened by sociology since it has the ability to give an overview from the social perspective to the other disciplines. The other criticism that sociology has faced is that it acts as a 'scavenger', i.e., sociology discusses as its content all the residues that the other social science disciplines do not discuss. This critique goes on to further suggest that sociology lacks any unique scope and subject matter because of its tendency to 'interfere' in many subjects. As a response to these criticisms, sociologists like Tom Bottomore emphasize on the 'encyclopedic' effect of sociology. The problem arises when students choose project topics and come up with different innovative ideas and say that since 'this' has an effect in society therefore it is a part of the sociology project. What they fail to incorporate is the theoretical dimension of the contemporary topic that they have chosen.

Where are the solutions to all the problems that sociology discusses?

A constant concern that students raise is that sociology makes a critique of many things in society, but does not always give solutions. Since law as a discipline has been primarily read from a positivistic method, therefore, the debunking method of sociology as a discipline comes across as alien in an environment of functionalists.

Optional courses that sociology teachers offer are 'softer'

The optional courses that sociology teachers offer in NUJS are Gender and Law, International Human Rights Law, Disability and Law, and Law, Culture and Pluralism. There is a market value of International Human Rights Law and therefore the course has become popular over the last few years. The other courses are neither 'marketable' nor 'hard' unlike 'masculine' law courses like International Trade Law or Petroleum Law or Biotechnology Law. Therefore, these 'soft' courses are not popular among most students. The set of students who would continue in academics or have a larger social responsibility agenda before them will be the students taking these courses. While, these courses are seen as 'soft', it is also regarded as very theoretical and 'heavy'. This again points to the lack of exposure to reading interdisciplinary materials consistently in all courses.

Hierarchy among the social science disciplines

There exists a hierarchy among the social science disciplines in law schools. The hierarchy that had been predominant in the disciplines of social sciences before this interface between social science and law, where economics was more dominant as a discipline than the other social sciences, seem to continue in law schools also. Here, a course in 'Law and Economics' adds value to the CV of a student, even if the course is theoretical as well as empirical, primarily because the knowledge of economics is desirable in many of the law courses like 'Corporate Law' or 'Banking Law' or 'Trade Law'.

Lack of available academic Indian socio-legal literature makes it very difficult to teach Masters' level Law-Social Science Interface Courses

There is very little literature on the interface between sociology and law in India. It is really unfortunate that eminent Indian sociologists have never really written much on the sociology of law in India, even though the Indian legal system has such an interesting sociological dimension as a product of colonial ideas, along with a liberal democratic legal structure being imposed on a culture which is by nature inegalitarian and stratified. What we do have today is some amount of journalistic writings on sociology of law, but a lack of both theoretical formulations and case studies. There is a dearth of autobiographies and biographies of judges and lawyers in India. Writing personal narratives among the people of this profession is not common in India and that has also left them outside the ambit of the discussion of common mass. Law as a discipline or a practice does not seem to have caught the attention of the social science academia in India and that has been one of the reasons why this disjunction between the two disciplines continues even today.

Identity crisis of a sociology teacher

This is an identity crisis one faces in a law school. Teaching in a law school has forced me to know the fundamentals of different kinds of laws that can be used for purposes of teaching sociology of law to first year students. To the community outside, therefore, who have very little knowledge of the law, I appear to be somebody who knows the law. At the law school, however, since I am a sociologist I am considered as incompetent to comment on Law, which is a technical discipline. Thus, to the community outside, I am a 'pseudo-lawyer' and to the community inside the law school I am a 'social scientist in a law school'.

III

Sociology and Its Significance in Legal Education

Different disciplines at different points of time have experienced more acceptability and marketability. If, in India, the 1960s and 70s gave emphasis to science and engineering, late 80s and 90s saw management personnel dominating the economy, and the mushrooming of business and management schools. Law schools are a growing phenomenon since the mid-1990s and law as a discipline now has a tremendous market potential in the contemporary global scenario. Law schools endeavour to give a five-year 'integrated' law course to its students. It is not that only a sociological perspective to the study of law is required. In fact a holistic social science perspective is what is necessary. Sociology has been a part of the engineering curriculum for a very long time, where the sociology of science and technology has been the focus. Similarly, management courses have also taught sociology, where specifically industrial sociology and labour relations has been the subject of discussion. Sociological knowledge is also required in Human Resource Management, in courses related to hospitality management, fashion designing courses, and media studies. Sociology as a subject has been popular among civil service examinees, possibly because of its encyclopedic nature. Traditional law universities taught sociology, but did not integrate it to the legal curriculum. Sociology was and still is a 100 marks paper in traditional law departments. Different social institutions and social problems comprise the subject matter of sociology. However, making connections between the legal system in India and abroad and the sociological issues remains a far cry. Moreover, on many occasions, a political science or a history teacher could be teaching sociology, indicating that one does not need a specialization in sociology primarily because it is 'commonsensical'. There are certain similarities and differences between law and sociology that need to be kept in mind. Law, as a professional practice, is concerned with the elaboration of the practical art of governing through rules. Its concern is prescriptive and technical.

Are we teaching sociology of law or sociology to law students? I think we are doing the latter, although the syllabus is designed in such a way that it seems to be couched in the theoretical orientation of the sociology of law. No established sub-discipline of sociology of law as emerged in India till now. Sociology of law must aim to interpret complexity, rather than replicate it or hide within it. It must seek to reveal the broadest significance of the social details it studies, to build bridges between the legal experience of individuals and of different social groups, to construct perspectives and connect disparate specialized or localized knowledge (Cotterral, 1992: 311). Cardozo's definition of law has the following four characteristics: (a) normative element, (b) regularity element, (c) courts, and (d) enforcement (Deva, 2005: 2). Sociologists consider law to be one of the several social codes. The primary function of social codes is to sustain the social order by upholding the basic values and norms of the society. Besides law, social codes include religious codes, institutions, customs and rules of etiquette and manners. Law is the structured and crystallized form of norms and values. Its study can provide a clue to the social values that are actually enforced but remain hidden from the public eye. However, it cannot be taken for granted that there is always a real consensus on the basic values underlying the legal system among all sections of the society. Though the legal system that prevails is binding on everyone, ingenious ways are found to circumvent it. The study of all such processes and mechanisms falls in the domain of sociology of law (Cotterrell, 1992: 3). However, since it is still a growing branch, its contours cannot be sharply demarcated. Through the study of prescriptions and prohibitions concretized in law, sociology is enriched by gaining insight into the operative values and attitudes. The analysis of the function of law adds to the understanding of the processes of social control. Considerations of policy cannot be excluded from the analysis since legal doctrine is continuously being shaped in the practice of courts and other agencies of interpretation by reference to assumed social purposes of law. A lawyer's analysis of law is often grounded in an array of philosophical assumptions – about the nature of responsibility, obligation, causation, and the autonomy of the individual – which often remain unexamined. Law as a scholarly professional practice is concerned with elaboration of the practical art of government through rules. Its concern is prescriptive and technical. Sociology is concerned with the scientific study of social phenomena; its concern is explanatory and descriptive. The lawyer is often a person entrusted with part of the apparatus of regulation of social relations, where the sociologist remains a relatively uncommitted observer. Law is a practical craft of systematic control of social relations and institutions; sociology is the scientific enterprise that seeks systematic knowledge of them (ibid.: 5). A sociological perspective of law does not require that law should somehow be subsumed as part of academic sociology's territory but that it should be viewed with a 'sociological imagination'. Such an imagination constantly seeks to interpret detailed knowledge of law in a wider social context, looks for relations between legal development and wider social changes, tries to understand law as interacting in complex ways with the social environment it purports to regulate and tries always to approach these matters systematically with a constant sensitivity to the need for specific empirical data and rigorous theoretical explanation (ibid.: 6).

It is increasingly becoming evident that the judiciary intervenes in nearly every aspect of an individual's and institution's existence. From confessing on parental abuse to taking decisions on which television channel will telecast cricket matches, to passing judgments on executive partiality and therefore shifting sensitive cases from one state to another, the judiciary is omnipresent. It is important therefore for law students to understand why laws are being passed at particular historical junctures and what role society plays in these laws. Since law is not made in a social vacuum but rather made in keeping with the larger social norms and imperatives of capital, sometimes to reinforce them and sometimes to change them, the knowledge of sociology is necessary for law students to appreciate the social imperatives of law making.

The extant sociological perspective helps understand macro-situations as well as micro-contexts. Thus sociology helps understand both the larger changes in legal education as a necessary must for globalization as well as the functioning of the courtroom from a micro-interactionist perspective. Any study would indicate that there exists a power dynamics in the designing of the courtroom. The actors involved in courtroom, the power dynamics from the dress of judges and lawyers, to the language used, to the architectural designing of courts. The study of sociology is also important because laws are not only the results of benevolence of the state and the judiciary, but many of them infact are a result of social movements.

Sociological knowledge can complement legal knowledge in the area of language. Law as a discipline is about technical specifications. This is because, there is a crucial requirement of application in the law and if the wordings are not clearly presented, it might create problems in implementation. The aim of legal language is exclusionist and limiting. On the other hand, sociology is a more philosophical and theoretical discipline, whose language is more encompassing. In conclusion, it can be said that sociological knowledge therefore enables law students to debunk the social reality given to 'defamiliarize the familiar'. Analytical and critical abilities are sharpened in law students with the knowledge of sociology, which is very necessary primarily because law is still understood in a positivistic manner. The knowledge of sociology challenges the methodological myth that law is about a division between a technical legal expert and lay person. A lawyer cannot consider the victim s/he is defending to be a mere 'thing', rather it is important to understand how s/he makes sense of the world. The basis of law is dialogic, but it is the knowledge of sociology which will enable this dialogue to happen as a critical engagement rather than a top-down discourse. Since law is about interpretation and primarily making qualitative interpretation of evidence, it is interesting to challenge the positivistic method of interrogation in a legal process. The entire objectivity of the legal system is based on the testimony of a set of actors, and the task of the lawyers is to interpret these testimonials. This means that a *verstehen* approach will best be able to make complete interpretation of evidences. The wide array of research methods that sociology has is helpful in legal research also because it is sociological methods that teach us to make qualitative assessments of evidence. Moreover a sociological knowledge would generate a sense of sensitivity and empathy in the lawyer to hear diverse 'voices' – it is important to give an empathetic hearing to the voice of the victim, in order for justice to be delivered.

There has been an effort to move from discontents to getting an insight from the experiences at NUJS. There had been an interesting exercise done by Vice-Chancellor Professor B.S. Chimni for the entire faculty in NUJS. Two committees were set up to review the curriculum of all subjects in the university and both these committees had a sociology teacher as a part of its members. The task of the committees was to suggest upgradation of the syllabus, suggest changes in the curriculum, introduce a law-social science interface in all subjects, and introduce human rights perspectives. The following are some of the observations from the experience of being a member of the Curriculum Review Committee. There were three sets of observations or attitudes that were noticeable among the members of the law faculty towards the suggestions given by sociology teachers on modifying the existing content in law subjects.

Rejectionist Approach

- Resistance to incorporate sociological readings mainly on the grounds that there was lack of time – most study materials lacked any social science readings, even where obvious sociological readings were available, like in Family Law, Labour Law, Information Technology Law, Media Law.

- When suggestions were made on the nature of interface that could be done, many responses argued that although these interfaces were done as a part of classroom discussions, they were never a part of the syllabus structure or the study material.
- Some responses received contended that 'softer' disciplines like sociology should ideally not get incorporated in disciplines like Banking Law, Petroleum and Mining Law, and Forensic Sciences, which are considered to be 'hard' subjects.

Accommodative Approach

- It is important to incorporate sociological perspectives in law courses, because law is not only a part of society but also affects society. However, there is very little perception beyond this elementary understanding about the need for social sciences.
- Even when an interface is accommodated, this is encouraged to be done in the first years, rather than in the later years when they start learning only the law subjects. So, the interface is encouraged in sociology classes, but not so much in the law classes. Sociology teachers, who discuss cases in sociology classes, lay emphasis on the interface. In a way, in spite of the accommodation, the onus is on the sociology teachers.

Interactionist/Integrationist Temperament

- Some law teachers actually made the efforts to bridge the divide and asked social science teachers to take a couple of preliminary classes on the interface between the specialized law subject and its connection with the social science.
- This interface was also encouraged in sociology classes where law teachers were asked to deliver a lecture in a sociology class. For instance, in a module on Class, Social Movements and Law, a teacher specialized in Labour Law will be best equipped be able to discuss the changing nature of the Supreme Court decisions on labour standards in a changing social and economic scenario.

The academic change was really noticeable the moment the interface happens between the social science subjects and legal studies. It was recommended to do this interface consistently in all the batches and in all the subjects, so as to help build a generation of lawyers who were more dialogic in their temperament and more critical in their perspective.

Sociology must study society to analyse 'the sum total of resources for all possible action', which are available to actors as the inventory of ends and the pool of means. According to Giddens,

> The practical impact of social sciences is both profound and inescapable. Modern societies, together with organizations that compose and straddle them, are like learning machines, imbibing information in order to regularize their mastery of themselves. Only societies reflexively capable of modifying their institutions in the face of accelerated social change will be able to confront the future with any confidence. Sociology is the prime medium of such reflexivity (cited in Bilton, 1996: 651).

It is this contribution to reflexivity and the generation of a critical temperament in the legal culture that needs to he recognized and forwarded for the creation of more interdisciplinary knowledge in Indian academia. In an environment where boundaries between disciplines are being broken, transdisciplinarity is here to stay and academics need to address this requirement. The law schools are a good place to experience and experiment with this transdisciplinarity and creating a new niche for sociology.

Notes

1. Some comments that I have regularly heard as a sociology teacher in the law school in Kolkata for five years are instructive:

   Why should one study sociology in a law school?

   What purpose does sociology serve in a law school?

   Sociology is interesting, it discusses the commonsense.

   Studying sociology did help in the knowledge of criminal law and constitutional law.

   An optional course which sociology faculty offers is very theoretical.

   Bringing social science teachers to classes in other law courses gives a broader perspective.

   Sociology generates a sense of social responsibility in students.

2. M.P. Singh, Vice Chancellor's Welcome Message to the Newcomers, http://www.nujs.edu/result/vc speech, last visited at 29th July, 2007.
3. Campus Recruitment (2007).

References

Bix, Brian. 2006. *Philosophy of Law: Critical Concepts in Philosophy*. London: Routledge.

Bilton, T. et al. 2002. *Introductory Sociology*. 4th edition. Hampshire: Palgrave.

Brest, Paul. 1995. "The Responsibility of Law Schools: Educating Lawyers as Counselors and Problem Solvers", *Law and Contemporary Problems*, Vol. 58, Nos. 3/4, pp. 5–17.

Chimni, B.S. 2005. "From the Vice Chancellor's Desk" in *National University of Juridical Science Bulletin*.

Cotterrell, Roger. 1992. *The Sociology of Law: An Introduction*. London: Butterworths.

—. 1989. *The Politics of Jurisprudence: A Critical Introduction to Legal Philosophy*. London: Butterworths.

Chaudhuri, Maitrayee (ed.) 2003. *The Practice of Sociology*. New Delhi: Orient Longman.

Deflem, Mathieu. 1996. *Habermas, Modernity and Law*. London: Sage Publications.

Deva, Indra (ed.) 2005. *Sociology of Law*. New Delhi: Oxford University Press.

Freire, Paulo. 1972. *Pedagogy of the Oppressed*. London: Sheed and Ward Ltd.

Frisby, David and Mike Featherstone. 1999. *Simmel on Culture: Selected Writings*. London: Sage Publications.

Jayanth, Krishnan. 2005. "Professor Kingsfield goes to Delhi: American Academics, the Ford Foundation and the Development of Legal Education in India", in *Legal Studies Paper Series*, Working Paper No. 3, William Mitchell College of Law, Minnesota.

Mehren, Arthur Taylor von. 1965. "Law and Legal Education in India: Some Observations", *Harvard Law Review*, Vol. 78, No. 6, pp. 1180–89.

Menon, N.R. Madhava. 2003. *From the Vice Chancellor's Desk*, in *National University of Juridical Science Bulletin* .

Menon, Nivedita. 2004. *Recovering Subversion: Feminist Politics Beyond the Law*. New Delhi: Permanent Black.

National University of Juridical Science, Bulletin and Brochures published between 2001 and 2006.

National University of Juridical Science, Campus Recruitment Brochure, 2007.

Singh, M.P. 2007. Vice Chancellor's Welcome Message to the Newcomers, http://www.nujs.edu/result/vc speech, last visited at 29th July.

Srinivas, M.N. 2002. "The Observer and the Observed in the Study of Cultures", in *Collected Essays.* Oxford University Press, New Delhi.

Swingewood, Alan. 2000. *A Short History of Sociological Thought* (3rd ed.). London: Macmillan Press.

11

The Challenges in Teaching Sociology at IIT

Are "Karl" and "Max" Relevant?

KUSHAL DEB

This paper is essentially a narration of my experience of teaching Sociology at the Indian Institute of Technology, Bombay (henceforth IIT-B) for the past seven and half years. But, before I begin, I must trace out briefly the trajectory of my teaching career. This is because I have seen both the worlds. I have taught in a fairly reputed mainstream sociology department in a state university and currently I am teaching at an elite technology institute where disciplines like Sociology are at the periphery.

After completion of my PhD, for ten years, I had taught at the postgraduate level at the Pune University. It was a very enriching experience and an equally frustrating one. In the initial years, in the midst of a beautiful campus, a reasonably good department, I managed to transform myself from a shy, tongue tied, inarticulate person with a thin voice into a reasonably good teacher. Two things helped in the transformation process: (a) my passion for Sociology, and (b) my love for my students. Sociology had transformed my life. For someone who had in a disinterested fashion pursued a Bachelor's degree in Science, spending more time in college canteens and for college politics, rather than in the classrooms and labs, the shift to Sociology at the Master's level had been an eye-opener. I had instantly taken to Sociology because it seemed to possess a strong subversive potential. Its strength seemed to lie in its ability to unravel the relations of power and domination implicit in everyday life, and in social processes and institutions. The insights one got into the nuances of human relations, and working of various social/political/economic institutions was for me enlightening and gave me a certain sense of emancipation. And, to gain that critical knowledge, I was and still am willing to traverse all disciplinary boundaries especially those classified under either the Humanities or the Social Sciences.

Second was my love for my students whom I have always looked at with great hope as on them rests the future of my country and of this world. My aim has always been to inculcate in my students a critical sensibility towards social issues and develop in them the sociological imagination, i.e., the ability to look at a social issue not in its isolation but learning to situate it in the larger social, economic, political and historical context in which it is embedded. Over the years I have also realized that unless one goes to the class with a positive attitude towards the students, the very task of motivating oneself into taking a lecture becomes extremely difficult. It is also probably for this reason that I would rate myself successful as a teacher but not so as a researcher. Although I am fully aware that teaching and research complement one another and one cannot be successful in one sphere without being successful in the other, over the years I have also realized that it is extremely difficult to maintain the balance. Many a time I have tried to convince myself that I would devote less time preparing for class lectures and spend time instead in my research work but I have failed. This is because there is an instantaneous evaluation which happens in every class and lack of preparation immediately gets reflected in bored visages or disappointment in the eyes of the enthusiastic ones and this is something which is very difficult to swallow for any conscientious teacher.

I

My Tryst at a State University

So, for a large part of my teaching career at Pune University, I spent totally immersed in teaching, interacting with students, and looking into not only their academic problems but sometimes even their personal ones. My life centred round my department, helping colleagues organize conferences and seminars and assisting successive heads in administration. My attachment to my department was so deep that a handful of students and I literally created a beautiful garden in front of the Social Sciences Block from a site full of rubble. We were like a family – the young faculty, the students and the administrative staff. Such was my attachment that I even picked up quarrels with colleagues with whom I otherwise had excellent equations because I felt that their personal, petty politics went against the larger interests of the department.

But, over the years, I learnt some bitter truths. I realized that academic bodies in state universities, which were essentially elected bodies, were run like personal fiefdoms and operated in terms of lobby politics. Attempts at changing the M.A. syllabus, which was 15 years old, nearly cost me my job. One or two colleagues who were reluctant to read up material on newly emerging areas initially used the bogey of Marathi medium students to thwart any attempts at syllabus change. The problem of Marathi medium students was genuine as the medium of instruction was English and books in Marathi were very few. But these teachers had never really bothered to look into the needs of these students by taking classes separately in Marathi. Unlike them, another colleague who along with me was pushing for change in syllabus used to also teach them whole course in Marathi on weekends. The colleagues who did not want a change in the syllabus lobbied with the Board of Studies (henceforth BOS). The BOS, which ratifies changes in syllabi, is an elected body and usually has members from affiliated colleges and hardly any member from the postgraduate centre (except for the Head of Department). The BOS initially asked us to cut down the reading list to a few books and when this was complied with, they wanted us to mention the relevant page numbers from these books. We even did that being desperate to get our syllabus revised. But, the whole process got us in conflict with the Dean of Social Sciences, who was a college principal with no idea about Sociology. His ego got involved and to punish me and my colleague who were pressing for change in syllabus, he got a separate statutory body called the Recognition Committee to derecognize both of us from being M.Phil and PhD supervisors and all the students who had completed or were in the process of completing their M.Phil under my supervision had to re-submit their dissertations as "independent research". The

Vice-Chancellor intervened to grant us back our supervisory rights but only after the whole issue spun out of control and we became pawns in bigger lobby fights. I also had an enquiry committee instituted by the University Executive Council because of alleged defamation of the university in an article written by me in *Sociological Bulletin* (Deb, 1998) on the travails of those teachers who want to do serious academic work in state universities.[1]

Before leaving the university, I also learnt another painful truth that notwithstanding the time and energy that one has given for one's department, it all adds up to nothing unless one is a big name in academic circles. I was told that "institutions can be built by only those who are 'institutions' themselves". I was too young and too small a person to be an institution builder but I realized that the advent of globalization had brought into focus a new breed of scholars whom I mockingly call 'corporate scholars' and who specialize essentially in 'networking'. So someone could aspire to be a big name in academics without essentially being a great scholar thanks to that person's capabilities in networking. The ideas one carried of inspiring students in class and doing at least one good academic work in one's lifetime were I realized old fashioned and passé.

As life became miserable at the university, I moved to IIT-B, with a world-wide reputation. I knew what I was getting into. I was aware that I would be mostly teaching B.Tech students and would therefore be denied the pleasure of debating and problematizing key sociological concepts with postgraduate students of one's own discipline except when I was teaching PhD students, whose number would be small. More importantly, I would also be robbed of the pleasure one got just from the thought that some of these postgraduate students would go ahead and take up sociology as their profession. But I was also aware that the Humanities and Social Science (henceforth HSS) Department at IIT-B was probably the most involved in B.Tech teaching compared to the rest of the IITs as it offered both core subjects and electives for the B.Tech students.[2] It also had an M.Phil programme in Planning and Development and one could in addition take PhD students from one's own discipline. Furthermore, I was aware that IITs provide excellent infrastructural facilities, academic freedom and various other incentives for both teaching and research like initial seed grant for research and funding for attending conferences abroad.

II

The Challenge of Teaching Sociology in an Overwhelming Technological Ambience

Within a few months of joining IIT-B I realized that the scenario and challenges were very different from my previous experience of teaching Sociology at the university. The first thing that struck me was that I would have to make a choice as far as my academic interests and priorities were concerned. This is because in the midst of an overwhelming technological ambience, my disciplinary and research interests seemed out of place. Quite a few of my HSS colleagues seemed to have given up pursuing core disciplinary areas and had shifted to applied specializations. Secondly, tying up with engineering faculty in research projects, running continuing education programme (CEP) courses, doing consultancies, getting massive funds, seemed to be the sure shot way of gaining recognition within the IIT systems.

I was also aware that although I would be teaching and supervising M.Phil and PhD students within the HSS department, the main challenge would be in teaching the core course in Sociology to second-year B.Tech students, a class of 140 students. These would be a big bunch of apparently very bright students, who would not be pursuing my subject in later years and who probably would be disinterested in whatever I had to offer. But teaching Sociology was my passion, and I also had tremendous confidence in the potential of my subject.

But it was a daunting task, keeping 140 students interested in one's lectures and it was important to know the expectations of the institution and, if possible, of the students. The HSS department website summarized in a way the role that the various disciplines were supposed to play:

> The Department of Humanities and Social Sciences plays a unique and distinctive role in an institute where the ethos of science and technology prevails. It is believed that engineering and science are, by their very nature, humanistic and socially derived enterprises. Hence, a complete science and technology education must include liberal arts, economics, social and behavioural sciences where the students unites application of scientific principles along with human, moral and social understanding. The undergraduate courses taught by the department faculty aim at making the science and technology students aware of the various issues concerning man and society.

They are meant to sensitize students to the broader social, cultural, economic, ethical and humane issues involved in social change.

After teaching the core course over a semester I also got some idea of the students' expectations. In the course evaluation forms many of the students had commented that they would like to have more discussions on current issues and wondered why they were being taught thinkers, like Marx, Weber and Durkheim, who had written in the 19th century. Secondly, some of them wanted more open-ended questions rather than being asked to answer questions on the handouts given in class. I also got some idea from a rather insensitive article which appeared in the students' newsletter[3] *Insight,* titled "Making Humans out of Technocrats?" Excerpts from the flippantly written article read as follows:

> HSS lectures are considered 'lukka,[4] lectures where one can sit back and laugh gleefully at the (apparent) simplicity of things, or scorn at an (occasional) metaphysical comment. A few restless souls will chuck planes, scribble on desks, or initiate classroom conversations in the hope of intellectual stimulation. Of the 'large' number of 'presentees' (on paper, of course) there are a few who fervently take notes in the hope of AAs and ABs and fewer still who attend lectures out of interest for the course. Are HSS courses about proxies, cramming from xerox notes and mindlessly writing foretold answers? Are they really being instrumental in achieving the all-round development of students, they are set to achieve?

I felt both hurt and angry after reading the article as it in no way reflected the situation in my class and nor in the classes of at least some of my colleagues. I called both the editor and the author and pointed out the insensitive tenor of the article. I told them that one did not mind criticism but it had to be constructive, especially when an article claims to be based on a survey but had no data to show that it reflected all shades of opinion among students. I asked them if they would have dared to write so casually about any engineering department. They apologized and accepted that they had been insensitive and requested me to write a rejoinder for the next issue. I did write a detailed rejoinder in which I tried to answer some of the issues raised in the article such as the accusation about encouragement of rote learning, grades not reflecting class interaction, commonsensical nature of disciplinary knowledge, etc. Interestingly, the article was supposed to be based on a general survey that was to be conducted among all the B.Tech students in IIT-B regarding various courses being run in their respective engineering departments and the relevance, efficacy of such courses. But, ironically the survey started and ended with an evaluation of HSS courses and neither the editors of the newsletter nor their scribes dared to take on the engineering departments.

Now, let me deal with some of the accusations made about HSS courses in that article. First is the point about rote learning and cramming from photocopied handouts given in class. There are various dimensions involved here and the accusation is not as straightforward as it looks. The students had a point when they pointed to the issue of cramming from photocopied handouts for examinations. Questions in examinations should definitely not test only their memorizing capacity but should also be able to test their analytical skills and social sensitivity. But, the issue involved here was also of differing methods of evaluation used in the engineering and science departments compared to the ones used by the HSS faculty. In the engineering and science departments certain concepts are explained in the class and then problems are given in examinations which require application of those concepts. But, in Sociology, for instance, you need to first understand Marx's concept of dialectical materialism or Durkheim's typology of mechanical and organic solidarity or various theories of nationalism before you can use these conceptualizations to understand issues concerning the present-day society. So questions in examinations for a Sociology core paper can be for example as follows: Explain Marx's materialist conception of history? Does it help you understand the present-day consumerism? Or explain Durkheim typology on suicides? Can you use this typology to understand the rising suicides among farmers in Vidharbha?

But many of the students unlike what they would do for their engineering papers would not like to study Marx or Durkheim but would like to write only about rising consumerism or about farmers' suicides in Vidharbha. They love to answer open-ended questions like (a) Why is female infanticide on the rise in urban areas? (b) Are big dams harmful for the environment? (c) Should IIT graduates settle abroad? or (d) Why is there increasing consumerism in urban India? These, usually English-medium educated students, have a good general awareness and can answer the above mentioned questions reasonably well and sail through the core Sociology course even without minimum attendance if only such open-ended questions are given.

Many of the rural-based or Hindi-medium students, whose numbers are increasing nowadays (probably due to a combination of studying in coaching institutes at Kota, having a strong background in the Science subjects which helps them clear the tough entrance test (JEE) in spite of being weak in English, introduction of Hindi as a medium for writing JEE, etc.) feel cheated as they diligently come for all the class lecturers, labour through the handouts which are in English but still end up getting lower marks than the others who have flair in the English language. One reason why some students complain about cramming is that given a chance they would like to sail through HSS courses without being forced to sit for lecturers. They would like to reduce Sociology to the level of commonsensical knowledge or journalistic writings.

Many students hate to study handouts because they feel that social scientists make long torturous arguments and do not come to the point straightaway. Given a chance they would like to deal only with facts and figures rather than read pages of convoluted arguments. These students therefore need to be explained that each discipline has its own style of presenting its arguments. In the Natural Sciences they build up their arguments starting from first principles and through mathematical equations whereas in the Social Sciences we present both sides of an issue, critically examine the work of other specialists within that given field and then finally present our own arguments. The students reluctantly see our point of view and therefore understand why it becomes important to sit for class lectures in which the teacher explains the nuances of each concept and simplifies some of the complex arguments. But given a chance some of them would rather indulge in 'Godgiri'[5] and try and master the handouts overnight just before the examinations without attending classes. Therefore, although I am principally against forced attendance for classes, I have been forcing the B.Tech students to attend my classes in the initial stages by threatening them with the rule on mandatory 80 per cent attendance. Or else I would not get the opportunity to make them realize that sociological understanding is different from the commonsensical knowledge that they have on issues.

Many students I realized also dislike the fact that they are forced to write long answers in Sociology unlike even Psychology where they have mostly objective-type tests. There is a temptation even within some of us teaching Sociology to give only objective-type tests because correcting 140 answer scripts repeatedly is an arduous and time-consuming task while objective-type answers can be handled by our teaching assistants.

Keeping all these issues in mind, I have had basically two goals while teaching the Sociology core course to B.Tech students. First, I need to make them understand the riches of my discipline, make them take it seriously and not treat it as a 'lukka' subject. Secondly, I want to inculcate in my students the sociological imagination, a critical sensibility, which would help them understand social issues in totality and therefore help them in later life to make more balanced judgements on social issues, which they would confront in their respective careers.

As far as the syllabus is concerned, given the flexibility and freedom which the faculty enjoy within IIT-B to develop their own curricula unlike in many universities (and for which I suffered at Pune University), we (i.e., the two teachers who are handing the two respective divisions of about 140 students each) teach foundational sociology topics like introduction to the discipline, basic concepts, conceptualizations on socialization process (Mead, Freud and others), classical thinkers (Marx, Weber, Durkheim) before the mid-semester examinations and then teach whatever issues which we think are relevant and according to our specializations in the second half. Keeping in mind the debates, which go on in the students' online discussion forums, I focus on issues concerning nationalism, communalism, secularism, gender, affirmative discrimination and environmental ethics in the second half of my course. I cannot claim to have been entirely successful but have managed to earn the students' respect.[6] The students have also accepted me as someone who would fight for their rights and if necessary put forward their point of view to the authorities on issues concerning them.

III

Some Pedagogical Techniques

I would now like to discuss some of the pedagogical techniques that I have used in my class so as to inculcate in my students a sociological imagination. I will also discuss some of the other interventions, which I feel are equally important both for bringing out the relevance of the discipline and for maintaining one's sense of dignity in an environment heavily dominated by the engineering departments. This involves interventions in the intellectual, social and cultural spaces available within IITs such as interventions in various web-based newsgroup discussions, in students' newsletters and in the various social issues, which crop up in the lives of residents in hostels and faculty quarters.

The first strategy that I used in my class was to adopt the method of 'inspired presentation of material'. For example, while teaching classical thinkers like Marx, Weber and Durkheim, I picked up only key theoretical concepts and presented them in a dramatized fashion. This is because I quickly realized that the attention span of many of the B.Tech students was limited and long elaborate theoretical debates and descriptions left them bored and they switched off mentally. Secondly, I realized that unlike students of M.A. (Sociology) who had been socialized to approach the classical thinkers with lot of reverence and respect, for many of the B.Tech students the names and their theoretical contribution meant nothing unless they could connect these theories to the contemporary scenario. In class tests, Karl Marx would be shortened to 'Karl' and Weber became 'Max' something which would be sacrilegious for Master's students in Sociology. I therefore prepared thoroughly for my class lectures and explained concepts as lucidly as possible, throwing in a lot of illustrations from the contemporary social and political scenario. I also tried to relate the concepts, wherever possible, to their everyday life situation and hoped that some of my enthusiasm would at least rub off on to them. At the same time, I saw to it that clarity was not achieved at the cost of losing out on the complexity and nuances implicit in sociological concepts. Then things would appear 'commonsensical' thereby dragging Sociology to the level of the mundane. This is a real danger, which is inherent in teaching Sociology because our subject matter often relates to the everyday life situation. In comparison, Philosophy seems esoteric to students, and Economics and Psychology are accepted as sciences because they use quantitative methods, formulas and experiments, while English is accepted as part of the aesthetic tradition. But Sociology has no such advantage. I would try to explain how a commonsensical understanding of the militancy problem in Kashmir becomes a Hindu-Muslim issue or a question of patriotism, while a sociological understanding essentially involves issues such as (a) the difference between nations and nation-states as analytical concepts, (b) the understanding, that formation of nation-states often leads to the encompassment of nations or sub-nationalities within nation-states, and (c) the issue of national identity, which becomes acrimonious because the majority community wants to identify the national culture and identity in terms of its own cultural and religious symbols and values, which in turn alienates the minority groups.

Even while teaching concepts from classical thinkers, care has to be taken so that the students do not end up with prejudiced inferences. For example, Durkheim's conceptualizations on mechanical and organic solidarity and their manifestation in different types of laws, fascinates the students. But some students immediately relate repressive laws to Islamic fundamentalism and therefore to backwardness or retrogressive systems. To avoid such stereotyped and prejudiced logic, one needs to not only explain the determining role of strong collective conscience behind repressive measures, manifest even in so called modernized and civilized societies, but also relate the issue to Foucauldian conceptualizations on discipline and punishment which show that control over the mind through surveillance, psychiatry or governmentality could be as repressive as control over the body through physical torture.

The second strategy that I have often used to inculcate in students a 'sociological imagination' is to use the pedagogical technique of "teacher as text".[7] This involves giving illustrations from my own lived experiences and helping them to understand that one needs to look beyond the immediacy of the issue, beyond one's personal gains and losses and understand the issue in terms of the larger context. For example, while discussing the issue of Kashmir, an issue on which students react emotionally, as their focus is on the Kashmiri Pandits who have become refugees, or the Hindus who were being gunned down by so-called terrorists, I narrate incidents from my life, of having suffered a personal tragedy in this turmoil. I then go on to explain how nation-states emerge, how they often enclose diverse nationalities, which in turn lead to sub-national movements. Similarly, when the issue of reservations or positive discrimination for members of Scheduled Castes (SG) and Scheduled Tribes (STs) is discussed in class, I usually find a majority of the students reacting in a very biased manner, essentially because they are from upper caste Hindu families and had to compete really hard to get into IIT, some of their batchmates having not made it. In comparison they feel that the entry is much easier for SC and ST students as the cut off entrance test marks is lower. The issue of affirmative discrimination therefore becomes a sensitive issue. I therefore take it up at the end of the semester as by then I have gained both their confidence and respect. I usually introduce it in a neutral fashion by first discussing Charles Taylor's seminal article on the "Politics of Recognition" in which he brings out the difference between 'politics of equal dignity' and 'politics of difference'. They understand these concepts and are able to apply them to understand that the issue of minority rights comes under politics of difference whereas the issue of affirmative discrimination or reservations comes under politics of equal dignity. But, when the actual debate on reservations policy in the Indian context comes up, the arguments again become personalized. They are unable to keep the critical distance, which is necessary when looking at the debate, although many had supported affirmative discrimination when the theories underlying it were discussed earlier in class. I therefore give illustrations from my life, of missing opportunities for promotions while teaching at a university because the few posts, which were advertised had to be reserved to make up for backlogs in implementation of the government's affirmative discrimination policies. I also relate an incident when a few hundred dalit students (galvanized from colleges outside the university campus) had sat on a hunger strike, demanding my removal because a rumour was deliberately spread about me having physically man-handled a dalit student and how I was saved by other dalit faculty members and the dalit students from within the university campus who knew the politics behind the canard. The idea is to make them realize that bitter personal experiences should not prevent them from understanding an issue in terms of the larger context in which it is embedded.

Discussions concerning gender or sexuality also lead to deadlocks and I have to often draw on my past, my personal experiences as a college student, to convince them that while I understand their point of view, having held them once in my college days, such views are biased, being based essentially on prevalent sexual stereotypes. One interesting discussion centred on a short story titled, "The Girl", written by a student for the alumni magazine *The New Insight.* The story had passages such as:

> Being well endowed with intelligence, she soon came to the realization that she was well endowed in other ways as well....former acquaintances of hers would have noticed the level of her nose rise along with her skirt line.....all this being possible, because a pair of long legs is synonymous with irresistible for majority of the male race...exploitation of the body is not an easy task, but given time and practice it can be achieved and this, she found added a new dimension to life. The bitter sweet sensation of mixing pleasure with business would attain the status of a derived taste.

The student claimed that it was not sexist but if anything, had the undercurrent of 'feminism'. In the discussions which followed in the class I had to explain what feminism essentially meant and that negative stereotypes about feminism were created by those who felt threatened by women fighting for their rights and dignity. The discussion inevitably shifted to the crucial role that their mothers who were housewives played at home. I then quoted to them a passage from a monograph written by Kamla Bhasin and Nighat Said Khan, which stated, "A woman who chooses to be a housewife and feels her individuality and talent are fully utilized by it can still be a feminist. Being a feminist does not necessarily mean working outside the home. All it means is having a real choice based on equal opportunities. The element of choice, of women's own wills, is what is important" (Bhasin and Khan, 2000). Discussing gender issues become important in an IIT set-up because usually only about 5 per cent of the B.Tech students are girls and many of the boys being just out of schools carry all kinds of notions about them.

As is evident from the above discussion, illustrations from the instructor's personal life, and his ability to empathize with the students' grouse, while simultaneously leading them to think beyond the immediacy of the issue, goes a long way in developing in them the ability to think critically.

The third strategy that I have adopted to bring out the relevance of a 'sociological sensitivity' and which takes me beyond classroom interactions is to intervene very actively in newsgroup debates on not only various socio-political issues of national interest but also on issues concerning life on IIT campus. Colleagues have often chided me for wasting time or have warned me of rubbing well-known engineering faculty on the wrong side. But I strongly feel that such interventions in the public domain are required because (a) it gives me a sense of equality as far as relations with other engineering faculty is concerned, and (b) often the debates need inputs from social scientists, especially when messages posted show a strong bias against the minority communities, as happened post-Godhra. But I have till now adopted differing strategies as far as intervention in web-based newsgroup discussions are concerned.

I usually do not intervene directly in students' newsgroup discussions. This is for two reasons. One, as stated earlier, some of the topics that I teach in my core course deal with contentious issues such as minority rights, secularism and reservations. I take up these issues only towards the end of the course as I have realized that it is very difficult to change people's mindset on such issues. They listen to you only after they start respecting you as a person. I therefore do not like to intervene in students' online newsgroup debates, as I would be revealing my political stand on issues and biasing their opinion about me even before they take up my courses. Secondly, once a debate is started off on an issue in students' newsgroups such as iitb.general or iitb.discuss, the number of postings is so rapid and voluminous that one can get mentally exhausted defending one's position. I usually scan the various issues being discussed so that I can understand the mindset of the students, get an idea about the topical issues and then take up the contentious issues in class. But post-Godhra, I was left extremely disturbed and shocked when I looked at the postings that were pouring in, especially in the site iitb.discuss, a site which was ostensibly created by a few senior students so that they could undertake serious political debates away from the light hearted discussions on iitb.general. But, in reality, it was a site dominated by some students with strong Hindu right-wing affiliations and they were literally pouring in hate mails against the minority community with captions such as, Indianization of Islam, Social Work by Santa Claus, The price of stone-walling Hindus, R we living in Hindustan, Correcting the anti-VHP stand, Frustrating, Pseudo-secular reporting by TOI, Conspiracy theory, Marxist engineering history, Some Pseudo-secular matters, Why conversions? etc. Although I felt terribly depressed reading those mails, I went through them and categorized them in terms of their intensity of hate and saved them for future research. But I did not intervene directly in the debate and instead galvanized secular-minded and highly respected professors from engineering departments, coaxing them to intervene in the debates, as their interventions would carry a lot of weight among the students' community. I also initiated meetings where some secular-minded faculty and students got together and discussed strategies. I talked to the Dean of Students Affairs and on his request wrote an article for the students' newsletter *Insight* titled, "The Need for Peace, Sanity and Secularism" in which I took up some of the contentious issues and explained why secularism was so important in Indian context. As stated above, my non-intervention in the web-based debates was a tactical move and not a fear of confrontation.

On the other hand, when it came to debates on communal issues on 'faculty-discuss', I was quite ruthless. I was simply appalled that some faculty members who were brilliant in their respective fields could harbour such prejudice against members of the minority communities. I would simply tear to shreds mails with a communal sub-text. I have been also engaging very actively in websites debates on issues concerning campus life such as controversies over sites for new constructions, issues directly affecting students such as banning of use of motorbikes, restrictions on entry of boys and girls into one another's hostels after a certain stipulated time, internet usage in hostels and the serious issue of students suffering from depressions and having large number of backlog. Interestingly and often embarrassingly, a lot of faculty members from the engineering departments seem to know me only though my mails on 'faculty-discuss'.

But sometimes debating with faculty members from the other departments can be exasperating as they are so caught up in the rationality and scientificity of their arguments that they forget the larger picture and do not realize that they are being one-dimensional. Recently, there was a debate on the environmental scenario on IIT-B campus with some faculty members showing concern about the cutting down of old trees that may happen due to the need for constructing new buildings. An highly erudite Mathematics professor took off with a tangential argument and wanted to know whether trees conduct better photosynthesis than grass. His hunch was that the surface area of grass on a given square piece of lawn was much more than that of a canopy of trees within the same area and therefore grass should conduct better photosynthesis than trees. He wanted scientific evidence for his hypothesis, which was not immediately forthcoming and he was literally ranting challenging people to prove him wrong.

I found his one-dimensional arguments irritating because somewhere he was taunting the environmentalists stating that we need lawns and not old forested areas. I therefore wrote a rather long posting taking ideas from the book *Dominating Knowledge* on how we humans operate using both a "personal map" and an "impersonal map" (Marglin and Marglin, 1990). These two maps give us a differing understanding of ourselves (issue of ontology), of our relationship with other life forms and other inanimate objects (issue of cosmology) and finally of what constitutes knowledge (epistemology). In our lives we need a balanced use of these two maps. I pointed out that while using the impersonal grid we have an 'instrumental' attitude towards other life forms. Other objects then have finite qualities and are replaceable. But when we look at other life forms using the personal grid, then our attitude is 'relational' and every life form is looked at being unique and irreplaceable. My point was that the Mathematics professor was taking an extremely instrumental and utilitarian stance and looking at different plant species from only one attribute – which one conducts better photosynthesis. So given a chance he would be replacing trees with lawns and if research shows some other species conducts better photosynthesis, he would be excavating the lawns and planting that species. Whereas when we use the personal map, even a Gulmohar tree may be deeply enmeshed in the biography of another professor, giving him/her deep aesthetic and poetic pleasure and may therefore seem irreplaceable.

My long posting I feel put off many faculty members (as my mail hardly evoked any response) who are more used to power point presentations (PPTs) and I got a nasty reply from the Mathematics professor who made a mockery of concepts like epistemology and ontology which I think completely put him off as he was not able to indulge in his usual "pop Sociology". I gave an equally sarcastic reply but somewhere deep inside I felt that I was arguing from the margins. Strangely scientific evidence seemed more important to many of these engineering and science professors than larger philosophical issues. Somehow carbon dioxide emission, chlorophyll, radiation and carbon dating seemed more important in this issue than larger philosophical questions. I gave up hoping that I must have made sense to at least a silent minority. I was left wondering whether the differing stance on issues was more a matter of disciplinary training which made us comprehend the same issue so differently.

I would therefore like to reiterate that although for faculty members from the Humanities and Social Science disciplines, working in a technology institute, there is often an anxiety for being recognized and being useful within that technological ambience, one should not attempt to achieve these goals at the cost of one's dignity and one's disciplinary interests. I accept that those who want to specialize in applied fields, which are directly related to the technological sphere, should be encouraged to do so. Networking and getting massive funding for projects remain important because these activities get the discipline visibility and employment for those research students who are without fellowships. But those like me who cannot hold CEP courses, do consultancies or get massive projects, also have a place within that framework. We are doing a very crucial job. We are training future technologists to think critically, to be sensitive to the conditions of the poor and oppressed sections of our society and inculcating in them secular and humanitarian values.

I would therefore like to conclude by quoting a passage from Paulo Freire's book *Teachers as Cultural Workers:*

> ...the task of a teacher, who is also a learner, is both joyful and rigorous. It demands seriousness and scientific, physical, emotional, and affective preparation. It is a task that requires that those who commit themselves to teaching develop a certain love not only of others but of the very process implied in teaching. It is impossible to teach without the courage to love, without the courage to try a thousand times before giving up ... We must dare so as never to dichotomize cognition and emotion. We must dare so that we can continue to teach for a long time under conditions that we know well: low salaries, lack of respect, and the ever-present risk of becoming prey to cynicism. We must dare to learn how to dare in order to say no to the bureaucratization of the mind to which we are exposed everyday. We must dare so that we can continue to do so even when it is much more materially advantageous to stop daring (2005: 5–6).

Notes

1. The enquiry committee gave its report a year after I had left Pune University and joined IIT-B and the report not only praised my article for its unbiased analysis but also mentioned that more such critical reflexive analysis was required if the university wanted to face up to new challenges.
2. At IIT, Bombay, presently, there are six disciplines within the department of Humanities and Social Sciences: Economics, Sociology, Psychology, Philosophy, English and Sanskrit. All students of B.Tech (about 450) have

to take Economic in their first semester. In the third semester they are divided equally into two groups who take Sociology and Psychology respectively. In fourth semester they again have the option of choosing between Philosophy and English. In their seventh and eight semesters they select electives offered by the HSS department and these include those from discipline of Sanskrit, which has been recently introduced.

3. *Insight: The Third Eye* (Vol. 4, No. 4, November 10, 2001).
4. "Time-pass" in students' parlance.
5. Within IITs, in every field whether it is academics, sports, organizing cultural activities, dramatics, music, computer software or initiating a start-up (their own entrepreneurial activity), they have their "Gods" who are exceptional in their respective fields and are worshipped by "aam junta". Every student dreams of doing some godgiri within their tenure at IIT.
6. I was awarded the Excellence in Teaching Award in 2005, an award which is essentially based on students' evaluation of classroom teaching.
7. Although I have been using this technique throughout my teaching career, the phrase '*teacher as text*' I have picked up from Walter R. Jacobs, 1998. "The Teacher as Text: Using Personal Experience to Stimulate the Sociological Imagination", *Teaching Sociology,* 26 (3).

References

Bhasin, Kamla and Nighat Said Khan. 2000. *Some Questions on Feminism and its Relevance in South Asia.* New Delhi: Kali for Women.

Deb, Kushal. 1998. "Teaching of Sociology in a Regional University: The Struggle for Survival", *Sociological Bulletin,* Vol. 47, No. 2, September.

Freire, Paulo. 2005. *Teachers as Cultural Workers: Letters to those Who Dare to Teach.* Cambridge: Westview Press, pp. 5–6.

Jacobs, Walter R. 1998. "The Teacher as Text: Using Personal Experience to Stimulate the Sociological Imagination", *Teaching Sociology*, 26 (3).

Marglin, Frederique Apffel and Stephen A. Marglin (eds.), 1990. *Dominating Knowledge: Development, Culture and Resistance.* Oxford: Clarendon Press.

Taylor, Charles. 1994. "The Politics of Recognition", *Multiculturalism: Examining the Politics of Recognition,* edited by Amy Gutmann, Princeton, New Jersey: Princeton University Press, pp. 25–73.

Part IV

New Sites and Modes of Doing Sociology

The practice of sociology in contemporary India is no longer confined to the university now. New institutions, such as the corporate and non-governmental organizations (NGOs), have emerged as sites of new knowledge production and dissemination, for instance the process of Social Compliance Audit (SCA) practised within the corporate sector or developmental research within NGOs. In both instances research is guided solely by agendas defined by the funding agency, more often international than national. Meanwhile, old institutions wherein sociology used to be practised are being reshaped both institutionally and intellectually. Institutionally, new practices and ideas of autonomy have come into being. Intellectually, new research and teaching agendas such as corporate sociology are being established. In all instances, the imperatives of the market appear to play a key role, at once reshaping the nature of the state and necessarily recasting the contours of higher education.

12

New Locations and New Articulations

Practice of Sociology in a Metropolitan Autonomous Institution

SHAJI VARGHESE AND R. SANTHOSH

Any academic engagement on the state of sociology in India has to contextualize the discipline within the multitudes of hierarchized academic, socio-cultural and geographical locations within India. Many recent self-reflexive accounts have observed the myriad contexts in which sociology is practised in India (Das, 1993; Deshpande, 1994; Shah, 2000; Chaudhuri, 2003). These diversities of contexts emerge from a number of factors including the diverse geographic locations, medium of instruction, rural/urban disparities, caste/class composition of the students, specific traditions and histories of certain centres of learning etc. These diversities make the task of addressing the 'practice of sociology' a rather difficult endeavour. Any discussion on the quality of sociological research and teaching has to keep these diverse backgrounds and different contexts in mind. The nature of syllabus, the rationale of curriculum setting, predominant pedagogical practices, quality of reading materials, inclusion of recent advancements in the discipline etc., have to be comprehended only by contextualizing the practice of sociology in the above mentioned settings.

The question of locating the discipline has become even more complex with the emerging trends in the field of higher education.

Internationalization of higher education with respect to the increased presence of foreign educational institutions in India, the structural changes with special reference to the emergence of autonomous institutions and deemed universities, the gradual withdrawal of the state from the realm of higher education and other factors are exposing the field of higher education in India to an unprecedented phase of rapid transformations. Hence, 'locating the discipline' within a clear and specific context informs us about divergent concerns and issues that the discipline encounters at divergent settings. This also informs us about the numerous ways through which the discipline negotiates and reorients itself. This paper focuses on the changes that the practice of sociology is undergoing in the context of academic autonomy. Closely examining the context of Christ College, an autonomous institution in Bangalore, this paper will explore the changing practice of sociology in this new location, thereby seeking to contribute to the existing knowledge about the 'field'. It would descriptively map out the larger institutional changes in general, and changes in the practice of sociology in particular, in the last five years, tracing these to the larger changes in the field of higher education and in the immediate context of economy and society in Bangalore.

I

Bangalore: The Metropolitan Context

The overall changes occurring in Christ College and the changes happening to the practice of sociology can be comprehended only if we look at the changes sweeping across the country and the city of Bangalore in particular. The changes in the practice of sociology at Christ College needs to be understood not only in the light of academic autonomy and the dynamics within the college, but within a broader context of changes happening in Bangalore and in the field of higher education in general.

The growth of Bangalore in the past two decades has been phenomenal in terms of economic activity, physical expansion and migration. The city, traditionally known as garden city, pensioners' paradise etc., was quick to adapt and utilize the opportunities provided through economic liberalization, which began in early 1990s. Bangalore's specific stakes in the era of liberalization was the field of information technology (IT) where the brand "India's Silicon Valley" paid rich dividends in terms of attracting foreign investments and harnessing the response of Indian state and domestic investors. Summing up the growth of Bangalore as a new IT destination, Hietzman observes:

> The region now had to project a public identity, an iconic presence, in order to attract certain transactional or national business. Bangalore, in the manner of urban regions globally adopted and adapted the language of the information society in order to pocket a brand name, a marketing logo. The great experiment that had always been Bangalore – the garden city, the industrial city, the science city achieved a new relevance within a renewed body of discourses rationalising patterns of capital formation...local players were quite avid in identifying a language that allowed the rationalisation of a liberal economic agenda, exercising their agency in the crafting of a new urban space (211: 2004).

The growth of Bangalore into a metropolitan city also influenced the scenario of higher education in the city. This growth also accompanied the emergence of new sections of affluent class, which looks for 'world-class education' and 'global exposure'. A whole range of professional courses and degrees, which would ensure immediate jobs in the corporate sector with unconventionally high salaries, started emerging. New professional educational institutions exclusively funded and managed by private organizations started mushrooming across the city. These institutions, functioning completely outside the purview of state funding, proved to be an important and emerging face of higher education. In this scenario Christ College emerged as an important educational institution that could foresee and capitalize most of these changes happening in the realm of higher education in Bangalore. Janaki Nair speaks about two contending forces that are staking claim over the city: "on the one hand are the newly renovated citizens, who are amply aided by a technocratic vision of change offered by the leaders of the new economy and on the other hand are those, including citizens-in-the-making such as women for whom democracy has come to have a different meaning in the urban setting" (Nair, 2005). The paper proposes to suggest that Christ College belongs to the former, capitalizing on the needs of this new section and catering to their educational aspirations.

II

Autonomy and the Institutional Context

Christ College is an autonomous institution offering both undergraduate and postgraduate courses and affiliated to the Bangalore University. In the academic year 2006–2007, it had a combined strength of 5,655 students studying in 46 undergraduate and 14 postgraduate departments with a combined faculty strength of 256 members, thus becoming one of the largest colleges in the country. It was re-accredited with A+ grade by the NAAC and has been selected under the 'Colleges with Potential for Excellence Scheme' of the UGC in 2006.

Established in 1969 by a Christian missionary congregation, the college aimed at offering general education in the field of liberal arts and science streams. It has been offering undergraduate courses in sociology from 1980 and a postgraduate programme since 1992. From a very modest beginning, the college began making rapid strides from 1985 onwards. Even while being in the university affiliated system, the college had begun its own initiatives to reflect over and address a number of issues pertaining to the system of education in the college. In 1997 it undertook the formulation of 'strategic planning' where the vision and mission statement of the college were derived. This was conceived as a four-year planning aimed at bringing about academic and administrative innovations in the college. This was the first organized attempt from the side of the college to look at the external context of the college and especially to understand the potential of a city like Bangalore and the fast emerging trends in the sphere of higher education.

Following the policy formulations of a number of educational committees at the national level, the college also began to offer a series of vocational courses. A whole series of new courses such as Hotel Management, MBA, BBM, MCA etc. were started along with the diversification of other traditional streams such as science and liberal arts. Most of these new programmes were started as 'unaided' courses, which did not require government salary for the staff. By early nineties itself the college had decided not to look for grant-in-aid from the state government for the new courses and began planning for economic self-sustainability. The college managed financial affairs in such a manner that the expenditure for day-to-day affairs, including salary for the teachers and financial requirements for the future development of the college, were derived from running these courses. While increasing the number of courses and diversifying degrees offered by the college, enormous attention is also paid in developing the infrastructure of the college. It is often pointed out that Christ College has extremely good infrastructural facilities and not many other colleges in India can claim such facilities. Huge investment is made to build new buildings, to develop computer/internet facilities, and to procure audio-visual teaching aids. The college has more than one hundred LCD projectors, most of them fitted permanently in the classrooms. Similarly, the Centre for Academic Excellence, housed within the campus, has more than eighty well furnished rooms to provide accommodation to the delegates coming for various programmes within the college. The recently built auditorium has a capacity of more than 1,9000 people and is equipped with the state-of-the-art audio-visual and lighting equipments. This is currently the largest auditorium in Bangalore. Construction for a new twelve-storied building has already begun on the campus.

Along with these infrastructural developments, the college also initiated a number of collaborative courses with foreign universities. Western Michigan University, USA, Ohio University, USA, Griffith University, Australia etc. have started a number of academic programmes with the college. Most of these programmes are operated as twinning programmes in which students spend half of the course duration at the college and the remaining at the foreign university. The foreign collaboration has developed to such an extent that two faculty members are managing the Office of International Affairs. Similarly, the college has established a research consortium with Liverpool Hope University in which twelve faculty members from the college are engaged in research in collaboration with the Liverpool University faculties. Christ College is constantly ranked high in the annual survey conducted by *Outlook* magazine in almost all the of three major streams of science, social sciences and commerce. Indeed, such surveys are itself a development of recent times. The MBA programme offered by the college is ranked just below that of IIM, Bangalore among different colleges within the city. Christ College has a campus placement cell which ensures most of the students who pass out of the professional courses are placed in reputed organizations.

Another important initiative was to establish a number of centres in the college campus focusing on specific areas for future development and plan of action. The Centre for Education Beyond Curriculum (CEDBEC), Centre for Social Action (CSA), Centre for Social Research (CSR) etc. were established during the late 1990s. CSA was conceived as an initiative to sensitize the student body of the college regarding various social issues and also to contribute for the community at large. Today, CSA has grown into an independent entity within the college, sponsoring almost 200 children of a nearby slum and undertakes community development works in four urban slums in Bangalore, 35 villages in Karnataka and 15 villages in Andhra Pradesh. It also aimed at carrying out independent commissioned research. The Centre for Publication of the college is bringing out three quarterly journals in Social Sciences, Sciences, and Commerce and Management streams. Another important initiative was to develop a curriculum for 'holistic development' aimed at imparting personal, interpersonal and societal skills to the entire student body of the college. This holistic education has components aiming at developing social awareness and a series of soft skills such as time management, communication skills, critical thinking etc.

As the college grew in terms of diversity of courses and the sheer size of the student body, more and more importance is laid on technology and management information system for effective administration and monitoring. Everyday attendance of students is fed into computers in a centralised Information Processing and Management (IPM) Unit and is uploaded in the college website every week. The parents of the students are given passwords and can check their wards attendance through the website. The Counselling Department, with more than ten full-time counsellors, monitor the attendance of the students and attend to all other disciplinary and personal problems of the students.

III

Autonomy at Christ College

A closer examination of the autonomous system and its relation, especially to curricular and pedagogical dynamics, is required to understand its impact on disciplinary knowledge, the resultant skews and its possible consequences. Such a careful examination would raise a series of questions of the problematic assumptions and conclusions such as academic freedom, quality syllabus, etc. Moreover, such an exercise would also inform us about the novel and interesting ways in which the discipline is trying to relocate and reposition itself within these changes.

Academic autonomy is increasingly seen as the best means to overcome the rigidity of the affiliating system, to improve curriculum and to introduce innovative teaching-learning methods. This trend is visible from the fact that a number of institutions opting for autonomous status have been steadily increasing. This need to be understood in the background of consistent efforts by the statutory and policy making bodies of the government to promote the idea of autonomy as a "structural solution intended mainly to provide an enabling environment to improve and strengthen the teaching and learning process" (CABE, 2005). The Central Advisory Board of Education, (CABE) Committee on Autonomy of Higher Education Institutions understands autonomy as characterized by curricular and pedagogic innovations, decentralized management culture and enhanced academic and financial accountability.

In Karnataka, though the proposal of granting autonomy to the colleges was pending for the past few decades, the actual implementation was done only in 2005. It is important to note that though any college could opt for the autonomous status, only a handful of colleges from Bangalore opted for it in 2005. The teachers, who feared that an academic autonomy will be followed by financial autonomy and grant-in-aid would gradually be stopped, voiced the main resistance against autonomy in many colleges. There was also apprehension about the eroding of teacher autonomy, possibility of outright commercialization of education, and the fear that access to these institutions will be limited only to the elite sections of the society. In 2005, all the colleges which opted for autonomy were managed by different Christian institutions, and in 2007, a number of other colleges in Bangalore decided to opt for autonomous status and currently there are around thirty colleges under autonomous scheme in Karnataka.

Christ College was in the forefront of demanding for the autonomous status and finally when the grant of autonomy was announced, it was received with both trepidation and relief. The college had always expressed its desire to adapt with the changing environments and capitalize the opportunities. "The ground realities of liberalization and globalization have not only affected economy and business, but also social life and culture of the people of this country. It is imperative that education also must keep pace with these changes"(Mathew, 2005).

Systematic efforts had begun almost two years before the actual grant of autonomy to study and understand 'best practices' from autonomous colleges all over the country. The in-house Centre for Education Beyond Curriculum (CEDBEC) conducted a survey of best administrative and academic practices[1] in 24 "highly reputed" institutions. The attempt was to identify the "best practices" followed in these institutions regarding "Institutional Leadership, Strategic Planning, Information Management, Human Resource Management, Social Responsibility and Resource Mobilisation" (Mathew et al., 2005). A committee of senior faculty visited a number of autonomous colleges in Chennai to study practices specifically in an autonomous system. It is with such meticulous preparation that the college shifted to the autonomous system. The Office of the Controller of Examinations now manages examinations, and the various departments are organized into three deaneries, one each for Humanities and Social Sciences, Sciences, and Commerce and Management. However, it is important to note that much of the administrative and academic restructuring began much before the actual grant of autonomy. The college was quick to respond to the changes that were happening in Bangalore in the last two decades.

The grant of autonomy provided a whole series of new responsibility and freedom with respect to the practice of curriculum and pedagogy. In the place of a university syllabus, which many times remained unchanged for years, autonomy provided space to formulate new syllabus for each institution. This reformulation of syllabi in each of these institutions reflects a number of concerns, priorities, and often mirrors a whole lot of wider dynamics within which the curriculum formulation takes place.

At Christ College this new space made available with the introduction of autonomy was used for radical reformulation of the syllabus in both undergraduate and postgraduate classes of sociology. An attempt was made to communicate the disciplinary perspective to the students in the introductory papers. Similarly, by highlighting the divergent schools of thought like functionalism, conflict and interpretive perspectives, the contested nature of sociological categories was highlighted in the undergraduate classes. For example, the paper on 'Indian Society' not only presents various theoretical arguments of different sociologists on Indian society, but also topics such as caste, class, gender etc. as very much a part of one's everyday life and social being. Similarly, contemporary social issues, such as caste inequality, crisis of development, sub-nationalism, development-related displacement, environmental movements, Naxal movement etc. now figure prominently in the undergraduate syllabus.

An attempt was also made to do away with textbooks, which were written keeping only examinations in mind – and specific readings – mostly original essays and books – were recommended. Similarly, a number of new assessment patterns were also introduced as the internal assessment carries fifty percentages of the marks. Along with written assignments, a series of assignment techniques like project exhibition, quiz, group work, book/article review, film review, research projects, internships in NGOs, dissertation etc. were also introduced. These wide varieties of assessment techniques and a new set of papers resulted in increased enthusiasm among the students towards the subject. Curriculum takes on a different meaning where classroom teaching/learning is supplemented with various co-curricular activities. The Sociology Department organizes at least two programmes every academic year. One of them is the Human Rights Festival, where students get an opportunity to study various human rights issues, and interact with activists/development professionals, film makers and writers. Another annual programme is the Inter-collegiate Sociology Students' Festival. Apart from these, students have an opportunity to interact with eminent guest speakers during workshops, conferences and lecture series organized by the department. These practices take the curriculum beyond the classroom.

The initiatives taken up by the college to make use of the changing scenario of Bangalore and to project it as a premier institution providing world class education has started providing rich dividends. The increased visibility and the reputation that the college has earned among the corporate circles is reflected in very impressive campus recruitment drives and increased industry-college interface at various levels. It would be relevant just to mention an instance of Microsoft Research Lab recruiting two sociology students as research assistants for their social research wing. Though it may be a single instance, it is definitely an indicator of changes in the offing.

Unconventional avenues and opportunities are being opened up for sociology students and the practice of sociology will be to a great extent influenced by these changes and what the new scenario have to offer.

IV

Freedom and Restrictions: The Anomaly of Autonomy

While examining the kind of freedom with respect to curriculum and pedagogy under autonomy at Christ College, it is also significant to note that autonomy brought in a number of restrictions and different types of controlling mechanisms to the practice of sociology in the college. Many of these restrictions emerged from the administrative compulsions of the college management, which often wants to streamline the academic programmes and its functioning within the college. The categories like 'academic validation', 'academic accountability' etc. became the most widely heard catch words in the day-to-day affairs of the college.

These two terms assumed significance in the college owing to the fact that the system of autonomy brought in the enormous responsibility of ensuring the worth and quality of the education imparted on the shoulders of the college. In this context, the ways in which these concerns are articulated and addressed are by adopting to a neo-liberal discourse of treating education as a merit good. Assessing the overall objective and relevance of education is narrowed down to the mere strategic approval and concurrence of the stakeholders of the college, basically comprising students, industry and a selective section of the wider society. Academic validation and academic accountability became the terms that facilitated the projection of education as branded commodity tailor-made for industry, which satisfies stringent quality checks and consumer satisfaction. Academic accountability of the teachers is operationalized as mere procedural requirements like timely completion of courses, regular engagement of classes, distribution of course plan etc. As Gray observes, "the rhetoric about 'driving up standards' can be read as an attempt to realign education to the commodity values that increasingly define worthwhile and legitimate knowledge in post-industrial societies, that is 'the task of education is not the dissemination of a general model of life, not to transform students' minds but to supply the system with merchandized needs in the form of information and skills" (1990: 204–23). A series of mechanisms and measures were introduced to ensure that these categories are easily getting translated into a number of specific procedures and practices.

Many a time, administrative convenience preceded sound educational rationale of academic decision-making. Assessment techniques were again restricted to limited types to ensure uniformity and written examinations assumed a prominent position within the internal assessment. Written examination is the most preferred form of internal assessment due to its objectivity as it is done in a centralized manner, with invigilators to monitor the examination, barcodes in the answer scripts to conceal the identity of the students. Objective questions are made more and more prominent in the question paper to make valuation more objective and foolproof. The examination system has been made so impersonalized that the teachers do not even get to know which class of students they are evaluating. This is made possible with the modification of answer papers where there is no space for the students to write their class name. Similarly, in an attempt to make examination system foolproof, the college has developed a question bank of all subjects from which the questions will be randomly selected with the help of a specially made software. This is also indicative of a wider process where the role of a teacher gets systematically marginalized and increasingly compartmentalized. So, the teacher's role is transformed from that of a facilitator with affective dimension seen as intrinsic to the teaching role to that of an instructor and evaluator with an emphasis on cognitive and managerial skills (Broadfoot and Pollard, 2006).

Benchmarking of syllabi and other academic practices becomes another important strategy through which the college strives to maintain its standard and quality. As Giroux (1997) points out that the ideological considerations that legitimate programmes in IT and management studies have become the model for evaluating other liberal arts and social science programmes. In a nutshell, it can be described as a series of new procedures which ensured the following processes: increasing managerialism, system orientation, greater rationalization of processes like benchmarking, quality standards, curriculum designs, validation etc. Autonomy also assumes greater administrative control over educational processes like curriculum, pedagogy and assessment. As these new contexts offer new possibilities to the practice of sociology, a whole new series of challenges and predicaments is also facing the discipline. Over the last decade new criteria have emerged for evaluating the significance of a discipline. Externally, the employability of students and internally, the capacity to generate revenue, drives the institutional view of a discipline. It is assumed that all disciplines must necessarily produce employable graduates. Understandably, this is seen as the only factor that will attract students to a course. Secondly, if the institution has to be financially sustainable, each department should generate enough revenue so as not to depend on cross-subsidies for other 'well-to-do' departments. As Giroux (1997) points out, "...Cost efficiency, restructuring and downsizing have become code words to tie education more closely to the ideological and economic imperatives of the labour market. This is evident, for instance, in the current conservative assessment of liberal arts programs as ideologically expendable and economically unfeasible". In the immediate context of the college, this trend inevitably leads to a stratification of departments, students and disciplinary knowledge. In this general atmosphere, where the success of an academic programme in the college is assessed on the basis of revenue generation, employability of the students, industry demand, on-campus recruitment etc., disciplines like sociology face very limited choices.

Another important consequence of these changes is the changing composition of students with respect to their socio-economic background. The academic and strategic initiatives taken by the college have succeeded in providing a brand name to the college in the city. This brand name and the visibility that the college acquired with respect to a number of above-stated factors has resulted in making the college a favoured destination for students from Bangalore and from other states as well. The institution attracts students from all over the country, almost entirely from English-speaking, upper caste and middle-upper class backgrounds. Christ College is often described as students' community epitomizing diversity as it has students on campus speaking more than thirty-two different languages and from thirteen different countries. But this diversity also masks a glaring homogeneity with respect to the aspects of caste and class. As Rudolph and Rudolph perceptively pointed out during the 1970s, "The college as community, even as 'happy family,' shaped by visions elaborated at the top by dedicated and competent teachers and willingly accepted by admiring and devoted students, is a paradigm of elite education as it existed prior to the democratic demand for expansion of higher education; prior to the revolution in generational relations that make the class and cultural diversity and the press of number that make 'community' increasingly difficult to perceive, much less to realize" (Rudolph and Rudolph 1972). The prevalence of a student body, predominantly belonging to the upper sections of the society, possessing considerable extent of cultural capital, is an important factor to be taken into consideration while discussing the process of curriculum formulation and teaching-learning practices within the college. The new experiments initiated in the light of autonomy and the nature of syllabus that is framed are influenced and conditioned by this factor that the college primarily caters to the elite students of Bangalore and the rest of India. This flow of elite students into the sociology classes also conditions the practice of sociology at Christ College in a specific manner. The theoretical orientation even in the undergraduate classes and the insistence on reading original articles and highly demanding internal assessment techniques are introduced and experimented upon only because of the presence of such a student body.

In the overall story of the college and its transformation under the conditions of autonomy and other changes is also the story of systematic exclusion. The emergence of Christ College as an institution with impressive infrastructural and an overall elitist atmosphere has excluded the lower caste/class students from the nearby locality from even seeking an admission in the college. Similarly, for the students who hail from Kannada-medium schools and colleges, Christ College is definitely not a choice. Before the grant of autonomous status, the college was required to admit 50 per cent of the students from the Bangalore University in all postgraduate programmes. Accordingly, the Master's programme in sociology also used to receive around twenty students each year from the university and invariably all these students hailed from Kannada-medium backgrounds. Lack of knowledge in English for these students used to be a major hurdle for them as well as for the teachers in the college. Yet, these students could benefit enormously from a number of other factors from the college. But with the grant of autonomy the college could refuse to admit any more students sent from the university and this has virtually sealed the possibility of Kannada-medium students sent by the government getting admitted into the college.

V

Conclusion

The above discussions regarding the functioning of autonomy in Christ College with respect to the practice of sociology in particular and the nature of higher education in general brings forth a number of issues that need careful analysis. Many of the claims made in favour of autonomy highlighting the academic freedom, innovations and quality improvement begin to appear more problematic. Disciplinary practices like curriculum development, teaching and assessment etc. are increasingly becoming fragmented and compartmentalized. The overall objective of education is reduced to the production of individuals with skill and attitudes required by the market economy. Increasing marginalization of teachers is amounting to what Naidoo and Jamieson call 'distortion of pedagogic relations'. "...the limited findings arising from various national contexts has indicated that the reconceptualisation of the complex relationship between students and teachers to that of 'service provider' and 'customer' is likely to be corrosive of both sides of the relationships" (Naidoo and Jamieson, 2005: 276–81). Similarly, autonomous institutions as a model of quality education belie the much needed democratization of higher education in India. The organizational restructuring based on market competitiveness in autonomous educational institutions simultaneously creates hurdles for socially and economically weaker sections to claim access to these centres of learning. The similar economic logic also leads to disciplinary hierarchies, where disciplines espousing humanistic perspectives such as sociology are subordinated to more instrumental and market-oriented disciplines.[2]

In 1972, Rudolph and Rudolph pointed out that college and university autonomy takes its meaning from the settings in which these institutions exist and from the goals they pursue. Like the meaning of values such as justice and freedom, that of autonomy varies with the society, institutional complex, and goals that give it meaning. Hence, it is imperative to analyse and understand the settings in which the present-day autonomous institutions function. Post-1990 liberalization era in its various manifestations define the present-day cultural and structural context of the higher education. This era brought about an erosion of social democratic values and welfare state concerns which were replaced by free market philosophy that stresses individual economic values and gains. In the field of education this trend is characterized by viewing education as a merit good instrumental in catering to the needs of a global knowledge society. According to educationists like J.B.G. Tilak (2005), this marketization of higher education is carried out through various measures like financial privatization of universities, establishment of private institutions and the provision of autonomy. Commenting on the same vein, Krishna Kumar has pointed out:

> Even as the discourse of education as empowerment and liberation continues to occupy centre stage in state rhetoric, ...the potential that education offers as a means of legitimising exclusion and oppression is being tested on a scale way ahead of what research can keep up with. The new super-schools are acquiring the character of export zones of industrial production where any normative supervision by law is perceived as bureaucratic intrusion which is harmful for the pursuit of quality and maintenance of the competitive edge. (Kumar, 2005)

Such being the setting within which autonomy needs to be located, it is evident that the decontexualized rhetoric about the virtues of autonomy needs to be contested. Such contestation would also inform us about how the disciplinary practices of subjects like sociology are increasingly transformed in these new contexts. On the one hand, autonomy is theoretically capable of offering newer pedagogic possibilities to these disciplines as curriculum formation and pedagogical practices are made more open. But, on the other hand, the specific neo-liberal context in which autonomy is practised diminishes and belittles the very relevance and significance of subjects like sociology. The critical and reflexive potential of the subject becomes a non-marketable and therefore unwanted good within the overall language of market economy. The intrinsic disciplinary qualities of sociology are evaluated and devalued against the techno-managerial subjects that are increasingly defining the field of higher education today.

Reviewing the practice of sociology in contemporary times is increasingly becoming complex. A multitude of new locations are emerging which influence the practice of sociology in different ways. The new locations of academic autonomy are one such context, which needs to be systematically analysed and studied. This paper offered one such modest attempt of reviewing the practice of sociology at Christ College, Bangalore. The geographic location of Bangalore and its new metropolitan status and the presence of an emerging new class of economic elites increasingly define the institutional context of a college like Christ College. Within this context the grant of autonomous status gets operationalized in a specific manner thereby making the claims about freedom etc. appear as highly problematic assumptions. The experience of this college indicates to the possibilities and a set of new challenges that the system of autonomy offers to the practice of sociology. The immediate context of the neo-liberal economic language has assumed greater significance in the conceptualization and operationalization of autonomy to increasingly influence the disciplinary practice of humanist subjects like sociology. The provision of autonomy many a time becomes the direct harbinger of an explicit market-oriented education system and thereby brings in a number of restrictions that goes very much against the academic and pedagogical spirit of subjects like sociology.

Notes

1. See Ravi Kumar for a critical commentary on the idea of 'best practices'.
2. This point has been argued by Ravi Kumar forcefully in this volume.

References

Broadfoot, Patricia and Andrew Pollard. 2006. "The Changing Discourse of Assessment Policy: The Case of English Primary Education", in *Education Globalization and Social Change*, edited by A.H. Halsey et al., Oxford: Oxford University Press.

Chaudhuri, Maitrayee (ed.), 2003. *The Practice of Sociology*. New Delhi: Orient Longman.

Das, Veena. 1993. "Sociological Research in India: The State of Crisis", *Economic and Political Weekly*, 27 (23): 1159–61.

Deshpande, Satish. 1994. "The Crisis in Sociology: A Tired Discipline?" *Economic and Political Weekly*, 29 (10): 575–76.

Giroux, Henry A. and Patrick Shannon. 1997. *Education and Cultural Studies: Toward a Performative Practice.* New York: Routledge.

Gray, J. 1990. "Quality of Schooling: Framework of Judgement", *British Journal of Educational Studies*, 38 (3): 204–23.

Heitzman, James. 2004. *Network City: Planning the Information Society in Bangalore.* Delhi: Oxford University Press.

Kumar, Krishna. 2003. "Judicial Ambivalence and New Politics of Education", *Economic and Political Weekly*, December, 6: 5163–66.

Mathew, Thomas C., Andrew Thomas Kennady and Grace Pais. 2005. *Best Practices in Higher Education.* Bangalore: Centre for Publication Christ College.

Ministry of Human Resources Development, Department of Secondary and Higher Education, Government of India. 2005. Report of the Central Advisory Board of Education. Committee on Autonomy of Higher Educational Institutions (CABE), New Delhi: Government of India.

Naidoo, Rajni and Ian Jamieson. 2005. "Empowering Participants or Corroding Learning? Towards a Research Agenda on the Impact on Students Consumerism in Higher Education", *Journal of Education Policy*, 20 (3): 276–81.

Nair, Janaki. 2005. *The Promise of the Metropolis: Bangalore's Twentieth Century.* New Delhi: Oxford University Press.

Rudolph, Susanne Hoeber and Lloyd I. Rudolph (eds.) 1972. *Education and Politics in India: Studies in Organization, Society and Policy.* Delhi: Oxford University Press.

Shah, A.M. 2000. "Sociology in a Regional Context", *Seminar*, p. 495.

Tilak, Jandhyala B.G. 2005. "Higher Education in 'Trishanku' Hanging between State and Market", *Economic and Political Weekly*, September 10, pp. 4029–37.

13

Social Research and the New Centres of Knowledge Production

RAVI KUMAR

The expansion of research and research institutions in the recent past has been one of the most significant developments in the academic universe of India. There are research institutes producing large volumes of research on contemporary issues and also generating, establishing and legitimizing many new ideas in the process.[1] I argue in this paper that this has redefined the nature of social science research. This paper rests on the assumption that different historical junctures produce different kinds of knowledge for "sociology as a body of knowledge cannot be separated from the specific social milieu in which it is produced" (Pathak, 2004: 31). And, the specific historical junctures have to be understood as specific global conjunctures of capitalism. The current rhetoric of 'freedom' and 'autonomy'[2] of colleges and institutions cannot be understood as abstract entities for their form and content are dependent on the needs of capital. In the current context, there is a major ideological reworking taking place, weakening dissent not by force but mostly through 'consent'. Consent is sought through two means: new centres of knowledge production (NCKPs) and co-option of university population within its fold through 'consultancies',[3] or through establishment of the TINA (there is no alternative) principle or through arguments of 'feasibility' and 'viability' flowing out of the TINA syndrome. In this process the actual role of capital in transforming the nature of research and academia almost gets unnoticed. It is in this context that the paper argues that the NCKPs can be fruitfully examined as hegemonic knowledge appropriators.

I

The Shift in Nature of Knowledge Production

The days dominance of the university, as a hegemonic centre of knowledge production, were largely the times when capital accumulation was being undertaken with the active role of the state. For instance, in post-independent India, the formulation of Bombay Plan (Mukherjee, 2002) was a clear reflection of the crisis of accumulation that the Indian private capital faced and wanted the state to develop infrastructure and invest in heavy industries while it expanded its reach in the market. This was the time, termed as the 'welfare state', when the state funded the universities and called for 'autonomy' and 'freedom' of academia. During this phase, the 'academic freedom' and liberty has been a part of the whole paradigm where the character of knowledge production was not challenging the state. Therefore, we find the Education Commission also emphasizing the need to provide freedom to universities, which needed to be differentiated from the profit-motivated management of commercial establishments or even government administrations (GoI, 1966). By 1970s the demand for opening of economy was being made as the private capital's accumulation needed new markets to invest. We witnessed new changes at policy level starting early 1980s (Kumar, 2006a). The withdrawal of state needs to be seen in this context.

The nature of knowledge production, seen in conjunction with the trajectory of capital, also started experiencing changes. Using the same vocabulary of 'production', global discourses which percolated down to India, began arguing for skill-based knowledge, and placed more emphasis on industry or market-driven knowledge, which will be useful in concrete material production processes. This had implications for social sciences as well. The interest in social sciences apart from economics declined. Research across the disciplines was affected as it came to be seen as a waste of time when one could earn more with less time taking technical education or training. Universities also started experiencing these changes. In some instances the course contents of sociology changed. In others new courses were added and new departments which could have very well been part of existing disciplinary framework were opened.

When one refers to the mushrooming of research institutions, it does not mean that there were no such institutions earlier. There has been a fundamental difference in the nature and aim of earlier institutions. Firstly and most importantly, they were not evaluation agencies, basing their work on the programmes run by the state. Rather, they undertook researches on diverse societal questions. For instance, the Centre for the Study of Developing Societies (CSDS), founded in 1964, focused on democratic politics, cultures and the politics of knowledge, critical discourses on science and technology, violence, ethnicity and diversity. The Centre for Studies in Social Sciences, Calcutta, founded in February 1973, began with the aim of promoting and coordinating research in social sciences, with special emphasis on the problems of the eastern region and West Bengal. It has contributed greatly in the area of social science research. Though there has been an increasing tendency towards evaluation-driven research in the institute, perhaps deriving from its mission statement which also said that it would "offer, on request, consultancy services to the Government of India, the Government of West Bengal and other State Governments and Union Territory Administrations, universities, colleges and other educational institutions and organizations in business, industry or trade" (see www.cssscal.org). In the 1970s the Council for Social Development was set up in Delhi, which has been largely dedicated to carrying out evaluation studies of government programmes, but characterizes itself as a research institute. Even in the 1990s some institutions came up focusing on basic social science research. For instance, the Centre for the Study of Culture and Society was established in 1996 by a group of scholars interested in developing new approaches to studying culture in India.

The space for institutions committed to understanding the social phenomenon or change has shrunk drastically. The new research institutions, managed by retired bureaucrats, unlike some of the institutions enumerated above, which are headed by academics, are dominating the field of new 'research'. They receive support from the Government of India, World Bank, UN agencies and many other international sponsoring agencies. Shripad Dharmadhikary, who is analysing the role of World Bank as a knowledge producer, estimates that its budget for research is about US$25 million, apart from which an additional US$20 million is spent on statistical capacity building.

> Bank researchers and their consultants produced nearly 4,000 papers, books, and reports between 1998 and 2005 including more than 2,000 articles in peer-reviewed journals. In addition, the World Bank publishes two peer-reviewed research journals, the *World Bank Research Observer*, and the *World Bank Economic Review*....In addition to research, the Bank produces enormous amounts of knowledge in its economic and sectoral work, technical assistance, country level assessments, project preparation studies, project evaluations, capacity building work and so on. Considering that in 2004, the Bank was involved in about 1,500 active projects we can see the extent of the project related knowledge generated by the Bank. ...
>
> As important as the Bank's in-house system are the many and extensive linkages and networks that the Bank has created with external researchers, research institutes, professionals and others. Some – like the Consultative Group on International Agricultural Research (CGIAR) with its 15 research stations – predate the Knowledge Bank. Others, like the Global Development Learning Network (GDLN), a partnership of over 120 learning centres in nearly 80 countries around the world, are more recent...The World Bank Institute (WBI), founded by the Bank in 1955, is one of the Bank's capacity development instruments. WBI delivered more than 700 learning activities to some 75,000 clients, and awarded 211 scholarships in fiscal year 2007 (Dharmadhikary, 2007).

The shift is immense. Every academic institution has gradually become a part of it either through direct funding or its members becoming part of such projects as consultants. This shift found support from those who argued that the state does not have resources to support such massive research and therefore it was justified that such massive inflow of funds should happen. Their argument helped exonerate the state of its responsibility to support research and allowed space for manipulation of knowledge production by those who could invest. Further, the growing economic distress also justified such research centres as job providers.

There is also a need to look at the current shift in disciplines of social sciences within the context of the above mentioned developments. The debate today is about being 'adaptive'. There is a rapid growth of sponsored research and the significance attached to this research. Such research is often conducted within a framework already provided tacitly or explicitly. For instance, if the Indian state provides a research institute with funds to organize a workshop with academics and bureaucrats (who are the new academics), its intention is very clear: it would not like a consensus against it to evolve. Take the case of one issue such as SEZs (Special Economic Zones) and displacement. The radical arguments in the workshop about SEZs being detrimental to common masses causing displacement, taking away livelihood etc., are all debated with the most spirited and revolutionary fervour but when it comes to understanding the issue, it is not understood as emanating out of the system, or of the relationship between capital, state and the nature of developmental politics. Rather, it is seen as the handiwork of a particular political party, or in many cases, the mal-intention of a particular minister. The reason is that questioning the system is not considered appropriate. Going against the system or moving out of the system for solutions are strictly avoided. Options are searched within the system. The point, however, is not so much about turning against the system but about an analysis that would address questions such as is the SEZ principle not connected to the interests of private capital? Why is the state all out in support of capital? Why do people's interest figure below that of capital for the state? Why do we see the current radical shift in the stand of state? Will SEZs fragment communities, as many activists-analysts argue, or will the process of capitalist individualization by its very nature transform the communities?[4]

II

The Politics of Knowledge Production

Central to the politics of new knowledge production is transformation of both extant university systems as well the proliferation of NCKPs. Traditionally universities have not only worked within the framework of state, but have also been centres of dissent and rebellion. Whether it was the students' movement of 1968, the students' upheaval of 1970s in

India, or later, on many issues universities have time and again demonstrated their vibrant democratic ethos (Kumar, 2007).

Expansion of the NCKPs is justified on the grounds that it has allowed expansion of research and has, therefore, democratized the access to knowledge. There is merit in the argument. But I contend that the resultant democratization of knowledge is seriously flawed. For democratization of knowledge would entail participation of individuals and communities in a process of knowledge production. What is actually taking place is a hierarchization of disciplines. Hence, management, technical and vocational courses are placed/located much higher than fundamental social science disciplines. This diminishes the relevance of fundamental disciplines and is linked to how well the market can expand itself in the sphere of education. While such courses allow capital a continuous supply of labour suited to its needs, the fragmentation of disciplines and encouragement of 'centres' in universities or 'research organizations' simultaneously create spaces for private capital to transform higher education. Social scientists in support of such initiatives need to come out with explanations about questions such as why cannot the minority, dalit, women, peace and conflict or religion studies form part of sociology, political science, economics or history? Why do we need separate centres to study these issues? The same resources could have been harnessed to develop these fundamental disciplines.

III

The New Research Practices: Some Trends

Since the 1990s research has witnessed unprecedented expansion. Earlier research was undertaken by the state-controlled institutions or a few non-state institutions. No doubt, there were international actors, such as the Ford Foundation, but the scale of operation today is very large. The new research today is overwhelmingly 'programme'-based. The different programmes, which are run by the government or the non-government agencies, form the object of investigation. They evaluate the ongoing programmes and suggest improvements in them. The validity of the programmes is seldom questioned. Hence, we find faculty members from reputed academic institutions in the country working for sponsoring agencies to record the 'best practices' in education. (They seldom record the worst practices.) This also ends up in diminishing spaces for critical researches. The findings and analysis tend to fall within the larger conceptual rubric, which the agencies construct. If someone wants to study whether the current policies of 'community participation' and 'decentralization' ignore the complex matrix of caste, class and gender in a village, essential to address the basic developmental questions, the possibility of funding diminishes.

Research therefore becomes a foreclosed exercise. It is not unheard of studies of hundreds of villages completed in a matter of three months. The new trends in research and institution building, I argue, emerge from deep-rooted necessities of capital. It is not coincidence or an evanescent tendency in academic world. They are indications of how knowledge is moulded in a fashion to suit the current needs of capitalism. Hence, what we come across is the tendency to obliterate all possibilities of developing critical knowledge. This is being undertaken within the state-managed institutions as well as non-state institutions. In the former the tendency towards promoting new centres or programmes such as one of peace and conflict studies, dalit and minority studies, gender studies or north-east studies are well-thoughtout strategies aimed at creating: (1) isolated, non-holistic, areas of enquiry; (2) thereby making it easier to suit the needs of the sponsors; and (3) hence, weakening the approaches which looks at phenomenon holistically and dialectically. It also creates, by employing, and therefore obliging, people, a force, which would argue that peace, conflict, religion, gender, religious minority could not be accommodated within existing social sciences. Such centres are also told to generate their own resources and therefore the element of privatizing higher education and reducing the role of state is also pushed through.

The non-state agencies, on the other hand, more freely and starkly pursue a repressive regime. The research which they undertake (for example, as on incentive in education), is 'awarded' to them after a 'bidding' process. In this bidding their technical and methodological ability is assessed. And, therefore, it is not surprising that private limited companies also participate in this whole process. This is also a common practice in many international agencies.

This kind of research necessarily dichotomizes theory and practice. There is an increasing tendency to divide the world of thought into distinct spheres of 'theory' and 'practice'. This distinction also become grounds for not accepting the much needed analysis of society and economy because it ends up in equating 'analysis' with 'theory'. And, the contexts of 'action-based research' in vogue in the so-called 'development sector' derives its legitimacy from this distinction. This situation leaves us with certain important questions that seek to understand 'theory' as 'practice' especially if we look at it from the ideological viewpoint, which demeans 'humanities' and creates a whole argument about 'relevance' and 'irrelevance' of disciplines and methods. Walter Benjamin's idea, though written in the context of art and the trends towards its reproduction, provides us an understanding of what statistics does. For instance, he writes:

> Every day the urge grows stronger to get hold of an object at very close range by way of its likeness, its reproduction. Unmistakably, reproduction as offered by picture magazines and newsreels differ from the image seen by the unarmed eye. Uniqueness and permanence are as closely linked in the latter as are transitoriness and reproducibility in the former. To pry an object from its shell, to destroy its aura, is the mark of a perception whose 'sense of the universal equality of things' has increased to such a degree that it extracts it even from a unique object by means of reproduction. This is manifested in the field of perception what in the theoretical sphere is noticeable in the increasing importance of statistics. The adjustment of reality to the masses and of the masses to reality is a process of unlimited scope, as much for thinking as for perception (Benjamin, 1935).

IV

The Discourse on Knowledge

There is a general feeling that education is the source of upward mobility and a medium to enhance livelihood options. Education is no longer seen as a tool to prepare good citizens, as carriers of democratic values, and as humans who would oppose injustice and inhuman traits in society. The students are being taught through different pedagogical sources – teachers, researches and curriculum – that education is about surviving as better consumers. In other words, the discourse on knowledge itself has changed.

In this discourse the world is seen as one where "knowledge supplants physical capital as the source of present (and future) wealth" (World Bank, 2000: 9). Because the aim of knowledge is to ensure survival of capitalism, it is important that it furthers the ethics of competition on which capitalism survives (Kay, 1979). And, the dominant discourse does not shun away from acknowledging this when it says that "the quality of knowledge generated within higher education institutions, and its availability to the wider economy, is becoming increasingly critical to national competitiveness" (World Bank, 2000: 9). There is a well-defined consistency in this discourse, which sees tertiary education as exercising "a direct influence on national productivity, which largely determines living standards and a country's ability to compete in the global economy" (World Bank, 2002: xx).

The emphasis is on building technical and professional capacity because then only an individual or a nation survives in this highly competitive world economy. The growth of market is seen as democratizing the opportunities and, therefore, everything is addressed in the context of encouraging the market (ibid.: 11). And it is from this point of view that directly or indirectly the courses and institutions of higher education are being encouraged to address the requirements of labour market (ibid.: ix). These developments therefore assign importance only to those disciplines or modes of learning which are effective for the market.

These developments are reflected in India as well. At the level of discourse while the Indian state made it amply clear that the "the universities must make greater efforts to supplement resources from the government" (GoI, 2002a: 17), it replicated the arguments being made by the World Bank and others about the nature of education:

> Higher education, whether in the general or the technical stream, must have links with all national goals and endeavours. To this end, a large number of centres for excellence to turn out quality manpower in areas relevant to industry and society need to be established with the triangular partnership of academia, industry and government. These institutes of excellence are essential to make India a knowledge superpower and would help in retaining our competitive edge in the global economy (GoI, 2002b: 64).

Though some committees have tried to ensure equity in higher education, ultimately their arguments failed to redefine education as one not necessarily connected to market (GoI, 2005). The recent CABE committee failed on same account when it also began its argument by stating that "investment in higher education makes vital contribution to accelerate the process and rate of economic growth, through increasing human productivity. Higher education is, therefore, regarded crucial to the development of developing countries, and to their ability to *compete in the global economy*" (GoI, 2005: 7, emphasis mine). The same report brings out the important functions of higher education as it follows: creation and dissemination of knowledge, supply of manpower, specifically knowledge workers, attitudinal changes for modernization and social transformation; formation of a strong nation-state, and promotion of higher quality of individual and social life. It is widely recognized that these traditional functions of higher education are ever relevant for all societies – modern as well as traditional, and developed as well as developing (ibid.: 8).

What is significant in all these debates is the following: (1) they talk of higher education as an instrument to propel development of market; (2) it is seen as enhancing productivity; (3) it is about skill development; (4) nowhere is the role of higher education seen as developing a critical faculty[5] that could analytically examine the nuances of social relations and social structure; and (5) it is all about how to survive, excel and serve the existing order of things because the ultimate aim is to add strength to national economy so that it marches ahead. The national economy is seen as coterminous with private capital. After all, one company such as Tata Group contributes more than 3 per cent to India's GDP (Singh, 2008). The nature of new knowledge is extremely relevant to understand the politics of knowledge production works through institutionalized forms, which is attempted here.

Theodor Adorno realized the tension between the two tasks of sociological education well, i.e., the tension between 'better understanding' of society and demands of 'livelihood'. He observed: "I have to tell you that the career prospects for sociologists are not good. It would be highly misleading to gloss over this fact. And far from improving, as might have been expected, these prospects have actually got worse" (Adorno, 2000: 1–2). The tension between the aims of acquiring knowledge for better understanding of society and the realities of livelihood do stare at us.

V

Functioning of the New Centres of Knowledge Production

The paper has already noted that there has been a spiralling growth of non-university research centres in the country. One seeks to understand their character and function better in this section. These are primarily of two kinds. One kind of research centres are registered under Societies Registration Act, 1860 and sustain themselves primarily on sponsorship from international and national funding agencies. They identify themselves as 'civil society organizations', which try to put the interests of the common masses first. The other constituents are private limited companies, which undertake evaluations, consultancies and even researches for sponsoring agencies. In both the organizations it is generally social science students which get employment because of the emphasis on the social sector in these organizations. Universities are identified as centres for 'theoretical' research where the nitty-gritty details of 'practical tasks' are not considered seriously. A disjunct is created between theory and practice and a hierarchy in terms of 'social relevance' is created wherein theories find no buyers. The immediate tasks as defined by the powers are seen as significant subjects of research. I seek below to diagrammatically illustrate the conceptual paradigm of NCKPs:

Figure 13.1
Conceptual Paradigm of NCKPs

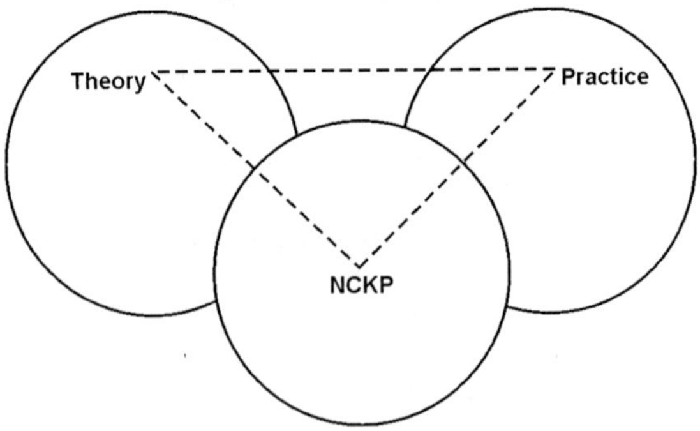

These organizations get funded for particular research projects if they fall in their priority area. A proposal is mooted with a "schedule of prices", as some agencies call it. Based on certain criteria the funding agencies sanction or reject these proposals. Because of the tremendous competition in the area, it is always considered better to include names of some well-known academics as consultants who can demonstrate certain amount of expertise in the area. Once the projects are passed, an MoU is signed which sets in certain terms and conditions of work. There is always a certain kind of pressure to undertake the research as agreed upon. The freedom to deviate is not allowed. In actual practice, when a research is carried forward, there is always a possibility that the researcher may stumble upon certain kinds of new social/cultural complexities of vital significance. This is difficult to incorporate for such changes are generally not permitted as the projects follow the proposals already submitted.

In a university, even though the character of research has been changing rapidly, there remains a possibility to critically explore the nature of disciplines itself or undertake researches through workshops such as the one that led to the making of this volume. It still has the spirit of liberal ethos, a fast receding space and a remnant of welfare capitalism, surviving in its last stage that allows this. But, if one approaches a funding agency to sponsor a workshop of this kind, it becomes difficult to muster resources. For it would not be fall in the priority area because of a perceived disjunct between theory and practice.

There are some deemed universities,[6] whose number have increased over years (Sharma, 2005) and more so rapidly after capital was unbound to perform its function of accumulation without any hindrance, which have emerged as one of the significant constituents of the NCKP.[7] The case of one such institution based in Delhi provides us an opportunity to understand their character. Apart from offering courses, which are definitely costlier and inaccessible to the vast majority, they undertake research as well. These researches are primarily sponsored projects, which they get from the Government of India as well as other non-state sources. In addition to this, they also implement programme-based projects in rural India. In order to multiply profit, the private 'academic' institutions as well as 'deemed' universities engage their faculty members in not only looking after these projects but also give them a target amount that they must bring to the institution through projects. There are short-term informational productions of knowledge 'resources', which hardly contribute to the understanding of societies in long run or even the disciplines that these institutions purportedly specialize in.

The Personnel

The NCKPs, depending on their area of specialization, attract students from disciplines such as sociology, economics, political science etc. However, another significant development that has occurred during the last two decades or so is the emergence of members of bureaucracy as the new academics. The participation of bureaucrats in the NCKPs should neither be mistaken for democratization of knowledge production and appropriation nor it be taken as a breach in the power-knowledge framework. It is rather a part of the dynamics of the framework within which an NCKP operates that produces knowledge for the system. The producers of knowledge, the researchers – seldom manage to hold on to their knowledge, which is appropriated by one or the other and sold in the market in tangible commodified forms of books, papers, articles etc. The institutional framework legitimizes this.

After their retirement, the bureaucrats who may have at one point signed the endorsement and supported the SEZs, dams or other such projects etc., spell out their implications. They are incorporated in the institutional framework of NCKPs because it helps them get more projects, augments their income and in a larger sense, strengthens the status quo. These people, by virtue of their location, the state, would have good relationship/connections with the sponsoring agencies. In context of research, their job profile ensures an experience of some familiarity with rural problems. A survey of the NCKPs and the recent literature that they have produced reveals the strong presence of ex-administrators, no doubt, some of them have been doing interesting work. The problem is not about shunning or outright rejection of the work that is being undertaken. That would be unjustified. The issue is that their presence which occurs at a historical conjuncture of capitalism perpetuates it more efficiently instead of transforming the nature of knowledge production.

Decades of experience in the government in many ways shape government personnel. For instance, the undemocratic ethos of the state's institutional framework, where the administrators hold the key, is many a time replicated. The lack of awareness about the developments in academic world, and the emergence of new schools of thought, deprive them of the vital inputs that the research would need when conducting any studies – be it on dalits, women, schooling, etc. This does not happen because of any innate character of bureaucracy but rather because of the absence of required training and familiarization with the subject. The problem gets compounded if the boss plays an interventionist role in the research work and more importantly prevents a liberal space for them to operate in. The NCKPs are assisted by people coming from diverse disciplines, with experience in research as the requirements are generally postgraduation or a doctorate. The working environment becomes difficult for any genuine fundamental research to take place as every member has to file his/her quarterly/monthly reports of activities, the projects they have undertaken and the plans they undertake or the seminars that they attend. This puts undue pressure to perform and become part of an order of things that survives on quantity, fast assimilation of what is asked to do or prescribed or, in other words, the world of the NCKPs.

Another significant aspect of the NCKPs is the participation of members from the academia as 'consultants'. The academics from the premier universities become busy writing reports for one sponsoring agency or the other or becoming consultants of the research projects that they undertake. In some of the instances it has also been found that the faculty members are involved in documenting 'best practices' of a programme. They seldom have much scope to alter the nature of the programme. They are only a cog in the wheel, having one specific pre-defined role. In some of the departments the situation has come to such a stage that faculty members are flooded with projects, hampering even the duties that they have as university faculty. Once the participation of the members of university academia becomes inseparable from the NCKP, the nature of disciplines is also bound to be affected.

This development, however, need not be taken as a surprise. It is part of the larger transformations that knowledge has experienced as an instrument of capital over years from welfarism to neo-liberalism. Autonomy gets scuffled significantly in this whole process, an autonomy which survives only as a remnant of welfare capitalism. The slogans of autonomy[8] traditionally attached with universities were products of a time when the state wanted the education to be its own estate and, more importantly, when Indian capital was not in a position to maintain or use directly the universities. It was a time of so-called nation-building which needed such a system. Today, when the state wants to withdraw and provide space to private capital to operate and produce knowledge that it wants to use, 'autonomy' gets redefined. From an era when academic freedom was seen in conjunction with autonomy (Kamba, 1993: 22) to today when it means commercial autonomy – the freedom to have the curriculum, fee and admission as desired by private capital.[9]

As pointed out earlier, the issues are not resolved through binary opposites whether the universities are more liberal or the NCKPs. It may help here to distinguish two forms of regeneration formal and informal. One method of control may be to institute certain rules, such as forty hours of compulsory weekly working at the department, generating own resources, instituting systems of daily attendance etc. These are formal or coercive modes of regimentation. Another way is to regiment indirectly, through bringing in an ethos where the actor is induced into modes of, for instance, self-censorship or acting as if more project-based research would be necessary for his existence. The university professors, when they begin undertaking extensive consultancies, extent into realm of NCKP (as the Figure 13.2 below shows). They get moulded to suit the demands of the market of knowledge. Their work is determined by what the market wants them to do.

Figure 13.2

The Overlapping Relationship of NCKPs and Universities

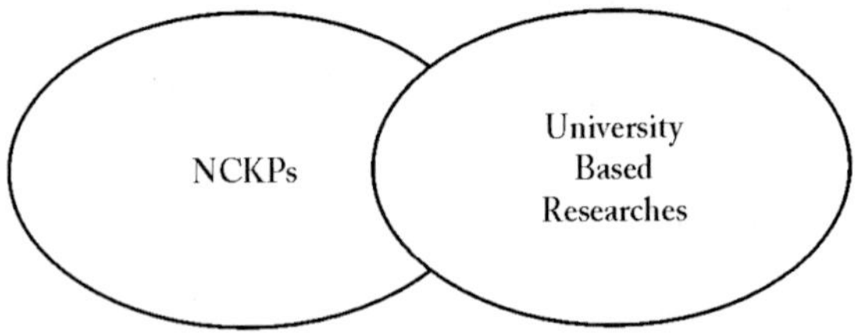

The Nature of Projects

As a part of the emphasis on programme-driven research,[10] proposals are invited to record the best practices of a programme. For instance, international sponsoring agencies invite proposals to record and demonstrate how successful have been the implementation of educational programmes so that it could be shown worldwide to gain and establish validity and stature. In these kinds of research the sphere of research is clearly defined and restricted. Any effort to critique the programme is not entertained. While this research establishes the validity of ongoing programmes, it also destroys the possibilities of critical engagement with social realities. Validity of ongoing programmes implies endorsing a particular paradigm and understanding of social problems, such as gendered exploitation, patriarchy, community etc. For instance, character of the state, nature of surplus accumulation in agrarian India, relationship between the nature of surplus accumulation, cultural symbols and localized ideological apparatuses are not explored to understand why the Mushars in Bihar are not even able to cross the 5 per cent literacy mark. It also means that the way the particular agency conceives of education, such as in terms of non-formal education centres for poor and girl child, also gets validated. It never raises the question that the two forms of education system – formal and non-formal – institutionalizes discrimination in education (Kumar and Paul, 2006; Kumar, 2006b).

After the 73rd and 74th amendments there is an omnipresence of discourse on community participation and strengthening of schooling system through community intervention and participation. In this context, nearly all the states have village education committees (VECs) in some form or the other. Community participation within the current development discourse implies that the rural/urban people participate in the management processes and make the school more efficient and accountable. The criteria used to assess the functioning of VECs are those they actually meet. Any critical social science research would reveal how heterogeneous communities are and, therefore, for a VEC to function and ensure equity and quality in schooling would mean confronting vital issues of social inequity and caste-class based hierarchies of the village. The dalits are not even able to speak before others. The symbolism, economics and politics of a village life, for instance, determine the nuances of actual participation. Most of the researches undertaken by the NCKPs are time-bound, short-term and pre-determined because of which they perforce have to make quick judgmental conclusions on the issues of 'empowerment' and 'participation'.

The way researches are formulated need to be considered seriously because it reveals how researches are pre-determined to serve a certain purpose. Quite interestingly, as already mentioned above, the researches are done through inviting bids, thus transforming research into a market, which gets determined by the price that one quotes (though marks are also given for methodology to demonstrate objectivity). A serious ramification of this is the kind of insecurity that it poses for the applicant research agency regarding the possibilities of winning the bid. Hence, the applicant makes every effort to go by what the sponsoring agency wants or would like in a proposal. This would even involve the objectives of research (which is in fact pre-determined because then only the bid can be invited) as well as methodology. For example, for a research on incentives on education, the sponsoring agency lays down the variables that are to be included in the study such as the political viability, effective targeting, administrative operability, adequacy, learning environment of children, impact of incentives, collateral effects, household level decision-making etc.

The NCKPs and their Role as Sensitising Agencies

The NCKPs, apart from engaging in research work, also undertake many other activities, extending from implementation of programmes to organization of workshops that would sensitize people on issues of social relevance such as domestic violence, displacement, gendered oppression etc. The NCKPs, as mentioned earlier, are spread across the country and even in hinterlands. Their 'research' though small in size would involve filling up questionnaires and collating information on many aspects. While they can be useful for any social scientist but the processes that they follow are more or less replications of the larger models that we have at the core of whole paradigm. Two examples will be of great significance in the present context.

While doing fieldwork in a village in the vicissitudes of Patna in Bihar, I came across an NCKP, which was organizing a sensitization workshop for village women on the relevance of Lokayukts. The District Judge had come to enlighten women, who were mobilized by the NCKP. The judge tried to appeal to women (who were shyly sitting there) to avoid conflicts in the household so that the need to go to court does not arise.

In the second example, workshops are organized to sensitize the personnel engaged in implementing the rehabilitation and resettlement programmes in Madhya Pradesh, Uttaranchal etc. In the workshops held for a week or some days, is it really possible to sensitize the personnel. Hence, if the patwari offers more compensation to the rich landed gentry of a displacement area by mischievously classifying his land in A category and brings the land of the poor peasantry into C category (to reduce the compensation) even if it is in A category, after attending the workshop does s/he become sensitive to his/her wrong actions?

Speakers in the workshop are critical of government policies, of displacing people, of not paying enough compensation, and of being dictated by the market. However, the raising of issues like why does the government do that, why were there no protests during the Nehruvian era on displacement and why are there more protests now, would clearly fall outside the protocols and parameters of NKPCs.

Notes

1. Archana Prasad's and Madhu Sharan's chapters on social audit and corporate sociology respectively are but two such instances.
2. R. Santhosh and S. Varghese's chapter is an interesting exploration of the rise of autonomous colleges.
3. This trend as evident in the volume extends to all regions. See Singh, V. Sujatha, Nanda, Deb, Ganguly, Jha, Nongkynrih, Mukhopadhyay, in this volume.
4. Amites Mukhopadhyay's discussion on the conceptual journey of 'community' in the volume is instructive.
5. See the discussion on the role of critical/liberal education.
6. There have been some deemed universities continuing before the liberalization of Indian economy began and one can very well question the need for such institutions when the state should have been providing the same functions of expanding higher education. However, the number of deemed universities has multiplied in an unprecedented manner in recent past due to the state's approval to the blatant privatization of higher education. The paper is referring primarily to these institutions.
7. Interestingly, another significant constituent in social science research in recent times has been some private limited companies, like New Concept Information Pvt. Ltd., Indicus Analytics Pvt. Ltd., etc. which also bid for research proposals.
8. Great amount of literature was produced by the international bodies such as the UN, which called for autonomy and defined universities' role in

terms of freedom for academics to teach and research and one can locate the changes in its language now when it calls for education for skill development, strengthening manpower resources, assisting economic growth etc. Seldom do we locate these changes. See Kamba (1993), Moor (1993) and Andren and Johansson-Dahre (1993) for the debates painting a happy picture of academic freedom and research.

9. An interesting aspect of this autonomy is also presented by Prasad (2005), where she argues about the mutation of the concept of autonomy itself from the days of Education Commission (1964–66) to now.
10. It is important to note to that the term used by the sponsoring as well as implementing agencies is 'research', and it is this aspect which has established that even evaluation of a State Resource Centre of literacy or documenting 'best practices' are counted as research work.

References

Adorno, Theodor. 2000. *Introduction to Sociology.* Cambridge: Polity Press.

Andren, Carl-Gustaf and Ulf Johansson-Dahre. 1993. "Academic Freedom and University Autonomy", in *Academic Freedom and University Autonomy.* European Centre for Higher Education, UNESCO: Romania, pp. 40–48.

Benjamin, Walter. 1935. The Work of Art in the Age of Mechanical Reproduction, available at http://www.arthistoryarchive.com/arthistory/modern/The-Work-of-Art-in-the-Age-of-Mechanical-Reproduction.html, downloaded on 12th August, 2007.

Beteille, Andre. 2006. "Sociology and Current Affairs", *Sociological Bulletin,* May–August, 55 (2): 201–214.

Chaudhuri, Maitrayee (ed.), 2003. *The Practice of Sociology.* Delhi: Orient Longman.

Dharmadhikary, Shripad. 2007. Manufacturing Consent through Selective Knowledge, available at http://www.indiatogether.org/2007/oct/opi-wbank.htm, downloaded on 18th October, 2007.

Deshpande, Satish. 2004. *Contemporary India: A Sociological View.* Delhi: Penguin Books.

Government of India. 1966. Education and National Development: Report of the Education Commission, 1964–66. Ministry of Education, New Delhi: Government of India.

—. 2002a. Tenth Five-Year Plan 2002–07. Vol. I, Planning Commission, New Delhi: Government of India.

—. 2002b. Tenth Five Year Plan 2002–07. Vol. II, Part I, Planning Commission, New Delhi: Government of India.

—. 2005, June. Report of the CABE Committee on Financing of Higher and Technical Education. National Institute of Educational Planning and Administration, New Delhi.

Kamba, Walter. 1993. "University Autonomy", in *Academic Freedom and University Autonomy.* European Centre for Higher Education, UNESCO: Romania, pp.18–23.

Kay, Geoffrey. 1979. *The Economic Theory of the Working Class.* London: Macmillan.

Kelsh, Deb and Dave Hill. 2006, March. "The Culturalisation of Class and the Occulding of Class Consciousness: The Knowledge Industry in/of Education", *Journal of Critical Education Policy Studies,* 4 (1), available at www.jceps.com/print.php?articleID=59

Kumar, Ravi. 2007. ''Relevance', 'Mobility' and 'Upgradation': It's Market All the Way in the Higher Education Policy Making", www.radicalnotes.com

—. 2006a, September. "When Gandhi's Talisman No Longer Guides Policy Considerations: Market, Deprivation and Education in the Age of Globalisation", *Social Change,* 36 (3): 1–46.

—. 2006b. "Equality, Quality and Quantity: Mapping the Challenges before Elementary Education in India", in Ravi Kumar (ed.), *The Crisis of Elementary Education in India.* New Delhi: Sage Publications, pp. 13–56.

Kumar, Ravi and Rama Paul. 2006. "Institutionalising Discrimination: Challenges of Educating Urban Poor in Neo-Liberal Era", in Sabir Ali (ed.), *Managing Urban Poverty.* New Delhi: Council for Social Development and Uppal Publishing House, pp. 253–289.

Moor, Ruud A. de. 1993. "Academic Freedom and University Autonomy: Essentials and Limitations", in *Academic Freedom and University Autonomy.* European Centre for Higher Education, UNESCO: Romania, pp. 58–66.

Mukherji, Partha Nath. 2005, "For a National Social Science Policy", *Sociological Bulletin,* May–August. 54 (2): 155–170.

—. 2006, "Sociology for What?: Rethinking Sociology in an Era of Transformatory Changes", *Sociological Bulletin,* May–August. 55 (2): 172–200.

Pathak, Avijit. 2004, "Teaching/Learning Sociology: A Critical Engagement with Modernity", *Sociological Bulletin,* January–April. 53 (1): 31–48.

Prasad, Madhu. 2005, November–December "Autonomy and the Commericialisation of Higher Education", *Social Scientist,* 33 (11–12): 43–48.

Sharma, Vijender. 2005. "Commercialisation of Higher Education in India", *Social Scientist*, 33 (9–10): 65–74.

Singh, Sandeep. 2008, "The Man…and his Dream Machine", *The Indian Express*, January 13. pp. 10–11.

Talib, Mohammad and Savyasaachi. 2003. "What Skills Can Students Acquire form Social Sciences?" in Maitrayee Chaudhuri (ed.), *The Practice of Sociology*. Delhi: Orient Longman, pp. 72–96.

World Bank. 2000. *Higher Education in Developing Countries: Peril and Promise* (The Task Force on Higher Education and Society), Washington DC: World Bank.

—. World Bank. 2002. *Constructing Knowledge Societies: New Challenges for Tertiary Education: A World Bank Report.* Washington DC: World Bank.

14

Why Choose Sociology?

Tamil Nadu in Global Times

MADHU SHARAN

Globalization has many dimensions (Stiglitz, 2002; Rodrik, 2002). In this paper I confine myself to rapid advances in information technology (IT), increased volume and variety of cross-border transactions and growth of employment in the state of Tamil Nadu. Tamil Nadu ranks third in foreign direct investment (FDI) approvals (cumulative 1991–2002) of $5,000 million, next only to Maharashtra ($8,100 million) and Delhi ($6,700 million). The state's FDI constitutes 9.12 per cent of the total FDI in the country. Most of the FDI has come in the automobile and auto components manufacturing, technology sector and in the manufacture of electronic equipment.

Many heavy engineering and manufacturing-based companies are centred in and around the suburbs of Chennai, which has earned it the nickname "The Detroit of Asia". Chennai boasts the presence of global vehicle manufacturing giants like Ford, Renault, Nissan, Hyundai, Caterpillar, BMW and Mitsubishi. Domestic heavyweights like MRF, Ashok Leyland, Royal Enfield, Mahindra & Mahindra, TAFE tractors and TVS too have set up large manufacturing capacities in the suburbs of Chennai.

Electronics manufacturing is a growing industry in Tamil Nadu. Companies like Nokia, Motorola, Sony Ericsson, Samsung, Cisco and Dell have all chosen Chennai as their South Asian manufacturing hub.

Ericsson also has a research and development (R&D) facility in the city. Big EPC companies have set up their engineering centres, which include Saipem I Project Services Ltd., Technip, Foster Wheeler, Petrofac and Technimont. The Austrian company, Austrian Energy and Environment has a design office here and there is a significant presence of the local giant Larsen & Tubro.

The growth of the IT and BPO sector in Tamil Nadu has been spectacular. The city employs over 1,00,000 computer professionals and software exports from Tamil Nadu rose from $1,600 million in 2003–04 to $2,400 million in 2004–05. Experts have opined that Tamil Nadu is well poised to emerge as the top IT state in India as well as a gateway to Southeast Asia.[1] The facts on ground lend credence to these conclusions.

Companies such as HCL, Infosys, TCS, Wipro, Satyam, Cognizant, Virtusa, Xansa and Verizon as also many others have offices in Chennai. Infosys Technologies has set up India's largest software development centre in Chennai to house 25,000 software professionals at an estimated investment of $270 million.

While outsourcing of production in the manufacturing sector, comprising largely blue-collar jobs has been going on for a while, recent years have seen significant amounts of offshoring of white-collar jobs in information and communications technology (ICT) enabled services activity, such as back office work processes, call centre operations, medical transcription, accounting, legal research, radiology jobs among others. A great deal of literature is available on the nature and implications of these developments. (Anderson and Cavanagh, 2004; Bardhan, 2006a; Bardhan and Kroll 2003; Bardhan, 2006b; Bardhan, 2003; Bhagwati et al., 2004; Blinder, 2005; Samuelson el al., 2004; Mckinsey, 2003; Hira and Hira, 2005; Dossani and Kenney 2004; Freeman, 2005).

Once again, Chennai is the preferred destination for companies outsourcing their high-end knowledge intensive operations. Testimony to this is the presence of major market research companies such as Frost & Sullivan and equity research companies such as Irevna in Chennai. Chennai is also a hub for e-publishing with over 45 e-publishing units registered in the city.

It is widely accepted that the presence of good infrastructure and tax incentives have played their role in attracting investment to Tamil Nadu. Similarly, the presence of a highly skilled labour force, especially specialists in the engineering discipline, has greatly influenced the choice of multinational firms when zeroing in on the state/city to create manufacturing capacities. Their presence, in turn, has further accentuated the desire of students, and their parents, to pursue science and technology related courses. The impressive statistics of employment in this sector has led to a 54 per cent increase in the intake of students in courses relating to the IT sector.[2]

It is against this backdrop that the recent changes that have occurred in the practice of social science subjects, particularly sociology in Tamil Nadu, have to be understood. There is an increased popularity of sociology as a choice of subject among students especially in the last three to four years. Two developments seem to be driving this change: a pronounced increase in the importance of corporate social responsibility (CSR) and greater awareness of the need to create an appropriate disaster management strategy, especially in the wake of the devastation caused by tsunami in December 2004.

I

The Changing Trends in Students' Choices

Tamil Nadu produces the highest number of engineering graduates in India (around 30,000) every year. The strong preference exhibited by students, and their parents, for science subjects shall perhaps ensure that the state's numero uno position on this count shall not suffer. The numerous IT and auto and ancillary companies have naturally hired a large number of individuals with backgrounds in engineering and applied sciences. An interesting development is the recruitment of students with degrees in Social Sciences to look after the companies' HR and CSR needs. This puts students of Social Work, Sociology and Anthropology at an advantage (as far as jobs are concerned) over students of other Social Sciences streams. Consequently, several colleges in Tamil Nadu, and particularly in Chennai, have altered their curriculum and introduced several skill-oriented courses to suit the growing demands of the market.

The CSR agenda of a company is no longer viewed as a liability on corporate resources. Companies have increasingly come to realize that CSR is an investment with multiple benefits for the corporate sector. Various empirical research findings point to a strong positive correlation between CSR and corporate profitability. This has furthered the growth of CSR.[3]

On August 26, 2006, the Confederation of Indian Industry (CII) announced that it would set up a Centre of Excellence for CSR in Chennai. The Centre will decide on instituting awards for corporates to encourage them to take up CSR. Speaking on the occasion, Prabhat Pani, Chief Operating Officer, Roots Group, explained that companies had moved away from the traditional view that firms were owned by shareholders and their money could not be deviated for CSR work. Today, the prevalent view is that business has an obligation to society that extend beyond its narrow obligation to owners and shareholders.

Earlier, in the same month, while accepting the Dr M.S. Swaminathan Award for Environmental Protection – 2006 on behalf of ITC, Y.C. Deveshwar, Chairman, ITC Limited said, "CSR can be a value proposition for companies". He spoke of a business model where customers would choose products based on the CSR portfolio of the company. "Profit is a by-product of business. The real aim is to do good for the society," he said.

In the context of India, it is becoming increasingly evident that this corporate activism is being viewed as sustainable, acceptable, and valuable as a change agent. In recent times, a number of foundations set up by leading firms in Andhra Pradesh and Tamil Nadu, including Nokia, Infosys, Wipro, Tata, Hyundai, Ford, TVS, IBM etc., have taken a keen interest in corporate activism to improve health care, education, living conditions, and to reduce poverty.

A visit to the websites of several organizations confirms that this is a growing trend. We look at two such examples:

- *SAP website*: "In line with SAP's commitment to the communities in which we live and work, Labs India has been actively driving and participating in various projects that focus on education and children. We also support disaster relief and rehabilitation projects, while engaging in community building with an aim towards all-round development of the community and its people. Employees at SAP Labs India are also enthusiastic about corporate giving, whenever the need arises."
- *Aventis Pharma website*: "At Aventis Pharma Limited in India, CSR is our passion. The company's commitment, aligned with that of the Group, extends beyond issues of health alone. We take pride not only in providing products that facilitate health and well-being, but also in giving back to society. It is our endeavour

to be recognized as a company that is socially responsible and that cares for people, and we regard the identification and implementation of humanitarian sponsorship programmes as key tasks in the leveraging of our company's equity."

An increased demand for individuals to handle CSR and HR portfolio in these large firms has led to a simultaneous increase in the demand for students with backgrounds in Social Sciences. Those recruited are expected to carry out research, understand, relate to and engage the wider community for developmental programmes for their firms and to secure a good brand image. Additionally, it has also led to a new branch in Social Sciences called 'Corporate Ethnography' to equip individuals to study, understand and handle issues of HR and social development in the corporate firms. Several colleges in Chennai have begun offering courses in 'Corporate Sociology' in their undergraduate and postgraduate streams. Madras University has, in fact, introduced a full-time postgraduate course called 'Corporate Sociology' to equip students with the requisite skills for the changing market.

The growing popularity of corporate ethnography has been written about widely in newspapers in Chennai and I quote from one of the articles by Sandhya U. that was published in *The Hindu,* on 6th December, 2006 titled, 'New gadget? Let the ethnographer see it first':

- "NEW SETS of gadgets have been given to your employees but there is a snag and they are finding it difficult to use them. A technician who was called in to fix the problem leaves saying that the gadgets are in perfect condition. For the employees the problem thus remains unsolved. So, what do you do? An ethnographer can tell you why your employees are unable to work with the gadgets and where the real problem lies.
- The field of corporate ethnography uses the sciences of Sociology and Anthropology to study the workers' lives, the way in which they work together and use the available technology. An ethnographer's job is to know how the customer handles a particular product, alterations that can be made to the existing product, the use the product could be put to, the influence of regional differences on the way it is used, the scope for additional innovation in that particular category etc. An ethnographer has to coordinate with the engineer and help them build a highly customer-specific

product. He finds out 'what people want from technology and how companies can cater to their needs'. This is why the role of ethnography is growing considerably and more and more companies are taking interest in it".[4]

Since various multinational companies view CSR as a critical function, hiring people to discharge this responsibility in an efficient manner has become equally important. In the last five years, at least 30 large corporate firms have established their presence in Chennai and its adjoining areas either by opening an office or by setting up manufacturing units and/or service facilities. Consequently, the demand for people possessing varied nature of skills has increased significantly. These opportunities are available both to individuals with an engineering/technical background and to students of social sciences, for placements in the core activities and HR and CSR functions respectively.

Tsunami and After

Another driving force, which has resulted in better career opportunities for students of Sociology, has been the growing realization of the need for an effective disaster management mechanism and structure. The tsunami, which struck the coast of Tamil Nadu on December 26, 2004, has had some unexpected fallouts. One such outcome was the increased demand for Sociology graduates emanating from the numerous external agencies and NGOs that came to be set up to deal with its after effects. It impacted the practice of Sociology in Tamil Nadu as a large number of them had their offices in Chennai and some continue to do so even as some others have withdrawn their services after the completion of their goals. For students of Sociology and Social Work, it opened promising career opportunities and good pay packets as most of these agencies received funding from international bodies.

II

The Practice of Sociology in Times of Change

To ensure that the skills being transmitted to students are in line with market demands numerous alterations have been made in the syllabus of Sociology offered by various institutions. To coordinate the placement of students to carry out/oversee HR activities in these multinational firms, placement cells have been set up in almost all colleges of Chennai offering courses in Sociology. This paper draws from both quantitative and qualitative data. It includes figures of enrolment from colleges, dropout rates and individuals recruited through placement cells in colleges. Qualitative data includes in-depth interviews of students and staff members of colleges offering graduate and postgraduate courses in Sociology and with senior functionaries of some corporate offices offering employment opportunities to these students. The study has also benefited from the material regarding the society and the practice of sociology in Tamil Nadu available on the Internet. Additionally, informal interviews were held with people residing in the state for generations and also with those who have come from other states to work in the firms operating in the state and with the state government. These included academics, social workers, government servants, students both from Tamil Nadu and those from other states etc. These talks proved immensely useful as they gave a good insight into the perceptions and thought processes of people located differently. As is evident, this paper has deployed a wide set of methods[5] and drawn upon a range of sources to both document and understand:

- *curriculum development* – understanding the demands of the market and the changes in the syllabus thereof. This section has excerpts of interviews of the faculty members and of the syllabus;
- *choices students make* – understanding the reasons for their choice to study the subject and their aspirations for the future;
- *role of the placement agencies* – their – coordination with the companies, institutions and their methods of recruitment;
- *the trends and perceptions* that emerge from the survey.

Information was drawn from a diverse range of participants, i.e., students, faculty of the sociology department of colleges, staff dealing with placement cell and the corporate organizations recruiting these students through these cells. The sample of the study included students, parents, faculty members as well as the employers of the corporate firms hiring students from such colleges.

- *Students:* A sample of 543 were students selected on a random basis and interviewed collectively in informal situations and from them a sample of 280 students were selected on a random basis and interviewed individually. These students belonged to the six colleges offering Sociology at the undergraduate and postgraduate levels. The students of both the colleges offering Sociology at the postgraduate levels, i.e., Madras University and Queens Mary College were interviewed. The sample details are given below:

- *Parents:* This category was the most difficult to interview as they were either not interested or not available for comments. Still structured interviews of some 54 parents were taken over the phone to get their views on the subject.
- *Faculty members:* Nearly all the faculty members of the sociology department in all the six colleges were interviewed. The heads of the department (HoDs) were interviewed in a more detailed, in-depth manner than the remaining staff. Staff members handling the placement cells of three colleges were also interviewed.
- *Corporate firms:* Heads and/or senior executives of four firms, which had hired students with a sociology background and the new recruits serving these institutions were also interviewed.

Data of colleges offering sociology: There are five colleges, which offer an undergraduate programme in sociology, and two that offer the course at the postgraduate level. For the undergraduate programme, the following data is relevant:[6]

Name of the college	*Year of inception of the sociology dept.*	*Total no. of students enrolled (all three years)*	*Type*	*Faculty members*
Queens Mary College	1978	112	All girls Govt. aided	7
Stella Maris	1971	180	All girls UGC aided	7
MOP Vaishnav College for Women	1996	188	All girls Self-financed	4
Loyola College	1983	194	All boys UGC aided	8
Kanika Parmeshwari College for Women	2003	No information available	All girls Self-financed	–

As far as postgraduate colleges are concerned only two colleges offer a degree course in Sociology, one being Madras University and the other is Queens Mary College. The table below gives us an idea of the type of courses offered by these colleges and the number of students enrolled therein:

Name of the college	*Type of post graduate programme*	*No. of students enrolled (Year 1 + Year 2)*
Madras University	(a) Sociology	20 + 18 = 38
	(b) Corporate Sociology	20 + 19 = 39
Queens Mary College	(a) Sociology	16 + 14 = 30
Loyola College	(a) Medical College	25 + 23 = 48
Stella Maris	(a) Social Work	32 + 28 = 60

Curriculum Development in Colleges

The growth of IT industry in the state has impacted all spheres of social and economic life, including higher education and its role in society. After interviewing several faculty members associated with teaching of Sociology, both at the undergraduate and postgraduate levels, it became evident that the job market requirements guide curriculum development in these institutions. The students too seem to be forsaking further research and academic pursuit in favour of skill-oriented courses available in almost all the colleges in Chennai to cater to the evolving needs of the market.

Detailed interviews with the HoDs and the staff members of the sociology department revealed that colleges usually revise their syllabus once every three years, when they make significant changes in it. However, they review it each year and minor changes can be effected during the annual review too, but in the presence of the syllabus committee. The syllabus committee in all the colleges comprises the Principal and subject faculty of the concerned college, a representative from Madras University and two external experts. These experts could be from the academia, development sector or even the corporate sector.

The HoD of Sociology of Stella Maris College, Sujatha remarked:

> Syllabus is designed keeping in mind the changing demands of society. It is both knowledge based as well as job oriented. All the papers focus on development issues. Topics that we felt were

> irrelevant, like rural and urban sociology were changed to rural and urban development, and were contextualized to suit modern times. The manner in which the study of caste was hitherto undertaken was changed and modernized to understanding "caste in the new avatar" comprising the linkages between caste and politics and its intrusion in other fields. We have tried to do away with everything that is traditional and does not fit in with the changing times except for Theory and Research Methodology which we feel will always be useful.

Padma Subramanian, who has been teaching Sociology in a leading private college, MOP Vaishnav College for Women, in Chennai for the last 14 years, expressed similar views:

> Ever since the Sociology Department became autonomous in 2004, the Board has been designing the syllabus and have made it more skill oriented by adding topics like Corporate Sociology, Media Sociology and a lot of project work with organizations in the development sector, NGOs and corporates. Importance of Research and Methodology has remained intact, as in the development sector and IT companies a great need will be felt to do research and write reports. A separate paper on Statistics has been added in Research and Methodology as also topics like Sociology of Organizations (NGOs) and Human Resource Management. In the 3rd year, a month long internship has been added for students during their summer vacations. Earlier it was with NGOs but now increasingly such internships are with HR Departments of firms. The subject thus has been value added and made more useful for the students.

The prospectus of the undergraduate course in Sociology of MOP College, which is given in Annexure I not only mentions the syllabus but also explicitly details the career that students can take up after graduating from the course. The final semester in Sociology has several skill-oriented courses to make it suitable for the market. The detailed syllabus of Human Resource Management and Corporate Social Responsibility is also attached in the Annexure II and gives a good idea of how "value addition" and "packaging of Sociology" has been attempted to reorient the subject to cater to market needs.

Similarly, a UGC aided college like Loyola also has incorporated papers like Human Resource Management, Sociology of Organizations, with an internship in the fourth semester (see table below) to make it relevant for the market. Here too, the prospectus mentions in the first page itself on why students should study the subject:[7]

Semester VI: Sociology: Loyola College for Boys					
VI	SO 6600	Urban Sociology (or)	MS	4	Both
	SO 6603	Rural Sociology	MS	4	Both
	SO 6601	Industrial Sociology (or)	MS	4	Both
	SO 6604	Community Development	MS	4	Both
	SO 6602	Urban Planning (or)	MS	2	Both
	SO 6605	Rural Planning	MS	2	Both
	SO 6650	**Skill Based Course:** – Human Resource Management – Sociology of Organization – Internship *	SK	10	CA

* One month training + field report + viva voce

The prospectus further deliberates on the need for introducing Medical Sociology as a full-time postgraduate programme:

> Master's programme in Medical Sociology was started in the year 2004–2005, keeping in view the fact that Tamil Nadu, particularly Chennai is fast becoming the Mecca for quality health care seekers. The need for sociologically informed technical man power in health care services/industries is the reason for this programme of study. This course, first of its kind in India, prepares the students into various areas of health care services management, which includes hospital human resources management, health outreach programme management, medical ethics and law to mention a few. The PG programme in Medical Sociology has internship in a multi-specialty hospital for six months as a course requirement for completing the programme.

The same trends are evident in the government-aided Queens Mary College. Kalavati, who has been teaching sociology for eight years in the college, observed:

> ...the current syllabus has been customized to include all the current topics and all the irrelevant topics (like theories) have been discarded. More fieldwork has been included and the syllabus has been made more 'job oriented' and 'relevant'. Topics like hospital management, gerontology, gender and society, industrial sociology have been included. Our intention is that the students should be able to get good job placement after they graduate from college. At the PG

> level, we have added Industrial Relations and HR Management. Even though there were protests from the University not to include Corporate Sociology to maintain the exclusivity of the subject, yet we have gone ahead and included it for the sake of the future of the students.

Nothing perhaps captures the packaging of the subject more than the introduction of a postgraduation course in Corporate Sociology in Madras University in 2003. The syllabus outline, mentioned in the Annexure III gives us an idea of the course content which reads similar to any course in Business Management.

According to D. Jaylakshmi, HoD, Madras University,

> The course was conceived three years ago and there were discussions with corporate firms. With a semester pattern and choice-based credit system, the course provides a strong theoretical foundation and practical inputs necessary for the corporate sector. Our focus on building a strong theoretical base and practical learning are evenly balanced. The practical learning comprises regular workshops, training programmes for skill building, and summer sessions in corporates.[8]

The focus clearly seems to be on equipping students for jobs in the corporate sectors. Elaborating further, Jaylakshmi said,

> Research and PhD does not hold much charm in Tamil Nadu, as there is no career in that as such. Students are not interested in going abroad for research. Also, students are not interested in doing fieldwork as they would rather sit in the comfort of the 'AC rooms' and manage HR problems in the corporate organizations rather than go to the fields and work in heat and dust amidst rural people. After the introduction of 'Corporate Sociology' even civil services seems to have lost some of its charm as very few qualify in them.

Choices students make: It would be interesting to study whether the efforts of the staff members to make Sociology more attractive by aligning the curriculum with market requirements have borne fruits. Is there any corresponding change among the students to make them opt in favour of Sociology in a society dominated by preferences for Science and allied subjects?

Students and faculty of four out of the five colleges offering undergraduate course in Sociology were interviewed. Similarly, students and faculty members of the two colleges offering postgraduate programmes were also interviewed. Of the 543 students interviewed, 170 were studying in the first year, 90 in the second year and 230 in the final year. The students studying in the final year at the undergraduate level were interviewed in larger numbers and at great length to ascertain their aspirations for their future. Besides, 53 students pursuing their postgraduation courses were also interviewed.

1. In-depth interviews with a cross-section of students from all the three years of undergraduation, both individually and in groups, and also the staff of these five colleges of Chennai, revealed that despite all efforts, Sociology still remains the second choice with most students. They opt to study Sociology because they failed to secure admission in the courses of their choice, which normally include Economics, Commerce and Business Administration.
2. Among those who have taken up Sociology as their first preference, the driving force appears to be a clear aversion to Science or any course involving Mathematics and are hence willing to experiment with a new subject like Sociology. Almost 45 per cent students of MOP Vaishnav College in Chennai revealed that they had taken up Sociology because they wanted to escape Science.
3. 10–12 per cent of the students were those who had initially enrolled in a Science course but within a year felt that it was too tough to pursue further or had failed in the first year and switched to Sociology.
4. A sizeable section from the 'sports quota' in all the colleges or those who plan to join 'priesthood' take admission into Sociology as it is perceived as a comparatively easy subject where one can score well even if one needs to miss a couple of classes.
5. Another 12–15 per cent of the students in all colleges are those who either want to join civil services or join NGOs and therefore have made a conscious decision to join the course.
6. In view of the foregoing, it can be inferred that Sociology is the preferred choice for a mere 7 to 10 per cent of the students studying Sociology in these five colleges at Chennai. For a majority of these students, the choice was made after surfing the Internet where they found the subject content interesting and decided to opt for it at the undergraduate level.

7. However, a recent trend among the choices made by students points that among the latest batch of students, i.e., the first year students in colleges, there would be around 25–30 per cent who have joined the subject out of their own will because they see a good future in it. An article in *The Hindu* published in August 2006, too expressed similar view (Sandhya, 2006). It stated that the Sociology Department at Stella Maris College received unprecedented attention this year during application time, with the Bachelor's course seats filling up at a speed rivalling the Commerce Department, one of the more popular courses at the college.

However, after having taken up the subject and having studied it for over two to three years both the second year and the third year students also seem to like the subject and see a promising future in it. This is applicable to students of all colleges. Coming to their aspirations for the future, it was found that:

1. Of the 230 final year students interviewed, (about 57 per cent) said they would like to go for higher studies but not in pure Sociology programmes. Of the remaining 43 per cent most said that they would like to go for direct job recruitment through the campus placement agencies while some said they would like to join their family business.
2. Coming to the 57 per cent who wanted to go for higher education, most of them said they would like to enrol themselves in programmes like Corporate Sociology, Medical Sociology or Communications and Media, or HR rather than pursue a Master's degree in Sociology. They clearly did not see any future in pursuing pure Sociology. Other courses that they were interested in included MBA, Law and Social Work. However, 80 per cent among them wanted to try their luck with the civil services at least twice.
3. Also, despite having a postgraduate programme in Corporate Sociology in Madras University, none of the girls from Stella Maris or MOP Viashnav or Queens Mary College were interested in going for it. Except for four boys from Loyola College nobody showed any inclination for Madras University or any other University in Tamil Nadu for pursuing Sociology in the Master's programme.
4. Another interesting point that emerged was that while the faculty prided themselves in making Sociology relevant for the market by

adding compulsory skill oriented papers and internships in the final year, the students were not happy with the new developments. They wanted "more of Sociology," as they put it. A group of final year students of MOP Vaishnav College remarked, "if we had to do so much of HR, we might as well have taken up BBA instead of Sociology".

This survey also throws up some interesting findings. First, despite making Sociology saleable and oriented towards the market, it still remained the second choice with the majority of the students. Second, a sizeable section among the final year students did not see any future either in Sociology or in Corporate Sociology and preferred to pursue diploma courses in more skill-oriented courses in their own colleges, wherever available. And, finally, students did not seem very pleased with so much of HR, CSR and internships thrown in into their undergraduate programmes. They wanted the course to focus on Sociology as they felt it would be more useful for the civil services examinations – many students admitted that they would like to sit in the examinations at least once.

We would however get a more holistic idea when we learn about the types of jobs available to the students from the placement agencies too.

Role of the placement cells in the colleges: A trend dating back four years has been the setting up of "placement cells" in several colleges of Chennai. A teaching staff who coordinates between the students and the recruitment firms usually oversees the functioning of the placement cell. These cells and agencies are active for only four months in a year, from November to January, as after that the students get busy with their final year examinations.

The placement cells are approached by IT companies for their HR and CSR needs, BPOs, call centres, banks etc. In some colleges, like Stella Maris, apart from a regular teacher, a group of ex-students also look after placement of fresh graduates and postgraduates. The shortlisted candidates are then called for a group discussion and the recruitment board then interviews for the final selection. Placement for students is done both after graduation and postgraduation. There is however a considerable difference both in the positions and salaries offered to these two sets of students. A remark made by a staff dealing with placement at Loyola College, Chennai is revealing:

> after undergraduation the kind of jobs available for students are usually from call centres, line department type jobs from garment companies or accounts related type jobs from IT companies. All these offer salaries ranging between Rs 8,000 – 12,000. At this level communication skills are of prime importance, and here students of Sociology have an advantage and do extremely well in the interviews. However, for senior positions for which postgraduate students apply, students of Economics and Commerce score over Sociology students as the demand is more for accounts related type of jobs. The pay packet too is high and ranges between 15,000 to Rs 20,000

The situation in girls college was somewhat different. According to the placement agency at Stella Maris College, "as far as placements in the firms are concerned, it is very rare that students who are looking for jobs fail to find one. It is only a matter of time rather than of qualifications as there is a great demand in and around Chennai for jobs, mostly the BPO types". Each year, some 200–250 students from all streams are able to find good jobs through the placement cell in the college and usually many students from the Sociology stream too apply for these positions.

Similar sentiments were expressed by Nitya Ghosh handling placement of students of Sociology at MOP Vaishnav College. There are four placement offices in MOP College unlike other colleges. There are separate placement cells for (i) School of Business, (ii) Sociology, (iii) BBA, and (iv) BISM, i.e., Information Systems Management. According to Nitya, who is in charge for placements for students of sociology:

> for CSR and HR type of jobs, companies look for good attitude, leadership skills, fluency in language as well as ethics and values. Companies who come for recruitment are able to judge the students on these parameters during their group discussions and personal interviews. Students of Sociology have an advantage over others because of their communication skills and a greater awareness of socio-political developments. They can talk on any topic, be it social, economic or political. I think the subject itself equips them for that. All these years, those who do not wish to go for higher studies but want jobs, manage to get it – all of them, and their starting salary varies between Rs 8,000 and Rs 12,000.

However, what clearly emerges from interaction with placement cells of the three institutions is that at the undergraduate level, none of the firms asked specifically for students of Sociology for the various jobs on offer. However, for the senior positions involving an element of HR management, they did ask for qualifications in Sociology, HR and/or Social Work. These jobs were specific in nature involving handling of personnel relations and CSR and were well-paid jobs. As far as the most sought-after subjects with the firms were concerned, it was agreed by all that Economics topped the list followed by Commerce, BBA, Corporate Sociology, Social Work and Sociology in that order.

Interviews with senior executives at four companies/organizations, namely, CII, Ford, Motorola and Intimate Fashions, revealed that for minor line department type of jobs they did not mind students from any stream as long as they had good communication skills and a positive attitude. However, for senior HR positions, they preferred postgraduates with knowledge in HR, CSR, Economics and with Business Administration skills.

When asked if they preferred students with background in Sociology, they said, "Yes, if they are well versed with HR management and have good communication and report writing skills".

However, the recruitment team from Ford which goes to all colleges in Chennai, including Law and the IIT, felt that for their HR requirement they prefer students with a background in Social Work and Sociology. Anand, a student of Sociology and now a member of the Ford Recruitment team, explained this by saying that "their subjects equip them with advanced research skills that allow them to design and carry out data collection, analysis and research".

Another noteworthy feature was that almost all the recruitment team members from the four companies said that a good academic record with good body language and a positive attitude were more important rather than the knowledge of any particular subject. This is because all the firms have a 3-month intensive training programme where they train the candidates. According to Prabhu, Manager HR, Motorola, "At the end of the day, it really doesn't matter what the backgrounds of the students are as long as their attitude is positive and they are willing to learn. Our 'on-the-job' training programme equips them with the skills required for their jobs. So, attitude is more important than the subjects they studied at the undergraduate or graduate levels."

III

Conclusion: Linking the Triad

Linking the triad between the forces of globalization, curriculum development and the choices students make, we can draw some interesting inferences from this survey. To begin with, in Chennai, an interrelationship does seem to exist between the forces of globalization and curriculum development. At the beginning of the paper one had clearly stated which features of globalization this paper focuses upon. However, this interrelationship has not really impacted the decision of the students in favour of Sociology to a great extent. The mindsets of the students are influenced by their parents who remain in the grip of Science and the numerous job offers that it brings. This explains why some parents still want their children to shift back to Science even after doing Sociology for two years in their undergraduation. "What is a loss of two years in front of a whole future," they reason.

The faculty of the sociology department echoes similar sentiment. As the HoD of Loyola College put it, "awareness about the subject is still very low among the parents. Most still feel that Sociology is a very general subject regarding the 'sociability of people' and since it is so general, there is no need to study it" . The comments from a senior faculty members at MOP Vaishnav College teaching Sociology for over 10 years, perhaps sums up the attitude of the society in Tamil Nadu towards Sociology: "the status of Sociology in Tamil Nadu can only go up if the name of the course is changed from Sociology to 'B.Sc. Social Engineering' as anything to do with 'science' and 'engineering' has a lot of value."

However, trends observed only in the last two years, i.e., post-tsunami show a shift in favour of the subject. A lot of international aid agencies and NGOs have set up offices in Chennai. They have hired students with a background in Sociology from Delhi, Mumbai and Pune. This has led to a change among the students who are more favourably inclined towards the subject. This explains why in the year of my study, as compared to the previous years, in all the colleges, a lot of applications forms were received for admission to the undergraduate course in Sociology. Also placement cells do confirm that students with a background in Sociology are picked up more readily then students from other streams because of their knowledge and communication skills. Research for academic pursuit, for the moment, however seems to be absent among the students in Chennai. Sociology, as it stands now among the cross-sections studied, i.e., the faculty, parents and the students, is 'another skill-based subject' preparing students for the market.

Notes

1. Studies by Harvard University, USA (Papers # 728, 729 and Readiness for the Networked World: A Quiet Information Revolution in Tamil Nadu; www.cid.harvard.edu/india/papers.htm.
2. Census Report 2005. Total number of jobs in the urban sector in Tamil Nadu between 2000–05 were 5,18,88,276 and intake of students in for employment in IT sector was 54 per cent.
3. Archana Prasad's chapter on Social Compliance Audit (SCA) explicates this relationship clearly.
4. This article by Sandhya U. in *The Hindu* (August 6, 2006) became the topic of debates among several colleges during their inter-college functions (also see Kalpana, 2005).
5. Readers would notice the manner that authors of this volume have used sociological methods innovatively to map the change and continuities in the practices of sociology.
6. This data has been compiled by facts given in the prospectus along with interviews with the administrative staff. In case of discrepancies between the two, the version of the staff has been given preference, as the prospectus has not been updated.
7. The department is clear on why it wants students to study Sociology. It mentions in the first page itself, "the undergraduate programme in Sociology at Loyola College is unique, for it incorporates the essential theoretic inputs together with on-site study programmes and a research study as practical components. The department is periodically revising and updating its curriculum. The Sociology graduates of our college are all well placed in the society. Our illustrious alumni include Manoj (IAS), Michael Kennedy (IRS), MGM Maran, the industrialist, Shriram, CEO of an IT Company."
8. See Corporate Sociology at www.madrasuniversity.edu

References

Albuquerque, Usha. 2005. "Smart in Skills", *The Hindu* (Chennai ed.), February 9.

Anderson, S. and J. Cavanagh. April 2004. "Outsourcing: A Policy Agenda", *Foreign Policy in Focus,* Vol. 9, No. 2

Bardhan, A.D. 2006a. "Managing Globalization of R&D: Organizing for Offshoring Innovation", *Human Systems Management,* Vol. 25, No. 2.

Bardhan, A.D. and C. Kroll. 2003. "The New Wave of Outsourcing", *FCREUE Research Report,* October.

Bardhan, P. 2006b. "Does Globalization Help or Hurt the World's Poor?" *Scientific American Journal,* April.

Bardhan, P. 2003. "Crouching Tiger, Lumbering Elephant: A China-India Comparison", in K. Basu et al. (eds) *Markets and Governments,* New Delhi: Oxford University Press.

Bhagwati, J., A. Panagariya and T.N. Srinivasan. 2004. "The Muddles Over Outsourcing", *Journal of Economic Perspectives.*

Blinder, A. 2005. *Fear of Offshoring.* Princeton University, CEPS Working Paper No. 119.

College Prospectus and Syllabus, Sociology (2004–2006). Loyola College, Chennai.

—. (2005, 2006). Stella Maris College for Women, Chennai.

—. (2005, 2006). MOP Vaishnav College for Women, Chennai.

—. (2005, 2006). Queens Mary College for Women, Chennai.

—. (2004–2006). Madras University, Chennai.

Dossani, Rafiq and Martin Kenney. 2004. "The Next Wave of Globalization? Exploring Relocation of Service Provision to India", *WP,* 156.

Freeman, R. May, 2005. "The Doubling of the Global Workforce", *The Globalist.*

Hira, R. and A. Hira. 2005. *Outsourcing America: What's Behind Our National Crisis and How We Can Reclaim American Jobs.* AMACOM Books, New York.

Kalpana, S. 2005. "Not a Dreary Area Anymore", *The Hindu* (Chennai ed.), June.

Rodrik, D. 2002. "Globalization for Whom?" *Harvard Magazine,* July-August.

Samuelson, Paul A. 2004. "Where Ricardo and Mill Rebut and Confirm Arguments of Mainstream Economists Supporting Globalization", *Journal of Economic Perspectives.* Summer 18, pp. 135–46.

Sandhya, U. 2006. "New Gadget? Let the Ethnographer See it First", *The Hindu* (Chennai ed.), December 06.

—. 2006 "Admissions at Stella Maris", *The Hindu* (Chennai ed.), August.

Stiglitz, J. 2002. *Globalization and Its Discontents.* New York: Norton & Co.

Wright, Sylvia. 2000. "Into New Territory", *UC Davis Magazine,* Winter 27.

ANNEXURES

Annexure I

Prospectus Sociology, School of Social Science, Department of Sociology, B.A. Sociology. MOP Vaishnav College for Women, Chennai

The department began its journey in the year 1996. Since its inception, the department has seen phenomenal and qualitative growth.

Objectives

- To impart knowledge in diverse areas pertaining to Sociology.
- To equip the students with sufficient knowledge and skills to effectively manage human relations.

Eligibility Criteria

A candidate, who has passed in Higher Secondary Examination, is eligible for seeking admission.

Entrance Test

Every student who wants to be considered for admission should take up an entrance test. The test will evaluate the following:

- Written Communication Skills in English
- Reasoning Skills
- General Awareness

Course Content

- English
- Languages (Tamil, Hindi, Sanskrit and French)
- Principles of Sociology
- Indian Society
- Social Psychology
- Social Issues and Social Problems in India
- Organizational Behaviour
- Sociological Theory – I
- Research Methodology
- Rural-Urban Sociology
- Sociology of Organization/Social Statistics
- Corporate Communication/Social Movements in India

- Project/Industrial Sociology
- Human Resources Management
- Media sociology/Population Studies
- Corporate Culture/Mass Media & Development
- Corporate social Responsibility/Rural Development in India
- Sociology of Marketing and Consumer Behaviour

Special Features: The department believes in multidisciplinary approach, which is reflected in the choice of subjects like Corporate Communication, Human Resources Management, Media Sociology, Sociology of Marketing and Consumer Behaviour.

Special Professional Courses: The department is offering the following courses:

- Basic Computers and Web Designing
- SPSS (Statistical Package)
- Social Entrepreneurship

Scope of the Course and Avenues for Higher Education

- M.A. Sociology
- M.S.W.
- M.A. Public Relations
- M.A. Communication
- M.A. Medical Sociology
- M.A. Corporate Sociology
- M.B.A.
- B.L.

Career Avenues

- Civil Servants (I.A.S.)
- Social Welfare Officer
- Community Development Officer
- Family Planning Department
- Non-Governmental Organizations
- Labour Welfare Department
- Personnel Department

Annexure II

Course Outline of Corporate Social Responsibility

School of Social Science, Department of Sociology, B.A. Sociology

MOP Vaishnav College for Women, Chennai

SEMESTER VI: CORPORATE SOCIAL RESPONSIBILITY

Unit 1. Philosophical Foundation of Social Responsibility

- Corporate social responsibility and trends and scope
- Approaches to corporate social responsibility-trusteeship approach and social enterprise approach

Unit 2. Theories of CSR

- Milton Freidmen
- Mahatma Gandhi
- Karl Marx
- Models of CSR
- Policies of CSR

Unit 3. Social Issues and Social Responsibility

- Stake holders – rights and safeguards
- Human factor in workplace
- Consumer interest
- Gender justice
- Environmental protection

Unit 4. Corporate Social Action

- Towards employees
- Towards customers
- Towards community
- Organizing social action programme
- Towards suppliers

Unit 5. Case Studies

Annexure III

Course Outline of Human Resource Management

School of Social Science, Department of Sociology, B.A. Sociology

MOP Vaishnav College for Women, Chennai

SEMESTER VI: HUMAN RESOURCE MANAGEMENT

Unit 1. Introduction

- Meaning, goals and importance of HRM
- Environment for HRM

Unit 2. Manpower Planning, Recruitment and Selection

- Nature, objectives, and importance of manpower planning
- Manpower audit
- Job analysis
- Sources of recruitment
- Methods of selection

Unit 3. Training and Development

- Significance of training and development
- Types of training – on-the-job, off-the-job
- Methods of training

Unit 4. Performance Appraisal

- Meaning and objectives of performance appraisal
- Methods of performance appraisal
- Essentials for a sound appraisal

Unit 5. Employee Grievances

- Nature and types of grievances
- Causes of grievances
- Procedure for grievances redressal

Annexure IV

New Course Outline of Corporate Sociology

M.A. CORPORATE SOCIOLOGY, MADRAS UNIVERSITY

Subject Code	Title of the Course	C/E/S	Credits			
			L	T	P	C
	I Semester					
SSSC601	Sociological Theory	C	3	1	0	4
SSSC602	Research Methodology	C	3	1	0	4
SSSC603	Sociology of Organisation	C	3	1	0	4
SSSC604	Globalisation and Society	C	3	1	0	4
SSSE602	Social Foundations of Management	E	2	1	0	3
SSSE603	Principles of Management	E	2	1	0	3
UOMS001	Soft Skill *	S				2
	II Semester					
SSSC605	Corporate Communication	C	3	1	0	4
SSSC606	Corporate Culture	C	3	1	0	4
SSSC607	Human Resource Development-I	C	3	1	0	4
SSSC608	Change Management	C	3	1	0	4
SSSE604	Organisational Analysis	E	2	1	0	3
SSSE605	Industrial Sociology	E	2	1	0	3
UOMS002	Soft Skill *	S				2
	Summer Internship	–	–	–	–	–
	III Semester					
SSSC610	Marketing and Consumer Analysis	C	3	1	0	4
SSSC609	Customer Relationship Management	C	3	1	0	4
SSSC614	Human Resource Development II	C	3	1	0	4
SSSC615	Industrial Relations and Personnel Management	C	3	1	0	4
SSSE607	Corporate Social Responsibility	E	3	0	0	3
SSSE608	Leadership in Organisation	E	3	0	0	3
UOMS003	Soft Skill *	S				2
	Summer Internship	–	–	–	–	–
SSSE606	Total Quality Management	E	3	0	0	3
SSSC613	Internship and Project	C	10	0	0	10
UOMS004	Soft Skill *	S				2
	Summer Internship	–	–	–	–	–

15

Sociology and the Practice of Social Compliance Auditing

ARCHANA PRASAD

The practice of any social science discipline, be its intellectual orientations or its institutional uses, changes from one social context to another. Sociology is no exception. In the late 19th and early 20th centuries, the founders of social sciences were deeply involved in analysing the social, political and economic changes that they observed in their own societies. This was also a period of path-breaking scientific discoveries and technological innovations. Not surprisingly, the dominant model that sociology, not unlike other social sciences, sought to emulate was the naturalistic model premised on the view that scientific methods applied to the natural and physical sciences could, with varying degrees of success, be applied to sociology too. This also rested on other domain assumptions, namely, the idea that sociological knowledge could be harnessed much like scientific knowledge to the needs of society.

The happy fallout of this vision was that social problems earlier being seen as givens or divinely ordained were sought to be explained socially. For example, poverty, so far seen as a 'natural phenomenon', began to be seen as a 'social problem' caused by human ignorance or exploitation. Poverty thus could be studied and redressed. One way of studying this was based on the belief that human phenomena can be classified and measured. Till date, and in today's India, the dominant technique of collecting data remains the survey method. It is potentially of immense use to have the kind of macro data that survey methods can generate. Neither the state, nor the corporate sector, nor the civil society can work without such data. But, unfortunately, within the practice of sociology, too often it takes the nature of what C. Wright Mills (1959) famously called 'abstracted empiricism'. Such an approach to empirical research most often proceeds with a purported non-theoretical premise, which in actual instance is a theoretical impossibility. However, the dominant ideology provides a certain space for such empiricism to be somehow above both theory and ideology. Dominant sociological ideology therefore also privileged this form of empiricism. In the contemporary context, this approach to data and data collection has been widely adopted by diverse agencies that collect and analysed data to serve the state, the market and often the growing sector of non-governmental organizations (NGOs).

However, along with this trend in sociology, there also was a growth of a critical approach that necessarily contextualized knowledge and privileged scrutiny of what Alvin Gouldner (1970) calls domain assumptions. Today, more than ever, we need to reclaim the critical and reflexive tradition in sociology in order to understand what some of the new practices of sociology mean both to society and to the practice of sociological theory. For we live in times of pragmatism where theory is viewed with suspicion.

Sociology in India has had long history of reflecting upon its own practice (Oommen, 1983; Singh, 1986; Chaudhuri, 2003). It is in keeping with that spirit that this paper is looking at the new practice of social compliance audit (SCA), which has accompanied the growth of globalization in India. Developments in this new context impacts the manner in which sociology is practised. New needs require new skills, usually understood simply as a set of techniques of data collection and what is broadly seen as greater sensitivity to social issues, that sociology is expected to provide. The larger intellectual resources of sociology most offer disappear to make space for a set of techniques of data collection that sociologists are expected to be equipped with. Significantly, the link between theory, methods and techniques of research likewise disappears. There have been numerous debates about the positive and negative effects of globalization on various countries, especially the developing ones. The concept has sparked debates not only among policy makers but also business groups and academics. A great deal has been written on globalization in India. But far too little on what it implies for the practice of social sciences and the changes wrought in the discipline of sociology.

The paper is based on personal experience of first, working as a social compliance auditor and then as a researcher working on social audit within the world of academic research. It seeks in part to document the new practice of social audit and the way sociology is deployed within it. Towards that, it also attempts to compare how sociology within defined prescriptions of auditors would operate and how critical sociology would look at the same phenomena but ask questions that would be different. Indeed, too often, there is a tendency to take these new practices as givens, without contextualizing their emergence or understanding its institutional purpose. Section I therefore seeks to understand the reasons for the emergence of the practice of social audit while Section II provides a map of what exactly social audit does and what are its limitations. A critical sociological perspective enables both the mapping of the process and the identification of why and what issues escapes its paradigm. Section III seeks to do so by revisiting one's personal experience as a social auditor and recounting how issues disappear from the focus of attention and how sociology if practised within its critical traditions can help us understand both the premises of social auditing and its operational strategies.

I

Emergence of Social Compliance Audit

The institution of social compliance audit (SCA) has to be understood in the context of the changing nature of both production and consumption. There is a new global division of labour and new global patterns of consumption. As this section seeks to show, consumers in the developed world are increasingly concerned about the conditions within which goods are produced, often in some other part of the world. Along with this greater consumer awareness, there has been the role of the media in reporting abusive practices, a pro-active civil society movement, and the need to protect an untarnished brand name in global business. It is within this context that social audit has emerged as an institutionalized process for the corporate sector.

The international trade union movement, NGOs and international buyers are now drawing up model codes. Although these model codes have different origins, they cover the same basic principles, which are based on key ILO conventions on core labour standards (Wick, 2003: 68). Besides, a large number of accreditation bodies have emerged in the West that offer labour certification to suppliers who have adopted the code of conduct and standards. The key factors responsible for emergence of the process are discussed below:

Avoidance of Media Report on Abusive Practices

The process of SCA has emerged in response to media reports against leading brand companies that used international contractors and sub-contractors. By the 1990s, due to media activism, most of these companies were being criticized for abuse of human rights established by their own ethical codes of conduct. The following abuses were reported which forced TNCs to take the initiative to make their business more ethical and abuse-free:

- 1992: The first report of abuse was recorded when a public scandal followed a report in the *Washington Post* about the production of Levi jeans by Chinese prison labour in the Island of Saipan. Levi-Strauss immediately reacted by drawing up a code on labour standards for all its overseas suppliers.[1]
- 1995: A famous American coffee house chain was appalled that its outlets were picketing because workers' rights were abused in the Central American coffee fields.
- EPZs in Noida (India) reported of having the following practices in the factories: locking workers in the factories, forcing them to work for 12 hours a day and all 7 days a week, paying no overtime, doing pregnancy test at the time of hiring, not giving maternity benefits, etc.

These media reports were coupled with reports from civil society and organizations who were working for labour rights. In recent years, some major international companies have faced growing protests against the work conditions in the factories. This has generated tremendous pressure on international buyers and retailers who are keen to avoid such abusive practices in their suppliers' factories, lest it draws unnecessary media attention and a bad reputation.

Civil Society Campaigns against Unethical Practices

The concern for environmental and social impacts of global manufacturing practices on workers in developing countries was initiated by civil society campaign. These campaigns focused on specific injustices of transnational companies (TNCs) in Third World countries (Clark, 2003). Most of the campaigns were against sweatshops manufacturing of products such as toys, electronics, garments and shoes. These campaigns demanded that leading companies stop abusive practices, improve overall conditions for workers and ensure the rights of workers to organize. Internet campaigns, NGO actions and demonstrations criticizing globalization enlarged the pressure on companies to behave according to human rights and enhanced the value of trustworthy statements of ethical behaviour (Neef, 2004). Under such pressure, TNCs started to project their concern for social responsibility.

Consumer Boycott of Goods Produce under Sweatshops

Consumer awareness of ethical issues in business has increased in the last five or six years. Consumers in developed countries became more concerned with the conditions under which goods are produced. In fact, surveys by agencies have shown that consumers in United States are willing to pay more if retailers guaranteed that their products are not made by child labour and that most would avoid goods made in sweatshops.

A national survey of 1,826 adults conducted by PIPA (1999) suggests that 74 per cent believe that they have moral obligation to ensure that people in other countries who make "products that we use ...do not have to work in harsh or unsafe conditions and 76 per cent said they would choose the sweat free garment".[2]

Similarly, Elliott and Freeman (2001) reports that over 80 per cent of consumers polled in the United States are willing to pay more for products that are made under 'good' conditions. And over 75 per cent report feeling a moral obligation to help improve workers' conditions, and over 90 per cent agree that countries should be required to maintain minimum standards for working conditions. A poll by Environics International (1999) found that 51 per cent of Americans reported 'punishing' a firm for bad social performance in their business.[3]

Consumers often boycotted goods on report of unethical practices under which they were produced. Thus consumers were in many ways at the root of the processes of SCA (Freeman, 1994). Increasingly aware consumers started demanding more information on the products they bought, and systems to help them avoid sweatshop products. Several initiatives were taken up by different organizations to increase awareness among the consumers about the conditions in the garment factories across the globe. The aim has been to raise awareness about how clothes are made and to pressurize retailers to take responsibility of labour conditions throughout the subcontracting chains.

> Global communication flows and civil society have made Northern consumers increasingly aware of the origin of the goods they purchase and the adverse circumstances in which they are produced. Consumer-led campaigns have put pressure on large brand name companies and retailers to address poor employment standards within the supply chain or risk adverse exposure that could damage their reputation and market share (Barrientos, 2002).

The access to information became easier with the development of new technologies like the Internet. Through the worldwide web, these activists could easily and quickly generate negative publicity that could tarnish corporate image and eat into market share and profit margin. As a result, consumer power was increasingly being wielded to affect company behaviour.

Protection of Brand Image

Today, as never before, an enterprise's public image is an asset, which must be protected and developed to the maximum. In highly competitive consumer markets, a company's public image often determines the decision of whether the consumers will buy its product or not. Companies face enormous difficulties in designing and enforcing global policies. Retailers and manufacturers risk damage to their reputation and the value of their brands, if workplace abuses at their factories or those of their contractors/suppliers are exposed. Therefore companies promote ethical concerns in order to project an image of a social responsible business. The ethical commitments undertaken by the company are communicated externally. It is strategically important that the message reaches the market.

The TNCs are under constant fear of media reports, boycott by consumers and bad publicity. Due to this large body of retailers in the United States and Europe these countries are now giving high priority to social responsibility, safety and environmental issues, besides corporate ethics. They try to respond to the requirements by establishing a code of ethics as an integrated part of the corporate culture and make it an essential business policy (Drury, 2000).

Firms are 'voluntarily' participating in or leading these programmes because of significant new pressures to improve their labour, environmental and social performance. Brand-sensitive firms are joining non-governmental initiatives or creating their own codes of conduct and monitoring schemes in response to direct pressures and demands from activists. Codes and monitoring systems are viewed as a strategy to reduce reputational risks in the market place (Conroy, 2001). One bad supplier can significantly damage a firm's reputation, and in turn its sales and stock value. Informed stakeholders view firms with suppliers in countries, having weak enforcement systems or a poor track record on child labour, with suspicion. These firms thus need independent means of establishing their 'good' performance. Many firms that source consumer goods from developing countries have adopted codes of conduct in order to protect their brand reputation (Jenkins, 2005).

II

The Process and Practice of Social Compliance Audit

The context and compulsions within which the practice of social audit emerged has been discussed above. It is important however also to look at the manner in which social audit is perceived and portrayed by the corporate world. This aspect is important for often this is taken at face value within the academic community. For instance, social audit is described as a term which refers to the growing interest in assessing the company's impact on community and society. The various developments that led to the emergence of SCA, discussed in the earlier section, suggest that the process of SCA is linked to the wider changes taking place in the economy, especially the increasing compulsions of the corporate sector to rework their response to social issues. However, it would be helpful to first look at the process of SCA which is a basic evaluation process through which the systems (procedures for achieving compliance) and actual compliance (actual performance) of a factory are examined. The nature of the evaluation process, as this paper will show, is structured by the objectives of SCA and would therefore be very different from an academic study of the conditions of work and of the labour force generally.

The core of SCA is to review social policies concerning work environment, compensation and benefits and to identify opportunities for positive changes. Through a review of the regulations governing a factory's operations, its records and its on-site inspection, auditors are expected to ascertain the level to which a factory conforms to applicable regulations as per the code of conduct laid. SCA can be defined as:

> a systematic and independent external assessment administered by a trained social auditor against a specific standard. To determine whether an entity is meeting those standards and complying with established policies, operating procedures and national and local laws. Results of a social compliance audit are not usually public.[4]

A social audit is undertaken by a company to evaluate the working conditions existing in a facility or supply chain (ILO, 2003). The term 'social accountability' is also used synonymously to refer to the commitment of business towards social life. It is a worldwide regulatory process adopted by all prestigious importers of goods in developing countries. It covers all aspects of the worker's welfare from health and safety conditions at the workplace to monetary benefits. In addition, the buyers are also required to ensure that the supplier (exporters) abide by all labour laws of their respective state.

Types of SCA

The different kinds of SCA prevalent in the garment factories are:

1. *Announced audits:* Announced audits are done with prior consultation with the factory managers. In this type the supplier is informed in advance about the date and time of audit. The advantage of this type of audit is that it gives the management time to prepare for the audit. Often it may happen that the factory is made clean and facilities provided only on the day of audit. There are a lot of arrangements made in advance to portray a positive picture of the factory to the auditor. The workers, during interview, listed the kind of arrangements made by managers before any announced audits. Following are some of the measures:

- Thorough cleaning of the company.
- Provision of first aid, medicine, protective tools like needle caps, gloves air mask etc.
- Workers are coached to quote low targets to impress the auditors while the targets are usually quite high, they are told to say that they do not work overtime, especially not on Sundays.
- Workers are drilled on how to present a good image of the company to ensure that the factory is passed to carry out the production orders.

Thus, announced audits presents a good picture of the factory even when in reality none of the code of conduct may be followed. As a result, the process of SCA appears almost as a total hoax.

2. *Unannounced audits:* Unlike announced audits, the unannounced audits are conducted without prior notice to the management. A surprise visit by the auditor is generally done on the basis of complaint against the supplier. A problem mentioned by many workers was that during an unannounced audit the auditor has a hard time entering the factory. It is argued that the management does not allow immediate entry into the factory. They ask the security posted at the entry gate to deliberately involve them in debating various procedures. Sometimes, they would keep the auditor caught in an argument for several hours. This act provides the management enough time to arrange the factory as per compliance standards.

Among experts, there are different views on whether audits should be announced or unannounced. Auditors often prefer announced audits because the factory is then capable of preparing the visit, for example, by making sure that the manager is available for an interview or that the relevant documentation is accessible.

Another reason why visits are often announced is that "retailers and audit firms do not want to jeopardize their relationship with their suppliers who tend to see unannounced visits, as part of the so-called 'policing approach', as impolite and inappropriate interference in their business". So, the practice of unannounced audits is uncommon in India. According to an employee for a large global social auditing firm: "Many of our suppliers will not be able to meet issues raised in social compliance if unannounced audits take place. Announced audits are thus in vogue. It will take time for our suppliers to meet high standards of labour conditions".

3. *First or second party audit:* It is done by the buying house/retailers by themselves by in-house auditors. In other words, they employ the personnel who are trained to conduct compliance audit. It is also referred to as in-house audit as the buying house performs SCA themselves and there is no involvement of any outside agency. The in-house audit is less expensive for the exporter. Big brands like GAP and Wal-Mart have their own system of audit and therefore spend less on getting services of auditing firms. Since the expenditure on SCA adds to the financial cost of their business, they take it in a serious manner. An auditor from GAP Inc emphasized that the fact of spending a big amount on getting audits done is a clear sign of their serious concern. In the words of the auditor, "So audit is a costly thing and brands such as GAP is spending a high amount of money on training auditors, taking care of their travel, so if one is spending so much money, one has to be serious about the work".

4. *Third party audit:* Unlike first and second party audit, third party audit is done by agencies on behalf of international buyers in home countries. This is usually more authentic as it is done more comprehensively. However, the third party audit is not one that is liked by factory owners and managements. The main reason for not preferring it is obviously the financial burden. Many factory owners consider it more expensive than the in-house audit. In the words of a factory owner, "SCA becomes a financial burden to the export unit when the audit is carried out by third party, in which case the auditing firm demands money from the firm to carry out the audit but in case of big brands like GAP, NIKE, H&M, audit is carried by their in-house auditors, no money is charged".

However, the cost of the process does matter to small manufacturers. On the other hand big brands and retailers who can afford to spend extra money usually ensures that the process is carried out effectively. Moreover, when a buyer makes SCA compulsory, it leads to more orders from international buyers and hence the earing of more profit. So for those who can afford the extra expense of SCA it entails more profit.

Irrespective of whether it is an unannounced or an announced audit, a first party or third party audit, the objectives, method and interestingly the possible range of findings of SCA remain the same. Though the clauses audited vary from buyer to buyer, there are certain core elements of SCA. These core elements are the main clauses against which compliance is verified. One examines the most relevant clauses that are audited during the SCA process below.

Key Clauses to be Audited

SCA is done to verify application of various laws, standards and clauses set up by the state (Indian Factories Act, 1948), International Labour Organization (ILO conventions on working conditions) and code of conduct issued by TNCs (GAP Inc). There is a lot of overlap among the three and below is a summary of the main clauses that are kept in mind while conducting a compliance audit. It is not simply a list of the clauses but also an examination of the clauses with reference to SCA. The key clauses that are audited during an SCA process are:

1. *No forced, bonded or prison labour:* Compliance demands that the factory should have contractor licences; it should maintain proper records and documentation of all workers like attendance register, time cards and logs. Factories are directed to be directly responsible for the workers' social security and working conditions.

Due to the high rate of migrant labour in urban areas, apparel factories tend to become sites for contract/bonded labour. Contract labour usually involves exploitation of workers who perform core activities but do not have any permanent status. Contract labour is characterized by abuses such as underpayment of wages, denial of overtime rates and social security even though local labour laws guarantee these rights. They usually have no proof of employment or any other documentation. Export factories generally employ workers as contract labour. This is considered more practical and more cost effective as they can be hired and fired at will when the work is less or when only certain workers are required. Since the problems of contract labour are acute, standards have been developed to avoid employment of labour that is exploitative.

2. *No child labour:* The code of conduct bans the use of child labour in garment factories. This is so because child labour has been recognized as a grave human rights violation across the globe. It is also considered as a criminal activity and therefore developing standards favouring unemployment of children below the age of 14 is an important step to eliminate child labour. While some argue that initiatives like social labelling in the carpet industry have been successful in

eliminating child labour, others argue that this may have forced child labour to those sectors that are not covered by such clauses leading to worse forms of exploitation.

The issue of child labour is complex. It is related to the socio-economic status of the family of children who are compelled to take up work to support their families. From the humanitarian point of view it is argued that child labour rather than being banned should be encouraged with alternative arrangement for the education and well-being of the working children. This is also taken care of by codes of conduct as it is stated that in case child labour is found, the employer has to ensure that they receive primary education, ensure that working hours do not coincide with school timings and that they are not engaged in dangerous activities.

3. *No discrimination in employment:* Non-discrimination as a principle of recruitment and appointment is an integral part of all codes of conduct. This is in keeping with an equitable social order. The focus is to guarantee equality and equity in employment and conditions of work. With regard to the employment of women, the main source of discrimination lies in the inequalities in wages paid to men and women.

4. *Wages and benefits as per labour laws:* The codes of conduct lay stress on the payment of wages as per the Minimum Wage Act, 1948.[5] It requires that the workers be paid the minimum wages as per the notification issued by the local government from time to time. This is considered relevant for the worker so that it allows him/her to live a life with at least the bare necessities. This is the most important standard that has to be complied with because the highest percentage of non-compliance is in terms of low rate of payment or non-payment of wages.

5. *Social security:* It implies monetary benefits given to the workers as part of employment. It is provided in the form of:

(i) Employees' State Insurance (ESI), which includes part of employer's income that is saved for meeting medical expenses due to illness or accidents.
(ii) Provident Fund (PF), which includes 12 per cent contribution each from the employer's and the employee's income. The amount goes into savings and is paid only after retirement.

(iii) Maternity benefits include both monetary and non-monetary benefits for pregnant women employees.
(iv) Disablement/death compensation and so on.

These are all parts of state policies for welfare and hence an integral part of all codes of conduct. These are well taken care of by all auditors as suggested in most studies of impact assessment of the code of conduct.[6]

6. *Normal working hours:* Working hours is an important issue in garment factories. This is a double-edged sword, that is, it is pursued both by the employer as well as the employee. The former emphasises the importance of extra hours of work to increase output and hence profit whereas the latter likes to work for more hours to increase income. This problem has been solved by setting limits to working hours. The Indian Factories Act specifies that a worker shall not perform more than 48 hours of work in a week. Any duration above 48 hours will be compensated with double overtime premium on normal wage rate. Setting a high overtime rate has dettered the employers to opt for extra working hours however the workers complain that it is against them as their incomes go down.

7. *Safe and hygienic working environment, no physical abuse:* It is mandatory for employers to maintain conducive working conditions that protect the health and safety of all workers. This includes clean working conditions, the provision of canteen facilities for workers, provision to fight fire accidents and other emergencies, and easy availability of medicines and medical aids. It also includes the non-existence of abusive working conditions, pollution-free environment, absence of sexual harassment at the workplace, and the availability of a forum to lodge complaints and discuss problems directly with the management. Compliance to these provisions guarantees that workers are not subject to ill-treatment by their employers.

8. *Establishment of regular employment relationships:* The employer has to ensure that employment is offered on a regular basis and has to also avoid seasonal or contractual employment to ensure employment security. This clause has been incorporated in order to prevent hiring of contract, sub-contract, part-time and casual workers. In actual practice, the employers do not prefer permanent workers in order to avoid litigation, and therefore employ contract and sub-contract workers. One of the reasons for not employing permanent workers is

the fear of employees' unions. During the SCA process all the workers are provided factory identity card to prove that they are permanent workers. Therefore, it is difficult to actually find out the contract and sub-contract workers through the SCA process.

9. *Freedom of association and the right to collective bargaining:* Freedom of association is unquestionably the key element in ensuring respect for other fundamental rights at work. The Indian Constitution guarantees freedom of association and workers are free to join trade unions of their own choosing. Various laws and regulations currently in force are very comprehensive and the labour relations system functions reasonably well in the formal sector industries. Therefore, the clause on collective bargaining is an integral part of all codes of conduct. Collective bargaining is the normal means of fixing wages and settling disputes in the formal sector, where trade unions are represented. However, with the absence of trade union in the garment factories, collective bargaining remains simply a clause on paper and is not implemented even during SCA.

To be more than pieces on paper, these clauses required a credible mechanism for verifying that firms or factories are implementing them in good faith. In creating such a mechanism of auditing compliance to standard codes/clauses, there was considerable pressure from consumers, media and civil society that led to the emergence of SCA.

Procedures involved in SCA

A veritable cottage industry of social compliance auditors has sprung up to help socially responsible companies to verify conditions at supplier's factories.

> Tens of thousands of social audits are commissioned annually by hundreds of brand-name companies or retailers. A whole industry of commercial social auditors, self-assigned experts, and quasi-independent ethical enterprises has jumped on the social audit bandwagon (Pruett, 2005).

The procedure of SCA is participatory, making use of questionnaires, interviews and involves a series of steps. The methods followed differ from buyers and auditing agencies, as there is no standard procedure laid down. An auditor from GAP Inc described the process of SCA as given below.

> Garment factory approaches sourcing department to take production order for GAP sourcing department. This department then contacts compliance department which in turn sends an electronic mail requesting details regarding factory license, area of production, health, safety measure and so on. Having got the details, an audit teams visits the factory and carries out the audit. Having noted the issues of non-compliance in the factories the audit team gives a notice of 15 days period to improve on areas of non-compliance. After 15 days the audit teams again visits the factory and if satisfied sends an audit report to the sourcing department to go on with their business.

Social auditors visit the factory to check out whether there is conformity with a labour standard laid out in the code of conduct that they have been given. The objectives include:

- Assessing the problems that exist in a factory.
- Developing a corrective action or remedial plan.

To achieve these objectives the following steps are followed during SCA. These steps are mentioned in the buyer's manual on SCA. However, prior to the actual audit, there is a pre-audit planning, where the authorized agency gets a request from the buyer to conduct the audit in the factory producing goods for the concerned buyer. This stage requires selecting the team of auditors who would be required to visit the factory and fixing the date and time of the audit.

On the day of actual audit, the following steps are followed:

(i) *Opening meeting:* On the day of the audit, the auditors have an opening meeting with the factory management. The management here means any manager or supervisor who has the authority and responsibility for the implementation of the code of conduct in the factory. During the opening meeting auditors are required to give a brief description of the audit process, the areas to be covered during the audit and the various tools to be used by them to complete the audit process.

This has a two-fold purpose: firstly, it offers a platform for the auditors to introduce the concept and process of SCA to the factory management and secondly, it allows the auditors to understand management structures and practices of the concerned factory. During the meeting the auditors review the following.

- *Factory facts and figures:* data and records of factory registration, obtaining of licence, the area of operation, the size of workforce employed, the nature of production and the name of buyers for whom production done.

- *Management practices:* the relationship between management and workers, mode of complaint redressal, system for allowing workers to interact among themselves and with management.
- *Payroll practices:* the salary structure, mode and time of payment of wages, whether giving salary slips or not, deduction being made and so on.
- *Health and safety:* the provision for taking care of the health and safety of workers, medical aid available, the provision of drinking water, toilets, canteen and crèche facilities.

(ii) *Factory tour and record review:* After talking to the management, the auditors take a round of the factory, including the place of work, to visually inspect the working conditions in terms of cleanliness, safety, freedom of movement, relation between the management and workers and other related aspects. While taking a factory tour some auditors also prefer to talk to the workers while they are working. The auditors make a close scrutiny of the following records:

(i) *Wage register:* to check whether the workers are paid as per the legal requirements, whether they are paid timely, whether they are paid social security benefits like Provident Fund, ESI etc.

(ii) *Time cards/attendance register:* to see the hours of work, the time of entry and exit, to verify that workers are not working beyond required working hours and if so are paid overtime as per the legal requirements.

(iii) *Personal files of the workers:* to review transparency in recruitment, to verify the age of the workers and the nature of employment. Also, to see if documents like ration card, birth certificates are verified at the time of recruitment to ensure that they are not below the age of 14, that is, not a child labour.

(iv) *Fire safety, first aid, medical and other records:* to review the health and safety provisions made available to the workers to ensure proper working conditions in the factories.

(iii) *Interview with the workers:* To cross-examine the information collected from factory record, the next step is to have a closed interview with the workers, in absence of the management. The workers are taken into confidence that it is for their benefit and that their name will not be disclosed. They are assured that they can speak freely and frankly about the existing conditions in the factory and also about the problems being faced by them. Around 20 to 25 interviews with different types of workers are conducted. Again, it is ensured that both males and females are covered. The tool for interview is structured and close-ended questionnaires. The auditors simply ask the workers to answer in 'yes' or 'no' on a whole range of issues ranging from the salary/wages they get to the nature of manager-workers relationship in the factory.

(iv) *Closing meeting:* At the end, the findings of the audit are shared with the management. The areas of non-compliance are explained to the management and corrective action plan offered for improvement. The action for transforming non-compliance to compliance is suggested. A time period of three months is generally given to improve non-compliance. And, after this period, a follow-up audit is done to verify the corrective action taken.

The task before the auditors after conducting the audit is to present a report to the buying agencies or retailers. The report is sent to the concerned buyer for further review. Based on the report the buyer asks the supplier to take necessary steps to improve the working conditions within the time limit. Under pressure to maintain high export order the supplier takes all action to do its best.

III

Role of Social Compliance Auditor and the Expected Role of Sociology

As stated at the outset, the central purpose of this paper is two-fold. The first is to map the new practice of SCA and understand the social, economic and political contexts of its emergence. Secondly, it aims to demonstrate how these new developments demand a certain kind of sociological skill and not another. My own experience both as a practising social auditor and then a researcher working on social audit brought to the fore how the two orientations would lead to very different kinds of data collection and understanding. In this section, I revisit my personal encounter with social audit and the subsequent journey.

A social auditor is required to undergo extensive training in labour laws of different states, codes of conduct of international buyers and ILO conventions on working conditions. This is in addition to the training on processes involved in audit process and behaviour expected from the auditor in the factory. During my three months' training, a common remark of the manager was, "A social science graduate can understand social issues very easily". This comment was based on the assumption that students of international marketing or management studies do not possess an adequate understanding of the society. He made a clear demarcation between me and other trainee – all from law and management background. He had a clear picture that law, science and management trainees had a 'technical mind' whereas I had a 'social' mind. By this he meant that I could understand issues of child labour, gender discrimination and sexual harassment better. The issues of payment of wages, overtime hours, technical details of factory ventilation etc. were technical and easily comprehended by the other trainees.

Students of social sciences, when taken in as compliance auditor, provide a more humane outlook to the overall process. Thus, the positive attributes of a social science graduate as a compliance auditor were sensitivity to social issues and ability to comprehend social reality. They would obviously not be equipped to look into the reasons for the non-functioning of powerloom in the factory, testing of quality of fabrics produced in the factory etc.

The differentiation between natural science and social science got reflected in the course of factory audits. While the social science graduates would be required to go in for workers' interview during which an attempt was made to understand the problem faced by the workers, the natural science graduates would be involved in checking the wage and overtime register that required technical skills. A problem faced as a sociologist in conducting workers' interview was the tendency to get involved with the workers that made the interview time-consuming. As mentioned above, the nature of work expected was mechanical in the sense that it required filling of the interview schedule as 'yes' or 'no'. Once I told him that in order to really know if workers are facing problem, we should spend more time than just getting monotonous replies. To this he replied that he had a more 'technical mind': "This interview seems very boring to me and then we are not investigative journalist that we go so deep. Our concern is to mark out violation that appears on the face that's it and nothing more."

His remark gave me the feeling that he was simply doing his work as auditor whereas I was more concerned at understanding the problem from the workers' perspective in order to find a feasible solution to their problems. I felt impelled to in C. Wright Mills' words that the sociological imagination requires us to "think ourselves away" from the familiar routines of our daily lives in order to look at them anew.

After the training when I went for audits to garment factories, in the beginning I found it tedious as it involved taking a tour of factory spread out over 500 square yard or more. The workplace, with powerloom, dyeing machine and sewing machine, was very noisy. The workers' interview was short and basic in the sense what was required was to fill in the questionnaire in 'yes' and 'no'. The workers appeared scared and would rarely speak on any issue with the fear that they were being watched. The auditors were aware of this but were unable to handle the problem due to paucity of time and the urgency to send the audit report in time. Once a auditor remarked, "see we can't be in the factory 24/7, we are not policing but trying to suggest changes for better business partnership with international buyers. In this process, the voice of the purported beneficiary gets relegated to the background. And, the priority becomes ensuring the better business partnership with international buyers".

As a social audit practitioner coupled with training in sociology became useful in arriving at a comparative study of the process of SCA. There were wide ranging differences in question raised as compliance auditor and as a sociologist. Some of them are discussed as under:

(a) Why is social compliance audit done? As a practitioner, it was generally accepted in the industry that the SCA is the outcome of the movement towards social corporate responsibility (CSR). It would be worthwhile to mention here that CSR as incentive became an integrated part of business in the neo-liberal paradigm. It stressed on the social obligation of transnational companies towards all its stakeholders. As a sociologist, it was imperative to critically examine the logic of CSR as expressed by different stakeholders. That it was not always the 'social obligation' that was a compelling factor to initiate SCA. Rather, it was the consumer and civil society movement that generated the pressure to protect brand image and reputation and therefore making the process a compulsory one for increasing business and profit margin. Or, as expressed above, a mechanism to pave way for better business partnership with international buyers.

Further, from a thorough examination of the process as practised in the garment factories, it was evident that the word 'social' often acts as a misnomer as the focus is on compliance with legal aspects. The process is legal rather than social because it deals with the laws that have been made by the respective state. Majority of the workers being illiterate do not understand the law.

(b) For whom the audit is done? As a practitioner it was suggested that the process was initiated to improve the working conditions of the factories so as to impact on the lives of the workers. As a result most of the codes of conduct were related to the workers and factory environment. As a sociologist I raised two important questions: Do workers for whom the codes are formulated understand them? Are they involved in the process of formulation and does the process really improve their working conditions? A sociological study revealed that the workers have no understanding of the process. The standards laid down are based on the international norms and many of them do not directly apply to the Indian society. For instance, take the case of the standards on 'discrimination', in the west. Audit reports highlight a high percentage of discrimination, but in India the female worker is not even aware of what 'discrimination' means, so how can she know whether she is being discriminated or not.

(c) How is the process carried out? As a practitioner auditors are trained to be well versed with the labour laws of the state and the codes of conduct issued by respective buyers and retailers. The tasks laid before the auditor involve record verification, physical observation of working place and interview with the workers in the absence of the management, thus making the process mechanical. In the interview the workers simply answer in 'yes' and 'no'. Many a time this is done without even understanding the question asked. They see the auditor as an outsider, as an inspector who has come to score their performance and hence should be replied to positively. As a sociologist, one felt that he or she ought to evolve a holistic approach of conducting the compliance audit by including the workers in the formulation of codes of conduct so that they are able to make sense of the process.

Looking at the ways in which compliance audit actually operates raises questions of accountability. This lack of accountability that one perceived makes the process limited in its impact. For many the codes simply do not work in reality. For example, as per the standards laid down, no employee should be discriminated on the basis of gender at the time of recruitment but in many factories there are only men employed on the pretext that the nature of job is either too 'technical' or tough for female employees. Likewise, in the case of maternity benefits, a female worker who gets pregnant would give up the job, unaware of her rights to avail of paid maternity leave.

A comparative view of the process as a practitioner and sociologist reveals the vast difference between practising sociology as simply a set of tools for collecting information through interviews, schedules etc. and that of understanding sociology as a discipline that enables one to develop a sociological imagination to critically examine the emergence and practice of SCA in the wider contour of economic, social and political changes.

Notes

1. See Jean-Paul Sajhau, 'Business Ethics in the Textile, Clothing and Footwear (TCF) Industries: Codes of Conduct', *ILO Bulletin*, No. II–9, June, 1997.
2. University of Maryland Program on International Program on International Policy Attitudes (PIPA), "Americans on Globalization", survey conducted during October 21–29, 1999 (survey results available at http://www.pipa.org/Online Reports/Globalization/contents.html).
3. See http://www.environics.net/eil/millenium/
4. The definition taken from http://www.interpraxis.com/social_audit_resources.htm
5. The Act provides for fixation of minimum wages for notified scheduled employment. Payment of wages is per different categories of workers in different industry. As per Delhi Minimum Wages, as on 1 February 2005 the wages for skilled, semi-skilled and unskilled workers in the textile industry are 133, Rs 123 and Rs 117 respectively (Source: Labour Department, Delhi).
6. The impact assessment study done by ETI, 'The ETI Code of Labour Practice: Do Workers really Benefit?', 2006 and CEC, 'Garment Industry and Labour Rights in India-the Post MFA Context by Sujana Krishnamoorthy, CEC, 2006.

References

Beteille, A. 2003. "Newness in Sociological Enquiry", in Chaudhuri, Maitrayee (ed.), 2003. *The Practice of Sociology*. New Delhi: Orient Longman.

Barrientos, A. 2002. "Extending Social Protection to Informal Workers in the Horticulture Global Value Chain", *Social Protection,* Discussion Paper 0216, World Bank, Washington, June, http://www.ids.ac.uk/idS/pvty/pdf-files/Chains_of_production.pdf

Chaudhuri, M. (ed.), 2003. *The Practice of Sociology*. New Delhi: Orient Longman.

Clark, J. 2003. *Worlds Apart: Civil Society and the Battle for Ethical Globalization.* London: Earthscan.

Conroy, M. 2001. "Can Advocacy-led Certification Systems Transform Global Corporate Practices? Evidence and Some Theory" (Working Paper Series No. 21), Amherst, MA: Political Economy Research Institute, University of Massachusetts.

Drury, C. 2000. *Management and Cost Accounting.* London: Thomas Learning Business Press.

Elliott, K. and R. Freeman. 2001. "White Hats or Don Quixotes? Human Rights Vigilantes in the Global Economy". NBER (National Bureau of Economic Research), Working Paper No. W8102), Cambridge, MA, January.

Freeman, R. 1984. *Strategic Management: A Stakeholder Approach.* Boston: Pitman.

Jenkins, R. 2005. "Globalization, Corporate Social Responsibility and Poverty", *International Affairs,* Vol. 81, No. 3, pp. 525–40.

Mills, C.W. 1959. *The Sociological Imagination.* London: Oxford University Press.

Neef, D. 2004. *The Supply Chain Imperative: How to Ensure Ethical Behavior in Your Global Suppliers.* New York: AMACOM Books.

Oommen, T.K. 1983. "Sociology in India: A Plea for Contextualization", *Sociological Bulletin,* Vol. 11, No. 32, pp. 111–36.

Pruett, Duncan. 2005. *Looking for a Quick Fix: How Week Social Auditing is Keeping Workers in Sweatshops* (last updated November, 2005), Clean Clothes Campaign. http:/www.cleanclothes.org/ftp/05-quick_foi pdf.

Singh, Y. 1986. *Indian Sociology: Social Conditioning and Emerging Concerns.* New Delhi: Vistaar Publication.

Wick, I. 2003. *Workers' Tool or PR Ploy? A Guide to Codes of International Labour Practice* (3rd ed.). Germany: Friedrich-Ebert-Stiftung/Boon.

PART V

Tracking Concepts: Mapping Intellectual Trends

Concepts are constitutive of societal processes and extant power relations. Here four central concepts, widely deployed in sociology, community, caste, tribe and gender are discussed. In each case the focus is on mapping the changed meaning and usage of the terms within sociological practice. The argument being made through this exposition is that these concepts get reconfigured in a curious conundrum wherein both the radical thrust of social movements and hegemonic drive of global capital play a role. In this process older nationalist frameworks are interrogated. The challenge however is to recognize the manner that the local critiques stemming from often radical social movements, women, tribal, caste or class are sometimes appropriated by international institutions far removed from the local and often operating (though not always) with antithetical ideological visions of the transformative potential of global capital.

16

Rethinking Community

In the Discipline and within Development Practices[1]

AMITES MUKHOPADHYAY

In 1951, when the United Nations declared its policy for the economic development of the underdeveloped countries, it set a high premium on rapid economic progress, declaring that:

> Ancient philosophies have to be scrapped; old social institutions have to disintegrate; bonds of caste, creed and race have to be burst; and large numbers of persons who cannot keep up with progress have to have their expectations of a comfortable life frustrated (United Nations, 1951: 15).

The relationship of Africa, Asia and Latin America to Europe and North America in the post-war period is more often than not couched in the language of development. Thus, it was development as western modernization that reigned supreme and it was in the interest of such modernization in the so-called developing countries that ethnic identities or communities needed to be dissolved, the comfort of living in homogeneous or harmonious world be sacrificed. Tradition was where age-old ideas or obscurant practices of the people seemed to perpetuate. It was in the interest of the few that many had to change their lives. About forty years later, the same United Nations in its Earth Summit held in Rio de Janeiro resolved that:

> Indigenous people and their communities and other local communities have a vital role in environmental management and development because of their knowledge and traditional practices. States should ... enable their effective participation in the achievement of sustainable development (United Nations, 1993).

Thus, no longer is tradition viewed as an obstacle to progress. Rather, it is increasingly being viewed as a site where people's age-old environmental wisdom lies hidden. And, ethnic collectivities were looked upon as carriers of such wisdom. 'Community' which was once perceived as a hindrance to modernity has been brought back onto the global agenda to contest the perceived discontents of modernity. The ghost of traditional community had only hovered over Comte's sociology; it has descended to occupy centre stage in current writings on development, environmental conservation and resource management (Agrawal, 1999: 92–93).

A penchant for community has always been central to sociology. It is not difficult to trace this in the theories of Auguste Comte, Ferdinand Tonnies, Herbert Spencer, Emile Durkheim and Karl Marx. For all these writers, ongoing social changes and the progressive disenchantment of the world implied a decline in earlier forms of solidarity. For Comte, Tonnies, Spencer and Durkheim, society has reached a final stage of evolution – a stage marked by the lessening of traditional communitarian ties. Marx saw community ties of the so-called oriental societies as obstacles to the spread of capitalist modernity. The influence of Darwinian theories of linear and progressive evolution is evident in the writings of these theorists. Therefore, community relations were written off as features of societies qualitatively inferior to modern western society. However, at the same time, many of these sociologists (particularly Tonnies and Durkheim) also attributed the growing dehumanization and instrumentalization of the modern society to the disappearance of community relations. Paradoxically, sociology of modernity also demonstrated a yearning for traditional community bonding.

It is perhaps needless to say that this tradition-modernity binary informed the development initiatives in the developing societies. The 1951 United Nations resolution mentioned earlier in the paper is only demonstrative of this. The Rostowan take-off stage (Rostow, 1960) can arrive only when traditional ties collapse completely and bonds of caste and race dissolve permanently. However, this continued as a dominant paradigm of development until the decade of eighties when the slogan of sustainable development gained currency and the World Commission on Environment and Development under Gro Harlem Brundtland alerted us to the ecological costs of mindless development. The decade of the eighties also saw the emergence of anti-modern discourse (also referred to as the neo-traditionalist discourse on Indian environment; see Sinha, Gururani and Greenberg 1997) in South Asia that added to the potency of sustainable development as a discourse. This neo-traditionalist scholarship, largely manifest in the writings of Ashis Nandy (1988), Vandana Shiva (1988, 1991), Claude Alvares (1988) and Shiv Visvanathan (1988, 1991), saw in the contemporary environmental movements a return of the native and valorized the idyllic community life in the face of growing modernization and instrumentalization of the Indian society. Shiva's portrayal of poor peasant women hugging trees to prevent their felling has become a global icon of popular protest against the exploitation of nature (Sinha, Gururani and Greenberg, 1997: 66). A representation of this kind has subsequently led multilateral agencies such as the World Bank to look for indigenous communities in the developing countries.

Although the neo-traditionalist perspective has gained considerable tactical leverage in its struggle against modernity (Chatterjee, 1998), the approach did not attempt a serious rethinking of the concepts such as tradition or community. In other words, the writers argued for the return of the native, but failed to examine how *native* the native was. They valorized the idyllic community life but did not bother to examine how *idyllic* the idyllic community was. This rethinking is absolutely necessary for the societies (in South Asia) undergoing rapid transformations and all-pervading modernization. While the modernist/positivist paradigm of earlier years celebrated communities' disappearance, the neo-traditionalists only celebrated their return into the development arena. But both provide a very reified view of community as bounded and impervious, occupying a space outside the sphere of the modern. It is this reified notion of community that I wish to question in this paper. Regardless of the growth and spread of institutions and practices of modernity in developing societies, they are believed to have retained their tradition. The use of the word 'indigenous' in the United Nations declaration at Rio de Janeiro is significant. Although the summit was viewed as having provided people everywhere with an opportunity to save the earth

(Tolba, 1992: 22), responsibility for achieving sustainability was devolved on to the so-called indigenous and localized communities of the Third World. No matter how community has been viewed – in negative or positive terms (whether an obstacle to progress or facilitator of it) – in the received history of social theory, societies in the East are always looked upon as potential/actual sites for producing indigenous communities.

I

Pedagogy in the Era of 'Turn to Community'

Under the influence of this 'turn to community' (Agrawal, 1999: 99) social science departments of the universities in West Bengal (especially Kalyani University where I teach and departments of other universities I am familiar with in West Bengal) are nearly flooded with funded or commissioned researches focusing on community involvement or participation in development projects. Similarly, designing of the teaching curriculum has also been informed by this trend towards 'turn to community'. Today, it is difficult to find a development studies course at the postgraduate level, which does not contain buzzwords such as 'community-in-conservation', 'community capacity building' and last but not least 'community empowerment'. The Department of Sociology of Kalyani University is no exception, for development studies here is offered as an optional course to the postgraduate students. The course intends to expose students to different paradigms of development and also to contemporary discourses of community development, participation, empowerment etc. However, despite being exposed to a wide ranging issues at stake in discourses of development, the dominant idea of community that guides them in their research is that of an essentialized, bounded and relatively impervious collectivity, waiting to be involved in the process of development initiated from outside. This is clearly reflected in the students' dissertation reports prepared (as part of the requirement of the course) on the basis of their specific field research. In my view the problem exists because more often than not the incorporation of contemporary issues in the curriculum is rather mechanical and as a result their dissemination remains far from comprehensive. Students also learn new concepts and theories rather mechanically. Rarely do they internalize them so as to be able to turn them into effective tools of meaningful research. Closely related to the above is the second problem. Students are hardly encouraged to adopt an integrated approach to the discipline. They are exposed to Michel Foucault's ideas or complex literature on postmodernism, but when it comes to approaching the 'field' or conducting fieldwork, they simply apply the techniques of social research (which they learn from an age-old course on social science methods).[2] Thus, a student may be familiar with the issues at stake in the domain of development, but when he or she steps out to empirically examine the community's role in development, he/she may adopt a very static view about community ending up surveying a few households. Very little attention is paid to the dynamics of community sustenance and formation in an age when communities are being shaped and reshaped by development interventions of different kinds.

The paper problematizes such a static, reified and essentialized notion of community. As argued earlier in the paper, the current valorization of community amounts to reifying the concept in exactly the same way as the teleological theories of progress of the earlier years did when they viewed it merely as an obstacle. Following Chatterjee (1998, 2004), I argue that instead of viewing communities as remnants of societies' (especially underdeveloped or less modern) pre-capitalist past, it is necessary that we view communities as products of people's increasing encounters and negotiations with the vast array of technologies of power deployed by the agents of development such as the modern state, global aid agencies, non-state bodies etc. In support of my argument, I present two cases – one based on my experience of supervising field research of students at my university and the other on my research in the Sundarbans. It is to the consideration of my first case study that I turn to in the next section of the paper.

II

A Dissertation on the Ruidas Community of Bilaspur[3] in Nadia

Apart from teaching the postgraduate optional course on development, I am responsible for supervising the dissertations of students. As part of the requirement of the course, the students are expected to carry out fieldwork (on a topic of their choice) to write up their dissertation reports. I supervise M.A. dissertations of about 5–6 students every year and I ensure that students submit their dissertations on time. A couple of years back, a student, who was working under my supervision, submitted her dissertation very late. This student of mine decided to work on an NGO and its role in community development in a village called Bilaspur in Nadia district, not far from where the university is located. According to her, apart from its awareness raising activities, the organization implemented government programmes on health and education fronts. Until recently, the NGO ran many non-formal education centres for school dropouts in Bilaspur and neighbouring villages under the Government of India funded scheme of non-formal education. In addition to providing government sponsored health services, such as organizing eye clinic for the old or polio vaccination clinic for the children, the agency was also implementing government funded housing scheme for the poor scheduled caste people. My student wanted to interview the beneficiaries of the housing scheme and evaluate the NGO's housing programmes in Bilaspur.

We had periodic supervisory meetings and she was pretty regular with her field reports. Therefore, her late submission left me wondering what went wrong. When I asked her why she took so long to submit she said that initially everything was fine but later her fieldwork got affected because the NGO got entangled with a problem concerning its housing scheme in Bilaspur. The organization suggested that she should stop her work till the problem was resolved. When I asked her about the nature of the problem, she narrated the incident as follows:

> The government housing scheme which the organization implemented provided a two-roomed house with an asbestos top and a kitchen and toilet for each *Ruidas* (cobbler) family who lived below poverty line. The NGO had about twenty such houses built under the scheme. However, the problem arose when a portion of the kitchen of a house collapsed and a member of the Ruidas family was seriously injured. The incident enraged the people of Ruidaspara. They brought charges of corruption against the organization. According to them, a deal was struck between the NGO supervisory workers and the contractor who had built these houses. The Ruidaspara people had apprehended this when the houses were being built because the building material used (particularly brick and cement) was of inferior quality. The NGO functionaries ignored this when the malpractice was brought to their notice by the beneficiaries. But, when the house collapsed, the villagers staged a sit-in

demonstration before the NGO office. The older section of Ruidas village made contact with the panchayat functionaries and tried to win their confidence. They approached the panchayat in order to take the NGO people to task.

The incident clearly put the NGO on the back foot. Fearing a possible backlash the NGO officials tried using their contact in the local party circles. To this end they employed their local level volunteers who were closer to the local panchayat and party people. The organization assured the Ruidas community that they would bear the medical expenses of the injured villager. However, this promise hardly satisfied the younger section of Ruidaspara. They, on the other hand wanted to cash in on this. As compensation they demanded that some of the youth of Ruidaspara be given employment in the organization. They further demanded that they be allowed to supervise and monitor the housing scheme in future. Through panchayat leaders they pressurized the NGO coordinator to give in to their demands. The older people of Ruidaspara persuaded the younger people not to put unnecessary pressure on the organization. They wanted to make the organization accountable for what they had done, but at the same time were cautious about not letting the crisis snowball into a proportion whereby the beneficiaries could run the risk of not benefiting from the scheme in future. They insisted on having meetings with the NGO functionaries and panchayat people in search of an amicable solution to the crisis.

She narrated the incident she heard from the NGO workers, but surprisingly, I did not find a mention of this in her dissertation. When I asked her about this she confessed that she did not realize that the incident itself was worthy of consideration and could have been an important part of her research findings. She viewed the controversy surrounding the housing scheme essentially as a problem for the NGO to settle, while her job, she thought, was to evaluate the success of the development programmes and their contribution to the economic and social well-being of the communities. She conducted a survey of the households who were beneficiaries of this housing programme and documented their perceptions about how the scheme contributed to their well-being. She treated 'the community' as given, a static entity waiting to be involved in and enlisted as a beneficiary of the government development programme.

However, the Bilaspur incident, which the student viewed mainly as an obstacle to her otherwise smooth research and failed to document in her report, offers a valuable insight into the dynamics of community formation. The incident and the subsequent negotiations it unfolded show that the Ruidas people are not the passive beneficiaries of development but active agents deeply aware of their entitlements. The disagreements and dissensions amongst the different sections of Ruidaspara make it difficult to see community as bounded, homogeneous and impervious entity. What explains the sustenance of community is no longer internal to the community itself. Rather, our case study suggests that communities are sustained and reshaped by a host of agencies working outside communities.

III

The Case of Sundarbans Adivasis

The first case study, my familiarity with which was via the dissertation I happened to supervise, provides only a glimpse of the dynamics of community formation. I wish to buttress my arguments about the realities of community formation a little further by focusing on my second case study based on my research among the tribals or *adivasis* in the Sundarbans of West Bengal. The Sundarbans, a heritage site and the largest mangrove delta, is not only the abode of the royal tigers but also a home to about 3.7 million people (as per 2001 census). The Sundarbans has substantial proportion of tribal population spread across different islands. However, the tribals are not indigenous people of the Sundarbans. Historically, the Sundarbans reclamation was carried out by the tribals indentured from Chotanagpur (Pargiter, 1934: 57; Mukherjee, 1981: 90). We know that colonial labour market, which came to operate in India, employed adivasis as coolies for the expansion of colonial capitalism (Mohapatra, 1985; Breman and Daniel, 1992; Bates and Carter, 1994; Prakash, 1992; Ghosh, 1999). We also know how discourses of aboriginality and primitivism operating in colonial labour market made possible ethnic stereotyping of labourers and fetishized the correspondence between aboriginality and physical strength as a crucial element in the construction of adivasi personhood. According to Choudhury and Bhowmik (1986), like indigo plantation in Bengal or tea plantation in Assam, the clearing up of large tracts of forest and marshy lands of the southern part of Bengal also required cheap labour. Naturally, the most tempting target was the adivasi who was a sturdy and hardworking person and able to live at a sub-human level of existence (ibid.: 331).

In the Sundarbans, reclamation and settlement through the clearing of forests took place before the natural process of siltation had raised the land sufficiently above the water level. Therefore, high earthen embankments were constructed to protect these settlements against daily inundation during high tides. The Bhumij and Santhal adivasis who cleared forests and reclaimed wetlands were engaged in embankment building activities as well. After the abolition of zamindari rule in the 1950s, when protecting and maintaining the Sundarbans embankments came under the purview of the State Irrigation Department, the department recruited the adivasis to the post of *Beldars* – government employees responsible for protecting and maintaining embankments. The rationale behind such recruitment was not only to employ local labour to maintain embankments, but also to pursue a wider government policy of uplifting 'socially backward' communities. Therefore, the obvious choice for these posts were the tribals (Sardars) of the Sundarbans. The adivasis, with their assumed aboriginality, physical prowess and historically defined role in the Sundarbans reclamation, qualified for the label 'indigenous people' – an oft-quoted phrase in contemporary government discourses of development.

It is interesting to note how discourses on primitivism and aboriginality continue to inform the present-day non-adivasis' perception of adivasis in the Sundarbans. During my research on an island (I named Kusumpur)[4] in the Sundarbans I often stumbled in on discussions among villagers agitated over frequent embankment collapse and their vulnerability. On the one hand they glorified the adivasis of yesteryears for their historic role as the Sundarbans reclaimers or embankment builders (thereby seeking to establish an unproblematic correspondence between aboriginality and labour power) and on the other, accused the present-day adivasis, who served as the government appointed *Beldars*, of not being aboriginals any more. The frequent embankment collapse is often attributed to laxity and negligence on the part of the *Beldars*.

During the period I carried out my fieldwork in the Sundarbans, embankments collapsed on a number of occasions in and around Kusumpur. Whenever embankments collapsed villagers living close by were found to initiate embankment repair activities. It was on one such occasion, when embankment collapsed in the southern part of Kusumpur island, I reached the site to find the villagers vociferously criticizing the *Beldars.* A portion of the embankment collapsed in the afternoon, but it was not before midnight, when water started receding during low tide, that repair work could be undertaken. On arrival I found that the place was lit up by a few lanterns (lamps burning on kerosene oil). The villagers started their work on a war footing. Some of them carried earth from the river bank while others were constructing the slope of the new embankment. Still others stood on the muddy river bank holding the lanterns aloft and closer to the mud wall of the new embankment so as to enable those repairing the slope to work in nearly invisible conditions. The villagers who gathered at the site were found to be in a belligerent mood. They accused the *Beldars* of being irresponsible and negligent. One could feel in their voices a sense of animosity towards the *Beldars.* They exchanged their displeasures amongst themselves. They compared the activities of the *Beldars* with those of their forefathers who played a significant role in the Sundarbans reclamation. I found myself drawn into the discussion more as a passive listener than as an active participant. What I gathered from their allegations and accusations was that the *Beldars* had become *sarkari baboos* who enjoyed a nice salary and did nothing to protect embankments. Unlike their ancestors they had lost the ability to toil and labour. Their ancestors had extraordinary physique and enormous courage. They were great embankment builders who laboured for hours in the sun, spent the night in the jungle and had only saline water to drink. It was they who reclaimed the land from the sea and made the Sundarbans habitable for us. They cleared the forest and fought the wild beasts. It was appalling to see how the present-day adivasi *Beldars* were wasting their body and strength which they inherited from their forefathers. They had become idle and alcoholic. Their only interest was in their monthly salary. At the beginning of every month they were found busy boozing and blowing away their money.

Not only are the present-day Sardars perceived as having failed as embankment builders, but they are also considered as having failed in reproducing their ethnic stereotypes. Here, it is interesting to observe further twists in the language of aboriginality and labour. We know that the colonial labour market encountered problems of drinking and idling among the aborigines (Mohapatra, 1985; Ghosh, 1999). This was the reason why the Santhal and Bhumij were considered undesirable for coal mines. The adivasis, who were the planters' favourite because of their expertise in clearing jungles and their ability to adjust to plantation life, were not considered suitable for coal mines where the need for cutting coal throughout the year required the labour to be more disciplined (Mohapatra, 1985: 265). However, what we observe in the Sundarbans seems to convey that drinking and idling, which once characterized adivasis and served as significant ingredients in constructing the Santhal or the Bhumij ethnic stereotype, are now seen by the non-adivasis in the Sundarbans as symptoms of tribals losing their ethnic stereotype, becoming estranged from their 'tribalhood'. The villagers' accusations and allegations seem to suggest that by becoming idle and alcoholic the adivasis fail to live up to the idealized image of the tribal as a labourer with uncanny strength and courage.

The incidence of embankment collapse discussed above and the villagers' anger provide an instance of how the villagers ventilate their grievances against the *Beldars*; how they perceive what *Beldars'* job ought to be. It was because of these accusations that I wanted to meet the *Beldars* of Sardarpara. To this end I contacted them beforehand and informed them of my intention to visit them for a chat. And it was decided that they would meet me at Bimal Sardar's (a *Beldar*) house at Sardarpara in Kusumpur.

The day I went to Bimal's house I found them discussing something amongst themselves. Seeing me they told each other, "Oh, he has come." Then Babulal, one of the *Beldars*, asked me, "How long do you think you are going to take?" "That depends on the time that you think you can spare," I answered. Babulal gave an awkward smile and said, "Actually a problem has cropped up." Then pointing to a boy sitting at a distance, he told me, "His father was a *Beldar* who died recently. Since he died while still in service, his son has a legitimate claim to his father's job now. But, the Irrigation Department is creating a problem on technical grounds. We have decided to take this boy to the Gosaba office and sort it out. Therefore, you need to let us off in an hour and a half." The boy sitting with a stick in his hand and clad in two pieces of cloth one to cover the lower part of his body and another piece wrapped around his bare chest, looked to me like someone whose father's formal funeral rites were not yet over. I told Babulal, "An hour and a half is okay, but it seems that his father's death rituals are not yet over." Babulal promptly replied, "That's precisely the reason why we want to take him now to the office and convince the officials about his bonafide claim."

With an hour and a half at my disposal I started conversing with the six *Beldars*. Except for Karna Sardar, the other five had all inherited their father's occupation. Initially, our discussion centred on their fathers and forefathers and their deeds during the time of the reclamation of the Sundarbans. They described the odds their forefathers and others who came with them faced in clearing forests during the early stages of settlement. While we were chatting Bimal Sardar kept drinking rice alcohol and nodding his head as a mark of his tacit support to what his colleagues were saying. He was drinking and at times passing his tumbler around to others for a sip. As soon as his tumbler was empty, his wife came to replenish it.

The moment I asked them about the allegations against them Bimal turned grave. Suddenly he got up as if the question shook him out of his inertia and asked, "Who told you this? Do these people know what our job and duties are?" He did not bother to wait for my response and continued, "We are not irrigation labourers, meant to add earth or repair embankments. Our job is to detect hidden holes (*ghog*) in the embankment. Detecting these holes is not everybody's cup of tea, you need to have trained eyes and ears to detect such holes." Pointing to the distant field dotted with houses and the horizon beyond he said, "These people [the villagers] think that anybody can become a *Beldar*." Bimal paused for a while, as he was short of breath. Babulal went up to pacify him and made him sit on the ground. He then turned to Karna and asked him to explain things to me. Karna said that such holes are made by crabs that come from the sea during high tide. According to him, it is only during high tide that they can inspect such holes because it is when the water rises that you can make out if seepage is taking place or not. Sometimes their eyes fail to locate them. Then they kneel down and use their ears to make out from the nature and sound of water flow whether holes have developed in the embankments. Holes can be detected only during high tide, but must be plugged when the water recedes.

Our discussion could not proceed further because Babulal and others wanted to go to the irrigation office. The next day I went to Upen Sardar's house, a few metres away from Bimal's house in Sardarpara. Upen was also present at Bimal's house when I met the *Beldars* there. Upen was sitting at Bimal's doorstep with a crutch by his side which clearly suggested that he was not physically fit. Later I came to know from Babulal that he had a cerebral attack which had paralysed his right limb. Upen could not sit through the entire discussion and before leaving Bimal's place he invited me to come to his house.

Upen's life was in shambles when I met him. He was slowly recovering from a cerebral attack. He was out of his job and fearing that he would not be able to work any more, he decided to stake his son's claim to his job. According to Upen, the Irrigation Office in Gosaba set its face against his claim on the ground that his son was still a minor. Initially, Upen could not make much headway and his repeated visits to the Gosaba office did not produce the desired results. Recently, he approached a panchayat member of his village who had contacts in the Gosaba irrigation office to pursue his son's case. Upen said, "Now, the wind seems to be blowing in my favour. I must ensure that my son gets the job before Kanu's son gets it." "Who is he?" I asked. "The boy you saw at Bimal's place yesterday was Kanu Sardar's son. But if the officers decide to recruit him first, who knows if they might once again create problems in taking my son in." "But don't you think Kanu Sardar's son should get his father's job?" I asked. "It's not that I do not support Kanu's son's claim and even I can be of help to him if need be. But all these can happen only when I feel secure. I need to look after my own interests as well," Upen answered. "For the last five months my salary has stopped and I do not have much land to my credit. My physical condition is such that working in the field is out of question. The villagers allege that *Beldars* do not work and it is because of their negligence that the embankment collapses, but did any of them bother to enquire how I am making my ends meet?" Upen looked visibly angry.

Beldars' narratives are significant in a number of ways. No matter how the identity of the *Beldars* is construed either as descendants of their illustrious forefathers, known for their legendary physique and strength, or as descendants who are no longer capable of producing their ethnic stereotype, Sardars as *Beldars* know exactly who they are answerable to. As agents of the state, the *Beldars* see themselves as protecting its interests. Not only did Bimal make it clear that he remained answerable to the irrigation department but the other *Beldars* present there also agreed with him. However, the way they decided that they would pursue the case of the son of their deceased colleague and establish his claim to his father's job indicates that their sense of identification with the state does not make them oblivious of their own rights and privileges. Their lack of familiarity with the detailed rules and regulations of the irrigation office is not a handicap. Their determination to present the deceased *Beldar's* son in person to the officials of the irrigation department proves that they are ready to counter any such technical problem with the strategies they have at their disposal.

Similarly, Upen was on the verge of losing his job, but this sense of loss does not condemn him to a state of utter despair. Rather, it imbues him with a sense of agency that is reflected in his determination to stake his son's claim and pursue it against all odds. To this end he has also established contact with the local panchayat leader who is believed to enjoy considerable clout among the engineers and officials. *Beldars'* narratives run contrary to the non-adivasis' imagination of the adivasis as forming a homogeneous and bounded community. This is not to suggest that Sardars as *Beldars* are not aware of their forefathers and their role in the Sundarbans reclamation. However, today, what keeps the community of *Beldars* together is not the idea that they are the descendants of adivasis who were once embankment builders and were known for their legendary physical prowess, rather what keeps them together is the possibility of their using to their advantage the resources that go with the office of *Beldar.* Whether Bimal and Babulal pursue the case of their deceased colleague's son collectively or Upen pursues his son's case individually, they all belong to this community of *Beldars* not as abstract descendants of his forefathers, but as individuals who are deeply aware of their predicaments and entitlements as *Beldars.*

IV

Conclusion

In the retreat of grand teleological theories of progress, 'community' comes to occupy a space of importance. But can indigeneity still be a useful concept in understanding the dynamics of community formation as it unfolds in contemporary Indian society? By documenting two specific case studies, I argued how communities, far from being idyllic and impervious, are actually the products of people's encounters with governmental rationalities of different kinds. The first case study clearly shows how difficult it is to understand community development through simple household surveys. The problems researcher faces and the circumstances under which a research is carried out are significant in that they may enable him or her to question many taken-for-granted assumptions about community and community development. The second case study raises the uncomfortable question of whether indigeneity can still be a relevant concept in understanding the tribal life in India. Protagonists who look upon the Third World as a prospective site for building bounded community relations fail to examine concepts such as state, society and community in the light of the specific experiences of modernisation in the non-western world.

Notes

1. This article is inspired by the ideas of Partha Chatterjee (1998, 2004) and Arun Agrawal (1999). However, the author is solely responsible for the arguments expressed in the paper.
2. As a student of Sociology one may learn diverse theoretical perspectives, but when it comes to approaching the 'field' or conducting empirical research, the model that prevails is that of social survey. Instead of theory and method being complementary to each other, there is a growing hiatus between the two. Often what goes by the name of methodology are actually techniques (nuts and bolts) of social research. However, this problem is not unique to Kalyani University. This has largely to do with the dominant perception of the discipline as an instrument of social reform. Also see discussion on abstracted empiricism in chapter 19.
3. Bilaspur is a fictitious name given to the place.
4. For the purposes of confidentiality I have named the Sundarbans village Kusumpur.

References

Agrawal, Arun. 1999. "Community-in-Conservation: Tracing the Outlines of an Enchanting Concept", in R. Jeffery and N. Sundar (eds.), *A New Moral Economy for India's Forests: Discourses of Community and Participation*. New Delhi: Sage.

Alvares, Claude. 1988. "Science, Colonialism and Violence: A Luddite View", in A. Nandy (ed.), *Science, Hegemony and Violence: A Requiem for Modernity*. New Delhi: Oxford University Press.

Bates, Crispin and Marina Carter. 1994. "Tribal Migration in India and Beyond", in G. Prakash (ed.), *The World of the Rural Labourer in Colonial India.* New Delhi: Oxford University Press.

Breman, Jan and E. Valentine Daniel. 1992. "Conclusion: The Making of a Coolie in Plantations, Proletarians and Peasants in Colonial Asia", *Journal of Peasant Studies,* Vol. 19, Nos. 3 and 4.

Chatterjee, Partha. 1998. "Community in the East", *Economic and Political Weekly,* Vol. 33, No. 6.

—. 2004. *The Politics of the Governed: Reflections on Popular Politics in Most of the World.* New Delhi: Permanent Black.

Choudhury, C. Niren and Sharit K. Bhowmik. 1986. "Migration of Chota Nagpur Tribals to West Bengal", in M.S.A. Rao (ed.), *Studies in Migration: Internal and International Migration in India.* New Delhi: Manohar.

Ghosh, Kaushik. 1999. "A Market for Aboriginality: Primitivism and Race Classification in the Indentured Labour Market of Colonial India", in G. Bhadra, G. Prakash and S. Tharu (eds.), *Subaltern Studies X.* New Delhi: Oxford University Press.

Mohapatra, Prabhu P. 1985. "Coolies and Collieries: A Study of the Agrarian Context of Labour Migration from Chotanagpur 1880–1920", in *Studies in History,* Vol. 1, No. 2.

Mukherjee, Shankarananda. 1981. "Peasant Uprising", in A.K. Das, S. Mukherji and M.K. Chowdhuri (eds.), *A Focus on Sundarban.* Calcutta: Editions Indian.

Nandy, Ashis. 1988. "Science as the Reason of the State", in A. Nandy (ed.), *Science, Hegemony and Violence: A Requiem for Modernity.* New Delhi: Oxford University Press.

Pargiter, Frederick E. 1934. *A Revenue History of the Sundarbans: From 1765 to 1870.* Bengal Government Press, Bengal.

Prakash, Gyan. 1992. "Science Gone Native", in *Colonial India Representations,* Vol. 40.

Rostow, Whitman Walt. 1960. *The Stages of Economic Growth: A Non-Communist Manifesto.* Cambridge: Cambridge University Press.

Shiva, Vandana. 1988. *Staying Alive: Women, Ecology and Survival in India.* London: Zed Press.

—. 1991. *The Violence of the Green Revolution.* London: Zed Books.

Sinha, Subir, Subhra Gururani and Brian Greenberg. 1997. "The 'New Traditionalist' Discourse of Indian Environmentalism", *The Journal of Peasant Studies,* Vol. 24, No. 3.

Tolba, Mustafa. 1992. "Two Vital Reasons for Rescuing Diversity", in *Earth Summit News*. London: United Nations Association.

United Nations. 1951. Measures for the Economic Development of Underdeveloped Countries. UN Department of Economic Affairs, United Nations, New York.

—. 1993. *Report of the United Nations Conference on Environment and Development at Rio de Janeiro.* June 3–14, Vol. 1, United Nations, New York.

Visvanathan, Shiv. 1988. "On the Annals of the Laboratory State", in A. Nandy (ed.), *Science, Hegemony and Violence: A Requiem for Modernity*. New Delhi: Oxford University Press.

—. 1991. "Mrs Brundtland's Disenchanted Cosmos", in *Alternatives*, Vol. 16, No. 3.

17

Tribes as Indigenous People of India

VIRGINIUS XAXA

The idea of 'indigenous people' is an issue of considerable contention in India today. This was hardly so till a few years ago. In fact, social workers, administrators, politicians and even scholars widely used the term to refer to a certain category of people. They hardly felt any unease in the use of native equivalent of this term, viz., 'adivasi'. G.S. Ghurye had of course some reservation to the use of such terms; the expression he used was 'so-called aborigines'. Again, it is they who took the term along with all the prejudices and conjectures to the masses. That is how the identity of adivasis has entered into the consciousness of the tribal people. The identity that was forced upon them from outside precisely to mark out differences from the dominant community has now been internalized by the people themselves. Not only has it become an important mark of social differentiation and identity assertion but also an important tool of articulation for empowerment.

The Term 'Tribe'

The Anthropological Survey of India under the 'People of India Project' identifies 461 tribal communities in India. They are enumerated at 67,583,800 persons constituting 8.08 per cent of the total population as per the 1991 census. The share of the scheduled tribe (ST) population to the total population in 1971 and 1981 was 6.94 and 7.85 per cent, respectively. The question of tribes in India is closely linked with administrative and political considerations. Hence, there has been an increasing demand by groups and communities for their inclusion in the list of STs of the Indian Constitution. That partly explains the steady increase in the proportion of the ST population in India, especially during the period between 1971 and 1981.

There has been more concern with the identification of tribes than with their definition. This does not mean that lists have been drawn without any conception of tribe whatsoever. There did exist some conception. This was obvious from the use of criteria that were adopted. These ranged from such features as geographical isolation, simple technology and conditions of living, general backwardness to the practice of animism, tribal language, physical features, etc. The problem however lay in the fact that they were neither clearly formulated nor systematically applied. One set of criteria was used in one context and quite another in another context. The result is that the list includes groups and communities strikingly different from each other in respect of not only size of the population but also the level of technology and other characteristics. Indian anthropologists have been acutely aware of a certain lack of fit between what their discipline defines as tribe and what they are obliged to describe as tribes. Yet they have continued with the existing labels.

The early ethnographers were not very clear about the distinction between caste and tribe in India. The 18th century writings, for example, showed synonymous use of the term 'tribe' with caste. Later it was even used in a cognate manner as one could see in the use of phrase 'caste and tribes of India' by Risley and many others in their writings. Efforts to make a distinction between the two began to be made after an initiative was taken to collect detailed information about the people for the census. The census officials were however far from clear with regard to the criterion of distinction. It is with the 1901 census that one finds a mention of criteria howsoever inadequate that may be. It defined tribes as those who practised animism. In the subsequent censuses animism was replaced by the tribal religion. Although the criterion so introduced was highly unsatisfactory, it continued to be used widely and extensively.

It is only in the post-independence period that more systematic effort was made towards distinguishing tribe from caste. Though the distinction between the two was made in both colonial and post-colonial ethnographies, the relation between the two was differently conceived. In the colonial ethnography, the concern shown by the British administrators/scholars was to mark off tribe from caste. Hence tribes were shown to be living in complete isolation from the rest of population and therefore without any interaction or interrelation with them. In contrast the main concern in the native ethnography has been to show close interaction of the tribes with the larger society or the civilization. Both Ghurye (1963) and Bose (1975), for example, stressed the nature of interaction between tribes and the larger Hindu society and the ways in which tribes have been drawn into the Hindu society. They stressed similarities between the two societies. Sinha (1958) even goes to the extent of viewing tribes as a dimension of little tradition that cannot be adequately understood unless it is seen in relation to the great tradition.

In view of such conception, tribes have come to be primarily studied in relation to features and characteristics of the larger society. The focus is on how tribes are getting absorbed into the larger society, the so-called mainstream, by becoming caste, peasant, class and so on. With such conceptualization, the identity of the tribal group or community is indeed put at risk. This is because of the way tribes have been conceptualized in anthropological literature and the reference with which tribal society in India is studied.

Tribes are primarily seen as a stage and type of society. They represent a society that lacks positive traits of the modern society and thus constitute a simple, illiterate and backward society. With change in these features on account of education, modern occupation, new technology, etc., tribal society is no longer considered to be tribal. If transformation is in the direction of caste society, then it is described as having become caste society. If the reference is peasant, then, it is posited as the peasant society and if the general direction of transformation is social differentiation, then, it is described as differentiated or stratified, and thus ceases to be tribal society. In the process it is forgotten that tribe besides being a stage and type of society is also a society alike and similar to any other kind of society, say, the Oriya or the Bengali. But it is precisely this that comes to be denied on account of the changed situation. Of course, it is true that the tribes are not of the same stage and type as Bengali or Oriya societies. There is then something clumsy about the use of the term 'tribe' in describing the Indian social reality.

Concept of Indigenous

Such conceptual and empirical problems inherent in the use of the term tribe or tribal society could to some extent be overcome by the use of the term indigenous but not without giving rise to other problems. The term indigenous or its equivalent has been used in anthropology to describe groups called tribes for quite some time. Its use now has however gone beyond the discipline of anthropology. The international agencies are increasingly and extensively making use of this term and concept in their deliberations and discussions. With this, the term has come to occupy wide currency in general as well as in the other social sciences literature. In the deliberations of the international agencies, the term was used for the first time in 1957 (Roy-Burman, undated). It gained wide currency after 1993 with the declaration of the year 1993 as the international year of the indigenous people.

In 1957 the general conference of the ILO passed a resolution concerning protection and integration of indigenous and other tribal and semi-tribal population in independent countries. The resolution framed general international standards for facilitating government actions towards protecting and promoting progressive integration of these people into the respective national communities (covenant, 107). By 1985 the ILO felt the need to revise the resolution on account of changes in attitudes and approaches towards these people worldwide. The ILO had earlier proposed integration as the desired objective but this was no longer being seen as appropriate. This was so because the international organizations and increasing number of governments were moving toward greater recognition of the rights of indigenous and tribal people to retain their specific identities and to participate fully in the planning and execution of the activities affecting their way of life. Accordingly, the ILO adopted a revised resolution (covenant, 169) in 1989 after the expert committee appointed by the ILO gave its recommendation and the same was passed in consultation with other international bodies.

The context of the discourse on the indigenous, initiated by the ILO and later accepted by the UNO, thus basically hinged on the twin concepts of 'need right' and 'power right' of a certain social category of people all over the world. People in this category were progressively being marginalized and dispossessed from their sources of livelihood and were vulnerable to cultural shock and decimation of their collective identity.

The ILO resolution referred to above, and the Working Group on Indigenous Population set up by the Human Rights Commission of the UNO, speak of the indigenous population as those tribal and semi-tribal people, who are regarded as having their descent from the populations which inhabited the country at the time of the conquest or colonization by Europe. They are in addition also those who irrespective of their legal status live more in conformity with their social, economic and cultural institutions that with the institution of the nation to which they belong (Roy-Burman, undated; Pathy, 1992b). The semi-tribal people are defined as those who are in the process of losing their identity but not yet integrated in the national community.

Thus, there are three aspects which are central to the conceptualization of the indigenous people. First, the indigenous are those people who lived in the country to which they belong before colonization or conquest by people from outside the country or the geographical region. Secondly, they have become marginalized as an aftermath of conquest and colonization by the people from outside the region. Thirdly, such people govern their life more in terms of their own social, economic and cultural institutions than the laws applicable to the society or the country at large. What is important here is that the notion of indigenous people, despite sharing attributes in common with the people described as the tribal and semi-tribal population, is seen as different from the latter in the sense that the indigenous are invariably marked out as a distinct international entity. That is, the indigenous are invariably seen as victims of conquest and colonization from outside the region, hence, the outsiders are easily identifiable.

Tribes as Indigenous

The term 'indigenous people', though of recent coinage at the international level, has been in use in India for a long time. In fact, the social workers, missionaries and political activists have been using the term 'adivasi', the Indian-language term for the indigenous people, freely to refer to the tribal people since the turn of the 20th century. The term, in conjunction with other related terms such as aborigines, autochthonous, etc., has also been extensively used by scholars and administrators in their writings and reports. It was used mainly as a mark of identification and differentiation, that is, to mark out a group of people different in physical features, language, religion, custom, social organization, etc. Even Ghurye (1963: 12), who otherwise talks of tribes as backward Hindus and has reservation about the use of the term 'adivasi', refers to them as the aborigines. He writes, "when the history of internal movements of peoples is not known, it is utterly unscientific to regard some tribe or the other as the original owner of the soil. It is possible to contend that even if the tribes are not aborigines of the exact area they now occupy, they are the autochthonous of India and to that extent they may be called the aborigines."

Thus, hardly any unease was felt by scholars in the use of the term 'indigenous people' to refer to these groups of people. No effort whatsoever was made to dispel the myth associated with the term then. The term however did not remain confined to only the scholars, administrators, politicians and social workers; it percolated down also to the people. Indeed, it is social workers, political activists and administrators who took the term and along with it all the prejudices and conjectures to the masses (Sengupta, 1988: 1003). The term thus came to be widely used to refer to the tribal people. It was hardly questioned, let alone debated. So long as it had not assumed a political dimension, it had remained an accepted term of description and designation of certain category of people.

It is only with the internationalization of the rights and privileges associated with it that the use of the term 'indigenous' has come to be critically examined or even challenged in the Indian context. The sense in which the term was used earlier and the sense in which it has come to be used today, are definitely not identical though they overlap in some sense. Today, aspects of marginalization are built into the definition of indigenous people. Only those people that have been subjected to domination and subjugation have come to constitute the component of the indigenous people. Yet, the use of the term 'adivasi' (indigenous) to designate certain category of people and not the other category clearly reveals that these aspects were not altogether lost sight of. It may be noted that even earlier the term was used to delineate people who were backward and cut off from the mainstream civilization. The basic mark of differentiation was between those who were part of the civilization and those who were not. Hence, the use of the term 'adivasi' to describe tribal people seems to have some validity even in the sense of marginalization. Historical antiquity may have been a more distant criterion, but the most immediate and proximate seemed to be the fact that they were not part of the civilization. In a certain sense then there was the aspect of marginalization that was taken note of while designating a group as 'adivasi'.

This seems all the more obvious when we take other aspects of Indian society. The coming of the Aryans has been invariably taken as the decisive historical factor to determine the original people of India. Yet not all the original people have been called the indigenous people. The groups speaking languages belonging to the Dravidian linguistic stock no doubt have been considered the inhabitants of India before the coming of the Aryans. Yet, they have never been described as the indigenous people, mainly because they do not constitute the marginalized groups. The Government of India had in fact placed no objection to the use of the term when it was deliberated upon in the ILO convention in 1957 and was tied to covenant 107. This was so because the term then had not raised such issues as empowerment and rights; rather it had articulated the need of integrating the indigenous and tribal people into the larger social and political system. By contrast, the focus had shifted from integration to one of rights and empowerment by 1989. And no sooner had the issue shifted than the argument ensued that a category such as this does not hold in the Indian context.

Arguments Against

Much of the discussion questioning the indigenous people's status in India has centred on the complex historical processes of the movement of the populations and their settlement in the subcontinent. It is said that unlike in the Americas, Australia and New Zealand with a recent history of conquest, immigration and colonization, in India, identification of indigenous people is not easy. Rather, there have been in India waves of movement of populations with different languages, race, culture and religions dating back centuries and millennia. Even groups or communities described as tribes have not been outside of this process. Given this, how far back should one go in history to determine people who are natives and who are immigrants. Indeed, any demarcation is going to be arbitrary and hence extremely contentious. And indeed so has been the case as we can see from the discussion below. It is also maintained that the communities described as tribes have been living in close proximity with the non-tribal people for over centuries leading to much acculturation and even assimilation into the larger Hindu society. The Indian experience, it is stated, is different from that of the new world where it was marked by conquest, subjugation and even decimation. It is hence argued that it is not only the point of departure that is problematic but also the Indian experience.

It is with the people described as tribes that the term 'indigenous people' has generally come to be associated in India. It is assumed that they have been the original settlers of what geographically constitutes India today or at least people who inhabited the region before the coming of the more dominant sections of the Indian society, viz., the Aryans. They are said to belong to social groups other than the Aryans and speak a variety of dialects belonging presumably to two main linguistic families, viz., the Dravidian and the Austric. The plausibility of groups speaking Tibeto-Burman languages is not altogether ruled out from the purview of the status of the original inhabitants in India. These groups have generally been described as 'adivasis' or the original people by social workers, missionaries, political activists, scholars and administrators since the beginning of the present century. Ray (1973: 124–25) writes: "The communities of people of today whom the anthropologists call tribals, happen to be the indigenous, autochthonous (adivasis, adimjati) people of the land, in the sense that they had long been settled in different parts of the country before the Aryan-speaking peoples penetrated India to settle down first, in the Kabul and Indus valleys and then within a millennium and half, to spread out in slow stages, over large areas of the country and push their way of life and civilization over practically the entire area of the country along the plains and the river valleys."

The question that is of central importance here is whether groups designated as tribes have been natives of India and non-tribes immigrants, and if they have not been natives whether their settlement is prior to that of the arrival of the major social group – the Aryans. Most of the scholars are of the view that tribes could hardly make legitimate claim that they are the only natives of India. They cite observations made by scholars, howsoever conflicting they may be, in support of their position. Hutton, for example, is of the view that only the Negritos may be considered as the original inhabitants of India though they do not have any marked presence now. He considers groups belonging to the Austric, Dravidian categories, etc. as much outsiders as the Aryans. Guha is also cited for making similar observation in the context of Austric-speaking people (Shah, 1982). But more authoritative sources on which such claim is questioned are the traditions of the tribes themselves as they speak. Dube (1977: 2) writes: "it is difficult to speak of 'original' inhabitants, for tribal traditions themselves make repeated mention of migration of their ancestors. There is considerable evidence to suggest that several groups were pushed out of the areas where they were first settled and had to seek shelter elsewhere. And there are several groups, now absorbed in Hindu society, which can make an equally tenable claim to being original or, at any rate very old inhabitants." Beteille (1998) makes similar observation on the point under reference.

There are two substantive points that have been made here. The first is whether one can speak of tribes as the original people especially in view of their migratory movement. This is indeed an important argument and cannot be brushed aside. The other makes reference to the claims that may be made by groups that have been absorbed into the Hindu society. The latter suffers from a certain flaws. Firstly, it is hypothetical. The second is that the groups lose the right to make such claim by virtue of their choice to get absorbed into the dominant, viz., the Hindu society.

If the issue of tribes as natives is questionable, is it so also with the second question? That is, are all tribal groups the inhabitants that settled the territory before the coming of the Aryans, the assumed cut-off point for demarcating the indigenous people in India? Whereas this is more or less the case, it cannot be said with certainty for all the groups described as tribes in India. It is said that there are tribes in India especially in the north-east whose settlement in the territories they inhabit today is an even later phenomenon than the settlement of many non-tribes in other parts of India. The Nagas, for example, are stated to have come to India around the middle of the first millennium BC first to Tibet and later to the territory where they live now – a period later than the coming of the Aryans. The Mizos are said to have settled in the territory where they live only in the 16th century. The Kuki settlement is considered even later than that of the Mizos. In contrast to this, the non-tribal groups like the Bengalis, Gujaratis, Oriyas, etc. have a much longer history of settlement than these tribes.

Given this, it becomes indeed problematic to say that all tribal people in India are earlier settlers than the Aryans and therefore tribes are indigenous and non-tribes, non-indigenous.

There is a need to make distinction between settlements in the context of country (India being the reference point here) as a whole and settlements within its parts or regions. In the discourse on indigenous people, the two aspects are either ignored or mixed or even interchanged. An argument valid at one level, for example at the local level, is often used to substantiate the argument at another level, such as the country as a whole. The Santhals may have settled in the territory where they live now – the Santhal Pargana or its adjacent areas, in the beginning of the 19th century. They may have even settled there later than the Bengalis. But that in no way negates the fact that their settlement in India is prior to that of the groups commonly referred to as the Aryans such as the Bengalis or Gujaratis. But to claim indigenous status on this ground is not so simple as one can see from the discussion that follows. Conversely, the settlement of the Mizos in the country called India may have been a later development than those of the Gujaratis or Bengalis, but the fact remains that they are the original settlers of the place where they live now.

It needs to be mentioned here that the tribal groups in India are not solely comprised of the Dravidian and Austro-Asiatic speaking groups. A very large number of the tribal groups in fact belong to the Tibeto-Burman speaking groups, many of whom can hardly be considered indigenous if the arrival of the Aryans is taken as the cut-off mark to decide who is indigenous and who is not. To restrict the term 'indigenous' to refer to only those groups of people who had entry prior to those of Indo-Aryan group would be to exclude many tribal groups of the Tibeto-Burman family from the status of indigenous people. There are also tribal groups like the Bhils that speak languages of the Indo-Aryan family. This poses the problem of their identification as indigenous people. Yet it is generally held that the groups so referred have been drawn into the languages they speak through the process of interaction and acculturation with the Indo-Aryan speaking groups. In terms of their culture and physical features, they are however still considered different from the Indo-Aryan population (Hermanns, 1957: 23).

What this means is that people identified and described as tribals are not to be necessarily treated as indigenous and that there are tribal groups which could be treated as indigenous and others which could not. In contrast many groups and communities, especially those belonging to the Dravidian language speaking group such as the Tamils, Telugus, Malayalis, could stake a claim of being indigenous people by virtue of the fact they have been inhabitants of India prior to the coming of the Aryans. They are however not recognized as tribals and share few attributes in common with the tribals who stand dispossessed, exploited and marginalized. Rather, they constitute a part of the dominant national community. In terms of other criteria that go to make up indigenous people, viz., marginalized status, loss of control over resources, etc., they can hardly be considered for the indigenous people status. The congruence between the term and the concept on which the tribal activists defend the application of the term does not stand valid in all situations.

There is still another ground on which the indigenous claim is contested in the Indian context. It is generally held that the Indian society is made up of a number of castes and groups and that many of these have been formed out of the process of fusion of various groups and communities including tribes. This is all the more true in case of the regional linguistic communities, such as Bengalis, Gujaratis, Oriyas etc. In view of this, it may become necessary that a segment of the same community be identified as indigenous and another as non-indigenous.

Arguments For

The extension of the term 'indigenous people' is however strongly defended by activists and other scholars – both tribal and non-tribals. This is done not so much on the basis of original settlement as on some other considerations. They, of course, trace the history of tribals in India much before the coming of the people who have been described as Aryans. They ask why tribals, whose ancestors lived here for some thousands of years prior to the Aryan invasion, a fact that can hardly be disputed, should not be considered indigenous people so that certain positive international instruments are made applicable to these marginalized and deprived social groups. But, the case is made more forcefully on another ground. Pathy (1992: 8), for example, writes that tribals in a way have been victims of conquest and colonization and hence share all the attributes of the colonized people such as ethnic identity, loss of control over customary territorial resources, cultural annihilation and powerlessness. He makes the case despite his recognition that insisting on original settlement in a territory is problematic and unreasonable.

But then even the issue of colonization and colonized status remains far from resolved. First of all, we do not have detailed and well-researched historical material on the nature of relations or encounter between groups that are designated as the indigenous people and the other social groups for the periods proceeding the coming of the British. Hence, it is difficult to say anything with certainty about the nature of relations between the two types of social groups. In general, the relation between tribes and non-tribes has been described as one of mutual coexistence rather than of subjugation and domination at least until the advent of British rule. In fact, this is the other important ground on which the term 'indigenous people' is contested in the Indian context. It is said that most of the studies of the history of Indian civilization show that the growth and expansion of Hindu society was a prolonged and complex process of assimilation. And, as stated above, the nature of interaction between the two has been broadly described as one of peaceful coexistence rather than one of conquest and subjugation (Bose, 1941; Beteille, 1998: 189).

Such a nature of interaction between tribals and non-tribals has also been endorsed by a scholar who otherwise talks of an aggressive absorption into the Hindu society with the onset of the colonial rule (Desai, 1977: 24). Pathy (1992a: 51) himself elsewhere talks of a symbiotic relationship between the tribals and the non-tribals rather than one of colonization and conquest. He writes, "majority of the so-called tribals of India had developed class structure over a long period of time and therefore had interactions with the other communities. Up to the time of colonialism, it was largely not a relationship of domination and subjugation". Not only is determining original settlement in the territory problematic, but also the question of colonization and subjugation as one can see from Pathy's observation. This means that the question of indigenous people could only be raised from the period of the arrival of the British and the subsequent processes of colonization and subjugation in India. If these processes are taken as the point of departure for demarcation of indigenous people, then, the issue of original settlement that is so central to the notion of indigenous people becomes redundant in defining indigenous people.

In fact, the whole exercise of identification of groups and communities as tribes during the colonial period was to a great extent contingent upon the differences tribes displayed in relation to the larger society. Thus tribes were by and large considered as those outside civilization. This means that they not only remained outside the politico-administrative structure of the larger society or the kingdom, but also outside the general social organization and worldview of the larger society. In short, they continued to be distinct because they escaped colonization and subjugation. Where people were subjugated, they became part of the larger social organization and failed to maintain their distinctiveness. Whether they lived in hills, plateaus or forests and lived by hunting, food-gathering or practised slash and burn cultivation followed from being outside civilization. Beteille (1986: 316) has forcefully brought this out. He writes that where tribes and civilization coexist, as in India and the Islamic world, being a tribe has been more a matter of remaining outside of state and civilization, whether by choice or necessity, than of attaining a definite stage in the evolutionary advance from the simple to the complex. The Indian practice of regarding as tribes a large assortment of communities, differing widely in size, mode of livelihood and social organization, cannot therefore be dismissed as anomalous. They are all tribes because they all stood more or less outside of Hindu civilization and not because they were all at exactly the same stage of evolution. In short, they are described as tribes and therefore even as indigenous people because they escaped colonization and subjugation processes.

The use of the term 'indigenous people' to refer to the tribal people is defended on yet another ground. It is argued that unlike antagonists who tend to take note of only historical realism, we have also to take note of critical realism. They state that irrespective of the place and time of origin or their occupation or their present habitat in India, there are certain communities, which until recently maintained practically autogenous sources of legitimization of cultural and social processes and were accentuated by the ideology of a self-regulated economy and had only marginal articulation with the external political structures. Their indigenous identity cannot be brushed away by juxtaposition of non-meaningful occurrences in space and time in systemic terms (Roy-Burman, 1992: 24).

Such claim is difficult to establish today. Not only have the tribal communities been brought under uniform administrative and legal structures under the British but they have also been drawn into the politico-economic process of the larger society, especially in the post-independence period of economic development. There are very few tribes, which have escaped such processes. The actual empirical reality is then too complex. It is not at all surprising then that elsewhere Roy-Burman (1983: 1172–74) writes, "even many of those with the simplest technology were integrated with the wider society". In short, the use of the term 'indigenous' to describe tribal people in India is fraught with difficulties. It does not reflect an empirical reality but is more of a political construction.

Though the question of indigenous people has been generally discussed in the context of the country as a whole, the discussion in the Indian context has also been drawn in relation to the regions or territories within the country. It has generally been observed that there have been so many migrations in and out of the region in the past centuries that no particular 'jati' can have genuine grounds for making a claim to be the original inhabitants (Beteille, 1998: 189; Hardiman 1987:15–16). In discussion of indigenous people in India, it is important that we do not mix the problems obtaining at two levels. Often, the problem at the level of the country is used to make a case against tribes being indigenous at the regional/local level and vice versa. Posing the question of tribes as the indigenous people in relation to territories within the country, rather than the country as a whole, indeed gives rise to problems of somewhat different nature. Movement of populations belonging to different races, ethnicities and linguistic groups, including those described as tribals, from one place to another is something that has been in process within India over the centuries. Thus, the groups which may be indigenous with respect to the country as a whole may not be indigenous in respect of their settlement in a given territory. It may also happen that the same group is indigenous and not indigenous at the same time. The Oraons, Mundas and many other tribes living in Jharkhand, for example, may have legitimate claim to be called the indigenous people in respect of their settlement in the country called India prior to that of the Aryans or even in respect of their settlement in Jharkhand, but it is not certain if they can claim to be indigenous in Assam or Bengal where they have moved in the course of last one century or so. Indeed, their claim of being indigenous is strongly contested in these places. Nowhere is this more true than in Assam where the migrant tribals' claim to be the indigenous people is being disputed by such tribal communities as the Bodos, Mishings and others who have a much longer history of settlement in the region than the tribals from Bihar, Orissa, Madhya Pradesh, etc. If however one takes India as a whole, then these migrant groups have a much longer record of settlement than the tribes in the north-eastern region. The tribals from this region have also moved in large numbers to Andaman Island and have settled there as cultivators after reclaiming land from the forest and in the process dispossessing the native Jarvas from their territories.

Adivasi Consciousness

In the context of India, as a whole, identification of indigenous peoples is indeed problematic. The problem emanates from the fact that the population movements and experiences in India have been different from those of the new world. It is true that the movement of population even in the new world has been, like in India, of different races, languages, regions, religions, cultures, etc. In the new world, however, these groups did not come to establish or have special relations with a given territory or region in the course of their movement. In India, the movement of the population was somewhat different. Here different communities came to develop distinct and definite association with certain territories in the course of the history of their movement.

Whether those especially associated with a given territory are indigenous to the territory or area they live in is a question that will always be contested. What however has come to be accepted that they have developed special relations with the territory in question. The communities in question have considered these territories as their own as against those of other communities. They considered themselves to have prior and preferential if not exclusive rights over the territory where they lived either on account of their prior historical settlement or numerical and other dominance. Following this they aspired to promote and protect the interests and welfare of their community and confer on the members of their community special rights and privileges. It was this aspiration among the members of the community that led to the desire to have a state of their own. And, after having realized this, they tend to promote the interests of their members by means of state patronage of various kinds.

The people living in their respective territories have thus come to see the states to which they belong as the culmination of the yearning of the members of a particular territory to have a homeland of their own. The Bengalis for example have a very strong sense of attachment to Bengal as Tamils to Tamil Nadu. There is in this an indication of the recognition, implicit though it may be, that certain people have prior right over others in the territory that they occupy. This is almost like saying that they are the original inhabitants of the territory that they inhabit. It is therefore not a coincidence that the dominant communities hardly feel the need to articulate issues in terms of rights of indigenous people. They have states of their own and therefore territories too. It surfaces only when they feel threatened from the movement of the population from outside the community. The threat is felt either on account of fear in the rise of number of members from outside the community or loss of control of power – economic and political. Nowhere is this identity with land or territory more crudely manifested than in the son-of-the-soil theory that has been raised from time to time by the dominant regional communities in India.

In short, people of India representing different languages, physical features, cultures, mode of social organizations, etc. identify and relate themselves in a special way with a given territory or region in the country. Attempts have been made to provide theoretical understanding to such developments in India. In doing so scholars have invariably made use of concepts such as nation and nationality. In the context of India, the two concepts refer essentially to the internal political arrangement of the Indian Union comprising a number of linguistic-territorial state units and components with a variety of regional pressures. At the same time, there has always been some kind of check-list of the objective criteria whereby a nation or nationality could be defined (Vanaik, 1988). And, in both of these conceptions, the element of territoriality assumes a central place.

The paradox is that whereas such privileges and rights are freely recognized in respect of the dominant communities in India, the same is denied to the tribal communities. In the process they are progressively getting dispossessed of their control over land, forest, water, minerals and other resources in their own territory and are increasingly subjected to inhuman misery, injustice and exploitation. If their status as indigenous people of India is problematic, and the problem indeed is both empirical and conceptual, the least the dominant regional communities could do is to recognize the priorities of rights and privileges of these people in the territories and regions they inhabit. It is the non-recognition of these rights and privileges by the dominant sections of the Indian society that has led to increasing articulation of the idea of indigenous people by the tribal people.

It is in the absence of such powers and rights that a new form of identity, viz., identity of adivasis or indigenous people, is crystallizing among the tribes of different parts of India. The term that was initiated mainly at a point of reference or description has become an important marker of identity articulation and assertion today. The designation or description of tribes as indigenous people had not emerged from self-identification or description by the tribal people themselves. It was not a part of positive identification and evaluation by the tribes. Rather, the outsiders had imposed it on the tribes. The identity that was forced from outside has now been internalized among the tribes. Today, it is an important mark of identity and consciousness of the people – an identity that evokes a sense of lowly and inferior society that often goes with terms like tribe or tribal. The people now use it to identify and define themselves. It is in relation to the identity of adivasi that tribes are increasingly differentiating themselves from the non-tribal population at least at the grass roots level. The declaration of the year 1993 as the international year of the indigenous people has only sharpened this identity for identity, since then, carries certain rights and privileges with it.

Further, the identity being expressed now by the term 'adivasi' is indeed an expanded identity cutting across tribes bearing different names, speaking different languages or dialects. It also goes beyond groups and communities or parts thereof that are listed in the Constitution of India. It is to be noted that there is an important gap in the sense in which the term 'tribe' is used and understood by others, especially administrators, lawyers and academicians. For the latter, communities are tribes only if they are so listed in the Constitution. Tribes on the other hand do not view tribes in the sense of politico-administrative category. Rather, they view them in the sense of belonging to the same community, irrespective of whether a group of segment of it is listed or not listed in the Constitution. And, by virtue of this bond of emotion, they are also adivasis or the indigenous people though the Constitution does not recognize them as tribes.

In many parts of India, the category has even taken political overtones. In Chotanagpur, for example, as early as 1939 it assumed the form of a demand for a separate state of their own for the adivasis.

Even the organization formed to spearhead this movement, viz., Adivasi Mahasabha, drew its inspiration from being described as the original people. Such a political overtone is not confined to Chotanagpur alone. It is catching up in other parts of the country as well but more prominently in the tribal regions of central and western India such as Madhya Pradesh, Gujarat and Rajasthan. It has already given rise to a number of organizations at local and regional levels that have been articulating the issues of the tribes in terms of the status of the indigenous people. There are organizations which are actively articulating the issue of the indigenous people at the national and the international levels.

The adivasi consciousness and the articulation of indigenous people's status is not so much about whether they are the original inhabitants of India as about the fact that they have no power whatsoever, over anything (land, forest, river, resources) that lies in the territory they inhabit. This is despite being the original inhabitants of India in relation to the others. The consciousness and the articulation are basically an expression of the yearning to have or to establish a special relation with the territory in which they live. It is the same kind of yearning that the various dominant communities of India articulated in the period before or after independence. That this is so becomes obvious if one maps the tribes or regions where such sentiment is strongly articulated. It is a fact that the issue of this identity is more strongly articulated in central, western and southern India than in the north-east India. This is because in the north-east people exercise some power over their territory. The scenario is just the opposite in other parts of tribal India. What this indicates is that the assertion of such identity is stronger where there is greater degree of marginalization and powerlessness.

There are however differences in the way this new identity is being conceptualized at different levels. The social workers/scientists have generally used the term in the sense of only the original inhabitants. The adivasi ideologues too primarily use this term in the sense of the original settlement, as this was the sense in which the outsiders described the tribal people. The aspect of the marginalized status that evolved in course of historical development has been added into it now. There are others, especially the radical scholars, who conceive it only in relation to particular historical development, viz., that of the subjugation during the 19th century of a wide variety of communities which before the colonial period had remained free, or at least relatively free from the control of outside states. This process, it is argued, was accompanied by an influx of traders, moneylenders and landlords who established themselves under the protection of the colonial authorities and took advantage of the new judicial system to deprive the adivasis of large tract of their land. Adivasi is hence defined as groups, which have shared a common fate in the past century and from this, has evolved a collective identity of being adivasis. It is not meant to imply that adivasis are the original inhabitants (Hardiman 1987:15–16). The use of the term 'adivasi' in the sense in which it is used by radical scholars hardly takes note of the sense in which people, either outsiders or the tribal themselves, use it. Not all who shared a common fate in the past century, in fact, identify themselves as the adivasis. The caste Hindu population howsoever deprived it may be invariably avoided being called adivasi for it was tied to the loss of status.

References

Beteille, A. 1986. "The Concept of Tribe with Special Reference to India", *European Journal of Sociology*, 27.

—. 1993. "Myth of Indigenous People", *The Times of India*, January 5.

—. 1998. "The Idea of Indigenous People", *Current Anthropology*, 39(2).

Bose, N.K. 1941. "The Hindu Method of Tribal Absorption", *Science and Culture*, (7).

—. 1975. *The Structure of the Hindu Society*. New Delhi: Orient Longman.

Desai, A.R. 1977. "Tribes in Transition", in R. Thapar (ed.), *Tribe Caste and Religion*. Meerut: Macmillan.

Dube, S.C. 1977. *Tribal Heritage of India*. Shimla: IIAS.

Ghurye, G.S. 1963. *The Schedules Tribe*. Bombay: Popular Prakashan.

Hardiman, D. 1987. *The Coming of the Devi: Adivasi Assertion in Western India*. New Delhi: Oxford University Press.

Hermanns, M. 1957. *Hinduism and Tribal Culture*. Bombay: K.L. Fernandes.

Pathy, J. 1992a. "The Idea of a Tribe and the Indian Scene", in B. Chaudhuri (ed.), *Tribal Transformation in India*, Vol. 3. New Delhi: Inter-India Publishers.

—. 1992b. "What is Tribe? What is Indigenous? Turn the Tables toward the Metaphor of Social Justice", *Samta, I.*

Ray, N. 1973. *Nationalism in India.* AMU, Aligarh.

Roy-Burman, B.K. 1983. "Transformation of Tribes and Analogous Social Formation", *Economic and Political Weekly.*

—. 1992. "The Indigenous Peoples and Their Quest for Justice", in B. Chaudhuri (ed.), *Tribal Transformation in India,* Vol. 2. New Delhi: Inter-India Publications.

—. (nd). "Indigenous" and "Tribal" Peoples and the International Agencies, Draft for Discussion, Rajiv Gandhi Foundation.

Sengupta, N. 1988. "Reappraising Tribal Movement", *Economic and Political Weekly*, May 14.

Shah, G. 1982. "Tribal Issues: Problems and Perspectives", in B. Chaudhuri (ed.), *Tribal Transformation in India,* Vol. 2. New Delhi: Inter-India Publications.

Sinha, S. 1958. "Tribal Culture of Peninsular India as a Dimension of Little Tradition in the Study of Indian Civilisation: A Preliminary Statement", *Journal of American Folklore*, Vol. 71, July–September.

Vanaik, A. 1988. "Is There a National Question in India", *Economic and Political Weekly*, October 29.

18

Teaching Caste and the Hindu Social Order

Dalits in Indian Sociology

VIVEK KUMAR

The practice of sociology in India has been marked by the world view and vocabulary of the so-called upper-caste male. In this context, T.K. Oommen has rightly argued, "All available evidence suggests that the Indian sociologists and social anthropologists, were predominantly drawn from the twice-born Hindu castes" (2001: 16). They therefore preferred a particular type of literature for establishing the subject matter of sociology. Adherence to *Sanskritic* texts for carving out the subject matter of Indian sociology was advocated by the first generation of Indian sociologists, most notable of them being G.S. Ghurye, often said to be the father of Indian sociology (Upadhya, 2002: 28–57). Likewise, D.P. Mukherjee, as a first president of the Indian Sociological Society, argued in 1955 that all our *Shastras* are sociological and Indian sociologists can acquire 'Indianity' by taking sociological training in Sanskrit language in which traditions have been embodied (Oommen, 2001: 17). Although Mukherjee also stated that Indian sociologists ought to be familiar with Indian lores both high and low, rarely have they used sources other than Sanskritic texts for teaching caste and Hindu social order.

If this was the source for the book view of so-called 'upper caste' sociologists, their field view was not very different. For instance, while doing field work in the village of Sripuram in Tamil Nadu, Andre Beteille wrote:

> I did my field work in Sripuram while living with the people as one among them. I was permitted to live in the *agraharam*, in a Brahmin house – a privilege ...I dined with the Brahmins and had access to most of their houses ...I was identified with the Brahmins by my dress, my appearance, and the fact that I lived in on their houses...I soon discovered that it made me suspect in the eyes of the non-Brahmins and Adi-Dravidas... (Beteille 1971: 9–10).

The passage is self-explanatory. It is in this context that one interrogates the manner that the Hindu social order is presented as a given in mainstream sociology. This paper attempts to highlight how this domination unfolds in Indian sociology. This paper takes the specific case of the dalits and contends that sociologists have not seriously included dalits in the curriculum of sociology.

I

The Dominant Theory of Hindu Social Order

Hindu social order as taught in the sociology classrooms is a construct, a handy work of certain sociologists and anthropologists. Some will argue that it is the handy work of 'Orientalists' (Thapar, 2002) and others that of 'Nationalists'. I am not going to enter that debate. The point I seek to make is that this construct is presented as the given reality in classrooms of sociology throughout the country.

According to a dominant theory, Hindu society can be divided into two races – Aryans who came from elsewhere and Dasas who were indigenous to present day India. The Aryans were fair in colour while the indigenous *Dasas* were dark (Ghurye, 1979: 46). The Aryans included only the twice-born castes. Yet there is little in common between the dalits of South India and Punjab. There are perhaps more similarities between the dalits and Brahmins of South India. Ambedkar had argued on similar lines:

> What racial affinity is there between the Brahmin of the Punjab and the Brahmin of Madras? What racial affinity is there between the untouchable of Bengal and the untouchable of Madras? What racial difference is there between the Brahmin of the Punjab and the

> Chamar of the Punjab? What racial differences are there between the Brahmin of Madras and the Paraiah of Madras? The Brahmin of Punjab is racially of the same stock as the Chamar of the Punjab and the Brahmin of Madras is of the same race as the Pariah of Madras…Caste system is a social division of people of the same race (Ambedkar 1979: 48–49).

Romila Thapar too argues that the racial construction of Hinduism is only a nineteenth century construction:

> …Its roots were provided by yet another nineteenth-century obsession, that the theory of Aryan race… concern with European origins was transferred to India… The notion of an Aryan race has now been generally discarded in scholarship and what we are left with is essentially a linguistic category: the Indo-Aryan speaking people (Thapar 2002: 81–82).

In the same vein, Trautmann has also questioned the validity of the racial theory of *varna*. He argues:

> The racial theory of Indian civilization was constructed by narrativizing the encounter of the polar opposites of Victorian racial thought, the fair-skinned Aryan and the dark-skinned savage, and by finding evidence for their encounter in the Vedic texts. It was the work of Sanskritists who were at the forefront in its construction. The leading texts were those of Max Muller…and John Muir's original Sanskrit texts on the origin and history of the people of India (1874: 84) (Trautmann, 1997: 206).

Sociologists routinely teach that the Hindu social order comprises of four *varnas* and thousands of castes. However, the *Rig Veda,* which is the basis for this four-fold so-called Hindu social order, mentions many other groups like Dasas, Dasyus, Rakshas, Panis, Nishads etc. (Mukherjee, 1988). Mukherjee himself argues that "from the evidence in the *Rig Veda* we find that besides the *Rig Veda* people there were other autochthonous groups in society …" But nobody knows why the details of these groups are missing from the sociology curriculum. The question that arises is, "What would have been the nature of the Indian society had the groups Dasas, Dasyus, Rakshas, Panis, Nishads etc. been included along with Brahmins, Kshatriyas, Vaishyas and Shudras?" The process of reducing the other groups into a blanket category Shudras has hidden a vast body of knowledge about society.

Hindu Social Order: Pan-Indian or restricted to Indo-Gangetic plains

The other fact about this construction of the four-fold social structure of Hindu social order is that it is found in its purest form only in the Indo-Gangetic plains. We can find the presence of Brahmins and ex-untouchables in every geographical area in the country but we will not find the equivalent of the Kshatriya and Vaishya of north India in other regions. Vincent Smith thus argues: "The Hindu theory that mankind is divided into four *varna*, ... was wholly foreign to the southerners. To this day Kshatriyas and Vaisyas do not exist among them" (Smith 1986: 42–42).

Hindu social order: Carving out a majority community identity

This construction of Hindu social order has serious implications for the structure and processes of the Indian society. At the outset, this has produced the identity of a majority community, i.e., Hindus. Second, this identity of Hindus subsumed other groups which had different belief, knowledge system, customs and culture. In this manner the Brahmanical culture, world view etc. got universalized and it became the hegemonic reference point for all others. It assumed an all-India character and therefore even where the Brahmins were not present their hegemony worked. In the words of Thapar, "The need for postulating a Hindu community became a requirement for political mobilization in the nineteenth century when representation by religious community became a key to power and where such representation gave access to economic resources...A Hindu community with common identity would be politically powerful" (Thapar 2002: 86).

When caste is recognized, and when denied

Caste has been for long understood in terms of purity and pollution. The dalits are called impure on the basis of their defiling occupation. But dalits argue that it is the dalits who keep the whole society clean then how is it then that it is they who become impure? Second, it is ironical that it is the caste of people who defecate and are unable to clean their own excreta, remove their dead animals, are unable to help their women to deliver their babies, cannot clean their clothes soiled by blood of menstruation, cannot dig graves for their dead who are deemed clean and pure? The very language of analysis is such that it articulates the domination of twice-born castes and negates the creativity and contribution of the dalits in the Hindu social order.

A number of sociologists have made their career by writing on caste. When they write and teach about caste in the academic world, they readily accept its presence in Indian society. They discuss at length about the nature of caste, its characteristics, adaptability, its role in politics and even mobility in the structure of caste. Shiv Vishvanathan (1990: 31–36) argues that based on the studies of many Indian sociologists a number of policies on caste have been formulated and many of them have themselves been members of the committees and commissions. Yet when it comes to the issue of policy formulation for the upliftment of the dalits or other backward castes (OBCs) the same sociologists virtually deny the existence of caste in public life.

II

Erroneous Conceptual Categories to Understand Indian Society

If Indian sociologists have constructed an imagined Hindu social order, they have also carved out other theoretical frame works and conceptual categories to understand the Indian society. One attempts to look at some of these.

Hindu social order: The ambiguous position of dalits

The Brahmanical hegemony is visible in the manner that the dalits are accorded an ambiguous position in the Hindu social order. No teacher ever explains how the metaphor fifth *varna* arose. It is very clear from the *Rig Veda*'s 'Purush Sukta' theory that there are four *varnas* in the Hindu social order (Ghurye, 1979: 44, Srinivas, 1985: 150–51). *Manu Smriti* which codified Hindu society, has also argued that there is no fifth *varna* (Dumont, 1999: 66–67). Why then do sociologists argue in the classrooms that "there are four *varnas* and there is a fifth also". For instance, Ghurye indirectly includes them in the four-fold *varna* hierarchy and argues that they are part of the Hindu social order. According to him, "The Scheduled Castes, formerly known as depressed classes, ... the fifth order of the four-fold society of Hindu theory" (Ghurye, 1979: 307). In this regard, Dumont has remarked "First and foremost, these texts were to mask the emergence, the factual accretion of a fifth category, the untouchables, each emulating the others in proclaiming that there is no fifth…" (1999: 68).

The existence of fifth *varna* – 'the dalits' – is further denied in the Hindu social order by its sacred texts in the way the functions and stages in the life of a Hindus are prescribed in them. Everyone is aware that the four *varnas* mentioned in the sacred texts have been assigned their duties or jobs (*dharma*) by these texts. For example in the hymns of the *Rigveda*, the job of the Brahmin *varna* was to read and write, teach and preach, offer and officiate sacrifices. The Brahmins were obliged by this tradition to undergo a life of study, mediation, and penetration into the mysteries of God and *dharma*. Ghurye argues that the occupation of Kshatriyas, "must have consisted in administrative and military duties…In the prayer for the prosperity of Kshatriya, he is said to be an archer and good chariot-fighter "(Ghurye, 1979: 48). The Vaishyas formed the third order and were supposed to be traders. Further, Ghurye argues, "The name of the fourth class, the Shudra…It seems …represented domestic servants, approximating very nearly to the position of slaves. The Shudra is described as 'the servant of another', 'to be expelled at will', and 'to be slain at will'. The *Panchvimsha Brahmana* defines this position still more precisely when it declares that the Shudra, even if he is prosperous, cannot be but a servant of another, washing his superior's feet being his main business… The Shatapatha Brahmana goes to the length of declaring that the Shudra is untruth itself"(ibid.: 50–51).

Apart from the aforesaid duties assigned to various *varnas*, the book view of caste system also prescribed an elaborate arrangement for various socio-economic, political and religious activities to be performed by an individual in various stages of his/her life. The dalits are completely excluded from this. These stages are termed as *ashrams*, which are four in number, namely, *brahmacharya*, *grihastha*, *vanaprastha* and *sanyasa*. The male members of Brahmin, Kshatriya and Vaishya *varnas* pass through these four stages in their life. The first *ashram* is called *brahmacharya ashram* from which the fourth *varna*, viz., Shudra and the women of the first three *varna*s were barred.

A number of questions emerge. First, even if we believe the sacred texts on the origin of caste/*varna*, where does the metaphor of the fifth *varna* originate? Second, accepting that there is a fifth *varna*, the natural corollary is what will be its *dharma* and which *ashrama* can its members follow? No convincing explanation is given by Indian sociologists, yet they treat dalits as part and parcel of the Hindu social order.

Dalit movements refutations of being part of the Hindu social order

The dalits have contested their inclusion in the Hindu social order. In the past they have launched a number of movements highlighting their independent identity and their status as the original inhabitant of this land. These movements included the Adi Hindu, Adi Dravid, Adi Andhra, Adi Karnataka and Ad Dharma movements. Through these movements they tried to moot a racial theory in which Aryans were depicted as outsiders who have subjugated the indigenous dalits who were the original inhabitants of this land. The term 'Adi Hindu' spread among a sizeable number of north Indian dalits during the 19th century. In Uttar Pradesh, Swami Acchutananda (1879–1933) launched the Adi Hindu movement.

The Adi Hindu movement with vision of a separate identity of the dalits got strengthened with four Adi Hindu conferences organized in Hyderabad between 1912 and 1924. The main organizers began to use the Adi Hindu nomenclature (Omvedt, 1994: 122). Radicalization among dalits throughout south India resulted in the emergence of 'Adi ideology'. In Hyderabad, Adi-Hindu movement emerged among Malas (an untouchable caste) who were led by Bhagyareddy Verma (1888–1939), a dalit steward from a Catholic family which educated him.

The dalit assertion in south India was also evident in Kerala where Pulayas – the untouchables – had organized, socio-cultural revolts, since the beginning of the 20th century under the able leadership of Ayyankali and Vellikkara Choti. The aim of such revolts initially was not economic gain but entry into educational institutions and other public places (Mathew, 1986: 102). Dalit organizations also came into existence in the erstwhile Mysore state where Murgesh Pillai led the Adi Dravida Abhi-Vrudhi Sangh, which was mainly supported by Tamils, although it did include the Kannadigas in its fold and programmes. An organization called Adi Jambava Sangha was exclusively formed and supported by the Madigas – now a major Scheduled Caste (SC) group in Andhra Pradesh. Although mainly a social organization, its leader convened a 'political conference' of the Panchamas in 1920, to which Ambedkar was also invited, although he could not attend due to a ban on his entry into the state. It is not known if the conference had adopted any political resolution. Other conferences were organized in 1923 and 1925 under the presidentship of M.C. Rajah. These conferences passed resolutions on various issues concerning the untouchables using the Adi Karnataka and Adi Dravida terminology. Their basic demands were admission of dalit students to educational institutions, access to water tanks, temple entry, etc. From the 1920s dalits also asked the government for allotment of waste and other fallow lands for cultivation and also for land to be allotted/leased/sold to them at reduced/concessional prices in the newly irrigated tracts around Irwin canal. In addition, demands were made that dalits be relieved from traditional caste duties. It was also argued that, if they were not relieved, the government should directly pay to them for their duties out of the cess collected from the peasants.

The Adi Dharam movement emerged in 1926 as an organized movement of dalits in Punjab, with Mangoo Ram as the President of the Executive Committee. Mangoo Ram was a folk hero and had lived with the activists of the Gadar Party. The main plea of the Adi Dharam movement was that the untouchables (dalits) constituted a *quam*, a distinct religious community similar to the Muslim, Hindu and Sikh communities, and that their *quam* had existed in India from time immemorial.

> Their ancient civilization was destroyed by the Aryans and they were subjugated to the point where they forgot their own identity. In restoring that lost identity Ad Dharmis held to a non-theistic view of divinity, worshipped low caste saints like Kabir, and especially their fellow Chamar Ravidas, collected their writings, and read them in their *Satsangs*, which resembled Sikh worship...A high point came early in Ad Dharm history when they gained recognition as a separate *quam* in the religion chapter of the 1931 census and recorded 418,789 Ad Dharmis (Webster, 2002: 27).

In the later stages, the leaders of the Adi Dharam movement were drawn by two models of social organizations and political influence. One was the example set by Muslim nationalists, who had demanded a separate territory of their own. The other was provided by political parties and religious-communal supports for electoral candidates. "Members of Dalit community in the Punjab adopted the first model along the lines of Muslim separatism and came up with the notion of Achutistan, a geographically distinct, "land of the untouchables". The idea was never worked out in any systematic way nor was there even a suggestion as to which area of India might be incorporated into such a nation.

In the end, we can argue that the 'Adi' movements through which dalits asserted that they have their own identity, separate from the Hindus, and the critique of Aryans who were responsible for their wretched condition in contemporary Indian society, could not emancipate dalits from their stigmatized identity and accord them a dignified position in the society. Therefore, these movements lost their influence among dalits in different parts of the country. Moreover, many alternative movements like those led by Ambedkar, Indian National Congress and Hindu Mahasabha. also emerged during this period, which attracted dalits towards their ideology and subsumed them and their leaders.

Assertion for exclusive existence from Hinduism

In modern times the assertion of the dalits can be seen in the following slogans which assert their brotherhood and proximity with the Muslims rather than Hindus, although it is in the realm of politics and movement. The first instance is of Agra in Uttar Pradesh where Republican Party of India contested election in alliance with Muslims in 1962 and coined the slogan:

Jatav Muslim Bhai-Bhai, Hindu Kaum Kahan se Ai (Lynch, 1969: 102).

Similarly, in central Uttar Pradesh, Rajendra Singh highlighted the proximity of dalits and Muslims in the land-grab movement of 1970. The slogan states:

Muslim Harijan Bhai-Bhai, Hindu Jati Khan se Ai (Singh, 2000: 137)

Ambedkar's critique of the Hindu social order and a possible Hindu nation is instructive.

> There is utter lack of what the sociologists call "consciousness of kind". There is no consciousness of kind…That is the reason why Hindus cannot be said to form a society or nation…Men do not become a society by living in physical proximity…Secondly similarity in habits and customs, beliefs and thoughts is not enough to constitute men into society. Things may be passed physically from one to another like bricks…Culture spreads by diffusion and that is why one finds similarity between various primitive tribes in the matter of their habits and customs, beliefs and thoughts although they do not live in proximity. But no one could say that because there was similarity the primitive tribes constituted one society. This is

> because similarity in certain things is not enough to constitute a society. Men constitute a society because they have things which they possess in common. To have similar things is totally different from possessing things in common. And the only way by which men can come to possess things in common with one another is by being in communication with one another... Parallel activity, even if similar, is not sufficient to bind men into a society. This is proved by the fact that the festivals observed by the different castes amongst the Hindus are the same. Yet these parallel performances of similar festivals by the different castes have not bound them into one integral whole. For that purpose what is necessary is for a man to share and participate in a common activity so that the same emotions are aroused in him that animate the others. Make the individual a sharer or partner in the associated activity so that he feels its success as his success, its failure as his failure is the real thing that binds men and makes a society of them. The caste system prevents common activity and by preventing common activity it has prevented the Hindus from becoming a society with a unified life and a consciousness of its own being (Ambedkar 1979: 50–51).

In a similar view Kancha Ilaiah emphasizes that dalits and backward castes (Shudras) are not Hindus. He also raises the issue of exclusion of dalits from the day-to-day life of the Hindu social order. In his own words, "I was not born a Hindu for the simple reason that my parents did not know that they were Hindus. This does not mean that I was not born as a Muslim, a Christian, a Buddhist, a Sikh or a Parsee" (Ilaiah, 1996: 1). Ilaiah further elaborates this by arguing that, "People belong to a religion only when they know that they are part of the people who worship that God, when they go to those temples and take part in the rituals and festivals of that region" (ibid.). Justifying the structural location of Shudras independent of Hinduism, Ilaiah remarks, "My parents had only one identity and that was their caste ...Their festivals were local, their Gods and Goddesses were local (the Hindu patriarchal Gods do not exist there) and sometimes these were even specific to one village. No centralized religious symbols existed for them" (Ilaiah, 1991: 1).

Village as a functional category

Village community is the most celebrated category of Indian society. It has been regarded as an ideal form of social organization to which there is no parallel anywhere in the world. Within it the unity of village is further magnified by Indian sociologists. While editing a volume of village studies conducted in the 1950s M.N. Srinivas (1978: 6–8) depicted this unity in Indian villages as a central theme in his works. Would the same unity be perceived by all castes? Ambedkar's observes:

> The Hindu village is a working plant of the Hindu social order. One can see there the Hindu social order in full swing...The Indian village is not a single unit. It consists of castes. But for our purpose, it is enough to say ...The population in the village is divided into two sections...Touchables and Untouchables...What are the terms of associated life on which the Touchables and Untouchables live in an Indian Village? In every village the Touchables have a code which the Untouchables are required to follow. This code lays down the acts of omission and commissions which the Touchables treat as offences...
>
> Another important thing to note is that the punishment for these offenses is always collective. The whole community of untouchables is liable for punishment though the offence have been committed by an individual...The right to beg for food from the Touchable is now the principal means of livelihood for ...Untouchables in India... Such is the picture of the inside life of an Indian village. In this Republic there is no place for democracy. There is no room for equality. There is no room for liberty and there is no room for fraternity. The Indian Village is the very negation of a republic. If it is a republic, it is republic of the Touchables, by the Touchables, and for the Touchables. The Untouchables have no rights...They have no rights because they are outside the village republic and because they are out side the so-called republic they are outside the Hindu fold. (Ambedkar 1989: 19–26)

The process of dalitization or 'hygienicaization'

According to the theory of sanskritization, caste is far from a rigid system in which the position of each component caste is fixed for all time. In this context, it would be worth mentioning Romila Thapar:

> In the process of articulation the perspective is generally limited to that of the *sanskritization* of the latter. It might be historically more accurate on occasion to view it as the reverse, as for example in the cult of Viththala at Pandharpur or that of Jagannatha at Puri. In such

> cases the deities of tribals and low caste groups become for reasons other than the purely religious, centrally significant and Brahmanism has to adapt itself to the concept of such deities... (Thapar 2002: 65–66).

The concept 'sanskritization' ignores the fact that dalits too may hold negative views about the 'upper castes' – a fact eloquently brought out by Ambedkar, quoting Abbe Dubois:

> Even to this day a Pariah is not allowed to pass a Brahmin street in a village, though nobody can prevent or prevent his approaching or passing by a Brahmin's house in town.

Furthermore, quoting the editor of the gazetteer of the Tanjore district, he argues:

> These castes (Paraayan abd Pallans or Chakkiliyan castes of Tanjore district) strongly object to the entrance of a Brahmin into their quarters believing that harm will result to them therefrom (ibid.).

Although the propounder of the theory of sanskritization delineates the cultural traits of the Brahmins and other twice-born castes he is not bothered to shed any light on the cultural traits of the dalits and Shudras. Is this a lapse on the part of researcher who hails from a particular social background or is it a deliberate attempt on his part to misrepresent. The second problem with this concept is, can we say that drinking alcohol, eating carrion, sacrificing animals etc. were prescribed and codified cultural traits of dalits and Shudras. Or put it differently, on what basis can we argue that living without non-vegetarian food, not drinking alcohol, not sacrificing animals to their deities becomes imitation of Sanskritic values.

The third problem with this conceptualization is that the researcher is concerned only with the upward movement of the lower castes in the caste hierarchy in the Hindu social order by imitating the Brahmins and other twice-born castes on the basis of very few case studies. But why did he remain silent or why could he not see so many Brahmins and other twice-born castes taking non-vegetarian food or not performing the rituals in day-to-day life etc. Therefore, logically, can we argue that at cultural level it is process of downward mobility for the twice-born castes, i.e., it is a process of *dalitization* though structurally the so-called twice-born castes maintain their higher status in the caste hierarchy?

The fourth problem in this concept is that the imitation of Sanskritic values is nothing but the imitation of values of Brahmins. And, the mobility can occur only in the Brahmanical framework, because only Brahmins were and still are the custodians of the so-called Hindu religion and culture.

Further sanskritization raises the question whether the dalits are part of a Hindu social order? Because had they been part of the same social order then there would have been similarities between them and the twice-born castes and hence there would have been no scope for imitation of the cultural traits of the so-called upper castes by the so-called lower castes. Last but not the least, the problem with the formulation of the concept is that while we do not see any such processes in contemporary times this process of sanskritization is still being taught in the classes as if it is still taking place.

Analyzing the concept of class in the Hindu social order

Sociologists have applied the concept of 'class' to measure the economic status of the people in general. In most cases the concept of class is exclusively identified with the economic status of individuals without any attention to the social aspects such as caste and religion which also play a dominant role in deciding the economic status of individuals and groups in India. As religion and caste play a dominant role in the social status of an individual or group, it is difficult to analyse the real social status of poor Brahmin and poor dalit through the concept of 'class' alone. Though there is a general understanding that the poor are all equal it can be easily argued that the poor of the so-called upper castes and lower castes are not similarly placed because of the contribution made by religion and caste in the formation of a class. Hence, we can objectively argue that the causes of poverty of dalits and upper castes are different and depend on their structural location in the social structure. For instance, a penury-stricken Brahmin who comes and begs is blessed by the donor. On the contrary, a cobbler who polishes shoes with his labour or a sweeper who cleans excreta is treated with contempt and usually people throw the money at them from a distance lest their touch defile them. Likewise, the richest industrialist goes and bows at the feet of a

Brahmin in Kasi or Haridwar. Similarly, a Rajput or Kshatriya landowner will never plough his land even though he is economically in a desperate situation because he will loose his caste. Likewise a hardworking dalit will not be allowed to open an eatery shop in the countryside even today.

III

The Construction of the Hindu Social Order and its Consequences

At the societal level dalits face an extreme form of exclusion and deprivation in society. They are not given any rights. This happens I agree on account of their forced co-option in the Hindu social order. Otherwise, how does one explain that a collectivity, which forms a part of the social order, is forced to live in isolation?

At another level the dalits have been excluded from the curriculum in social sciences in general and sociology in particular. And when represented, there is a serious misrepresentation of dalits. This happens because neither have they been able to justify their exclusion from the Hindu social order nor their inclusion in the Hindu social order in the academic literature. As far as their exclusion is concerned, they are totally excluded from the Hindu social order. One can infer even from the book view of the Hindu social order as taught in the class rooms, that there is denial of every right whatsoever to the dalits – no place in *varna* hierarchy, non-existence of any *Ashrama Dharma* to follow for them, denial of *Purusharthas*, or any *Rinas,* denial of access to the gods pantheon of denial to perform a clean occupation and the oppressive existence of caste endogamy.

I therefore agree strongly that the sociologists have tried unsuccessfully to include the dalits in the Hindu social order. Usually, they are treated as a fifth *varna* although they are a conglomeration of number of a hierarchically arranged castes. Usually, in the *varna* hierarchy, there are sub-castes, having at least a number of social ties with touchability. But dalits do not have any avenue of interaction with other castes as well as castes which are considered as untouchables. Then, how can one contend that they are a part of the *varna* system in the scheme of Hindu social order?

On the other hand, the sociologists have again unsuccessfully tried to hide the exclusion of the dalits from the Hindu social order by not discussing the real nature and scope of exclusion in the curriculum of sociology. The aforesaid phenomenon has brought to fore the real nature of Hindu social order in which dalits occupy a status "excluded but included in the collectivity". This unique status of dalits has never been recorded by the Indian sociologists earlier. A combination of developments have forced Indian sociology to grapple with this. One is the process of democratization of the society on the basis of constitutional rights. Then, equipped with these constitutional rights, there has been dalit assertion in every realm of Indian society whether religion, politics, culture etc. More recently the market has played a role in marketing the dalit literature written both by the dalits and non-dalits.

This exclusion of the dalits from the curriculum of sociology in India can be captured through five simultaneous processes which are deployed by the Indian sociologists to analyse the dalits by placing them in the imagined Hindu social order. These five processes are:

- Cognitive blackout
- Forced availability
- Chequered accessibility
- Pseudo inclusivity
- Lack of reflexivity

Cognitive Blackout

At the outset the exclusion of dalits in the subject matter in sociology takes the shape of a 'cognitive blackout'. It is a well-known fact that the description of dalit's society, their icons, their movement, world view or contribution of their labour in the annals of Indian sociology is rare. Dalits have their own vibrant culture and literature. They have their own folk songs and dance and art forms but all has been blacked out in the annals of sociological discussions and literature. This has been eloquently portrayed by Oommen. He writes:

> There has been a cognitive black-out in Indian social science, until recently, as far as knowledge regarding the life – world of Dalitbahujans. The fact the life-styles of upper castes and *Dalitbhujans* vary dramatically in terms of food habits, worship patterns or gender relations is tacitly acknowledged. But instead of squarely recognizing these variations and explaining why they exist, the dominant tendency in Indian Sociology, at least until recently, has been to

suggest that the *Dalibahujans* are abandoning their way of life in favour of the life-styles of caste Hindus. This is what *sanskritization* is all about. In this perspective, not only the norms and values of caste Hindus are privileged but they are also christened as norm-setters and value-givers for the society as a whole. Conversely, the norms and values of *Dalitbahujans* are knocked out, ignored, stigmatized and de-legitimized" (Oommen, 2001: 21).

In this context, Gough had argued that there is (1956: 846) a difference between the cultures of untouchables and Brahmins. According to her, there is a tacit opposition between the inhibiting 'culture' of the Brahmins and the free 'nature' of the untouchables. Both differ in their attitudes towards sexuality, and aggression towards elders and peers. Engaged in the practical business of earning a living through manual labour, the low castes care more for health and prosperity in this life. Indian sociologists have failed to record this.

Forced Availability

Forced availability means that the availability of dalits as subject matter in sociology has been forced by an external agency and it has not emerged out of conscious effort made by the Indian sociologists. In this regard, we have to observe the fact that till yesterday the Indian sociologists never bothered to study the dalit society. If we take 1914 as the starting point when the first department of sociology was established in India at Bombay University, we find that it was only in 1970s that few studies on delits were taken up by the sociologists of Indian origin and that too at the behest of Indian Council of Social Science Research (ICSSR). That means, it took 56 years before 'dalits' could become a worthy category and also a subject of enquiry for the Indian sociologists although many of the anthropologists or sociologists from Europe and America had already done some very fine work on dalits. Another aspect of this forced availability is that by 1970 dalit society, its movements, its icons, its production of knowledge etc. had become so visible that it was not possible for the mainstream sociologists of Indian origin to not to consider dalits as the subject-matter of their study, Yet they did succeed in not including the dalits in mainstream sociology curriculum.

It is astonishing to note that till late 1995 or so the dalits could not become the part of curriculum of sociology in most of the universities both at the graduate and postgraduate levels. The teaching community argued that there is dearth of quality material on the topic which can be taught in the classroom. But as time passed the abundance of literature related to the dalits forced the sociologists to take cognizance of the dalit society. This material on dalit society belongs to the three streams – one stream included the material written by the foreign authors like O.M. Lynch, Robert Hardgrave, Michael Moffat, Eleanor Zelliot, Mark Gallentar etc., the second stream included material written by the so-called the upper caste Indian writers like G.S. Ghurye, Sachidanand Sinha etc. and the third one by the dalit themselves like Ambedkar, C. Parvathamma, Nandu Ram etc. to name a few. Therefore, the state agency, the dalit assertion and abundance of dalit literature forced Indian sociologists to include the topics related to the dalits in the curriculum. The forced nature of the inclusion of dalit study in the curriculum is evident in the manner that a topic on the dalits in a book is usually given a place in the end of the book. In all, probability the write-up will be by a dalit scholar.

Chequered Accessibility

This brings to the next point of chequered accessibility of the subject matter of dalits. Even if the subject matter related to dalits is available in the curriculum, it is quite common to find that teachers and students have no access to the relevant material. The nature of accessibility is also very different. The Indian sociologists would like to access relevant material written either by the so-called upper castes or by foreign authors. The indexes and bibliographies of books and references of different articles would also suggest that the works of dalits by dalits are seldom referred.

Pseudo-inclusivity

If the subject matter related to dalits is available and is also accessible, then, we have to analyse the nature and manner in which it has been included in the curriculum taught in the classrooms. A key question that needs to be asked is: Does the teacher have a reductionist attitude towards the dalits as the subject matter? A look at how dalits are placed in the curriculum would be instructive. They have been understood through the vantage point of reservation, atrocities, educational status, poverty etc. Seldom has their contribution in running the economy and polity of this country been understood. They have been reduced to the status of dirty drunkards, devoid of any merit, *sarkari* Brahmins, burden on this earth, etc. The process of reductionism of the dalit society has been noted by Viswanathan, who writes: "The privileging of Gandhi as an emblem of non-partisan feeling has, as its inverse, the demonization of Ambedkar as a purveyor of sectarian politics. The view that 'the national hagiography in India has rarely conceded a space for Ambedkar alongside Gandhi' is borne out by amazing exclusion of Ambedkar from several well known literary works about untouchability "(Vishwanathan, 2001: 220).

Lack of Reflexivity

There is also a lack of reflexivity on the dalits as a subject matter in sociology because the subject matter has not been treated seriously. From the definition of the term 'dalit', the language used to describe them (Kumar, 2005: 520–521), is all tentative. We have yet to find a concrete definition of the term 'dalit' to be sure which collectivity we are talking about. Some sociologists usually define dalits without taking any difference of caste, gender or class into account. Therefore, their definition of dalit includes all the economically poor persons. Most of the times they include scheduled castes, scheduled tribes, other backward castes, and also women of both general and dalit groups. I have read research proposals without any concrete definition of the collectivity called dalits. The whole approach towards evolving a clear-cut definition of dalit is very casual. Whosoever wants can explain the term 'dalit' in whatever manner he/she deems it fit to define. It is interesting also to note the student's response to the teaching on dalits. It has been observed that the students are not particularly interested in the topics related to dalits. They do not actively participate in the discussions on the topic and remain more of less passive or indifferent in the classroom. Further, they do not attempt the questions given on the topic in the examinations unless they are compulsory.

IV

Conclusion

The central argument of this paper is that the Hindu social order as taught in sociology classes by Indian sociologists is a mere social construct. Through this construction a majority community, namely, 'the Hindus' has been carved out. This has led to the marginalization of dalits not only in the society but also in the sociology curriculum. This is the basic reasons for the alienation of dalits. from the curriculum of Indian sociology. They have been raising a number of perplexing questions whether they meet you as students or as the conscious member of society. They ask why one should study sociology when we do not teach about the life and world views of a majority of the population? Why should one study 'Indian' culture and society, which is about the so-called castes that have always discriminated the lower strata and dominated the Hindu social order? Why should we not study the cultural traits and elements of the dominated and discriminated groups? The dalits ask why one should study India's social reform movements led by Raja Ram Mohan Roy, Dayanand Saraswati, or Mohandas Karamchand Gandhi only? Why can't we also include social reform movements led by a number of dalit and backward caste social reformers like Jotiba Phule, Narayana Guru, Achutanand, Ambedkar, or Periyar E.V. Ramaswamy, Uda Devi? Similarly, why does one have to study social thought of icons like Gandhi, Aurobindo, Tagore, only? Why has the social thought of aforesaid social reformers belonging to the dalits and backward castes not been included in the sociology curriculum? Why should we study the origin, development of Indian National Congress party only, why not the history and development of Bahujan Samaj Party?

Therefore, the paper humbly submits that if the practice of sociology in India has to reflect and project a total picture of Indian society, and if it has to remain relevant for Indian society, then its subject matter and teaching has to become more inclusive. It has to be more representative of the cultural traits of the discriminated dalit group. Sociology curriculum as taught at the various levels should include studies related to the life of dalits, their culture, world view, sufferings, discriminations and humiliation. The sociology curriculum has to move beyond tokenism and symbolic representation of the dalits with concrete studies on their achievements, their contribution in running the economy, polity and society of the country. We have to question the existing concepts and theories through which Indian society and structures are understood. We have to also ask questions about the existing concepts and theories regarding the basic structures and processes propounded by Indian sociologists in India. For instance, we have to question basic institutions like village, evaluate the feasibility of concepts like class in Indian society and analyse the process of sanskritization to name just a few. We have to analyse the lopsidedness and limitations of the tools and methods of data collection with which sociological data about Indian society has been collected. It is on the basis of such data that generalizations on India has been made and the same is being taught in classrooms. This has to change.

References

Ambedkar, B.R. 1979. "Annihilation of Caste", in *Dr Babasaheb Ambedkar Writings and Speeches*, Vol. 1, Education Department, Government of Maharashtra, Mumbai.

—. 1989. "The Indian Ghetto-The Centre of Untouchability", in *Dr Babasaheb Ambedkar Writings and Speeches*, Vol. 5, Education Department, Government of Maharashtra, Mumbai.

—. 1990. "The Untouchables: Who Were They and Why They Became Untouchables", in *Dr Babasaheb Ambedkar Writings and Speeches*, Vol. 7, Education Department, Government of Maharashtra, Mumbai.

Beteille, Andre. 1971. *Caste, Class and Power: Changing Patterns of Stratification in a Tanjore Village.* Berkeley: University of California Press.

Dirks, B. Nicholas. 2004. *Castes of Mind: Colonialism and the Making of Modern India.* New Delhi: Permanent Black.

Dumont, Louis. 1999. *Homo Hierarchicus: The Caste System and Its Implications.* New Delhi: Oxford University Press.

Ghurye, G.S. 1979. *Caste and Race in India.* Bombay: Popular Prakashan.

Gooptu, Nandni. 1993. "Caste and Labour: Untouchable Social Movements in Urban Uttar Pradesh in the Early Twentieth Century", in Peter Robb (ed.), *Dalit Movements and the Meanings of Labour in India.* New Delhi: Oxford University Press.

Gough, Kathleen. 1956. "Brahmin Kinship in Tamil Village", *American Anthropologist*, 58: 826–53.

Ilaiah, Kancha. 1996. *Why I am Not a Hindu.* Delhi: Samaya.

Lynch, Oven M. 1969. *The Politics of Untouchability.* New Delhi: Oxford University Press.

Kakar, Sudhir. 1982. "Setting the Stage: the Traditional Hindu View and the Psychology of Erik H. Erikson", in Sudhir Kakar (ed.), *Identity and Adulthood.* Delhi: Oxford University Press.

Kumar, Vivek. 2003. *Dalit Leadership India.* New Delhi: Kalpaz Publications.

—. 2005. "Locating Dalits in Indian Sociology", *Sociological Bulletin.*

—. 2005. "Situating Dalits in Indian Sociology", *Sociological Bulletin*, Special Issue on South Asia, Vol. 54, No. 3, September–December 2005, New Delhi.

—. 2006. *India's Roaring Revolution: Dalit Assertion and New Horizons.* New Delhi: Gagandeep Publications.

Lorenzen, David N. (ed.), 1996. *Bhakti Religion in North India.* New Delhi: Manohar Publishers and Distributors.

Mathew, Joseph. 1986. *Ideology, Protest and Social Mobility: Case Studay of Mahars and Pulayas.* New Delhi: Inter-India Publications.

Mukherjee, Prabhati. 1988. *Beyond the Four Varnas: The Untouchables in India.* Delhi: Motilal Banarsidass.

Oommen, T.K. 1990. *Protest and Change: Studies in Social Movements.* New Delhi: Sage Publications.

—. 2001. *Understanding the Indian Society: The Relevance of Perspective from Below.* Department of Sociology, University of Pune, Pune.

Omvedt, Gail. 1994. *Dalit and the Democratic Revolution: Dr Ambedkar and the Dalit Movement in Colonial India.* New Delhi: Sage Publications.

Singh, Rajendra. 2000. "Peasant Movements in Uttar Pradesh", in M.S.A. Rao (ed.), *Social Movements in India.* Delhi: Manohar.

Singh, Y. 1986. *Indian Sociology: Social Conditioning and Emerging Concerns.* New Delhi: Vistaar Publications.

Smith, Vincent A. 1986. *The Oxford History of India*, edited by Percival Spear, New Delhi: Oxford University Press.

Srinivas, M.N. 1978. *India's Villages.* Bombay: Media Promoters & Publishers Pvt. Ltd.

—. 1985. *Caste in Modern India and Other Essays.* Bombay: Media Promoters & Publishers Pvt. Ltd.

Thapar, Romila. 2002. *Interpreting Early India.* New Delhi: Oxford University Press.

Trautmann, R. Thomas. 1997. *Aryans and British India.* New Delhi: Vistaar Publications.

Upadhya, Carol. 2002. "The Hindu Nationalist Sociology of G.S. Ghurye", *Sociological Bulletin*, Vol. 51, No. 1, March, New Delhi.

Vishwanathan, Gauri. 1998. *Outside the Fold: Conversion, Modernity, and Belief.* Delhi: Oxford University Press.

Wankhade, M.N. 1992. "Friends, The Day of Irresponsible Writers is Over", in Arjun Dangle (ed.), *Poisoned Bread (translated from the Modern Marathi Dalit Literature).* New Delhi: Orient Longman.

Webster, John C.B. 2002. *Religion and Dalit Liberation: An Examination of Perspectives.* New Delhi: Manohar.

19

The Concept of Gender

Its Travels and Travails

MAITRAYEE CHAUDHURI

This paper seeks to understand how the concept of gender has emerged, travelled and acquired new meanings. It forms part of my larger and longer interest in exploring how concepts and theories acquire ascendancy within the social science academia, how they arise, journey, nestle into curriculums and enter the classroom, how students deploy them, and how the infamous but influential 'guidebooks' incorporate and appropriate them (Chaudhuri, 2002, 2003, 2010). My own experience as an evaluator of answer scripts of students who sit for the entrance examination for the Master's Programme in Sociology at the Jawaharlal Nehru University (JNU), has in many ways helped me map this process. There have been important changes in the manner that questions pertaining to 'gender' have been addressed over the years. For instance, I recall an answer almost a good two decades ago where a student had elaborated on the grammatical use of gender in response to a question on gender studies. People from my generation will remember a time when the term 'gender' was indeed exclusively deployed with reference to grammar. This has changed both rapidly and dramatically since. In this journey many actors have played their part, not least the women's movement, the state, and increasingly today influential international institutions, non-governmental organizations (NGOs), the academia and the corporate sector.

I begin the story with the late 1970s for this is the point that marked the beginning of institutional women's studies and intellectual theorizing of gender within the academia.[1] This is also the point when many of my generation and I personally were drawn to research in the area. The 1970s saw the rise of what is often termed the "second wave of the Indian women's movement" that brought attention back to the gender question. However, 1975 was also the year that marked the declaration of the International Women's Year and Decade by the United Nations. Contending narratives of women's studies in India have either begun with the women's movement or with the institutional declaration by the UN. The latter appear to be the preferred mode initially within the developmental sector. Over the years, however, this idea was gained ascendency even within the academia. This may appear a small matter to quibble over. But I do think that it indicates a divide between contending narratives and priorities. As we would see in this paper, we have today two very different kinds of studies using gender as a central concept. One is critical, theoretically equipped, often historical and more intellectually if not otherwise allied to the struggles of women's movements and other radical social movements. The other more empiricist and both more institutionally and intellectually allied with the practical tasks at hand – be it the tasks set by the state or by an NGO or by an international institutions. And they would probably trace their legacies and genesis in different ways. Significantly both trends coexist within the same time frame. In a way both engage with the new conditions of globalization and its model of development but while one debates key political and theoretical issues pertaining to it, the other works within the given frame often as research evaluators of some programme of the other. I explicate this in Part II and Part III respectively.

I argue here in this paper that the role of international institutions in the institutionalization of the gender and developmental discourse has been enormous though until the 1970s the state had an important role to play. This role of international institutions has acquired a scale and complexity of a very different order in the contemporary context where complex processes that a neo-liberal driven mode of globalization has ushered in, has redefined not just the character of classes, nations and states but necessarily also ideological sites such as universities and civil society organizations. I have also argued that new sites of knowledge production ranging from corporate-driven social research to developmental agencies have not only emerged, but proliferated. Significantly, for both, gender research is important. But, the nature and logic of such research may share little except the use of gender as a term. Further, often today, a close relationship exists between international institutions, non-governmental organizations and some academics in the traditional universities, who are increasingly part of the global network of researchers and 'activists'. I use the term 'activists' in quotes for in many ways the term has undergone a makeover from a radical to a professional one. Feminism in such a context gets easily transfigured from a radical political movement to sometimes a developmental profession, sometimes to a niche marketing strategy by corporations and sometimes a lifestyle statement. I will only draw upon illustrative evidence here.[2] This has been one central mode by which feminism and gender has been mainstreamed. It can be read as a co-option by the corporate sector or international institutions or the state as the case may be. It can also be read off in a somehow glib fashion as simply a generational shift of feminist visions. This however is not my central contention here. It however is central to the context within which I seek to map the journey of the concept of gender.

My central contention in this paper is that the analytical category of gender has produced a very large but uneven and disparate body of research in India. I confine myself in this paper to two very different trajectories that women's studies have taken and the very different deployment and understanding of gender with which they have operated. We have an incredibly rich and intellectually sophisticated body of writing on gender across social science boundaries.[3] We also have, if I may say, utter travesties of gender studies. Capturing this uneven and incongruent journey is a daunting task and I am tempted to suggest that if this paper appears a bit all over the place and disjointed this is of course my failing but also partly reflective of the state of research and teaching of gender.

This paper is broadly divided into four parts. Part I seeks to outline the paradigm shift that the Indian state adopts in the early 1990s with its new economic policies. Part II focuses on different aspects of the new developmental questions that globalization throws up. Part III discusses the nature of the growing body of evaluative research, widely associated with women's studies, which emerge within such a developmental regime. Part IV looks at a very different body of rich historical and sociological writings on gender.

I

The Paradigm Shift from the 1990s

The premise upon which this paper rests is that broader social developments impinge upon social movements as well as on research. In much of independent India's history there was a broad commitment to a model of growth that was committed to equity. The state had a commanding role in this model. Much of this changed with the new economic policies of the 1990s. Many of these developments stem from a certain neo-liberal notion of economic growth. But, importantly, many of them are linked not just with actual economic policies but also to an all-encompassing ideology of the good life, of the free person, of the autonomous woman, of the middle class consumer, who increasingly appears to subsume the nation. The nation is reconfigured as the 'middle class' poised to be the biggest consuming market and the rest are no longer the toiling masses, the peasants or workers, often posited earlier as icons of the nation, but simply a problem of poverty. Often today the nation itself is referred to as India Incorporation or Brand India and there has been an incredible move towards corporatization in all spheres including that of the academia and other centres of knowledge production.[4] The corporate language has acquired such legitimacy that critiquing it sometimes appear churlish.

Apparent in the dominant neo-liberal paradigm in India is a discursive displacement of workers by the 'heads of industry' as key nation builders. I mention two instances from the recent past. In both the events, which were actually media hosting award ceremonies, the Finance Minister and Prime Minister were present to honour heads of industries. In one, the Finance Minister made an interesting distinction between what he called an earlier era of organic development of capitalism where Indians built industries and the present stage where they should buy off already established industries in major global takeovers. The issue of employment clearly did not feature in this model. The other was a television broadcast of its awards for the Indian of the Year 2008, hosted in Hotel Taj Mansingh on 17 January 2008 and attended by among others industrialists, politicians, the Prime Minister and Finance Minister. The anchor Barkha Dutt introduced the event mentioning that "India's best and brightest have come together in the room" and that "today it is economics, not politics, that drives the world". I think, both statements emerge as the apparently unproblematic common sense of the neo-liberal era. Indeed, politics is seen as disruptive to development. Not surprisingly, "women's empowerment" is viewed as constructive, "women's unionization and political movements" as obstacles to the furthering of neo-liberal policies, now termed "reforms". Further, there is an emptying out of politics from the present economic model. It transforms itself simply as a technical decision – above ideologies, above politics and therefore necessarily universal, representative of all sections.

Not surprisingly, the gender question and feminism itself has also been subject to reconfigurations (Chaudhuri, 2000). This is not my focus here but I am tempted to draw from two advertisements: one for a feminist professional in an international organization and the other of a workshop for female executives. The first, an advertisement of an "international feminist organization working to strengthen the voice, impact and influence of women's rights advocates, organizations and movements *internationally*" captures what can be termed professionalization[6] and globalization of gender and feminism, requiring as it does a Research Associate to work with the "Young Feminist Programme" who will be engaging "with the youth sector *globally*". ...The language skills required were in "*French and/or Spanish*" and "*some experience living and/or working in the Global South*" was preferred. The second advertisement is of a *workshop targeted at working women to raise awareness of the importance of work life balance policies at the level of the enterprise*....I quote:

> ...Within the past decade or so, the global workplace has seen increased numbers of working women; dual-career and single-parent families, and increased numbers of employees with eldercare responsibilities; a decrease in job security; and a blurring of work-family boundaries due to technological change. ...Life is a balancing act. Striking the right balance is the key to a fulfilling life. *Female executives have multiple responsibilities, diverse needs, and often, conflicting priorities. Organizations are becoming increasingly conscious of the important role that work-life balance policies play in attracting and retaining high calibre staff.* Striving to achieve a better work-life balance should become a national obsession (emphasis mine).

The above advertisements capture a very different world of women's movements and gender awareness from India of the 1970s. I quote from Vina Mazumdar, the pioneering women's studies scholar who iterates time and again the embryonic relationship between women's studies and gender studies. She writes:

> The revival of the women's movement in the late 1970s brought *new dynamism and directions to women studies.* Issues of *violence* – domestic and social, sexual exploitation in old and new forms, identification of *complex structures of domination and their reassertion in new forms in the ideology of revivalist, fundamentalist, communal and ethnic movements* – are some of the most significant of these new dimensions that the movement has brought into women's studies. Similarly, *investigations of peasant women in the rural economy* and of their undiscovered history have prompted new questions and *drawn women studies closer to issues being also raised by ecological and environmental movements.* Investigations ... *have turned women's studies into one of the major critics of the pattern of "development" and the choice of strategies* (Mazumdar, 1994: 44; emphasis mine).

Significantly, this very focus on women in the rural economy and in the unorganized sector brought forth new conceptualization of 'work' as well of the public and private domain. Developments thereof were however not always as intended by the pioneers. The next section elaborates on the manner that feminist findings and interventions are appropriated by international agencies operating with very dissimilar agendas of gender justice and development.

II

Debating Development and Gender

One of the crucial texts to come out of the decade of the 1980s was the *Shramshakti* report on self-employed women and women in the informal sector that was published in 1988. The report was intended to show women's extremely vulnerable working conditions across diverse occupations under high levels of discrimination, as well as the range of health hazards that women were exposed to on an everyday basis. The recommendations of the report were addressed to various ministries and departments at the central and state levels, but possibly also to international agencies (John, 2004).

Mary John has argued that:

> ...The World Bank report draws directly from the efforts of the National Commission on Self-Employed Women and Women in the

> Informal Sector as well as from most of the literature on women and development produced in India and elsewhere over the last decades. In other words, it is not based on case studies of its own. *By drawing upon the past years of research, activism and government action in India, however, it is able to perform a remarkable feat; lay claim to an overall consensus on the nature of women in poverty, while in fact coming to often diametrically opposite conclusions from prior feminist concerns* (John, 2004: 247; emphasis mine).

The 'agency discourse' of international institutions argues that the informal sector is at the heart of the market economy and represents its prime model. In their view, although 'restrictive' Third World state regulations are responsible for the growth of the informal sector in the first place, it is nonetheless here that high productivity is possible with low capital costs. Most important of all, since women are seen to predominate in this sector, it is their creativity and potential that needs special attention (John, 2004: 247).[7] Findings of women's long and hard work in difficult conditions are no longer arguments about *exploitation* as much as proofs of *efficiency*. As the World Bank report concluded, poor women are clearly more efficient economic actors, with greater managerial and entrepreneurial skills than men. Women therefore require greater access to resources, especially credit and social services. But as Mary John points out, they do need "the conditions of employment that obtains in the formal sector, which would only stifle productivity". Development, therefore, is reconfigured as a *social* issue, rather than an economic or political one.

Not surprisingly, therefore, a great deal of development gender discourse is now exclusively addressed within the micro-credit framework. Many studies have suggested that it develops banking habits among poor women and leads to increase in deposit accounts (Varman, 2005). A recent work is a collection of micro-finance activities and women's empowerment interestingly initiated by UNDP and ICICI Bank.

> Micro-credit, as a tool of poverty alleviation and empowerment, particularly of women, has gained credence in development dialogue the world over. The provision of micro-credit involves initiatives on the part of the state and non-state organizations in making available very small amounts of credit to poor citizens. There is an acute need among the poor for credit, both for consumption and production, which often forms the deciding line between survival and

> succumbing to poverty. In other words, credit is sought for basic requirements such as food, as well as for income generation activities. *The rationale of micro-credit is based on the hypothesis that the poor can be relied upon to return on time the money that they borrow. It has been proved that the poor are capable of thrift and savings* (Deshmukh et al., 2005: 31; emphasis mine).

In the discourse on poverty and micro-credit, the categories of 'class' and 'class relations' completely disappear. The 'poor' and 'poverty' appear to be self-contained entities with no structural connect with production relations.

Central to the neo-liberal frame is the informal sector as we saw and one needs to foreground the political implications of this. Naila Kabeer, who has a more careful take on the role of micro-credit, however, does not dispute the point that the "imperatives of cost-recovery and financial sustainability which drive the financial systems approach clearly resonate neo-liberal orientation to market principles" and that "it is not surprising therefore that it has come to assume a hegemonic position in international development thinking about micro-finance as a tool for poverty reduction" (Kabeer, 2005: 4709). The political implications of making the informal sector, where the greater proportion of women workers are the hub of the new economy, are spelt out by Breman:

> ...the informalisation of gainful employment which has become a major trend especially in developing countries in this late phase of capitalism hampers steady increase in the wretchedly low wages and regular employment with casual, spasmodic work arrangements, paid not in time-based wages but on piece rates. *An economic regime of this kind discourages militancy and obstructs the mobilization of the labouring poor into other unions and other representative organizations* (Breman, 2004: 3872; emphasis mine).

This is only one of the takes on globalization and its implications on the dispossessed in general and on poor women, in particular. But, this, it has to be emphasized is not the only take. Not all within the women's movement feel similarly about a globalization driven by neo-liberal forces. Gail Omvedt comments that being 'anti-globalization' has become the correct standard of political correctness. She agrees with Rohini Hensman (2004) who argued that in a globalized world, labour needs global regulation, and therefore the left should argue for the extension of these and not of withdrawing from the world system. But if one looks at the processes that Breman and John are delineating, the very assumptions of the growth of a global labour movement need to be rethought. Debates on outsourcing in the US are instructive in this regard.

Omvedt contents that the only meaningful question for a Marxist (or dalit, or feminist) activist, is what advances the revolution, "that is, the movement towards a non-caste, non-patriarchal, equalitarian and sustainable socialist society?" (Omvedt, 2005: 4881) She argues that:

> ...the increasing extraction of natural resources and their channeling to the world market via multinationals, the state and local powerholder... means that resources will be extracted more sustainably, that local people will get a share of the profits and raise their standard of living. It does not mean that they will resist the world market and extraction or listen to the activists when they try to tell them to do so; self-determination after all does mean just that, that they will do what they want. And this will primarily mean getting a better deal from world capital (Omvedt, 2005: 4883).

The two very different positions on globalization and gender from within the women's movement demand a more serious analysis than this perfunctory mention. That however is not my intent here. My aim is more limited, to illustrate the complex and, if I may use the term, 'intersectional analysis' that gender studies in India has demonstrated. In contrast to this nuanced approach, we also have, and unfortunately in abundance, a fast growing body of studies which shows complete disengagement with history, theory, politics and functions simply as technical operators of data collection for a problem that has already been defined. This kind of studies has always existed and not simply in our parts of the world going by C. Wright Mill's celebrated critique of abstracted empiricism. However, I would argue that with the proliferation of developmental projects sponsored research in the current context, the scale and extent of such studies generally and on gender specifically have been given a serious fillip. Both institutionally and intellectually the time is right.

III

Evaluation Research, Abstracted Empiricism and Gender

The time indeed is right for the proliferation of a kind of research that is that is geared to evaluate the functioning of specific projects.

However, this kind of research is not new to sociology in India. It is important to highlight the fact that sociology in independent India was seriously influenced by American sociological theory and methods. Mills, in his chapter on "Abstracted Empiricism", quotes from a Bernard Berelson, who provided a statement on this method that may help us look back to *where and what* that legacy is which has had such a lasting influence in Indian sociology and women's studies. He writes with reference to the study of public opinion but one that is relevant for much of sociological and gender studies in India.

> ...the field has become technical and quantitative, – a-theoretical, segmental, and particularized, specialized and institutionalized, 'modernized' and 'group-ized' – in short, as a characteristic behavioural science, Americanized.... Today, teams of technicians do research projects on specific subjects and report findings. (Berelson quoted in Mills, 1959: 65).

Sharmila Rege describes the pervasive nature of this influence as she describes what sociologists do when they do sociology:

> The expansion began in 1952, as the knowledge/methods of sociologists became 'usable' by the state. Sociologists were required to outline the social determinants and consequences of state sponsored development issues that did not fall within the purview of economists- became the prerogative of the sociologist and as the need for trained personnel increased...It is important to note that this expansion, courtesy CDP (1951–70), courtesy the Ford Foundation *meant a strong dose of modern survey research methods imported from the United States. Research technology became the 'need of the day' (state?) and there was neither the inclination nor the time to reflect on substantive issues in methodology* (Dhanagare, 1993). This period of visibility for the sociologist saw its estrangement from history, economics and political science (Rege, nd: 5; emphasis mine).

Though sociology in India has had diverse and rich traditions of scholarship, it remains a fact that the widely and commonly expected skills of sociologists are familiarity with a set of techniques to collect and analyse quantitative data. Not surprisingly, the employability of sociologists in research institutions has arisen precisely because this is broadly the order of research skills that they require. Institutionally many developmental programmes run by non-governmental and governmental agencies require essentially evaluative research where even the parameters of evaluation have already been laid down. In a great deal of research a few indicators is all that is required to collect data whether it be 'poverty alleviation' or 'empowerment' to assess the impact of any intervention to alleviate 'poverty' or lead to 'empowerment' of women.

Maithreyi Krishnaraj's insightful comments on such women's studies show how techniques take precedence with less attention in the formulation of research:

> ...Women studies scholars are expected to move away from this narrow academic view. NGOs claim that they on the other hand constantly keep in view the subjects of their research. However, *women studies research is not just for locating immediate problems or seeking immediate solutions.* It has a wider scope. It seeks to delve into history, to understand other disciplines by a careful reading of their theories attempting thereby to locate biases and shortcomings in mainstream disciplines in the way they articulate women's lives and hopefully, and thereby evolve new theories and methodologies. *While immediate problems are indeed necessary, these broader engagements are equally important as an intellectual enterprise for creating new knowledge,* that form the basis for understanding issues and formulating action. Hence, all women studies research need not only be empirical research. Both theoretical work and empirical work constantly complement each other (Krishnaraj, 2005: 3008; emphasis mine).

She emphasizes the importance of identifying and formulating the problem of research. She rues the fact that by and large, the 'topics' are chosen for the following reasons: (a) they are currently fashionable; (b) falls in line with the government's or policy-maker's interest; (c) funding agencies' preferences; (d) issues that find publicity in current literature – media, journals, conferences; and (e) individual choice which is itself often influenced by current fashion. Expectedly, the majority of studies that have made their appearance today are on micro-credit, self-help groups, unorganized sector, panchayati raj and violence (Krishnaraj, 2005: 3008).

The paper began with a cursory mention of times when the concept of gender meant little more than its grammatical avatar. Today, it has wide presence and considerable visibility. But not quite the way it was intended. To go back a few decades, the Indian

Association for Women's Studies, established in 1982, aimed to further the perspectives of women's studies within and beyond educational institutions. Since the association came into existence the University Grants Commission (UGC) has drawn attention of the universities to promote an understanding of women's issues through the teaching, research and extension activities of various disciplines. In the early 1990s alone nearly forty universities entered the field. The UGC has been promoting a speedy expansion of women studies centres in the country but with a vision, *not always* in consonance with "...the pursuit of a more comprehensive, critical and balanced understanding of social reality". During the Bharatiya Janata Party (BJP)-led regime, there were active plans in place to reformulate the women studies centres as family studies programmes. If this reveals core conservative patriarchal visions, other trends display a broader shift to extension activities rather than the kind of women's studies that sought to "persuade the social science community to re-examine the methodology, concepts, theories, and analytical apparatus of social research...". Significantly, Women Studies in the Tenth Plan within the UGC was placed in the Non-Formal Education Sector underlying the assumption that the business of women studies was really about schemes for extension activities and ameliorating women's conditions (assumed to be already understood and given) and not quite on par with other academic disciplines which as the volume notes anyway is seen as 'useless' if not of immediate and tangible "practical use". It is not unheard, therefore, that such programmes get women involved in the business of the now growing beauty parlour business as income-generating activities. Contrast this with the vision of women's studies in the 1970s.

> A new programme for Women's Studies, initiated by the Indian Council of Social Science Research (ICSSR), emerged after the report with three distinct objectives: (1) to identify and work for needed policy change; (2) *to persuade the social science community to re-examine the methodology, concepts, theories, and analytical apparatus of social research, which had successfully excluded women's role, status, and situation from the entire arena of social investigations*; and (3) *to revive the social debate on the women's question*, which had emerged as a major issue during the freedom struggle but had faded in the post-Independence period (Mazumdar, 1994: 43; emphasis mine).

IV

Interrogating Dominant Narratives of Nationalism, Nation-State and Gender

The last section has noted the a-historical emphasis of abstracted empiricism due to an epistemological preference' (Mills, 1959: 73). Significantly, some of the finest work using gendered analysis in India has emerged from historical works, some done by sociologists (Uberoi, 1996). This is not accidental. Our own erstwhile colonial condition and negotiation with western feminism partly accounts for this. I return to this later. But I would argue that the legacy of American sociology of one kind also foreclosed the possibilities of the kind of women's studies that sociology could legitimately do. Sociology was caught in the modernization framework and a great deal of energy was spent on either role conflicts of middle class women or identifying indicators of modernization of Indian women (Chaudhuri, 1982). Both were inspired by the need to be technical. Problems of investigation were often chosen with regard to how readily amenable it could be to statistical investigation. Contemporary events, a-historically addressed, became the necessary chosen fields. In contrast historians in India, were influenced by sociological and social anthropological approaches that allowed for a holistic and intersectional analysis. Not surprisingly a historical going back provided new insights to categories such as caste and region, community and tribe – key categories in sociology.

In this section I hope to only indicate at the barest how women's studies in India have been at the forefront of questioning mainstream and widely accepted understandings of some of the central categories of analysis in social science research. I necessarily have to return to the story of women's movements. It would be perfectly in place to question why do I return here to mapping histories of women's movements. This I argue is prompted by two reasons. One, that much of the intellectual challenge that women's studies in India have thrown up has been simply by unearthing buried and forgotten accounts of struggles and the politics that bypassed them from the pages of history. The other and a related reason is that these new accounts of history also opened up new questions and takes on what were thought as accepted and consensual understandings of nationalism and colonialism.

There has been considerable interrogation from the dalit viewpoint about the nationalist framework as well as the purported role of colonialism. Sharmila Rege writes:

> History of late colonial India has always prioritized Indian nationalism, such that it came to be assumed that the world of political action and discourse can be comprehended only through the categories of nationalism, imperialism and communalism. The radical historiographies of colonial India, though they emphasized the autonomous role of peasants, labour and other subaltern groups, equated the historiography of colonial India with that of Indian nationalism (Sarkar, 1997). The non-brahmanical re-constructions of historiography of modern India in the works of Omvedt (1976, 1993, 1994), Patil (1982) and Alyosius (1997) have underlined the histories of anti-hierarchical, pro-democratising collective aspirations of the lower caste masses which are not easily encapsulated within the histories of anti-colonial nationalism. In fact these histories have often faced the penalty of being labeled as collaborative and have therefore being ignored in a historiography which is dominated by narratives of nationalism (Rege, 1998).

The debate on the women's question in the public sphere of colonial India has been scrutinized carefully from different perspectives. We thus have a Latha Mani questioning whether the debate on *sati* was about women or about reconfiguring tradition and culture; we have as Rege points out questions on why dalit women's public initiatives and intervention went unwritten about; we have arguments that suggested social reforms were more about efforts to introduce new patriarchies rather than about women's right and gender justice. Much of this questioning is of recent times. For long, the nationalist rendering of an account of social evils and the unproblematic role of male reformers persisted and perhaps still does, given our very uneven spread of new knowledges in the country.

However, one did have other accounts and orientations even if they were not the dominant strands. What readily comes to one's mind is the document "Role of Women in a Planned Economy"(WREP) which revealed a curious mix and jostling for space of three dominant ideas of liberalism, socialism and cultural revivalism, within the same text. It contained substantial data on conditions of women workers in the unorganized sector, in agriculture and the public and private issues that they faced (Chaudhuri, 1997). It could be argued however like

Rege does that even such accounts of labour and other subaltern groups still privileged the role of nationalism. Such critiques of a dominant nationalist framework have played an important role to rethink the limits and constraints of a purportive nationalism that spoke for all sections. I would however hesitate to contend that an anti-imperial nationalism and subsequently a 'nationalist' state did not have any role to usher in the historical possibility of the excluded voice from actually emerging.

Talking about women/gender studies, we need to clarify what we mean by studies. For much pulling out the hidden history swept under social reform or nationalism involves new ways and approaches of reading old texts and ofcourse discovering new texts. Thus while at one time (and this is but one illustration) Tarabai Shinde's, *Stree Purush Tulana* (1882), a text against women's subordination as well as against Brahmanical patriarchy, would not be thought of when one mentions women studies, it would be considered a key pioneering feminist text today. This rethinking of history and the rich body of research that has emerged in India is as I mentioned earlier, of course not accidental. I have argued earlier that "if I had been searching for writing on Indian feminism per se on the lines of debates in the West between radical and socialist feminism for example, I was obviously on the wrong track. I was also obviously on the wrong track because I felt troubled about my reliance on western theoretical sources while teaching a course on gender. My own hands-on attempt at resolving the dilemma was to emphasis the specific history of the women's question in India" (Chaudhuri, 2002). I had further argued that *historical research has laid the ground for theorizing feminism.* A great deal of feminist theorizing interrogated the imagining of a nation that conflated itself with a sanitized image of Hindu upper caste women. While writings on modern India has explored the recasting of women in colonial India (Sangari and Vaid, 1989; Chaudhuri, 1993; Tharu and Lalita, 1993) scholars of ancient India have interrogated the Altekarian vision of the high and noble status of women in ancient India (Chakravarti 1989; Roy, 1996; Chaudhuri, 2004: xiii). Women's studies and feminist perspectives therefore involve not just an adding of more information *but* necessarily imply new modes of interrogation and new perspectives to approach the study of society. Reges' recent work (2006) documenting narratives of dalit women as testimonies bears witness to this increasing body of writings that have opened up ideas about the nation, feminism and caste.

V

Conclusion

The main argument of this paper has been that when we teach and research concepts, in this case, gender, we need to understand its biography. My attempt to map this biography may be uneven. This task has been even more formidable for the journey of 'gender' entailed both radical local movements and global intervention by international institutions. Acknowledging this limitation, I would hope that one has communicated the complex processes by which a concept finally arrives in the classroom, in the textbook or in the workshop. I contend that this exercise is important as for too often concepts in both teaching and research are accepted as sacred givens, abstracted from the structural context of its production.

In this paper I look at the kind of gender debates in Part I and III, which may not have any direct or immediate relationship to developmental agendas, but would go a long way to strengthen the critical and reflective tradition of social sciences in India. This is in keeping with the broader argument that I made in the introduction, namely, that at different points in the trajectory of capital, class formations and nations, the place and role of the social sciences and not surprisingly gender studies tends to get redefined. A central argument that this volume has expressed is that a liberally educated person should be capable of principled judgement, seeking to understand the origins, context, and implications of any area of study, rather than looking exclusively at its application.

Notes

1. I qualify 'the academic context' because I believe that considerable intellectual theorizing was done earlier but usually within a context of political action (see Chaudhuri, 2004).
2. I have dealt in some detail the reconfiguration of feminism in Indian print media elsewhere (Chaudhuri, 2000). For the use of gender in corporate research see Chaudhuri 2010.
3. See detailed bibliography in Chaudhuri (2004). Also see Rege (2005) and John (2008).
4. You will recall our discussion on the corporate vision in the Introduction.

5. See Chaudhuri 1996
6. Precisely at the point that the paradigmatic changes of the 1990s that I describe above were taking place, a parallel process was taking place within the classroom as I taught a paper on women and society in India. I quote:

> In the early years the course was new and expectations veered from the serious to the trivial to what could be read as voyeuristic. …Over the years …expectations were more grounded on some familiarity with feminism. *And more recently I discern a certain professionalisation in the interest in gender studies. …A lot of NGO and international organisations want specialisation gender and development issues* (Chaudhuri, 2002; emphasis not in the original).

7. For a fuller discussion, see Kalpagam (1994).

References

Agnihotri, Indu and Vina Mazumdar. 1995. "Changing Terms of Political Discourse: Women's Movement in India, 1970s–1990s", *Economic and Political Weekly*, 30 (29), July 22: 1869–1878.

Agnes, Flavia. 1997. "Women's Movement in a Secular Framework: Redefining the Agenda", *Economic and Political Weekly*, 29 (19): 1123–1128.

Breman, Jan. 2004. "Return of Social Inequality: A Fashionable Doctrine", *Economic and Political Weekly* (34-35), August 28, pp. 3869-3872.

Butalia, Urvashi. 1993. "Communalism, State and Gender: On Women's Agency During Partition" *Economic and Political Weekly*, April 24 1993, WS-12, WS-25.

—. 2000. *The Other Side of Silence: Voices from the Partition of India.* Durham: Duke University Press.

Chakravarti, Uma. 1989. "Whatever Happened to the Vedic Dasi? Orientalism, Nationalism and a Script for the Past" in Kumkum Sangari and Sudesh Vaid, Eds. *Recasting Women: Essays in Colonial India.* New Delhi: Kali for Women, pp. 27–87.

Chaudhuri, Maitrayee. 1982. "Sociology and Women's Studies", *Social Scientist*, October.

—. 1993. *The Indian Women's Movement: Reform and Revival.* Delhi, Radiant.

—. 1995. "Citizens, Workers, Emblems of Culture: An Analysis of the First Plan Document on Women", *Contributions to Indian Sociology*, 29, Nos. 1 and 2, 211–34.

—. 2000. "'Feminism' in Print Media" *Indian Journal of Gender Studies*, 7:2 pp. 263–288.

—. 2002. "Learning Through the Teaching the Sociology of Gender", *Indian Journal of Gender Studies,* 9,2: 245–261.

—. 2003. "Culture and Globalization: In My Classroom and Outside" in Maitrayee Chaudhuri, *The Practice of Sociology.* New Delhi: Orient Longman, pp. 370–402.

—. 2010. "The Family and Its Representation: From Indology to Market Research" in Yogendra Singh (ed.), *Social Sciences: Communication, Anthropology and Sociology, History of Science, Philosophy and Culture in Indian Civilization,* Vol. XIV Part 2, Delhi: Pearson, 2010, pp. 363–389.

Dennis, Ann. 2008. "Review Essay: Intersectional Analysis: A Contribution of Feminism to Sociology", *International Sociology,* Vol. 23, No. 5, pp. 677–694.

Deshmukh, Ranadive. 2003. "Placing Gender Equity in the Family Centre Stage", *Economic and Political Weekly,* 38(17).

Hensman, Rohini. 2004. "Globalisation, Women and Work: What Are We Talking About?" *Economic and Political Weekly,* March 6, 39, (10), pp. 1030–1084.

John, Mary E. (1996a) *Discrepant Dislocations: Feminism, Theory and Postcolonial Histories.* Berkeley: University of California Press.

—. (1996b). "Gender and Development in India, 1970s–1990s: Some Reflections on the Constitutive Role of Contexts", *Economic and Political Weekly,* 31 (47): 3071–3077.

John, Mary (ed.) 2008. *Women's Studies in India: A Reader.* New Delhi: Penguin.

Kabeer, Naila. 2005. "Is Microfinance a 'Magic bullet' for Women's Empowerment? Analysis of Findings from South Asia", *Economic and Political Weekly* (40: 44-45), 29 October, pp. 4709-4715.

Kalpagam, U. 1994. *Labour and Gender: Survival in Urban India.* New Delhi: Sage.

Krishnaraj, Maithreyi. 2003. "Challenges before Women's Movement in a Changing Context", *Economic and Political Weekly,* October 25–31 38(43): 4536–4546.

—. 2005. *Economic and Political Weekly,* July 9, pp. 3008 –3017.

Kumar, Radha. 2008. *Infochange Defining Development,* October 15th 2008 infochangeindia.org

Mani, Lata. 1989. " Contentious Traditions: The Debate on Sati in Colonial India" in Kumkum Sangari and Sudesh Vaid 1989 *Recasting Women: Essays in Colonial India.* New Delhi: Kali for Women. pp. 88–120.

Mazumdar, Vina. 1994. " Women's Studies and the Women's Movement in India: An Overview", *Women's Studies Quarterly* 3 and 4, pp. 42–53.

Mazumdar, Vina and Kumud Sharma. 1979. "Women's Studies: New Perspectives and Challenges", *Economic and Political Weekly* 14, 3, 113–20.

Menon, Ritu and Bhasin, Kamla. 1998. *Borders and Boundaries.* New Jersey: Rutgers University Press.

Mills, C. Wright. 1959. *The Sociological Imagination.* London: OUP.

Misra, Yamini and Subrat Das. 2006. "Gender Budgeting Statement", *Economic and Political Weekly,* 41.

Omvedt, Gail. 1990. *Violence Against Women: New Movements and New Theories in India.* New Delhi: Kali for Women.

Rege, Sharmila (nd) "Feminist Sociology: Disenchanting Sociology or For Sociology?" Draft Copy.

Roy, Kumkum. 1996. "Where Women are Worshipped, There the Gods Rejoice: The Mirage of Ancestress of the Hindu Woman", in Tanika Sarkar and Urvashi Butalia (eds.) *Women and the Hindu Right: A Collection of Essays,* New Delhi: Kali for Women, pp. 181–215.

Sangari, Kumkum and Sudesh Vaid. 1989. *Recasting Women: Essays in Colonial India.* New Delhi: Kali for Women.

Tharu, Susie and K. Lalitha. 1993. *Women Writing in India: 600 B.C. to the Present,* Vol.1 and 2, Delhi: Oxford University Press.

Varman, Mahendra P. 2005, "Impact of Self-Help Groups on Formal Banking Habits", *Economic and Political Weekly,* Vol. 40. No. 17, April 23 pp.1704–1713.

Uberoi, Patricia. 1996. *Social Reform, Sexuality and the State.* New Delhi: Sage.

Index